The Supreme Court and the Commerce Clause, 1937-1970

Paul R. Benson, Jr.

The Supreme Court and the Commerce Clause, 1937-1970

Foreword by
Maurice G. Baxter

DUNELLEN

International Standard Book Number 0-8424-0018-4.

Library of Congress Catalogue Card Number 74-136244.

Printed in the United States of America.

342.73
B474s

72-1453

Dedicated to my wife,
Joan Rosalie Whitton Benson

THE CONSTITUTION OF THE UNITED STATES
OF AMERICA
ARTICLE I

Section 8. "The Congress shall have Power . . . [clause 3] To regulate Commerce with foreign Nations, and among the several States, and with the Indian Tribes."

Contents

Foreword

Nearly two centuries ago the framers of the Constitution met at Philadelphia to form a more perfect union during a period of great commercial difficulty. Every student of history will recall that one of the leading reasons for convoking this convention was general dissatisfaction with shortcomings of the existing governmental system in securing and facilitating commerce among the states and with foreign nations. From the perspective of the present, one may say that the founding fathers dealt with the problem simply and effectively by adopting the brief clause in the first article of the Constitution which empowers Congress to regulate such commerce. For many years, it is true, the brevity of the provision puzzled politicians, lawyers, and judges who sought explicit answers to various questions concerning its meaning: Was national power exclusive; if not, to what extent and under what circumstances could the states also regulate interstate and foreign commerce; and, indeed, what facets of American economic and social life could properly be classified as commerce? After numerous twists and turns of theorizing, the Supreme Court has arrived at positions on those questions which have met the needs of the country— to regulate enormously powerful business corporations, to carry forward programs of social welfare and economic justice, to safeguard the rights of individual citizens, and to allow that diversity of state legislation so necessary in a federal system of government.

Though there have been a few monographs and innumerable essays on the history of the Commerce Clause, until now no one has undertaken a full-scale study of the subject for the modern era, especially the years since the "constitutional revolution" of 1937. Surely an account of judicial expositions on the uses of this very important constitutional power in the mid-twentieth century will interest many readers. Paul Benson has written an account of this kind, and more. He has placed his story in the context of earlier, nineteenth-century landmark cases (notably *Gibbons v. Ogden*); he has traced the lines of development of formulas for dividing state and national powers over commerce; and he has analyzed the bases of contemporary judicial doctrines with great skill. In short, he has performed the constitutional analyst's task well. He has gathered the evidence industriously and has explored the relationships and implications to be found there. This work should become the standard reference on the topic for some time to come.

What emerges from the present investigation is a view of the Constitution, and of the Commerce Clause in particular, as a remarkably adaptable, practical instrument of public policy. Rather than dominating the nation as if they were Scripture, the constitutional words have provided the freedom for each generation to use such powers as it requires to manage its affairs. This charter has permitted two levels of government to operate simultaneously without either Balkanizing the Union or producing a monolithic tyranny. No one could expect more from a constitution.

Maurice G. Baxter
Professor of History
Indiana University

Acknowledgments

I wish to express my personal appreciation to the several persons who directly or indirectly made this book possible.

The dedication to my wife says all that is necessary about her contribution. Had it not been for her constant encouragement and support and her expert typing of the two drafts, the work would never have seen the light of day.

Milton Hobbs, Associate Professor of Political Science, University of Illinois, played a significant role in the development of my intellectual abilities, particularly my capacity to reason logically and objectively.

Maurice G. Baxter, Professor of History, Indiana University, was on sabbatical leave for the first semester of 1968-1969 but spent much time which could have been his own to read and criticize the first draft as it was written; his many comments and suggestions made an invaluable contribution to the final product. In addition, I am grateful to him for the ensuing foreword.

Warner O. Chapman, Professor of Government, Indiana University, took time from his many duties as teacher and as Dean in the School of Arts and Sciences to read the first draft; he offered numerous helpful criticisms which improved immeasurably the logic and tightness of the final presentation. He also acted willingly and ably as my chief mentor.

Finally, my thanks go to Gladys G. McNerney, in the Archives of The Citadel Museum, who typed the final copy under severe pressure for time and who patiently and uncomplainingly put up with my demands for perfection, and to Paule H. Jones, Executive Editor of The

Dunellen Company, who made a number of excellent suggestions as to manuscript form and style.

A last word is in order on my special indebtedness to Dr. Chapman and Dr. Baxter. The former taught me constitutional law; the latter taught me constitutional history. Both of them are splendid teachers, and they not only imparted knowledge and an appreciation of their subjects but also stressed by personal example the qualities of intellectual discipline which make the scholar-careful and unbiased research, logical reasoning, and the ability to analyze and criticize. My debt to them can never be paid, except as I attempt to emulate in my professional activities the high standards of excellence which they set. In sum, it has been my privilege to study and to work under them. Whatever is of merit in the following pages is due to their training and influence; I alone am responsible for any errors of fact or interpretation.

Paul R. Benson, Jr.

Introduction

This study concerns the ways in which the United States Supreme Court has interpreted the Commerce Clause of the Constitution (Article I, section 8, clause 3) over the past third of a century. Commerce, or commercial enterprise, is a vast and complex area comprising many and varied activities and presenting many constitutional questions of major importance to the American political system. Obviously, no one book could treat the subject exhaustively, even for the relatively short span of time indicated; and this effort will be no exception. Accordingly, the work will focus on five major aspects of the development of constitutional law in connection with the Commerce Clause.

    1. A careful analysis of *Gibbons v. Ogden* (1824) will be made.[1] This was the first case under the Commerce Clause to be brought before the Supreme Court, and it is imperative that Chief Justic John Marshall's original exposition of that clause in his majority opinion be illuminated with care and accuracy. In a sense, all subsequent development and use of the Commerce Clause hinges upon the principles there laid down by Marshall; the importance of *Gibbons* cannot be overestimated. The development of the clause up to, and including, *Cooley v. The Board of Wardens of the Port of Philadelphia* (1852) will also be outlined briefly.[2] The *Cooley* doctrine, as set forth by Justice Benjamin R. Curtis, marks one of the major turning points in constitutional interpretation; therefore, it will be dealt with in some detail.

    2. A brief history of the Commerce Clause will cover the main trends from 1852 to 1937. Included here will be (a) the consequences

of the *Cooley* doctrine, which opted for a partial "concurrent" state-power theory; (b) the expansion of the federal commerce power after the beginning of the twentieth century; and (c) the rise of "dual federalism" between 1895 and 1937. These subjects will be covered only to bring the reader up to the point at which the main body of the study begins. Consequently, many recognizably important issues in this period of time will not be examined; to do so would be to go beyond the scope of this treatise.

3. The "constitutional revolution" of 1937-1942 will be analyzed in detail, even though this event has been treated elsewhere.[3] Specifically, the great watershed cases of *National Labor Relations Board v. Jones & Laughlin Steel Corporation* (1937)[4] and *United States v. Darby* (1941)[5] will be used to illustrate the almost complete unfettering of the federal commerce power and the consequent demise of "dual federalism." *Wickard v. Filburn* (1942)[6] will complete this trilogy of cases which gave to the national government virtually unlimited power to regulate the commercial enterprise of the United States, no matter how "local" it might be in nature. Since 1942 (with but one exception, which will be noted) the scope and magnitude of the federal commerce power have not been seriously questioned. It will be helpful, though, to examine a number of the more important cases in the last twenty-five years or so in which this vast power has been reaffirmed and reinforced by Supreme Court decisions. But, let it be added, anyone familiar with American constitutional law will find no surprises here.

4. One of the most explosive issues in constitutional law as well as in public policy generally in the 1960's is the issue of civil rights for American minorities. Accordingly, opponents of the federal Civil Rights Act of 1964 (which, in its final form, was based on the Commerce Clause) have presented the most serious and determined attack on the power of Congress over commerce since the days of the New Deal. Thus this congressional use of, and positive Supreme Court reaction to, the Commerce Clause as a basis for furthering civil rights will be accorded some extensive attention. Some earlier cases in which the Supreme Court took the lead in using the clause to uphold civil rights will be considered in order to round out the picture.

5. If the extent of congressional power over commerce has now been settled, the same cannot be said of the power of the states to regulate aspects of what is admittedly interstate commerce. This complex topic will be covered in three parts: (a) a comparison of the conflicting constitutional views of Chief Justice Harlan Fiske Stone,

2

Justice Hugo L. Black, and Justice Robert H. Jackson on the proper scope of state power over commerce, together with a survey of state power in the absence of federal legislation; (b) an intensive study of state power where there is alleged "conflict" with prior congressional "occupation of the field"; and (c) a quick review of state taxation of interstate commerce. The focus will be upon the first two parts and thus upon the way in which the Court marks out and maintains the boundary line between national and state power. Two conclusions will emerge from this. The first is that at the same time the Court has sanctioned vast federal power, it has greatly expanded the reach of state power over many subjects of interstate commerce and business activities of "foreign" corporations; the second is, on the other hand, that the Court will still act to invalidate what it considers a particularly obnoxious state interference with, or discrimination against, commerce. In sum, it will be shown that the Supreme Court continues to play its constitutional role as final arbiter of the American federal system in regard to the power to regulate commerce.

These five major topics, then, will represent the central components of this study. The overriding objective will be to treat them in such manner that the reader will have a clear picture of where the Commerce Clause stands today. Certain aspects, however, will not be covered. The whole area of antitrust cases under the Sherman Antitrust Act will be omitted, except for a few cases which are especially relevant to the two major lines of development of federal power up to 1937 and which illustrate the present scope of that power. Cases which involve the transportation industries, the communications industry, the power-transmission companies, and the securities markets will also be omitted primarily because the study does not extend to a consideration of the federal regulatory commissions. Nor will the interesting historical controversy raised by William W. Crosskey as to exactly what the framers of the federal Constitution meant by the word "commerce" be joined,[7] beyond what is necessary to a precise understanding of Marshall's opinion in *Gibbons v. Ogden*. Finally, with respect to the chosen topics, even these will not be treated exhaustively in the sense of examining all of the relevant cases; rather, only the most important cases, which furnish good grounds for broad generalizations in a particular area, will be analyzed in detail to show the direction of interpretation which the Court has followed in the last third of a century.

A word, perhaps, is in order on the subject of methodology. The general approach of the study will be from a legal-historical point of view, but with an emphasis on analysis rather than mere description. In other words, there will be no attempt to fit the various parts of the study into one, overall theoretical framework or theory of judicial decision making. This is not meant to imply any antiscientific bias on the part of the present author or any intimation that the judicial process is not a proper subject for scientific inquiry. In fact, the author would argue for the possibility of a science of politics and for the validity of what may be called the behavioral approach to politics; and it will become clear that this work itself is oriented along scientific lines in the sense that, from the important decisions in each area, appropriate generalizations (or laws) will be drawn. But this will not be done with an eye to formulating some comprehensive theory to explain the way in which the United States Supreme Court decides Commerce-Clause cases.

Finally, the reader is entitled to know the author's biases or prejudices. He has two which are relevant. The first is that he subscribes to the tenets of analytical jurisprudence as put forward by the English jurist John Austin; the most basic of these is that law is the command of the sovereign and that it is the function of the judge merely to interpret and apply that law as given and not to read his own personal predilections into it. In other words, the judge is to be concerned only about what is the law, not about what it ought to be. In the American system of government, sovereignty rests in the combination of people and amending process, and the Constitution represents the supreme law or command of that sovereign. Therefore, as an example, the delegated powers of Congress in Article I—including the commerce power—must be read as the full or plenary powers that they are and may not be diminished by spurious reasoning based upon the particular social, economic, or political philosophies of individual justices.

The second bias is that the author espouses an intelligent and rational nationalism and the concomitant of a strong central government. He believes that a careful reading of American constitutional history shows that, by and large, it is the federal government which has remained true to the founding principles of the nation and which has acted consistently to secure the best interests of all its people. If he had to defend his nationalistic philosophy in a few words, he would rely upon a statement made by Justice Joseph P. Bradley in *Ex Parte Siebold* (1880): "It seems to be often overlooked that a National Constitution has been adopted in this country, establishing a real government therein, operating upon persons and territory and things; and which, moreover, is, or should be, as dear to every American citizen as his State Government is."[8]

With the author having now admitted to being both an Austinian and a modern-day Federalist, the real tasks which were outlined above begin.

Notes

1. 9 Wheaton 1.

2. 12 Howard 299.

3. See, for example, Robert H. Jackson, *The Struggle for Judicial Supremacy* (New York: Vintage Books, 1941), 197-285; Robert L. Stern, "The Commerce Clause and the National Economy, 1933-1946," *Harvard Law Review*, LIX (1946), 645 and 883; Bernard Schwartz, *The Supreme Court: Constitutional Revolution in Retrospect* (New York: The Ronald Press Company, 1957), 16-48.

4. 301 U.S. 1.

5. 312 U.S. 100.

6. 317 U.S. 111.

7. William W. Crosskey, *Politics and the Constitution in the History of the United States* (2 vols., Chicago: The University of Chicago Press, 1953), I, 17-292.

8. 100 U.S. 371, 394.

Part 1: Early History of the Commerce Clause

The story of the Commerce Clause of the United States Constituion begins where many another important development in American constitutional law was conceived—with the powerful pen of Chief Justice John Marshall. Consequently, Chapter 1 will be devoted primarily to an in-depth examination of Marshall's original exposition of the clause in *Gibbons v. Ogden* (1824) and to the far-reaching implications of that decision. A second milestone in Commerce-Clause history, *Cooley v. The Board of Wardens* (1852), will also be analyzed and evaluated. Chapter 2 will then trace the main facets of constitutional development from 1852 through 1936 and will cover such topics as state power, congressional power, and the flowering of the doctrine of "dual federalism" as a restraint upon national power over commerce. Finally, Chapter 3 will record the decline and fall of "dual federalism" in the period 1937-1942 and the concomitant rise of almost absolute congressional authority over the national economy. These three broad subjects will be dealt with at some length in order to provide a comprehensible (but not comprehensive) background to the succeeding two parts of the book, which cover federal and state power over commerce from 1942 to 1970 and which, of course, provide the major focuses of attention.

1   Gibbons v. Ogden

The purpose of this chapter will be to review and analyze the great steamboat case, *Gibbons v. Ogden* (1824)—the first case in which the Supreme Court, under Chief Justice John Marshall, interpreted and applied the Commerce Clause of the United States Constitution.[1] Specifically, this examination will be limited to the following areas: (1) the background, resulting litigation, and two United States Circuit Court precedents preceding *Gibbons v. Ogden;* (2) the Supreme Court case, including the arguments of counsel, Marshall's majority opinion, and Justice William Johnson's concurring opinion; (3) an analysis of Marshall's opinion and some possible reasons for his holdings, together with their far-reaching importance to the American constitutional system; and (4) a rather brief survey of the constitutional development of the Commerce Clause up to, and including, *Cooley v. The Board of Wardens* (1852).[2] No other commerce cases will be dealt with in any great detail, although several will be mentioned to show the general direction taken by the Court in the first few decades after *Gibbons v. Ogden;* and the important implications of the *Cooley* case as a landmark in judicial interpretation will be made clear.

Background, Litigation, Precedents

As early as March 19, 1787, the New York legislature passed an act "for Granting and Securing to John Fitch, the sole right and advantage of Making and Employing, for a limited time, the Steamboat by him lately invented."[3] Nothing came of this; and on March 27, 1798, the

9

legislature repealed the act and transferred "the sole and exclusive privileges for navigation by fire and steam on all the public waters within the territorial jurisdiction of New York" to Robert R. Livingston, socially prominent and politically powerful New Yorker.[4] When Livingston was United States minister to France, he met Robert Fulton, a professional inventor and skilled technician, who was experimenting with propelling a boat by means of a steam engine. On October 10, 1802, the two men became legal partners in the state franchise.[5] By a series of acts in 1803, 1807, 1808, and 1811, the New York legislature extended the exclusive right of steamboat navigation to the Livingston-Fulton enterprise up to the year 1838 and provided increasingly stringent penalties for intruders. On April 19, 1811, the legislature of the Territory of Orleans granted the partners exclusive privileges to navigate the Mississippi River; the monopoly now controlled two of the greatest commercial waterways of the country.

As events were to prove, the steamboat monopoly was very unpopular, invoked recriminations, and attracted open competition. In May, 1811, James Van Ingen and some associates built a steamboat, the *Hope,* and began to carry passengers. Livingston and Fulton promptly petitioned the New York Court of Chancery to enjoin the Van Ingen interests from using the *Hope.*[6] Chancellor John Lansing denied the injunction on the common law grounds that the legislative grant invaded certain natural rights to the use of air and water which were incapable of alienation or restraint by positive legislation. He added, as an afterthought, that it was a possibility that the state grant invaded the authority of Congress to regulate commerce.

The Livingston interests appealed to the New York Court of Errors.[7] Here the opposing arguments centered upon constitutional issues.[8] Counsel for Van Ingen asserted that the New York grant was void under the federal Constitution because the power to regulate commerce was vested exclusively in the national government and therefore could not be exercised by the states; otherwise, there would be the old confusion and diversity of state commercial regulations which the Constitution had been adopted specifically to end. Counsel for Livingston emphasized that the commerce power could not be exclusive for two reasons: (1) since the states retained all powers not explicitly divested in favor of the Union, they had a concurrent jurisdiction over commerce; and (2) authority in the national government over trade could not be exclusive because so many aspects of that power involved activities affecting the social and community interests of the states at the purely local level.

The higher court unanimously reversed Chancellor Lansing. Chief Justice James Kent wrote the most important *seriatim* opinion.[9] He was distinctly unimpressed with Lansing's natural law limitations upon the authority of the legislature. The only proper question was whether the legislature had the constitutional power to grant the exclusive franchise. Kent admitted that "powers [granted to the general government] whether expressed or implied, may be plenary and sovereign, in reference to the specified objects of them";[10] but the Constitution had created a federal system, and he reasoned that every power was reserved to the states that had not been taken away and vested exclusively in the national government. The question was whether the power to regulate commerce was "exclusive" or "concurrent," and to answer it Kent looked to Alexander Hamilton's discussion of federal power in *Federalist 32.* There Hamilton had argued that there were only three classes of exclusive powers delegated by the Constitution: (1) those which "in express terms granted an exclusive authority to the Union"; (2) those which "granted in one instance an authority to the Union and in another prohibited the States from exercising the like authority"; and (3) those which "granted an authority to the Union, to which a similar authority in the States would be absolutely and totally *contradictory* and *repugnant,*" that is, those which were exclusive in their nature.[11]

The federal commerce power obviously did not belong to either of the first two classes, and Kent could find no reason to think that it fell into the third category. Thus New York possessed a concurrent authority over commerce, and the Tenth Amendment justified the continuation of such state power until Congress clearly suspended it or until the Supreme Court formulated a national law which would be binding upon the states.[12] Then Kent summed up this argument: the federal commerce power was limited to activities not wholly in one state; "all internal commerce of the state . . . remains entirely and . . . exclusively within the scope of its original sovereignty."[13] Therefore the New York statutes did not violate the United States Constitution and did not come into conflict with any laws of Congress. A permanent injunction was issued against the interlopers, and the steamboat monopoly was secure in its legal rights for another twelve years.

If the decision in *Livingston and Fulton v. Van Ingen* had settled the legal status of the monopoly, it had not guaranteed it immunity from harassment. Colonel Aaron Ogden, former United States senator and governor of New Jersey, acquired a steamboat, the *Sea-Horse,* for use on New York Bay. After the *Van Ingen* case, he obtained an exclusive right from the New Jersey legislature to navigate her territorial waters.[14] He made life so uncomfortable for the monopoly that in 1815 he obtained from it an exclusive license to operate the *Sea-Horse* between New York and New Jersey. About this time, another commerce-minded man entered the picture. Thomas Gibbons, a resident of Elizabethtown, New Jersey, had an interest in a ferry property which he leased to Ogden for the latter's new venture. The arrangement should have been an amicable one, but Gibbons was an adventurer after bigger game. He soon bought two steamboats of his own and began to operate a rival ferry service to New York with no legal authorization. These machinations led to trouble between Ogden and Gibbons and to the litigation which would culminate in the famous Supreme Court case.

As Gibbons became increasingly offending, Ogden sued him, asking for protection of his exclusive grant from the monopoly.[15] Chancellor James Kent granted Ogden an injunction and almost a year later Gibbons filed an answer for review of the decree. In it Gibbons set up two defenses, the more important of which was that he had a right to navigate the nation's public waters (which included those of New York) by virtue of a federal license issued under an act of Congress for the enrolling and licensing of ships or vessels to be employed in the coasting trade.[16]

Kent disallowed Gibbons' legal claim under the license.[17] He did not find that the Federal Coasting Act of 1793 conferred any right of navigation because the statute merely determined by registration that the ships were American in character and thus entitled to certain statutory privileges concerning tonnage duties. Furthermore, an explicit invalidation of the state laws would have had to have been written into the congressional act in order to sanction Gibbons' claim. Then Kent drove his point home: "There is no collision between the act of Congress and the acts of this state, creating the steamboat monopoly."[18] The injunction stood.

Gibbons appealed to the New York Court of Errors.[19] His counsel, in addition to pleading the federal license, argued that the exclusive right of the monopoly was inconsistent with the power of Congress to regulate commerce among the several states. The contention was put succinctly: "The right to regulate the coasting trade is solely and exclusively vested in Congress. No state can, therefore, restrain or prohibit the exercise of that right."[20] Counsel for Ogden relied upon the precedent set in *Livingston and Fulton v. Van Ingen* and upon Kent's Chancery Court opinion concerning the license.

Justice Jonas Platt wasted no time in upholding Kent.[21] He made two main points: (1) New York had the power to grant the exclusive privilege because the Commerce Clause per se did not negate or restrict the sovereign power of the state in such matters; and (2) the coasting license was designed only to establish a criterion of national character. Thus the federal statute gave no right of navigating the nation's waters and did not come into collision with the state laws. From this decision, Gibbons appealed directly to the United States Supreme Court.

Before coming to the Supreme Court case itself, it is necessary to notice two United States Circuit Court cases which were precedents for, and had a bearing upon, the steamboat case. The first is *The Brig Wilson v. United States*,[22] which was decided in the Circuit Court of Virginia in 1820 with John Marshall presiding. The details of this admiralty case are unimportant; what is important and relevant is what Marshall said about commerce:

> From the adoption of the constitution, till this time, the universal sense of America has been, that the word "commerce," as used in that instrument, is to be considered a generic term, comprehending navigation, or, that a control over navigation is necessarily incidental to the power to regulate commerce.[23]

Here was a clue, then, to the way Marshall would interpret the word "commerce"; it included navigation, at the very least.

The second case has even greater relevance. It concerned a free British national, a Negro seaman named Elkison, who was being held in jail in Charleston, South Carolina, under an act which allowed the seizure, incarceration, and sale into slavery of any free citizens of color who entered the state.[24] The British captain retained counsel and appealed to the Circuit Court for the release of Elkison on the ground that the state law was in conflict with the power of Congress to regulate commerce.[25] Justice William Johnson, a South Carolinian himself, held that the state statute was unconstitutional and therefore void. His chief reasoning was as follows: "But the right of the general government to regulate commerce with sister states and foreign nations is a paramount and exclusive right. . . . [The very words of the grant to Congress] sweep away the whole subject, and leave nothing for the states to act upon."[26] The significance of this case, which created a storm of local protest, lies in the fact that Johnson held the power over commerce to be exclusive in the national government and thus denied, in its entirety, to the states.[27]

In the Supreme Court

Arguments of Counsel

Following his defeat in the New York Court of Errors, Gibbons appealed his case to the Supreme Court. Because of a technicality,[28] the appeal was dismissed, refiled, continued, and finally set down for argument in the February term, 1824. Meanwhile, Gibbons hired Daniel Webster and William Wirt (United States Attorney General) to represent him; Ogden retained Thomas J. Oakley and Thomas A. Emmet as counsel. With these formidable opponents facing each other, the great steamboat case, *Gibbons v. Ogden*,[29] was argued the first part of February, 1824.

Daniel Webster opened the argument for the appellant.[30] He found that the case raised two substantial questions: (1) Did the New York legislature have the power to pass the monopoly laws; and (2) if so, did the laws interfere with any right enjoyed under the federal Constitution and laws of the United States, and were they therefore void? On the first point, he contended that the power of Congress to regulate commerce was complete and entire and, to a certain extent, necessarily exclusive; furthermore, the state acts in question were regulations of commerce, "in a most important particular," and affected commerce in those respects in which it was under the exclusive authority of Congress and forbidden to the states.

Webster turned to the history of the Confederation to support his argument. He thought nothing was clearer than that the primary motive of the framers at the Philadelphia Convention was to achieve national regulation of commerce in order to rescue it from "the embarrassing and destructive consequences resulting from the legislation of so many different states" and to place it under the protection of a uniform law. This uniform law required that at least the "higher branches" of commercial regulation must be committed to a single hand; and that these high and important powers over commerce were vested exclusively in Congress was apparent from a reading of the Constitution. Such powers could not be concurrent with the states; otherwise, all the old confusion and divisiveness would return, and this was not to be tolerated. Concurrent power in the states would be "insidious and dangerous."

Webster explained away all the state statutes respecting roads, toll bridges, ferries, and so forth as regulations of police rather than commerce. These kinds of laws represented "internal legislation" over

14

which the states had complete control, but the New York grant was not of this nature. All legislative acts which created monopolies of trade or navigation were regulations of commerce, and such grants were included in the "higher branches" of commercial regulation which had been exclusively delegated to Congress; it would be "totally contradictory" for the states to exercise a similar authority. Then he summed up the first and, to his mind, most important part of his argument:

> If, then, the power of commercial regulation, possessed by Congress, be, in regard to the great branches of it, exclusive; and if this grant of New York be a commercial regulation affecting commerce, in respect of these great branches, then the grant is void, whether any case of actual collision ha[s] happened or not.[31]

Having argued this "selectively exclusive" doctrine of the federal commerce power, Webster turned his attention to the Federal Coasting Act of 1793 and the license which Gibbons held under it. He interpreted the Act as follows: The enrollment had the effect of ascertaining the ownership and character of the vessel; the license conferred the right to navigate freely the waters of the United States and to carry on the coasting trade. Thus Gibbons had a right, as a United States citizen, to go from New Jersey to New York; and no act of the New York legislature could deprive him of it. Therefore a case of actual collision had occurred between the state grant and an act of Congress; and the state grant was inoperative under the supremacy clause of the Constitution.[32]

Such was the gist of Webster's argument. In retrospect, it contained two main points: (1) the power of Congress to regulate commerce depended upon a doctrine of "selective exclusiveness"; in its "higher branches," commerce was solely under the authority of the federal government, and the states were without power to enact laws affecting it; and (2) the New York laws creating the monopoly came into direct conflict with the Federal Coasting Act and were therefore void.

Thomas Oakley made the leading argument for the respondent.[33] The bulk of it concerned the issue of "exclusive" versus "concurrent" power in order to show that the commerce power was concurrent between the national government and the states. Oakley began with the proposition that the states, by their own act in the Declaration of Independence, had created themselves as sovereign and independent nation-states. On the other hand, the United States Constitution was one of limited and expressly delegated powers, which could only be exercised as granted, or in the instances enumerated; this derived from the nature of the Constitution itself and from the express stipulation in the Tenth Amendment. These delegated powers were of two types: (1) those exclusively vested in the federal government and (2) those concurrent with the states. Here Oakley followed Hamilton's formulations in *Federalist 32* in order to contend that the commerce power had to be concurrent. It had been fully possessed and exercised by the states after the Declaration of Independence; it had not been granted, in exclusive terms, to Congress or prohibited to the states; and finally, there was nothing in 'the nature of the power which rendered it exclusive. Several proofs of the last statement could be adduced: (1) the specific prohibitions on the states of Article I, section 10, would have been unnecessary if the commerce power had not been considered concurrent by the framers; (2) the commerce power was limited in Congress to the regulation of commerce "among the several States" and did not extend to regulation of the internal commerce of any state; and (3) the long practice of the states in regulating many objects of commerce showed that the power had always been thought to be concurrent.

Having established to his satisfaction that the commerce power was a concurrent one, Oakley turned to the matter of the supposed repugnancy of the New York laws to the power of Congress to regulate commerce. First, he argued that the foundation of the right of intercourse among the states was the *jus commune* of nations and that the Constitution had not changed this. All the regulations of a state, then, which operated within its own limits, were binding upon all who came within its jurisdiction. Second, he argued that the statutes in question were nothing more than regulations of the internal navigation of the state; they applied only to the territorial waters of the state. As a sovereign entity, New York had a clear right to regulate its internal trade and transit; and the coasting license did not affect this sovereign right. In short, there was no conflict between federal and state law.

Thomas Emmet covered much the same ground as Oakley, but he stressed three considerations in particular.[34] First, he argued for a narrow definition of commerce. The proper acceptance of the term was "the exchange of one thing for another; the interchange of commodities; trade or traffic." Congress might have an incidental power to regulate navigation, but only insofar as that navigation was used for these limited purposes of commerce. Second, Emmet went into an extensive review of the legislation of different states on pilotage, light houses, inspection, health and quarantine, bridges, ferries, and turnpikes in order to show that the individual states had always exercised the power of making very material regulations respecting commerce. Third, he made a detailed examination of the Federal Coasting Act to prove that the license issued under it only gave "some privileges as to payment of tonnage duties, and less frequent entries at the customhouses." But even if the congressional act gave a right of entry or navigation, the exclusive state grant did not prevent this; it merely provided that no unfranchised vessels could use "the force or agency of steam or fire" on New York waters.

William Wirt made the closing argument.[35] He reiterated the most important of Webster's propositions and contended for a broad definition of commerce which would include navigation, the hauling of passengers, and any kind of intercommunication or intercourse. And he expanded upon the "selectively exclusive" doctrine which his colleague has proposed:

> Some subjects are, in their nature, extremely multifarious and complex. The same subject may consist of a great variety of branches, each extending itself into remote, minute, and infinite ramifications. One branch alone, of such a subject, might be given exclusively to Congress, (and the power is exclusive only so far as it is granted,) yet, on other branches of the same subject, the States might act, without interfering with the power exclusively granted to Congress. Commerce is such a subject. . . . One or more branches of this subject might be given exclusively to Congress; the others may be left open to the states. They may, therefore, legislate on commerce, though they cannot touch that branch which is given exclusively to Congress.[36]

> . . . It was viewing the subject in this light, that induced his learned associate to assume the position . . . not that all the commercial powers are exclusive, but that those powers being separated, there are some which are exclusive in their nature; and among them, is that power which concerns navigation, and which prescribes the vehicles in which commerce shall be carried on.[37]

At the end Wirt waxed melodramatic; he cited the retaliatory laws of New Jersey, Connecticut, and Ohio and asserted that here were three states almost on the verge of commercial civil war with New York. Then he pleaded with the Court to interpose its "benign and mediatorial influence" to prevent the breakup of the Union.

Opinions of the Court

On March 2, 1824, John Marshall handed down the majority opinion.[38] He began by briefly, but firmly, rejecting the premise that the expressly granted powers of the Constitution should be construed strictly. This would have the effect of denying to the national government those powers which the words of the instrument clearly imported, would cripple it, and would render it unequal to the ends for which it was instituted. Then he turned to his famous delineation of the Commerce Clause.

First, he took up the word "commerce" and gave it a broad definition. Commerce was a general term, applicable to many objects and not restricted to traffic, to buying and selling, or to the interchange of commodities: "Commerce, undoubtedly, is traffic, but it is something more; it is intercourse." Furthermore, all America had uniformly understood from the time of framing the Constitution that commerce included navigation; and "a power to regulate navigation is as expressly granted as if that term had been added to the word 'commerce.' "[39]

Second, to what commerce did this power extend? Commerce, as the word was used in the Constitution, was a unit and had to carry the same meaning throughout the clause. Commerce with foreign nations comprehended every species of commercial intercourse; the same was true with the states: "The word 'among' means intermingled with. . . . Commerce among the states cannot stop at the external boundary line of each state, but may be introduced into the interior."[40]

But were there any limits to the reach of the power? Yes. "Comprehensive as the word 'among' is, it may very properly be restricted to that commerce which concerns more states than one. . . . The completely internal commerce of a state, then, may be considered as reserved for the state itself."[41]

Third, what was this power? Marshall gave wide scope to the constitutional grant in these sweeping terms: "It is the power to regulate; that is, to prescribe the rule by which commerce is to be governed. This power, like all others vested in Congress, is complete in itself, may be exercised to its utmost extent, and acknowledges no limitations, other than are prescribed in the constitution."[42] Recognizing the import of these words and the possibility of future abuse of this vast power by Congress, Marshall added a prophetic answer to those who would restrict legislative choice and action:

The wisdom and the discretion of Congress, their identity with the people, and the influence which their constituents possess at elections, are, in this, as in many other instances, . . . the sole restraints on which they have relied, to secure them from its abuse. They are the restraints on which the people must often rely solely, in all representative governments.[43]

Having thus dissected and interpreted the Commerce Clause, Marshall focused on the problem of whether the commerce power was exclusive or concurrent. But he did not resolve it. He noted that counsel for Gibbons had contended that the word "regulate" implied in its nature "full power over the thing to be regulated" and that this necessarily excluded "the action of all others that would perform the same operation on the same thing"; and he hinted that he was strongly inclined toward such an exclusive-power doctrine: "There is great force in this argument, and the court is not satisfied that it has been refuted."[44] But Marshall became uncharacteristically cautious and guarded at this point and refused to commit himself. Instead, he stated that whether the power was still in the states or not, the question could be dismissed because Congress had already acted. The sole question which remained was whether a state could regulate commerce among the states while Congress was regulating it. But here again Marshall was equivocal. He avoided a direct declaration by holding that if a state, in legislating on subjects acknowledged to be within its control, adopted a measure of the same character as an act of Congress, it did not derive its authority from the delegated power, but from some other power which was reserved to the state. This was the first oblique reference, in a constitutional law case, to what would come to be called the "police power" of the states.

Marshall was now in a position to move to the easier question of whether the laws of New York came into collision with any act of Congress. He addressed himself to the Federal Coasting Act of 1793 and had no trouble in finding that section one granted to the vessels which it described the privilege of carrying on the coasting trade. The process of enrollment conferred an American character upon them; the license granted the authority or permission to trade and hence the right to navigate the coastal waters of the United States. The final question was whether a steam engine, in actual use, deprived a ship of the right conferred by the license. Marshall could not have been more explicit: "If the power reside in Congress . . . to regulate commerce, then acts applying that power to vessels generally, must be construed as comprehending all vessels.[45] . . . [T] he laws of Congress, for the regulation of commerce, do not look to the principle by which vessels are moved."[46]

At long last he sealed the fate of the monopoly: "[T]he act of a state inhibiting the use of either [wind or fire] to any vessel having a license under the act of Congress, comes, we think, in direct collision with that act",[47] because of the supremacy clause, the state laws would automatically have to fall.

This decided the case. The New York laws creating the great steamboat monopoly were declared void, and the injunction against Gibbons was annulled. Commerce was free.

Justice William Johnson wrote his own concurring opinion.[48] He thought that one of the main reasons for the adoption of the federal Constitution was that the states during the Confederation passed "iniquitous laws and impolitic measures, from which grew up a conflict of commercial regulations, destructive to the harmony of the states."[49] In order to preserve harmony, Congress was granted the power to regulate commerce among the states, and that power was exclusive. This meant that all state laws concerning commercial regulations dropped lifeless from the statute books; the grant of power carried with it the whole subject and left nothing to the states. Furthermore, the scope of the commerce power was wide; an integral part of it was the power to control navigation. Thus the New York laws were clearly unconstitutional and void.

Johnson went on to disagree with the Court's view of the effect of the federal coasting license; he held that it was only meant to confer certain privileges of lower and less frequent tonnage duties on American vessels. But this did not affect the outcome of the case; in fact, the act itself represented a full expression of Congress on "commerce coastwise," and the power of the states here was at an end.

Finally, Johnson, like Marshall, recognized in the states the "municipal power" of superintending their own internal concerns. He also recognized that the two levels of government might exercise their distinct powers over the same objects. When this kind of collision occurred, "the question must be decided how far the powers of Congress are adequate to put it down";[50] but the real remedy in such cases was frank and candid cooperation on both sides for the general good.

Analysis of Marshall's Decision

Gibbons v. Ogden raised three major constitutional questions: (1) what did the term "commerce" comprehend; (2) was the federal commerce power exclusive or concurrent; and (3) were the New York monopoly laws in conflict with an act of Congress and therefore void? Each of these will be considered separately, but there is one point to be made before proceeding. When the Supreme Court first confronted the task of interpreting the Commerce Clause, it had to evolve its doctrines without substantial guidance from previous precedents, analysis, or discussion; even the records of the Federal Convention provided little help in expounding its meaning or scope.[51] In a very real sense, the justices were writing on a virtually clean slate.

First, take the meaning of the word "commerce." Marshall had no difficulty in finding that commerce included navigation and the transportation of passengers for hire. He took this for granted because he believed in an "organic theory" of commerce, that is, that commercial intercourse covered a wide variety of subjects and could not be restricted to a few specific activities. But was Marshall justified in construing commerce so broadly? All of the available evidence indicates that the framers intended the commerce power to include control of navigation.[52] In fact, one of the reasons which Edmund Randolph of Virginia gave for his refusal to sign the Constitution was that it omitted a provision that national maritime laws should require a two-thirds vote of Congress for passage.[53] More important to the legitimacy of Marshall's holding, however, is the common-sense argument that the decision in *Gibbons* was necessary to the basic health of the American economy. In 1824 steamboat transportation was an efficient and economical mode of moving goods and people. The New York monopoly controlled two great water routes and impeded the growth of steamboat traffic;[54] a narrow ruling that commerce did not include navigation would have been absurd, totally unrealistic, and very detrimental to the national economic interest. Marshall's interpretation of commerce was thoroughly warranted with respect to both historical precedent and contemporary circumstance. Whether in 1787 and 1824, commerce was generally understood to comprehend all gainful business transactions (as has been claimed) is another question and one which is beyond the scope of this study.

The second question raised was whether the federal commerce power was exclusive or concurrent. This was really the crucial issue at stake in the case; accordingly, it will be examined in some depth from a number of points of view. As has been said, a careful reading of Marshall's opinion reveals that he skirted the issue and made no clear resolution of it. Now this presents two problems: (1) how did Marshall himself regard the commerce power; and (2) why did he leave the question unanswered? To begin with, Frederick D.G. Ribble, Felix Frankfurter, and William W. Crosskey all take the position that Marshall thought the commerce power was exclusive in the national government.[55] Ribble argues that in 1824 the ideas of natural law were still very predominant in legal reasoning and that, consequently, judges sought to discover, not choose, fundamental principles which could be applied to specific cases. In constitutional law, these principles were sought in the intentions of the framers and in the nature of the delegated powers. Furthermore, there was the general belief that a governmental power was an organic whole which could not be divided between competing sovereignties. Thus when Marshall considered the reasons for the adoption of the Constitution and looked upon commerce as an indivisible unit, he could easily conclude that the power to regulate it must be exclusive. Crosskey analyzes Marshall's opinion exhaustively to arrive at the same conclusion, but he is the only one who argues that Marshall really did hold the power to be exclusive in his *Gibbons* opinion.[56] It is true that Marshall expressed a decided sympathy in this direction, but that was as far as he actually went.[57] However, there is absolutely no evidence to show that Marshall ever thought the power was concurrent, and it is certainly a tenable conclusion that he did indeed regard it as exclusive and indivisible.

Now why did Marshall not use either his own theory of exclusive power or Webster's theory of "selective exclusiveness"? Frankfurter argues very convincingly that he rejected Webster's theory for two reasons. First, it was too flexible; it could be used to secure state autonomy as well as to restrict state authority. In other words, in the hands of a states' rights judge, the "higher branches" of commerce might be pushed so "high" that Congress would have very little left to control; and this prospect did not appeal to the highly nationalistic Chief Justice. Second, Webster's formula would reveal all too clearly the large discretion of the justices in construing and applying the Commerce Clause. This would only serve to arouse unnecessary popular condemnation of the Court, and one of Marshall's great objectives was to build the prestige of the judicial department in the American scheme of government. It was not that he did not want wide scope for judicial action; he did, but he also wished to cloak it from the public eye.

Why, then, did Marshall not use his own theory of exclusive national power? There appear to be at least three considerations which militated against this. First, unpopular as the steamboat monopoly was, any such sweeping, unqualified assertion of national power over commerce would almost certainly have brought the Court under heavy political attack, particularly from the Southern states with their "peculiar institution." Marshall followed very closely the events of the day; he was well aware of the bitterness of the debates in Congress over the Missouri Compromise and of the hornets' nest that Justice Johnson's *Elkison* decision had stirred up the previous summer. Apropos the latter, he expressed himself to Justice Joseph Story as not being "fond of butting against a wall in sport,"[58] in other words, as not being willing to take unnecessary risks with his judicial position. In sum, it seems fair to say that the political explosiveness of the slavery issue at the time was the most important factor in restraining the Chief Justice's hand.

But in addition to political realism, there were two doctrinal objections which compelled forbearance. First, as Frankfurter points out, while Marshall may not have been overly solicitous of states' rights, he had a hard-headed awareness of the federal nature of the Union, that is, he appreciated the complexities involved and recognized the practical necessity of allowing the member states to continue to regulate many local concerns. If he had held the commerce power to be exclusive, and this doctrine had been rigorously applied, the states would have been too drastically restricted in their powers and activities to have remained viable units in the federal system; this would have been true even though they would have retained the exercise of their inherent police powers. Second, if Congress were conceded to have exclusive authority over commerce, this would leave the Court with very little latitude in which to draw the boundary line between national and state power; and since another of Marshall's prime objectives was to increase the decision-making power of his tribunal, it is reasonable to suppose that he wished to reserve (but not presently announce) this important interpretative function for the Court so that it might play a large role in the development and future use of the Commerce Clause. Thus, as has been shown, Marshall sidestepped the central issue in the case and brought in the Federal Coasting Act to decide it.

The third and final question raised by the *Gibbons* case was whether the New York laws were in conflict with the act of Congress. No detailed examination of the latter can be attempted here, but it would appear that it was passed in the context of an intention by Congress to set tariffs and tonnage duties and to give American ships special tax advantages within the new revenue system. The Act of 1793 merely revised two earlier acts passed in 1789;[59] a study of the *Abridgement of the Debates of Congress* and the *Annals of Congress* (2 Congress, 2d session) reveals no debates on it; and it would seem that Kent, Platt, Emmet, and Johnson all made the correct interpretation of it. Thus Webster and Marshall stretched its meaning considerably when they found that it conferred the right to engage in the coasting trade and to enter any of the navigable waters of the United States. Yet it was on this supposed national right that Marshall held the New York statutes to trespass and so to be null and void.

In conclusion, several comments are in order as to the constitutional implications of the case. First, and undoubtedly foremost, Marshall gave a broad and comprehensive meaning to the word "commerce" and wide scope to the power "to regulate." This meant that as new technology created new methods of transportation and communication, all of these could easily be brought under the control of Congress. It also meant that as industrialization and urbanization created new commercial activities and new economic problems, Congress would have a vast reservoir of power with which to meet the needs and demands of the day. It was the old theme of *McCulloch v. Maryland* (1819) with respect now to the Commerce Clause: "this provision is made in a constitution, intended to endure for ages to come, and consequently, to be adapted to the various *crises* of human affairs."[60] Second, by leaving open the question of exclusive versus concurrent power, Marshall did not saddle the nation with a rigid pattern of commercial regulation. Instead, he introduced the concept of the police power of the states into American constitutional law;[61] this concept became clearer in *Willson v. The Black-Bird Creek Marsh Company* (1829) and showed up clearly in *Mayor of New York v. Miln* (1837). But third, because of this Marshall was forced to deform the Federal Coasting Act in order to reach the desired decision. There is evidence that he did this again with the Federal Tariff Act in *Brown v. Maryland* (1827) to strike down the Maryland license law;[62] obviously, he was wary of giving the federal commerce power an exclusive character. It might be asserted, as Maurice G. Baxter has written, that:

> *Gibbons v. Ogden* would have been a more satisfactory precedent if Marshall had stood firmly on broad national authority operating from the Constitution itself, regardless of Congressional action, instead of backing away from that position toward which he leaned in the first two-thirds of the opinion [that the commerce power was exclusive in the national government]....
> He would have been on even better ground if he could have overcome his usual reluctance to divide political power and had

adopted the option proposed by Webster and Wirt that only the "higher branches" of the power were exclusive. Surely interstate steamboat traffic, in those days very important economically, was a "higher branch" admitting only national legislation.[63]

But for the reasons already given, he did neither.

Constitutional Development, 1824–1852

Gibbons v. Ogden marked only the beginning of the long history of the Commerce Clause in constitutional adjudication. In *Brown v. Maryland* (1827)[64] Marshall formulated the "original-package" doctrine to strike down a state license tax on wholesalers who were importing and selling foreign goods; as long as the goods were in the possession of the importer, the state could not reach them (via the importer) because of the prohibition in Article I, section 10 of the Constitution against state imposition of any imposts or duties on imports or exports. Then Marshall went on to hold that the state act was hostile to a Federal Tariff Act, which had been passed under the commerce power, on the theory that an express authorization to import articles (as he construed the Act) included the right to sell them free from state interference; whenever state action disrupted that which was designed to be a uniform whole under the control of Congress (such as the importation of foreign goods), the state action must fail. Marshall added in *dictum* that these principles applied equally to importations from sister states, but he left the unanswered question of *Gibbons* still unanswered.

Two years later in *Willson v. The Black-Bird Creek Marsh Company* (1829)[65] Marshall sustained a Delaware act which authorized a dam across a navigable tidal creek flowing into the Delaware River, even though the dam obstructed navigation of the creek by a vessel sailing under a federal coasting license identical to that held by Gibbons. Marshall looked to the "circumstances of the case" and found that the state statute was a valid regulation designed for the improvement of health and the enhancement of property values in the area; it was not "repugnant to the power to regulate commerce in its dormant state," and it was not in conflict with any act of Congress on the subject. Marshall's language in this brief opinion indicates that he probably regarded the statute as an exercise of the state's police power.

Marshall died in 1835, and Roger Brooke Taney, a Jacksonian, succeeded him as Chief Justice. In 1837 the Court decided its next important commerce case. *Mayor of the City of New York v. Miln*[66] involved the validity of a New York law requiring masters of ships arriving in the port of New York to report certain data on all immigrants and to give bond that the latter would not become charges upon the city. The law was attacked as an interference with congressional authority over foreign commerce, but Justice Philip P. Barbour, speaking for five of the seven justices, held the law valid as a legitimate exercise of the state's police power. The statute was aimed at the internal welfare of the state and was not in conflict with any act of Congress. Three of the five (not a constitutional majority of the seven justices) held the view that New York was properly regulating commerce, and Justice Smith Thompson opted for such a concurrent power in a concurring opinion. But Barbour sidestepped the old question of whether the commerce power was exclusive or concurrent.

The Court then fell into what may best be described as a state of confusion regarding both the commerce power itself and its relation to the police power of the states. The *License Cases* (1847)[67] concerned the validity of three statutes of Massachusetts, Rhode Island, and New Hampshire, which required a license of those importing and selling intoxicating liquors. The state acts were unanimously sustained in each case; but the justices were badly divided in their reasoning, and six of them wrote nine different opinions. There was general agreement that the fact that a state tax law levied for internal police purposes had an incidental effect upon interstate commerce did not thereby invalidate it. Taney contended that the states had a concurrent power to regulate such commerce in the absence of federal action: "[T]he mere grant of power to the general government cannot, upon any just principles of construction, be construed to be an absolute prohibition to the exercise of any power over the same subject by the States."[68] And he uttered his classic definition of state police power: "the power to govern men and things within the limits of its [the state's] dominion."[69]

Then in 1849 the *Passenger Cases*[70] were decided. New York and Massachusetts had imposed a head tax upon alien passengers arriving in their ports. The constitutionality of the statutes was questioned; and the Court, in a five-to-four decision, held them void. But again there was great disparity in the reasoning of the justices, and no one view commanded a majority. Justice John McLean stated flatly that the commerce power was lodged exclusively in the national government; Taney, in dissent, repeated his theory of concurrent state power over commerce in the absence of positive congressional action.

Finally, in the watershed case of *Cooley v. The Board of Wardens of the Port of Philadelphia* (1852),[71] the Court cleared up much of the confusion surrounding the Commerce Clause. At stake was the validity of a Pennsylvania Act of 1803 which required vessles entering or departing the port of Philadelphia to take on local pilots. Justice Benjamin R. Curtis first held that a rule which is a regulation of commerce when enacted by Congress is equally such a regulation when enacted by the states; he did not evade the crucial issue by labeling the act an exercise of the state's police power. The question then became "whether the grant of the commercial power to Congress, did per se deprive the States of all power to regulate pilots."[72] He answered this as follows:

> The grant of commercial power to Congress does not contain any terms which expressly exclude the states from exercising an authority over its subject-matter. If they are excluded, it must be because of the nature of the power, thus granted to Congress, requires that a similar authority should not exist in the states.[73]

> . . . But when the nature of a power like this is spoken of, when it is said that the nature of the power requires that it should be exercised exclusively by Congress, it must be intended to refer to the subjects of that power, and to say they are of such a nature as to require exclusive legislation by Congress.[74]

> . . . Either absolutely to affirm, or deny, that the nature of this power requires exclusive legislation by Congress, is to lose sight of the nature of the subjects of this power, and to assert concerning all of them, what is really applicable but to a part.[75]

Having turned from the nature of the power to its subjects, Curtis found that the power to regulate commerce involved a vast field which contained many subjects. Some of these were national in character and demanded uniform regulation; here federal power was properly exclusive. Others were local in nature (though still parts of interstate commerce) and demanded a diversity of regulation; here the states had concurrent power over commerce, exercisable only where Congress had not yet acted. Curtis focused on the specific matter in hand and discovered an Act of Congress of August 7, 1789,[76] which provided that pilotage should continue to be regulated by the states until there was further legislation by Congress. He had no difficulty in finding that the Pennsylvania statute was fully in accord with the express will of Congress and that pilotage was a local subject which could best be regulated by as many designs "as the legislative discretion of the several states should deem applicable to the local peculiarities of the ports within their limits."[77] But Curtis was careful to confine his ruling to "these precise questions" on pilotage, and he emphasized the point that the majority opinion did not extend

> to the question what other subjects, under the commercial power, are within the exclusive power of Congress, or may be regulated by the states in the absence of all congressional legislation; nor to the general question, how far any regulation of a subject by Congress, may be deemed to operate as an exclusion of all legislation by the states upon the same subject.[78]

Two comments are in order on the immediate importance and future implications of *Cooley v. The Board of Wardens*. First, in adjudicating the force of the commerce clause, the Supreme Court finally compromised the question of exclusive versus concurrent power by adopting, in effect, the "selectively exclusive" theory of Webster in *Gibbons* and holding that certain subjects of national importance demanded uniform—or exclusive—congressional regulation, while others of strictly local concern admitted of diverse—or concurrent—state regulation. This theory of the commerce power, based as it was on "facts" rather than philosophical or legal abstractions, proved to be very practical and very viable; it gave to the federal government all the power needed to regulate an expanding, increasingly technologically sophisticated, industrial economy, without at the same time obliterating the states in the process. From the standpoint of the development of constitutional law, the case is a landmark second only to *Gibbons v. Ogden;* and the *Cooley* rule is still in use today.

Second, in turning its attention away from questions concerning the nature of the commerce power (which had predominated in Marshall's thought) to a consideration of the *subjects* of that power, the Court reserved to itself the power of ultimate determination with respect to the classification of those subjects and thus retained the constitutional prerogative which Marshall had historically established for it—that of being the final arbiter of the boundaries of national and state power. This is the great significance of the *Cooley* case; for in the final analysis, the Court reserved for itself great and far-reaching power to make decisions which would affect the very core of the American federal system. In short, Marshall's primary objectives had been fulfilled; the Commerce Clause represented a potential source of tremendous centralized authority which could be used to weld the diverse parts of the country into a single Nation, and the Supreme Court occupied a position of impressive power and prestige *vis-à-vis* both the coordinate branches of the national government and the states of the Union.

Notes

1. 9 Wheaton 1.

2. 12 Howard 299.

3. *New York Laws,* II, 472.

4. *New York Laws,* IV, 215.

5. George Dangerfield, *Chancellor Robert R. Livingston of New York 1746-1813* (New York: Harcourt, Brace and Co., 1960), 405. The historical discussion here relies mainly upon four sources: the one just cited, 403-22; George Dangerfield, "The Steamboat Case," in John A. Garraty (ed.), *Quarrels That Have Shaped the Constitution* (New York: Harper & Row, Publishers, Inc., 1964), 49-61; W. Howard Mann, "The Marshall Court: Nationalization of Private Rights and Personal Liberty from the Authority of the Commerce Clause," *Indiana Law Journal,* XXXVIII (Winter, 1963), 117-238; David W. Kendall, "Mr. Gibbons and Colonel Ogden," *Michigan State Bar Journal,* XXVI (February, 1947), 22-25.

6. *Livingston and Fulton v. Van Ingen,* 9 Johnson 507 (New York, 1812).

7. Full name: New York Court for the Trial of Impeachments and the Correction of Errors.

8. 9 Johnson 507, 536-56.

9. Ibid., 572-89.

10. Ibid., 574.

11. Alexander Hamilton (Publius), *Federalist 32,* in Jacob E. Cooke (ed.), *The Federalist* (Cleveland: The World Publishing Company, 1961), 200.

12. 9 Johnson 507, 574-75. For later reference, it is important to note that Kent did not argue that the reserved powers of the states served per se to reduce an enumerated power; and he recognized that is was the unique function of the Court to formulate national rules from the authority of the Constitution.

13. Ibid., 578.

14. *New Jersey Laws,* 38th Session, 1st Sit., 61.

15. *Ogden v. Gibbons,* 4 Johnson Ch. 150 (New York, 1819).

16. *U.S. Statutes at Large,* I, 305.

17. Johnson Ch. 150, 156-64.

18. Ibid., 158.

19. *Gibbons v. Ogden,* 17 Johnson 488 (New York, 1820).

20. Ibid., 502.

21. Ibid., 508-10.

22. *Federal Cases* 239.

23. Ibid., 243.

24. *Statutes at Large of South Carolina,* VII, 461.

25. *Elkison v. Deliesseline, 8 Federal Cases* 493 (1823).

26. Ibid., 495.

27. For further information on the case and on events immediately following it, see two sources: Mann, "Marshall Court," *Ind. Law J.,* XXXVIII (Winter, 1963), 131-48; Donald G. Morgan, *Justice William Johnson: The First Dissenter* (Columbia, S.C.: University of South Carolina Press, 1954), 190-206.

28. The record was incomplete because it did not show that the New York Court of Errors had made a final decree in the state case. 6 Wheaton 448 (1821).

29. 9 Wheaton 1.

30. For his complete argument, see ibid., 3-33.

31. Ibid., 26-27.

32. "This Constitution, and the Laws of the United States . . . shall be the supreme Law of the Land . . . any Thing in the Constitution or Laws of any State to the Contrary notwithstanding." U.S. Constitution, Article VI, paragraph 2.

33. For his complete argument, see 9 Wheaton 1, 33-78.

34. For Emmet's complete argument, see ibid., 79-159.

35. For his complete argument, see ibid., 159-86.

36. Ibid., 165.

37. Ibid., 180-81.

38. For his complete opinion, see ibid., 186-222.

39. Ibid., 193.

40. Ibid., 194.

41. Ibid, 194-95.

42. Ibid., 196-97.

43. Ibid., 197.

44. Ibid., 209. One of Webster's several arguments was that the framers of the Constitution had intended that "the commerce of the States was to be a *unit*" and so had vested the commerce power exclusively in Congress. See ibid., 9-11.

45. Ibid., 217.

46. Ibid., 219-20.

47. Ibid., 221.

48. For his complete opinion, see ibid., 222-39.

49. Ibid., 224.

50. Ibid., 239.

51. It should be mentioned that the extensive notes which James Madison took at the Convention were not published until 1840.

52. Albert S. Abel, "The Commerce Clause in the Constitutional Convention and in Contemporary Comment," *Minnesota Law Review,* XXV (March, 1941), 432-94. Even though Abel argues that the commerce power was meant to be a "mild, modest little power," he is clear on the point that it was intended to cover navigation and maritime affairs. Three other authors confirm this, except that they argue that

the commerce power was intended to have wide scope and give Congress great power: Robert L. Stern, "That Commerce Which Concerns More States Than One," *Harvard Law Review,* XLVII (1933-34), 1335-66; Joseph A. Roper, "The Constitution: Discovered or Discarded," *Notre Dame Lawyer,* XVI (January, 1941), 97-124; George L. Haskins, "John Marshall and the Commerce Clause of the Constitution," *University of Pennsylvania Law Review,* CIV (October, 1955), 23-37.

53. See "Edmund Randolph to the Speaker of the Virginia House of Delegates," October 10, 1787, in Max Farrand (ed.), *The Records of the Federal Convention of 1787* (4 vols., New Haven, Conn.: Yale University Press, 1911), III, 123. Randolph complained about "the submission of commerce to a mere majority in the legislature, with no other check than the revision of the president." Ibid., 127. For further proof that he believed commerce included navigation, see Abel, "The Commerce Clause," *Minn. Law R.,* XXV (March, 1941), 432, 452-56. The two-thirds requirement was part of the Pinckney Plan and was rejected by the Convention. But years later Charles Pinckney recalled that "the power was given to Congress to regulate the commerce by water between the States" and cited the restrictions on Congress in Article I, section 9 of the Constitution as the clearest proof of "what the power to regulate commerce among the several States means." See "Charles Pinckney in the House of Representatives," February 14, 1820, in Farrand (ed.), *Records,* III, 439, 444.

54. This point may be supported by reference to two sources: Albert J. Beveridge, *The Life of John Marshall* (4 vols., Boston: Houghton Mifflin Company, 1929), IV, 446-47; Dangerfield, "The Steamboat Case," in Garraty (ed.), *Quarrels,* 57.

55. For the discussion which follows, see three sources: Frederick D.G. Ribble, *State and National Power over Commerce* (New York: Columbia University Press, 1937), 3-52; William W. Crosskey, *Politics and the Constitution in the History of the United States* (2 vols., Chicago: The University of Chicago Press, 1953), I, 229-92; Felix Frankfurter, *The Commerce Clause under Marshall, Taney and Waite* (Chapel Hill, N.C.: The University of North Carolina Press, 1937), 12-45.

56. Crosskey, *Politics and the Constitution,* I, 252-80. As further proof that Marshall did this, he cites the case of *North River Steamboat Company v. Johnson R. Livingston,* 1 Hopkins Ch. 149 (New York, 1824), 3 Cowen 711 (New York, 1825). This case involved purely intrastate movement on the Hudson River. Chief Justice John Savage struck down the monopoly and refused an injunction on the narrow ground that the Hudson was a public navigable river not included in the wholly internal commerce of the state; such navigation composed a part of the coasting trade and was subject to the regulation and control of

Congress alone. Then he went on to add in dictum that Marshall had held the commerce power to be exclusive and not split between the two levels of government. (Rather than really proving the point, this case merely demonstrates the ambiguity of Marshall's remarks on whether the commerce power was exclusive or concurrent.)

57. Maurice G. Baxter, *Daniel Webster & the Supreme Court* (Amherst, Mass.: The University of Massachusetts Press, 1966), 204-05. For a full analysis of Marshall's opinion, see ibid., 202-07. A word of explanation is indicated here. It will readily be seen that the present chapter makes several points identical to, or parallel with, those presented in Baxter's book. Thus the author makes no claim to any special originality of analysis; he does, however, assert that his own extensive research confirms the accuracy and soundness of those views.

58. Marshall to Story, September 26, 1823, Story Papers (Massachusetts Historical Society), quoted in Baxter, *Webster,* 206-07.

59. *U.S. Statutes at Large,* I, 55 and 94.

60. 4 Wheaton 316, 415.

61. George Haskins (footnote 52) agrees with Frankfurter on this matter, as does Wallace Mendelson, "New Light on *Fletcher v. Peck* and *Gibbons v. Ogden,*" *Yale Law Journal* LVIII (1948-49), 567-73.

62. Frankfurter, *The Commerce Clause,* 20.

63. Baxter, *Webster,* 206.

64. 12 Wheaton 419.

65. 2 Peters 245.

66. 11 Peters 102.

67. 5 Howard 504.

68. Ibid., 579.

69. Ibid., 583.

70. 7 Howard 283.

71. 12 Howard 299.

72. Ibid., 318.

73. Ibid., 318.

74. Ibid., 319.

75. Ibid., 319.

76. *U.S. Statutes at Large*, I, 54.

77. 12 Howard 299, 319.

78. Ibid., 320.

2   From Cooley to the New Deal

The period from 1852 to 1937 saw the unfolding of several significant trends in Commerce-Clause adjudication before the Supreme Court. While it would be impossible to cover every aspect of these developments in a purely transitional chapter, three areas in particular warrant—and will receive—some attention: (1) the constitutional scope for state regulation of interstate commerce; (2) the increased exercise of the commerce power by Congress, particularly after 1900, to create, in effect, a federal police power; and (3) coincidentally with this second phenomenon, the rise of the doctrine of dual federalism as a limitation upon national power.

State Power

In *Cooley v. The Board of Wardens* (1852) the Supreme Court shifted the focus of its inquiry from the nature of the commerce power to the subjects upon which it operated. Those subjects which were national in scope demanded uniform regulation and came under the exclusive control of Congress; those subjects which were essentially local in character acknowledged multiform superintendence and might be left to state authority. In other words, the *Cooley* rule furnished a way whereby a limited state power could be exercised over local aspects of interstate commerce, provided there was an absence of conflicting federal legislation and provided the matters were otherwise within state power to regulate.[1] This three-pronged doctrine gave to the states a partial concurrent power over commerce, including activities which would ordinarily be classed as interstate commerce. But it left to the Court, as the final arbiter between national and state power, the all-important task of working out a system of adequate declarations with respect to the precise limitations on state action. The result was that various judicial formulas had to be devised to decide the steady flow of litigation which involved questions of state power. Some of these more important formulations will be considered and specific cases used to illustrate their application, but no attempt will be made to be definitive either as to the propositions themselves or as to the complete lines of cases which flow from them.

Direct and Indirect Effects

One of the first broad formulas was that of the direct and indirect effect upon interstate commerce. This reinterpretation of the *Cooley* rule was designed basically to determine when a recognized local activity could remain under state control and when it had to come under federal authority. The general idea was this: if the Court considered the activity to be of more than local interest, state regulation of it was held to exert a "direct" effect on commerce and had to fall; if, however, the Court viewed the activity as merely local in scope, continued state control was regarded as having an "indirect" or "incidental" effect and might stand, as long as the other requirements of the *Cooley* rule obtained. Closely related to this direct-indirect dichotomy was the concept of a burden upon commerce. The Court often took the position that a state regulation which had a direct effect on commerce *ipso facto* placed an unconstitutional "burden" upon it. A corollary of both these propositions was the final determination, fatal to any state action, that the subject was national in character; that is, if a state enactment were found to affect interstate commerce directly or to burden or obstruct it unduly, the Court frequently came to the conclusion that the subject demanded that uniform regulation which only Congress could dispense. A few illustrations will be useful.

In *Reading Railroad Company v. Pennsylvania* (1873),[2] often referred to as the *State Freight Tax Case,* the Supreme Court reviewed a Pennsylvania act of 1864 which required transportation companies to pay a tax at specified rates on each two thousand pounds of freight, whether carried wholly within the state or in interstate trade. Justice William Strong reasoned that the Pennsylvania legislature had made the payment of the tax a condition for transporting goods into or out of the state and that this constituted a "burden" on the prosecution of such commerce; it was of national importance that "over the subject there should be but one regulating power," and the tax was invalid as applied to cargo which moved interstate. The same idea as expressed three years later in *Henderson v. Mayor of New York* (1876).[3] In striking down a statute requiring a fee of $1.50 for every alien passenger arriving at New York from a foreign port, Justice Samuel F. Miller said, "A regulation which imposes onerous, perhaps impossible, conditions on those engaged in active commerce with foreign nations, must of necessity be national in its character."[4]

Hall v. DeCuir (1878),[5] another case of this era, also illustrates the Court's thinking. An 1869 Louisiana law prohibited discrimination between white and colored passengers in accommodations furnished by common carriers within the state. In refusing to hold it applicable to an interstate steamship, Chief Justice Morrison R. Waite first admitted that it was not always easy to draw the line between state power and the "exclusive power of Congress" over commerce. Then he continued:

> But we think it may safely be said that state legislation which seeks to impose a direct burden upon interstate commerce, or to interfere directly with its freedom, does enroach upon the exclusive power of Congress. The statute now under consideration, in our opinion, occupies that position. It does not act upon the business through the local instruments to be employed after coming within the State, but directly upon the business as it comes into the State from without or goes out from within.
>
> . . . It was to meet just such a case that the commercial clause in the Constitution was adopted. The River Mississippi passes through or along the borders of ten different States, and its tributaries reach many more. The commerce upon these waters is immense, and its regulation clearly a matter of national concern.[6]

Waite pointed out the "great inconvenience and unnecessary hardship which would follow if each state could regulate interstate carriers as it chose. Commerce could not flourish under such conditions; uniformity of regulations was a necessity, "and to secure it Congress, which is untrammeled by State lines, has been invested with the exclusive legislative power of determining what such regulations shall be."[7]

Two cases decided some years apart illustrate the Court's favorable view of state legislation. One is *Greer v. Connecticut* (1896),[8] which sustained a state act making it an offense to have in one's possession, for the purpose of transportation beyond the state, certain species of game birds lawfully killed within the state. The Court thought that the law only "indirectly" affected interstate commerce and upheld it. A similar example is *Hygrade Provision Co. v. Sherman* (1925),[9] which validated a New York statute prohibiting the sale of meat misbranded as kosher. The Court held that the regulation: (1) did not impose a direct burden on interstate commerce, (2) came fairly within the range of the state's police power, (3) did not conflict with any federal legislation, and (4) was not invalid because it might "incidentally" affect commerce in meat.

However, the Court often struck down state regulations of commerce. Thus in *Seaboard Air Line Railway v. Blackwell* (1917)[10] a Georgia statute which required trains to slow down to nearly a full stop at grade crossings was held invalid as "a direct burden upon interstate commerce." A typical case is *DiSanto v. Pennsylvania* (1927).[11] The state had made it a misdemeanor for any person or corporation (other than a railway or steamship company) to engage in the business of selling steamship tickets without first having obtained a license from the Commissioner of Banking. The license was granted upon proof of good moral character and fitness to conduct the business; it could be revoked for fraud, misrepresentation, or failure to account for funds received. The statute was designed primarily to prevent exploitation of the poor and of immigrants who were interested in buying trans-Atlantic passage for relatives. Its validity was challenged before the Supreme Court.

Justice Pierce Butler made short work of the state license requirement; it was "a direct burden" on a well recognized part of foreign commerce and thus was a constitutionally prohibited regulation, "regardless of the purpose with which it was passed." Justice Louis D. Brandeis, joined by Justice Oliver Wendell Holmes, protested that the statute was a valid exertion of Pennsylvania's police power to protect its citizens, particularly "persons of small means, unfamiliar with our language and institutions," from fraud and sharp practice and that it affected foreign commerce only "indirectly."

But a more cogent dissent—one which was a harbinger of things to come—was filed by a justice who had come on the Court only two years before. Harland Fiske Stone spelled out his objection to Butler's reasoning thus:

> In this case the traditional test of the limit of state action by inquiring whether the interference with commerce is direct or indirect seems to me too mechanical, too uncertain in its application, and too remote from actualities, to be of value. In

thus making use of the expressions, "direct" and "indirect interference" with commerce, we are doing little more than using labels to describe a result rather than any trustworthy formula by which it is reached.[12]

To his mind, state regulations were to be sustained,

not because the effect on commerce is nominally indirect, but because a consideration of all the facts and circumstances, such as the nature of the regulation, its function, the character of the business involved and the actual effect on the flow of commerce, lead to the conclusion that the regulation concerns interests peculiarly local and does not infringe the national interest in maintaining the freedom of commerce across state lines.[13]

In this case the interference with commerce was "local in character" and interposed no prohibited "barrier to commerce." Holmes and Brandeis concurred with the future Chief Justice, but for the time being the mechanistic Butler view prevailed.

Discrimination

A second formula used by the Court involved the matter of discrimination against commerce. If it found that a state regulation "discriminated against" extrastate commerce in favor of local business, the act was likely to fail. At the same time, the Court often considered the purpose of the state act or the beneficial effect which would accrue to the state from its application. It then weighed the anticipated benefit against the detriment to interstate commerce to determine the validity of the local regulation. Thus a good purpose could help save a relatively severe law, while a bad purpose could invalidate a much more harmless interference with commerce. Intimately associated with these ideas was the concept of freedom of commerce—the proposition that the Commerce Clause in and of itself demanded "free" commercial intercourse within the United States and automatically prohibited state attempts to interfere with or restrict the flow of goods and services interstate. These formulas gained increasing judicial favor as national economic activity expanded rapidly following the end of the Civil War and Reconstruction.

An early application of the no-discrimination doctrine came in *Welton v. Missouri* (1876),[14] in which the Court struck down a state law which required any person selling merchandise not grown, produced, or manufactured in Missouri to obtain a peddler's license; no such license was needed by those dealing in goods which were produced within the state. Justice Stephen J. Field held that the license tax amounted to an impost on goods coming into the state, that it could operate as an "absolute exclusion" on such goods, and that it could give rise to "all the evils of discriminating State legislation . . . which existed previous to the adoption of the Constitution." Admitting the difficulty of "drawing the line precisely where the commercial power of Congress ends and the power of the State begins," and refusing to state any universal rule, he concluded:

> It is sufficient to hold now that the commercial power continues until the commodity has ceased to be the subject of discriminating legislation by reason of its foreign character. That power protects it, even after it has entered the State, from any burdens imposed by reason of its foreign origin. The Act of Missouri encroaches upon this power in this respect, and is therefore, in our judgment, unconstituional and void.[15]

The *Welton* case has other implications which will be discussed a little later.

A similar case is *Robbins v. Shelby County Taxing District* (1887),[16] in which the Court invalidated a Tennessee statute (applicable only to the city of Memphis) which provided that all "drummers" and other persons "not having a regular licensed house of business in the taxing District," and offering for sale or selling goods by sample, should be required to pay ten dollars per week, or twenty-five dollars per month, "for such privilege." Justice Joseph P. Bradley wrote an extremely nationalistic opinion. He discussed at some length the means by which a merchant or manufacturer of one state could feasibly sell his goods in another state, and he concluded that the only practical way was to solicit orders through traveling salesmen (or drummers) sent interstate. Thus it did not matter that the statute did not discriminate between "domestic and foreign drummers"; that did not solve the problem, and he could hardly have been more blunt or sweeping in his condemnation of the state-exacted fee: "Interstate commerce cannot be taxed at all, even though the same amount of tax should be laid on domestic commerce, or that which is carried on solely within the state."[17]

However, Bradley thought that discrimination against merchants and manufacturers of other states could in fact be shown. They could only sell their goods in Memphis by use of drummers, while local com-

40

petitors did not need such agents; and if local businessmen were being taxed for their licensed houses, so, presumably, were the out-of-state businessmen in their places of residence. The tax had been imposed to protect local business from foreign competition, and it erected a forbidden barrier to free commercial intercourse.

In *Minnesota v. Barber* (1890)[18] the Court voided a state statute which made it mandatory that cattle, sheep, and swine designed for slaughter for human food and sold as fresh meat be inspected by state officers within twenty-four hours before being slaughtered. Justice John Marshall Harlan disregarded the asserted purpose of the state legislature to protect the health of its citizens and looked instead to the actual effect upon commerce. He found that the act necessarily excluded from the Minnesota market all fresh beef, veal, mutton, lamb, and pork from other states; and he thought it was obvious that such legislation discriminated against "the products and business of other States in favor of the products and business of Minnesota" and that therefore the act unconstitutionally interfered with and burdened interstate commerce.

A case decided in 1911 well summarizes the reasoning behind the no-discrimination doctrine. In *West v. Kansas Natural Gas Company*[19] the Court declined to allow Oklahoma the right to keep for its own domestic users natural gas produced within the state. Justice Joseph McKenna explained why the attempted retention of the gas could not stand:

> If the states have such power a singular situation might result. Pennsylvania might keep its coal, the Northwest its timber, the mining States their minerals. . . . And yet we have said that "in matters of foreign and interstate commerce there are no state lines." In such commerce, instead of the states, a new power appears and a new welfare,—a welfare which transcends that of any state. But rather let us say it is constituted of the welfare of all the states, and that of each state is made the greater by a division of its resources, natural and created, with every other state, and those of every other state with it. This was the purpose, and it is the result, of the interstate commerce clause of the Constitution of the United States.[20]

Intent of Congress

The third formula adopted for determining the extent of permissible state power was that of the intent of Congress and its corollary, the silence of Congress. To understand the development of this doctrine it is necessary to look at the broad sweep of Commerce-Clause philosophy for a moment. Marshall looked upon the interstate commerce power as exclusively national (even though he did not so decide cases) because he thought in terms of the nature of the power and its indivisibility. It is a logical extension of this theory to categorize regulatory state laws as being "burdens" on interstate commerce, as "directly affecting" such commerce, or as "discriminating" against it. Taney, on the other hand, viewed the power as concurrent between the states and the federal government and denied that the mere grant of it to Congress operated to limit state power. He silently acquiesced in the majority opinion in the *Cooley* case because there Curtis' application of the doctrine of selective exclusiveness led to the same result as would have been achieved by a frank recognition of a concurrent state power.[21] But a natural outgrowth of this theory is an increased attention to the intent of Congress to decide whether particular subjects are "national" or "local" in character.

This is in fact what happened after the *Cooley* ruling. The Supreme Court assumed the role of arbiter over the division of subjects and, therefore, over what belonged to the nation and what to the states. One means by which it could arrive at a conclusion in a given instance was to refer to congressional intent, if any. If Congress had spoken on a subject, this usually settled the issue. If Congress had remained silent, however, then the Court could assume that its judicial wisdom in the matter would coincide with the unexpressed will of the legislative branch. Since in actual practice Congress took little commercial action before 1900, the latter state of affairs more often prevailed, and the Court was left free to exercise wide discretionary power over state regulatory measures.

The first reference to the intent-of-Congress doctrine came in the case of *Welton v. Missouri* (1876). After striking down the discriminatory state license tax, Justice Field added, "The fact that Congress has not seen fit to prescribe any specific rules to govern interstate commerce does not affect the question. Its inaction on this subject . . . is equivalent to a declaration that interstate commerce shall be free and untrammeled."[22] But this "deference" by the Court to the "will of Congress" is best seen in the line of cases flowing from the formation of the "original-package" doctrine. It will be recalled that in *Brown v. Maryland* (1827) Marshall held that a state could not levy a tax on an import from a foreign country as long as it remained "the property of the importer, in his warehouse, in the original form or package in which it was imported." At the end of the opinion he observed in *dictum,* "It may be proper to add, that we suppose the principles laid down in this case, to apply equally to importations from a sister state." As it turned out, however, later justices were unwilling to apply the doctrine to the purely interstate movement of goods. Two cases in particular will illustrate this judicial forbearance.

In *Woodruff v. Parham* (1869)[23] the Court upheld a local ordinance of Mobile, Alabama, which imposed a tax upon all sales of merchandise within the municipality. Woodruff, an auctioneer and commission merchant, claimed that he was not liable to the tax on goods brought in from other states and sold at wholesale in their original and unbroken packages. Justice Miller looked to the history of the formation and adoption of the Constitution and to its language to conclude that reference by use of the word "imports" to goods imported from one state into another was "altogether improbable" and that no intention existed to prohibit "the right of one State to tax articles brought into it from another." He pointed out that Marshall's "casual remark" did not constitute a binding decision on the matter, and he thought that it was inapplicable here; the tax was imposed upon all sales made in Mobile, "whether the sales be made by a citizen of Alabama or of another State, and whether the goods sold are the product of that State or some other." Thus there was no attempt to fetter commerce, and the tax was valid.

In *Brown v. Houston* (1885)[24] the Court sustained a Louisiana annual tax on movable property which had been levied upon coal brought from Pittsburgh to New Orleans on flatboats and left afloat in its original condition and package awaiting sale to whatever customers might appear. Justice Bradley first took occasion to express his characteristic nationalist sentiments and to make a very deep bow to the controlling nature of congressional intent:

> The power to regulate commerce among the several States is granted to Congress in terms as absolute as is the power to regulate commerce with foreign nations. If not in all respects an exclusive power . . . still . . . the power of Congress is exclusive wherever the matter is national in its character or admits of one uniform system or plan of regulation; and is certainly so far exclusive that no State has power to make any law or regulation which will affect the free and unrestrained intercourse and trade between the States. . . . So long as Congress does not pass any law to regulate commerce among the several States, it thereby indicates its will that commerce shall be free and untrammeled;

and any regulation of the subject by the States is repugnant to such freedom.[25]

The question then became whether the property tax amounted to an actual interference with the free movement of coal from Pennsylvania to Louisiana, and Bradley answered in the negative. The state exaction was not imposed "by reason of the coal being imported"; rather, it was imposed because the coal had come to rest in New Orleans and had become part of "the general mass of property in the state." As such, it could be taxed in the same way as all other comparable property therein.

Three years later the Court deviated from its previous policy. In *Bowman v. Chicago and Northwestern Railway Company* (1888)[26] it invalidated an Iowa law which imposed a fine of $100 upon any railroad which knowingly brought intoxicating liquor into the state without first obtaining a certificate that the consignee could lawfully sell it. Justice Stanley Matthews held that the sweep of the statute was not confined "to the purely internal and domestic commerce of the State." Instead, the act was "a regulation directly affecting interstate commerce in an essential and vital point," and it therefore constituted "an unauthorized breach and interruption of that liberty of trade which Congress ordains as the national policy, by willing that it shall be free from restrictive regulations."[27]

The apex of the use of the silence-of-Congress doctrine and its implied "freedom-of-commerce" concomitant came in *Leisy v. Hardin* (1890).[28] An Iowa statute prohibited the manufacture, sale, or dispensing of intoxicating liquors except for specified purposes which required a permit. Leisy, an Illinois brewer, shipped beer in barrels to Keokuk, Iowa, where it was offered for sale in the original packages; Hardin, the city marshal, seized it. The prohibition on selling the beer went beyond the previous ban on transportation, and Leisy sued to recover it on the ground that the state enactment was an invalid regulation of interstate commerce.[29]

Chief Justice Melville W. Fuller wrote the majority opinion. He began with a general discussion of the federal commerce power and the efficacy of the *Cooley* rule to uphold state power. Then he turned to the inferences to be drawn from the silence of Congress:

> Whenever, however, a particular power of the general government is one which must necessarily be exercised by it, and Congress remains silent, this is not only not a concession that the powers

reserved by the States may be exerted as if the specific power had not been elsewhere reposed, but, on the contrary, the only legitimate conclusion is that the general government intended that power should not be affirmatively exercised, and the action of the States cannot be permitted to effect that which would be incompatible with such intention. Hence, inasmuch as interstate commerce . . . is national in its character, and must be governed by a uniform system, so long as Congress does not pass any law to regulate it, or allowing the States so to do, it thereby indicates its will that such commerce shall be free and untrammeled.[30]

Fuller pointed out that beer was a subject of purchase and exchange and so undeniably an article of commerce. He relied heavily upon the *Bowman* precedent to hold that Leisy had a right to import the beer into Iowa and sell it, "by which act alone it would become mingled in the common mass of property within the State" and thus become subject to state control. No state could, however, interfere with the original importation and sale of a particular article, since this would, in effect, concede to a majority in that one state the power over commercial intercourse which had been granted by the Constitution to "the people of the United States."

The decision in *Leisy v. Hardin* met with general public disapproval, and within three months Congress acted to nullify it. The Wilson Act[31] provided that all intoxicating liquor upon arrival in a state or territory should "be subject to the operation and effect of the laws of such State or Territory enacted in the exercise of its police powers . . . and shall not be exempt therefrom by reason of being introduced therein in original packages or otherwise." The constitutionality of this exercise of congressional power was immediately challenged and sustained in *In re Rahrer* (1891).[32] Chief Justice Fuller admitted that Congress could neither "delegate its own powers nor enlarge those of a State." But he disagreed with the proposition that the Commerce Clause guaranteed complete freedom of commerce and thus made any governmental restraint (congressional or state) inoperative: "In surrendering their own power over external commerce the States did not secure absolute freedom in such commerce, but only the protection from encroachment afforded by confiding its regulation exclusively to Congress."[33] Furthermore, in legislating the Wilson Act Congress had not attempted "to delegate the power to regulate commerce, or to exercise any power reserved to the States, or to grant a power not possessed by the States," but it had steered "its own course and made its own regulation, applying to these subjects of interstate commerce one common rule, whose uniformity is not affected by variations in state laws in dealing with such property."[34] Fuller summed up his defense of the federal statute in broad terms:

> The power over interstate commerce is too vital to the integrity of the nation to be qualified by any refinement of reasoning. The power to regulate is solely in the general government, and it is an essential part of that regulation to prescribe the regular means for accomplishing the introduction and incorporation of articles into and with the mass of property in the country or State.[35]

But seven years later in *Rhodes v. Iowa* (1898)[36] the Court restricted the scope of the Wilson Act by holding that the word "arrival" meant "arrival at the point of destination and delivery there to the consignee" and not merely physical arrival in the state of destination. The effect of this decision was that state power did not become operative until after the consignee had his liquor. So the mail-order sale of liquor to residents of "dry" states flourished, a situation which is graphically illustrated by the anecdote which Thomas Reed Powell relates about an expressman in Urbana, Illinois, who remarked to a consignee, "Professor, your box of books is leaking."[37]

In 1913 Congress sought to close this loophole by passing the Webb-Kenyon Act,[38] which prohibited the shipment of transportation in interstate commerce of any intoxicating liquor "intended to be received, possessed, sold, or in any manner used, either in the original package or otherwise," in violation of the laws of any state. The constitutionality of this statute was questioned and upheld in *Clark Distilling Company v. Western Maryland Railway Company* (1917).[39] Chief Justice Edward D. White noted initially that there was no dispute about the fact that Congress could have prohibited "the shipment of all intoxicants in the channels of interstate commerce" and thereby have prevented all interstate movement of liquor. As he saw it, the issue related not to a lack of congressional power but to the method used, that is, to the condition that the Act "submitted liquors to the control of the states" and hence was wanting in necessary uniformity of regulation. White denied the objection about nonuniformity on two grounds: (1) the Act did provide uniform regulation in that it applied "to all the states"; and (2) if the Act permitted the existence of varying state regulations, there was no restriction in the Constitution "that the power to regulate conferred upon Congress obtains subject to the requirement that regulations enacted shall be uniform throughout the

United States."[40] Nor would the Court "engraft" such a requirement onto it.

The Chief Justice went on to point out that the Webb-Kenyon Act was merely an extension of the Wilson Act, for the purpose of "making it impossible for one State to violate the prohibitions of the laws of another through the channels of interstate commerce," and that it would be curious indeed if the Court should hold that

> because Congress, in adopting a regulation, had considered the nature and character of our dual system of government, state and nation, and instead of absolutely prohibiting, had so conformed its regulation as to produce co-operation between the local and national forces of government to the end of preserving the rights of all, it had thereby transcended the complete and perfect power of regulation conferred by the Constitution.[41]

The foregoing discussion outlines in rough form the important ways in which the Supreme Court handled cases involving state regulation of commerce. Three summary comments are now in order. First, the Court did not keep its several formulas neatly separate and independent of one another; in many of the cases it employed various combinations of principles to strike down or sustain the challenged state act. Second, the decisions in these cases underscore the frequently restrictive policy of the Court toward state power; this result was due partly to the logical implications of the *Cooley* rule and partly to the dominant philosophy of the justices which ran toward a negative view of state (or any) governmental interference with business and commerce.[42] Third, in exercising its broad discretion in this area, the Court strongly reaffirmed its historical prerogative to fix the boundaries of national and state power. This last conclusion, however, is subject to some attack and requires additional consideration.

Frederick D.G. Ribble contends that in the late nineteenth century, the Court lost to Congress its role as final arbiter over the division of commercial subjects and that in interpreting the intent of Congress, the Court honestly sought to be consistent with the policy ascertainable from outstanding congressional action.[43] Now it is true that the Court accepted both the Wilson Act and the Webb-Kenyon Act as valid, but these were specific exercises of federal power under the Commerce Clause and had to be judged under the broad standards laid down by Marshall in *Gibbons v. Ogden*. It is one thing to say that the Court will defer to an express act of Congress; it is surely quite a different thing to say that because the Court refers to the "intent of Congress"—or its "silence"—to determine questions of state power, it has relinquished its role as arbiter of the federal system. The whole sweep of Commerce-Clause history would seem to dispute this last conclusion. Pertinent here is Thomas Reed Powell's spoof of the practical effect of this formula:

> Now congress has a wonderful power that only judges and lawyers know about. Congress has a power to keep silent. Congress can regulate interstate commerce just by not doing anything about it. Of course when congress keeps silent, it takes an expert to know what it means. But the judges are experts. They say that congress by keeping silent sometimes means that it is keeping silent and sometimes means that it is speaking.[44]

It is not being invidious toward the justices or disrespectful toward an expert like Ribble to argue that, in general, the Court utilized the formula to substantiate its own policy choices and that it remained firmly entrenched as final arbiter on the constitutional limits of national and state authority.

Congressional Power

The period after the Civil War saw a tremendous expansion of the national economy as America turned its energies primarily to the business of creating material wealth. This was also the heyday of the doctrine of laissez-faire in economics—let business alone, let the freemarket forces of supply and demand determine businessmen's entrepreneurial decisions, free from any governmental regulation. With this rapid growth of the economy, however, came the concentration of individual industries in a few hands and the development of great business trusts and monopolies. Instead of a free market place open to all, the trend was toward artificial price fixing of goods and services, discriminatory treatment of customers, and the practical exclusion of any viable competition. Nowhere, perhaps, was this more evident than in the railroad industry with its multitude of sharp practices—rebates, pooling agreements, basing-point systems, and so forth—all of which were designed to exploit shippers and the general public alike.

The Interstate Commerce Act

In response to a growing popular pressure for reform, Congress, on February 4, 1887, passed the Interstate Commerce Act,[45] which

48

provided for "reasonable and just" rail rates, prohibited the worst of the abuses and the discriminatory arrangements, and established a five-man Interstate Commerce Commission which was charged with enforcement of the Act. However, because of the narrow way in which the courts interpreted the statute's regulatory provisions, it was some years before the ICC became an effective instrument for governmental control of the railroads;[46] indeed, it required the Hepburn Act of 1906, the Mann-Elkins Act of 1910, and the Federal Transportation Act of 1920 to transform the Commission into an effective regulatory body.[47]

As the ICC began to be invigorated, not the least of its successes came in cases in which the Court recognized its right to control intrastate rail rates where these had an effect upon interstate commerce. The first intimation of such authority came in the *Minnesota Rate Cases* (1913).[48] At issue was the validity of an order of the Minnesota Railroad Commission which prescribed maximum charges for passengers and freight between points within the state. These rates were below the level of interstate rates with which they had previously been on a parity. Represented by Pierce Butler among others, stockholders of three affected railroads charged that the state order resulted in discrimination against interstate commerce and thus was unconstitutional. Justice Charles Evans Hughes rejected his future colleague's claim. He devoted most of his opinion to emphasizing the paramount authority of Congress over interstate commerce; but, under the *Cooley* rule, he held that there was an area of commerce open to state regulation, provided the federal government had not yet occupied it. The state order fell within that sphere and was valid. Then Hughes added an explosive proposition. Pointing out that commerce was becoming more and more a unit, he presaged national control of state activities:

> If the situation has become such, by reason of the interblending of the interstate and intrastate operations of interstate carriers, that adequate regulation of their interstate rates cannot be maintained without imposing requirements with respect to their intrastate rates which substantially affect the former, it is for Congress to determine, within the limits of its constitutional authority over interstate commerce and its instruments the measure of the regulation it should supply.[49]

A year later this view of the wide scope of the federal commerce power became constitutional law in the significant *Shreveport Case* (1914).[50] Railroads in the Louisiana-East Texas region were charging more for haulage between Shreveport and points in East Texas than for longer hauls from those same points west to such cities as Dallas and Houston; businessmen in the latter thus enjoyed an unfair economic advantage over their out-of-state competitors. To remove this discrimination the Interstate Commerce Commission issued an order forbidding the railroads to charge a higher rate from Shreveport to East Texas than from Dallas or Houston eastward for an equal distance. This meant in practice that the railroads had to raise their intrastate rates and thereby ignore orders of the Texas Railroad Commission. The carriers appealed the federal order on the grounds that the ICC had no jurisdiction over intrastate rates. The stage was set for a clash between national and state power.

Justice Hughes again spoke for the Court. He first emphasized heavily the paramount power of Congress "to provide the law for the government of interstate commerce." This included the power to "promote its growth and insure its safety" or, conversely, to control and restrain it if need be. Congress possessed a right of regulation which was broad and penetrating:

> Its authority, extending to these interstate carriers as instruments of interstate commerce, necessarily embraces the right to control their operations in all matters having such a close and substantial relation to interstate traffic that the control is essential or appropriate to the security of that traffic, to the efficiency of the interstate service, and to the maintenance of conditions under which interstate commerce may be conducted upon fair terms and without molestation or hindrance.... The fact that carriers are instruments of intrastate commerce, as well as of interstate commerce, does not derogate from the complete and paramount authority of Congress over the latter, or preclude the Federal power from being exerted to prevent the intrastate operations of such carriers from being made a means of injury to that which has been confided to Federal care. Wherever the interstate and intrastate transactions of carriers are so related that the government of the one involves the control of the other, it is Congress, and not the state, that is entitled to prescribe the final and dominant rule....[51]

Since a clear case of unjust rate discrimination had been shown and since this constituted an undeniable evil to interstate traffic, "abundant ground" existed for federal intervention, and the ICC order was valid.

The *Shreveport Case* marked an important milestone in Commerce-Clause adjudication. The decision stood for the proposition that federal authority could reach to purely intrastate commerce if the regulation of such commerce were necessary to the effective protection or control of interstate commerce; and it was Congress (cr one of its designated agencies), and not the states, which was empowered under the Commerce Clause to decide the necessity of intervention in any given case, based upon a determination of the effect of the offending obstruction. Hughes' opinion endorsed one basis for the exertion of federal power—the right to deal with local discriminations against commerce, and it intimated a second more extensive basis— the essential unity and interdependence of state and national economic life in the twentieth century and the impracticability of isolating or separating out the intrastate elements. The revolutionary effect of the *Shreveport* doctrine was to provide constitutional sanction for the future expansion of national sovereignty over the American economy at the expense of state power.

The Sherman Antitrust Act

At the same time that Congress began regulation of the nation's railroad system, it also took action against the gigantic trusts which dominated the economic scene in almost every major industry and which were viewed by the public as a menace to the free enterprise system. On July 2, 1890, the Sherman Antitrust Act[52] became law. The major provisions of the Act were contained in the first two sections: Section 1 provided that: "Every contract, combination in the form of trust or otherwise, or conspiracy, in restraint of trade or commerce among the several States, or with foreign nations, is hereby declared to be illegal." Section 2 made it a misdemeanor for any person to "monopolize, or attempt to monopolize, or combine or conspire with any other person or persons, to monopolize any part of the trade or commerce among the several States, or with foreign nations." Appropriate punishments were provided for violations of these provisions, and it was stipulated that the law might be enforced by bringing suits in equity to dissolve illegal combinations. But the crucial constitutional question of whether trusts which produced goods destined for interstate markets could be held to restrain commerce in violation of the Act was left open by its somewhat vague language.

In the first antitrust case, *United States v. E.C. Knight Co.* (1895),[53] the Supreme Court answered this question in the negative. But in spite of a general judicial reluctance to subject private enterprise to governmental regulation, two early cases did result in victory for the federal government and in an expanded concept of its commerce power. In *Northern Securities Company v. United States* (1904)[54] Justice Harlan applied the Sherman Act to a railroad holding company which controlled both the Northern Pacific and Great Northern lines. Rejecting the defense argument that Northern Securities was merely a stock investment company, not in itself commerce, he held that the Act of 1890 declared illegal "every contract, combination, or conspiracy, in whatever form, of whatever nature, and whoever may be parties to it, which directly or necessarily operates *in restraint* of trade or commerce *among the several states or with foreign nations.*"[55] Thus the combination in question did not have to be in commerce; it was necessary only to show that it operated in restraint of commerce, and the government had made such a factual showing.

The further contention was made that Northern Securities was lawfully organized in New Jersey, that it had violated no state laws, and that if the Sherman Act in fact applied to the combination, the federal statute was unconstitutional under the Tenth Amendment as an invasion of the sphere of state sovereignty. Harlan attacked this line of reasoning as invalid; it constituted (1) an assertion that a state could grant immunity from an exercise of federal power and (2) a denial therefore that the federal government was supreme in its own sphere. He drew the inescapable conclusion: "It means nothing less than that Congress, in regulating interstate commerce, must act in subordination to the will of the states when exerting their power to create corporations."[56] But such a crippling view of national authority could not be "entertained for a moment." The congressional Act was valid as applied.

Another notable case was *Swift & Company v. United States* (1905).[57] The government had sued to enjoin Swift and other meat packers from conspiring to control the price of livestock in the stockyards and other places of slaughter. The combinations had taken place in local yards where the livestock were temporarily at rest, and the companies urged that the sales transferring title to the animals were strictly local transactions which were insulated from federal control. Speaking for a unanimous Court, Justice Holmes emphasized the extensive interstate movement of live animals and dressed meat and suggested a broadened definition of commerce:

. . . commerce among the states is not a technical legal conception, but a practical one, drawn from the course of business. When cattle are sent for sale from a place in one state, with the expectation that they will end their transit, after purchase, in another, and when in effect they do so, with only the interruption necessary to find a purchaser at the stock yards, and when this is a typical, constantly recurring course, the current thus existing is a current of commerce among the states, and the purchase of the cattle is a part and incident of such commerce.[58]

Thus the application of the Sherman Act was valid, and an injunction could be issued against the conspiring packers. The "stream-of-commerce" doctrine marked a new extension of the commerce power and became an important peg upon which to hang an expanded exercise of congressional authority.

In spite of the decision in the *Swift* case, Congress later found it necessary to enact additional legislation to regulate the monopolistic conditions in the meat-packing industry. The Packers and Stockyards Act of 1921[59] prohibited the packing companies from engaging in "unfair, discriminatory, or deceptive practices" in their interstate business, proscribed any attempts to establish market monopolies, and imposed certain controls upon transactions in the stockyards. The Secretary of Agriculture was given authority to enforce the Act by issuing cease-and-desist orders which were subject to review in the courts. The constitutionality of the Act was challenged and upheld in *Stafford v. Wallace* (1922).[60] Chief Justice William Howard Taft wrote the majority opinion. He first focused on the facts of the situation and found that the stockyards were not "a place of rest or final destination" for the livestock; instead, they were "a throat through which the current flows, and the transactions which occur therein are only incident to this current from the West to the East, and from one State to another."[61] The stockyards (and the sales made in them) were "necessary factors" in the orderly and unimpeded flow of this stream of commerce, and because of this Congress had treated these facilities as "great national public utilities," subject to federal authority.

The only question which remained was "whether the business done in the stockyards between the receipt of the live stock in the yards and the shipment of them therefrom is a part of interstate commerce, or is so associated with it as to bring it within the power of national regulation."[62] The controlling precedent was *Swift & Co. v. United States,* and Taft amplified upon Holmes' opinion:

> The application of the commerce clause of the Constitution in the *Swift Case* was the result of the natural development of interstate commerce under modern conditions. It was the inevitable recognition of the great central fact that such streams of commerce from one part of the country to another which are ever flowing are in their very essence the commerce among the States and with foreign nations which historically it was one of the chief purposes of the Constitution to bring under national protection and control. This court declined to defeat this purpose in respect of such a stream and take it out of complete national regulation by a nice and technical inquiry into the non-interstate character of some of its necessary incidents and facilities when considered alone and without reference to their association with the movement of which they were an essential but subordinate part.[63]

Nor would the Court do differently in the present case.

Then the Chief Justice sounded a note consonant with the nationalistic decision in the *Shreveport Case.* Looking to the possible and even probable effects of the prohibited activities on commerce, he said, "Whatever amounts to more or less constant practice, and threatens to obstruct or unduly to burden the freedom of interstate commerce is within the regulatory power of Congress under the Commerce Clause, and it is primarily for Congress to consider and decide the fact of danger and meet it."[64] But this was not all. In the best Austinian tradition, Taft closed with a complete endorsement of the philosophy of judicial self-restraint with respect to federal regulation of business: "This court will certainly not substitute its judgment for that of Congress in such a matter unless the relation of the subject to interstate commerce and its effect upon it are clearly non-existent."[65] Only Justice James C. McReynolds dissented from this strongly worded opinion which solidified the "current-of-commerce" doctrine and thus sanctioned broad congressional power under the Commerce Clause[66]—exercises of which the justices seemingly would not question on the basis of their own personal predilections and prejudices.

Federal Police Power

About the time that Congress was legislating to correct the economic abuses of American private enterprise, it also undertook to exercise its delegated powers to create what may be called a federal police power. While the states had always been conceded an inherent power "to govern men and things" for the health, safety, good morals, and general welfare of their citizens, constitutional theory held that the national government (a government of enumerated powers carved out of the original powers of the states) had no such inherent power. However, Congress was faced with a rising public demand for the solution to various national problems of an essentially social and/or moral nature, and it decided to attack these under its powers to tax and to regulate commerce, particularly the latter.

Congress moved first to control gambling by passing the Federal Lottery Act of 1895,[67] which prohibited the importation, mailing, or carriage of lottery tickets from one state to another. This unusual exercise of the commerce power elicited sharp reaction from those opposed to any extension of federal power to matters which traditionally had been reserved to state authority. Opponents challenged the constitutionality of the Act on several grounds: (1) lottery tickets were not items of commerce, and their shipment from one state to another did not constitute "commerce" within the meaning of the Constitution; (2) the power of Congress to regulate commerce did not include the power to prohibit and thereby totally destroy it; and (3) the Act invaded an area of state sovereignty and therefore was repugnant to the Tenth Amendment.

By a close, five-to-four decision the Supreme Court upheld the federal regulation in *Champion v. Ames* (1903),[68] often referred to as the *Lottery Case*. Justice Harlan spoke for the majority. He went straight back to Marshall's opinion in *Gibbons v. Ogden* for its definition of commerce as "intercourse" and for its broad construction of the power to regulate, that is, "to prescribe the rule by which commerce is to be governed." Harlan came down hard in his emphasis on the supreme and plenary power of Congress over commerce as enunciated by Marshall:

This power . . . is *complete in itself*, may be exercised *to its utmost extent*, and acknowledges *no limitations, other than are prescribed in the Constitution*. . . . If, as has always been understood, the sovereignty of Congress, though limited to specified objects, is plenary as to those objects, the power over commerce with foreign nations, and among the several states, is vested in Congress as *absolutely as it would be in a single government*. . . .[69]

He added meaningfully that "in determining the character of the regulations to be adopted Congress has a large discretion which is not to be controlled by the courts, simply because, in their opinion, such regulations may not be the best or most effective that could be employed."[70]

Against this backdrop of sweeping national power and judicial self-restraint, Harlan took up the specific charges against the Act. He noted that the lottery tickets in question showed on their face that they might be good for a large cash prize; consequently, they were subjects of traffic which could be bought and sold. This made them "subjects or commerce," and the regulation of their shipment interstate was "a regulation of commerce among the several states." He then argued that the power to regulate necessarily included the power to prohibit. Congress might constitutionally impose absolute prohibitions upon parts of interstate commerce if it chose to do so. Harlan made his point with the help of two powerful rhetorical questions:

> If lottery traffic, *carried on through interstate commerce,* is a matter of which Congress may take cognizance and over which its power may be exerted, can it be possible that it must tolerate the traffic, and simply regulate the manner in which it may be carried on? Or may not Congress, for the protection of the people of all the states, and under the power to regulate interstate commerce, devise such means, within the scope of the Constitution, and not prohibited by it, as will drive that traffic out of commerce among the states?[71]

Lastly, he considered the Tenth-Amendment objection and gave it short shrift: "If it be said that the act of 1895 is inconsistent with the Tenth Amendment, reserving to the states respectively, or to the people, the powers not delegated to the United States, the answer is that the power to regulate commerce among the states has been expressly delegated to Congress."[72] Expanding upon this curt statement, he drew an analogy between the police power of the states and congressional power over commerce:

> It [Congress] has not assumed to interfere with the completely internal affairs of any state, and has only legislated in respect of a matter which concerns the people of the United States. As a state may, for the purpose of guarding the morals of its own people, forbid all sales of lottery tickets within its limits, so Congress, for the purpose of guarding the people of the United States against the "widespread pestilence of lotteries" and to

protect the commerce which concerns all the states, may prohibit the carrying of lottery tickets from one state to another. . . . We should hesitate long before adjudging that an evil
of such appalling character, carried on through interstate commerce, cannot be met and crushed by the only power competent to that end.[73]

To the argumentum ad horrendum that Congress could arbitrarily
exclude any article (no matter how useful or valuable) from commerce, Harlan replied that it would be "time enough to consider the
constitutionality of such legislation when we must do so." He added
that "the possible abuse of a power is not an argument against its
existence" and that the remedy for "unwise or injurious" legislative
action lay, as Marshall had said, with the people at the polls.

Champion v. Ames was another landmark decision in Commerce-
Clause history. Harlan was on solid ground in his interpretation of
congressional power over commerce. In stressing the plenary and
unitary nature of that power, he put himself squarely in line with the
best Marshallian tradition. The same may be said of his staunch
refusal to limit the scope of "the power to regulate" by separating it
from the necessarily concomitant power to prohibit. And his view
that the Tenth Amendment presented no barrier to the exercise of a
delegated power merely echoed a statement made by Marshall in
McCulloch v. Maryland. All in all, Harlan's opinion in the *Lottery
Case* provided strong new underpinnings for a broad and far-reaching
federal commerce power.

Congress did not delay long in capitalizing upon the invitation to
utilize this power to reach other evils. In 1906 it passed the Pure
Food and Drug Act,[74] which barred adulterated and misbranded
foods from shipment in interstate commerce. This measure was sustained unanimously in *Hipolite Egg Co. v. United States* (1911).[75]
Justice McKenna emphasized the wide sweep of the commerce power
and held that no trade or traffic could be "carried on between the
states to which it does not extend." The power was "complete in
itself" and "subject to no limitations except those found in the
Constitution." He did not find it necessary to discuss the motives or
purpose of Congress as a factor in determining the validity of the
statute.

Four years later Congress attacked the growing problem of prostitution with enactment of the White Slave Traffic Act of 1910.[76]
Commonly called the Mann Act, it prohibited the transportation of

57

women in interstate or foreign commerce for immoral purposes. In *Hoke v. United States* (1913)[77] the constitutionality of the statute was affirmed. Again speaking for the Court, Justice McKenna based his decision upon such precedents as *Champion* and *Hipolite Egg Co.* To the old contention that the Act invaded the police powers of the states in violation of the Tenth Amendment, he answered with the explicit proposition that Congress could use the commerce power to protect the morals and promote the well-being of all the American people:

> Our dual form of government has its perplexities, state and nation having different spheres of jurisdiction, as we have said; but it must be kept in mind that we are one people; and the powers reserved to the states and those conferred on the nation are adapted to be exercised, whether independently or concurrently, to promote the general welfare, material and moral.[78]

This powerfully worded statement should have disposed of any future question of congressional intent or motives; the purpose of federal regulation needed only to be the general welfare of the people. That this was not to be, however, will appear shortly.

One further example will round out this chronicle of the rise of a federal police power under the Commerce Clause. In 1919 Congress passed the National Motor Vehicle Theft Act,[79] which forbade the movement of stolen automobiles across state lines. The statute was clearly designed as a police measure, and it enforced an absolute prohibition on the interstate movement of the specified article. Speaking for a unanimous Court, Chief Justice Taft sustained the enactment in *Brooks v. United States* (1925);[80] he referred to *Hipolite Egg Co.* and *Hoke* as controlling precedents. In reality the law was aimed at preventing automobile thievery before any movement took place, but the Court made clear its approval of the moral purpose behind the Act and therefore had no trouble in finding it constitutionally acceptable. A "good" motive was still helpful in securing judicial approbation for an exercise of the commerce power in behalf of the public welfare.

The preceding accounts show that, around 1900 and thereafter, Congress made increasing use of the Commerce Clause to regulate the national economy and to erradicate certain evils from American society. In the process the Supreme Court gradually gave an expanded interpretation to the scope of national authority contained in that delegated power. But as solidly as the decisions reported above supported the concept of extensive federal power, the Court was composed of too many essentially conservative justices to give Congress completely free rein with respect to Commerce-Clause legislation. This circumstance led to one of the most important developments in American constitutional law—the rise of the doctrine of dual federalism.

Dual Federalism

The term "dual federalism" was coined by Edward S. Corwin, who reasoned that its genesis rested upon four propositions: (1) the national government is one of enumerated powers only; (2) the purposes which the national government may constitutionally promote are few; (3) the two levels of government—national and state—are "sovereign" and hence "equal" within their respective spheres; and (4) the relation of the two levels to each other is one of tension rather than collaboration or cooperation.[81] Corwin blamed James Madison (the later Madison) for the paternity of the doctrine.[82] Writing in criticism of Marshall's great nationalistic decision in *McCulloch v. Maryland* (1819), Madison expressed the fear that the Court had relinquished "all control on the legislative exercise of unconstitutional power." The central vice in the Chief Justice's reasoning was that he regarded the powers of the general government as "sovereign powers," the result of which was "to convert a limited into an unlimited Gov't." Madison thought that there must certainly be

> a reasonable medium between expounding the Constitution with the strictness of a penal law, or other ordinary statute, and expounding it with a laxity which may vary its essential character, and encroach on the local sovereignties with which it was meant to be reconcilable. The very existence of these local sovereignties is a controul on the pleas for a constructive amplification of the powers of the General Gov't.[83]

Corwin pointed out that in the House debate in 1791 on Treasury Secretary Alexander Hamilton's proposal to establish a national bank, Representative Madison had said: "Interference with the power of the States was no constitutional criterion of the power of Congress." By 1819, however, ex-President Madison had fashioned a new criterion: *"the coexistence of the states and their powers is of itself a limitation upon national power."*[84] The essence of the doctrine of dual federalism, then, is the canon that the delegated powers of the federal government are limited at some points by the reserved powers of the states, or to put it a little differently, that the Tenth Amendment represents a restriction on the enumerated powers of Congress.[85] Three prime examples of the application of this principle will now be recounted; comment on all of them will be reserved to a general analysis at the conclusion.[86]

The first case in which the Supreme Court used dual federalism to defeat an exercise of congressional power was *United States v. E.C. Knight Co.* (1895).[87] Under the Sherman Act the government sought a court order to cancel an agreement by which the American Sugar Refining Company had purchased the E.C. Knight Company and three other companies and thereby obtained control of more than ninety percent of the production of all refined sugar in the country. Chief Justice Fuller wrote the eight-to-one majority opinion which refused to grant a dissolution order. He began by making a sharp distinction between manufacturing and commerce. "Commerce succeeds to manufacture, and is not a part of it," he said; and he went on to argue that the power to regulate commerce was "a power independent of the power to suppress monopoly." A monopoly in manufacturing could be dealt with only under the police power of the states, and Fuller emphasized the necessity of keeping the two separate:

> It is vital that the independence of the commercial power and of the police power, and the delimitation between them, however sometimes perplexing, should always be recognized and observed, for while the one furnishes the strongest bond of union, the other is essential to the preservation of the autonomy of the states as required by our dual form of government; and acknowledged evils, however grave and urgent they may appear to be, had better be borne, than the risk be run, in the effort to suppress them, of more serious consequences by resort to expedients of even doubtful constitutionality.[88]

Furthermore, it was no help to argue that a combination or conspiracy to control domestic production might tend ultimately to restrain trade among the states; any such result (or effect) would be merely "indirect" and beyond the reach of federal regulation. The Sherman Act could not be extended to monopolies in manufacturing because of the serious limitations this would put on state power. Fuller painted a black picture: "Slight reflection will show that if the national power extends to all contracts and combinations in manufacture, agriculture, mining and other productive industries . . . comparatively little of business operations and affairs would be left for state control."[89] The federal government was powerless to deal with the Sugar Trust.[90]

The Court again affirmed the doctrine of dual federalism in *Hammer v. Dagenhart* (1918).[91] At stake was the validity of the Child Labor Act of 1916,[92] which prohibited the shipment in interstate commerce of products made with the use of child labor. By a vote of five to four the Act was declared unconstitutional. Justice William R. Day handed down the majority opinion. He first resurrected the distinction between the power to regulate and the power to prohibit. In a "reinterpretation" of Marshall's exposition on the commerce power Day said, "In other words, the power is one to control the means by which commerce is carried on, which is directly the contrary of the assumed right to forbid commerce from moving and thus destroy it as to particular commodities."[93] It was necessary, of course, to distinguish the present case from those in which Congress had been allowed to prohibit commerce—*Champion v. Ames* and *Clark Distilling Co.,* and this he did by asserting that those cases rested upon "the character of the particular subjects dealt with," that is, the restricted products were themselves "harmful" and prohibition of them was necessary to protect commerce itself from contamination. This element was wanting here because the goods shipped were "of themselves harmless."[94]

Day then turned to the issue of congressional purpose. The Act did not regulate commerce but was designed in its effect "to standardize the ages at which children may be employed in mining and manufacturing within the states." Employment in production was not part of commerce and thus not subject to federal control. He invoked dual federalism explicitly: "The grant of power to Congress over the subject of interstate commerce was to enable it to regulate such commerce, and not to give it authority to control the states in their exercise of the police power over local trade and manufacture."[95] The statute invaded a sphere of state sovereignty in violation of the Tenth Amendment; in amplifying this contention, he actually misquoted that article: "In interpreting the Constitution it must never be forgotten that the nation is made up of states, to which are intrusted the powers of local government. And to them and to the people the powers not expressly delegated to the national government are reserved."[96] Thus the Child Labor Act was repugnant to the Constitution in a twofold sense, and to sustain it might have a devastating effect upon the federal system:

> It not only transcends the authority delegated to Congress over commerce, but also exerts a power as to a purely local matter to which the Federal authority does not extend. The far-reaching result of upholding the act cannot be more plainly indicated than by pointing out that if Congress can thus regulate matters intrusted to local authority by prohibition of the movement of commodities in interstate commerce, all freedom of commerce will be at an end, and the power of the states over local matters may be eliminated, and thus our system of government be practically destroyed.[97]

The United States was impotent to control child labor!

A case decided in the mid 1930's revealed starkly the extent to which the national government could be crippled by judicial adherence to dual federalism. *Carter v. Carter Coal Co.* (1936)[98] involved the validity of the National Bituminous Coal Conservation Act of 1935[99] (popularly known as the Guffey Coal Act), which attempted to bring some stability to the chaotic price structure of the soft-coal industry. The Act created a Bituminous Coal Commission which was given authority to draft an industry-wide Coal Code and to establish minimum and maximum coal prices. To gain compliance, a tax of fifteen percent was levied on all coal sold at the mine head, nine tenths of which was to be refunded to producers who complied with the Code provisions. A separate section of the Act guaranteed collective-bargaining rights for workers and provided for setting up maximum-hours and minimum-wage agreements. The Act specifically stated that the labor provisions and the price-fixing provisions were separable and that the possible unconstitutionality of one should not affect the validity of the other.

The Guffey Coal Act immediately became the subject of a stockholder's suit to set it aside. The Supreme Court by a vote of six to three struck down the labor provisions of the Act; by a vote of five to four it also voided the price-fixing provisions.[100] Justice George Sutherland wrote the majority opinion. He began with what is undoubtedly the most beautiful judicial defense of dual federalism on record. It bears quoting at some length:

> The general rule with regard to the respective powers of the national and the state governments under the Constitution, is

not in doubt. The states were before the Constitution; and, consequently, their legislative powers antedated the Constitution. Those who framed and those who adopted that instrument meant to carve from the general mass of legislative powers, then possessed by the states, only such portions as it was thought wise to confer upon the federal government; and in order that there should be no uncertainty in respect of what was taken and what was left, the national powers of legislation were not aggregated but enumerated—with the result that what was not embraced by the enumeration remained vested in the states without change or impairment. . . . While the states are not sovereign in the true sense of that term, but only quasi-sovereign, yet in respect of all powers reserved to them they are supreme—"as independent of the general government as that government within its sphere is independent of the States." . . . And since every addition to the national legislative power to some extent detracts from or invades the power of the states, it is of vital moment that, in order to preserve the fixed balance intended by the Constitution, the powers of the general government be not so extended as to embrace any not within the express terms of the several grants or the implications necessarily to be drawn therefrom.

. . . State powers can neither be appropriated on the one hand nor abdicated on the other.[101]

The government had admitted that the validity of the Act rested not upon the taxing power but upon the commerce power, and Sutherland turned his attention to that issue. He had no difficulty under the *Knight* precedent in concluding that the mining of coal was not commerce within the constitutional meaning of that term. But did the production of coal "bear upon and directly affect" commerce as the government had contended? This called for a discussion of direct and indirect effects, and Sutherland obliged. Holding that "the local character of mining, of manufacturing, and of crop growing is a fact, and remains a fact, whatever may be done with the products," he explained the nature of the dichotomy and pushed it to its logical conclusion:

The distinction between a direct and an indirect effect turns, not upon the magnitude of either the cause or the effect, but entirely upon the manner in which the effect has been brought about. If the production by one man of a single ton of coal intended for interstate sale and shipment . . . affects interstate commerce indirectly, the effect does not become direct by multiplying the tonnage, or increasing the number of men employed, or adding to the expense or complexities of the business, or by all combined.[102]

Thus, with respect to the labor provisions, the alleged evils of labor-management disputes (even though they might lead to curtailment of production and a reduced volume of coal in commerce) were "all local evils over which the federal government has no legislative control. . . . Such effect as they may have upon commerce, however extensive it may be, is secondary and indirect."[103]

Finally, dismissing congressional intent to separate the provisions of the Act, Sutherland took up the price-fixing provisions and held that they were "so related to and dependent upon the labor provisions" that the fall of the latter carried the former down with them. The Guffey Coal Act had been completely eviscerated.

These cases deserve a few summary remarks. First, the categorical distinction which the Court drew between manufacturing or mining and commerce was not based on economic reality; with the rise of an industrialized, highly interdependent economy, businesses were forced to organize on a nation-wide basis, and the processes of production became intimately intermeshed with commerce and were in fact dependent upon it, both for supplies of raw materials and end markets. Integration of economic functions had made obsolete any factual separation thereof, and the Court was simply perpetuating a mechanistic, legal illusion.

Second, the distinction between "direct" and "indirect" effects on commerce was equally unrealistic in terms of practical economic cause and result. But beyond that it had an amorphous and metaphysical quality which made it totally incapable of any precise definition. On what grounds or by what criteria could one determine in advance whether an effect upon commerce would be classed as direct or indirect? In actual practice what appeared on the surface to be an objective standard for deciding questions of national power was in fact a highly subjective test under which the justices retained wide discretion to base decisions on their personal social and economic philosophies.[104]

The most pernicious result of the doctrine of dual federalism was the body blow it struck at national supremacy. In *McCulloch v. Maryland* and *Gibbons v. Ogden,* Marshall had expressed the view that the federal government was supreme in its own sphere, that is, that the enumerated powers of Congress had been delegated in their entirety and could be exercised as if they belonged to a single government. This meant that Congress could constitutionally enter and occupy the sphere of authority ordinarily reserved to the states whenever necessary in order to control matters which affected a legitimate national interest. The powers of Congress were thus paramount in the federal sphere, and those of the states had puissance only so long as they did not intrude upon federal authority. As Corwin has summed it up:

> *[W]hen the supremacy clause is given its due operation no subject-matter whatever is withdrawn from the control of the delegated powers of the United States by the fact alone that the same subject-matter also lies within the jurisdiction of the reserved powers of the States; for when national and State power, correctly defined in all other respects, come into conflict in consequence of attempting to govern simultaneously the same subject-matter, the former has always the right of way.*[105]

However, the neat severance of production from commerce, and the nice distinction made between direct and indirect effects upon the latter, served to impair seriously the power of the federal government to regulate interstate commerce effectively and to impose the uniform controls needed for its protection and advancement. And this occurred simultaneously with the growing incompetency of the individual states to regulate business and industries organized on a national scale. In short, dual federalism was a perversion of the American federal system; it resulted in an absence of power at both levels of government to meet and solve the most pervasive and pressing problems of the times. Again, as Corwin has so cogently expressed it: " 'Dual federalism' thus becomes triple federalism—inserted between the realm of the National Government and of the states is one of no-government—a governmental vacuum, a political 'no-man's land.' "[106] Such constitutional heresy, so inimical to effective government and therefore so destructive of the general welfare, had to be curbed and soon.

Notes

1. There is some disagreement among experts as to the exact implications of the *Cooley* case. The view taken here is essentially the one held by three commentators: Alpheus Thomas Mason and William M. Beaney (eds.), *American Constitutional Law: Introductory Essays and Selected Cases,* 4th ed. (Englewood Cliffs, N.J.: Prentice-Hall, Inc.,

1968), 161; Alexander Smith, *The Commerce Power in Canada and the United States* (Toronto: Butterworths, 1963), 217-18. For a different slant on the case which is slightly more favorable to state power, see Maurice G. Baxter, *Daniel Webster & the Supreme Court* (Amherst, Mass.: The University of Massachusetts Press, 1966), 224-26.

2. 15 Wallace 232.

3. 92 U.S. 259.

4. Ibid., 273.

5. 95 U.S. 485.

6. Ibid., 488-89.

7. Ibid., 489-90.

8. 161 U.S. 519.

9. 266 U.S. 497.

10. 244 U.S. 310.

11. 273 U.S. 34.

12. Ibid., 44.

13. Ibid., 44. Stone's views on the scope of state power over commerce will be examined in some detail in Chapter 7.

14. 91 U.S. 275.

15. Ibid., 282. Note that in these state cases the justices often used the word "foreign" to mean extrastate.

16. 120 U.S. 489.

17. Ibid., 497.

18. 136 U.S. 313.

19. 221 U.S. 229.

20. Ibid., 255.

21. Felix Frankfurter, *The Commerce Clause under Marshall, Taney*

and Waite (Chapel Hill, N.C.: The University of North Carolina Press, 1937), 56-57.

22. 91 U.S. 275, 282.

23. Wallace 123.

24. 114 U.S. 622.

25. Ibid., 630-31.

26. 125 U.S. 465.

27. Ibid., 498.

28. 135 U.S. 100.

29. In *Mugler v. Kansas,* 123 U.S. 623 (1887), the Court had upheld, as a proper exercise of the state's police power, a statute which forbade the manufacture of intoxicating liquor for sale or barter within the limits of the state.

30. 135 U.S. 100, 109-10.

31. *U.S. Statutes at Large,* XXVI, 313.

32. 140 U.S. 545.

33. Ibid., 561.

34. Ibid., 561.

35. Ibid., 562. Notice that Fuller's sweeping statements sound very much like the exclusive-power doctrine.

36. 170 U.S. 412.

37. Thomas Reed Powell, *Vagaries and Varieties in Constitutional Interpretation* (New York: Columbia University Press, 1956), 157.

38. *U.S. Statutes at Large,* XXXVII, 699.

39. 242 U.S. 311.

40. Ibid., 327.

41. Ibid., 331. For a favorable review of White's opinion, see Thomas Reed Powell, "The Validity of State Regulation under the Webb-

Kenyon Law," *Selected Essays on Constitutional Law,* compiled and edited by a committee of the Association of American Law Schools (4 vols., Chicago: The Foundation Press, Inc., 1938), III, 881-901.

42. See John B. Sholley, "The Negative Implications of the Commerce Clause," *Selected Essays on Constitutional Law,* III, 933-73. See also the discussion later on the use of dual federalism to deny federal power over parts of commerce.

43. Frederick D.G. Ribble, *State and National Power over Commerce* (New York: Columbia University Press, 1937), 81-85 and 106-09.

44. Thomas Reed Powell, "The Still Small Voice of the Commerce Clause," *Selected Essays on Constitutional Law,* III, 931, 932.

45. *U.S. Statutes at Large,* XXIV, 379.

46. See Alfred H. Kelly and Winfred A. Harbison, *The American Constitution: Its Origins and Development,* 3rd ed. (New York: W.W. Norton & Company, Inc., 1963), 550-52.

47. Ibid., 606-11 and 681-82.

48. *Simpson v. Shepard,* 230 U.S. 352.

49. Ibid., 432-33.

50. *Houston, East & West Texas Railway Company v. United States,* 234 U.S. 342.

51. Ibid., 351-52.

52. *U.S. Statutes at Large,* XXVI, 209.

53. 156 U.S. 1. This extraordinary decision will be examined in some detail later.

54. 193 U.S. 197.

55. Ibid., 331.

56. Ibid., 345.

57. 196 U.S. 375.

58. Ibid., 398-99.

59. *U.S. Statutes at Large,* XLII, 159.

60. 258 U.S. 495.

61. Ibid., 516.

62. Ibid., 517.

63. Ibid., 518-19.

64. Ibid., 521. See Alpheus Thomas Mason, ·*William Howard Taft: Chief Justice* (New York: Simon and Schuster, Inc., 1964), 242-48 and 260-62, for the argument that while Taft appeared to endorse a broad, Marshallian concept of the commerce power, he did not at heart accept Marshall's general views on the plenary nature of the delegated powers, unqualified by the Tenth Amendment; as partial evidence of this, Mason cites and analyzes Taft's opinion in *Bailey v. Drexel Furniture Company*, 259 U.S. 20 (1922).

65. Ibid., 521.

66. The following year the Court upheld the Grain Futures Act of 1922 (*U.S. Statutes at Large*, XLII, 998). In *Board of Trade of Chicago v. Olsen*, 262 U.S. 1 (1923), Chief Justice Taft rested his opinion squarely on the current-of-commerce doctrine as formulated in the *Swift* and *Stafford* cases.

67. *U.S. Statutes at Large*, XXVIII, 963.

68. 188 U.S. 321.

69. Ibid., 347.

70. Ibid., 353.

71. Ibid., 355.

72. Ibid., 357.

73. Ibid., 357-58.

74. *U.S. Statutes at Large*, XXXIV, 768.

75. 220 U.S. 45.

76. *U.S. Statutes at Large*, XXXVI, 825.

77. 227 U.S. 308.

78. Ibid., 322. For fuller coverage of this entire subject up to the

Child Labor Act of 1916, see Robert E. Cushman, "The National Police Power under the Commerce Clause of the Constituion," *Selected Essays on Constitutional Law,* III, 36-90.

79. *U.S. Statutes at Large,* XLI, 324.

80. 267 U.S. 432.

81. Edward S. Corwin, "The Passing of Dual Federalism," in Robert G. McCloskey (ed.), *Essays in Constitutional Law* (New York: Vintage Books, 1957), 185, 188-89.

82. Edward S. Corwin, "The Power of Congress to Prohibit Commerce," *Selected Essays on Constitutional Law,* III, 103, 107-10.

83. Quoted in ibid., 108. Corwin gives the original sources as *Writings of James Madison* (Hunt, ed., 1906), VIII, 447-53; *Letters and other Writings of James Madison* (Philadelphia, 1867), III, 143-47.

84. This is Corwin's interpretation, ibid., 108.

85. It should be noted that this doctrine would also limit severely the exercise of concurrent national and state powers. (See the analysis at the end of the chapter.)

86. Some commentators would include a fourth example, *A.L.A. Schechter Poultry Corp. v. United States,* 295 U.S. 495 (1935), in which the Court unanimously invalidated the National Industrial Recovery Act of 1933. But Chief Justice Hughes concentrated two thirds of his opinion on showing that the Act was an unconstitutional delegation of legislative power, an issue which is irrelevant here. It is true that he went on unnecessarily to hold that the Schechter brothers' poultry operations exerted only an "indirect" effect on commerce and so were beyond the power of Congress under the Commerce Clause. But the case was not a good one, the effect on commerce was not dramatic, and even Justices Cardozo, Brandeis, and Stone could not swallow the NRA—an indictment in itself. For a pro-NRA view, see F.D.G. Ribble, "The 'Current of Commerce': A Note on the Commerce Clause and the National Industrial Recovery Act," *Selected Essays on Constitutional Law,* III, 184-97. For a dissent from the *Schechter* decision, see Frank Freidel, "The Sick Chicken Case," in John A. Garraty (ed.), *Quarrels That Have Shaped the Constitution* (New York: Harper & Row, Publishers, Inc., 1964), 191-209.

87. 156 U.S. 1.

88. Ibid., 13.

89. Ibid., 16.

90. Only Justice Harlan dissented from this incredible decision; see ibid., 18.

91. 247 U.S. 251.

92. *U.S. Statutes at Large,* XXXIX, 675.

93. 247 U.S. 251, 269-70.

94. The distinction was purely artificial. The majority simply closed its eyes to the fact that the interstate sale of the cotton goods in question perpetuated the "evil" of child labor and contaminated commerce quite as much as lottery tickets or liquor. The latter are not evil in themselves; it is the use to which they are put that may be "immoral." Here it was the abuse of children. See Justice Holmes' famous dissent in this case; ibid., 277.

95. Ibid., 273-74.

96. Ibid., 275.

97. Ibid., 276.

98. 298 U.S. 238.

99. *U.S. Statutes at Large,* XLIX, 991.

100. Chief Justice Hughes concurred on the labor provisions and dissented on the price-fixing provisions. Justice Cardozo, joined by Justices Brandeis and Stone, dissented on the price-fixing provisions and found it unnecessary to rule on the labor provisions.

101. 298 U.S. 238, 294-95.

102. Ibid., 308.

103. Ibid., 308-09.

104. The same criticism can be made of the distinction made in *Hammer v. Dagenhart* between "harmful" and "harmless" goods. In that case the Court disregarded the plain fact that the profitable use of child labor depended upon free access to interstate markets, that is, that interstate commerce per se supported the "evil." For a biting critique of this case, see Thomas Reed Powell, "The Child Labor Law, The Tenth Amendment, and the Commerce Clause," *Selected Essays on Constitutional Law,* III, 314-36.

105. Edward S. Corwin, *The Commerce Power versus States Rights* (Gloucester, Mass.: Peter Smith, 1962), 12-13.

106. Corwin, "The Power of Congress to Prohibit Commerce," *Selected Essays on Constitutional Law,* III, 103, 123.

3 The Demise of Dual Federalism

This chapter will record and analyze a major development in judicial interpretation of the Commerce Clause: the demise of the doctrine of dual federalism and the resulting enlargement of the scope of federal authority. As previously shown, by the end of 1936 the Supreme Court had developed two distinct lines of precedent which could be used to decide cases arising from the exercise of congressional power over commerce. The question which it then faced was whether to retain these two options, to be used in the future as the justices might see fit, or to pursue one line of precedent to the exclusion of the other. What happened was earthshaking, not so much in terms of strict constitutional law but in the general attitude of the Court toward its supervision of federal economic regulation. The Court not only repudiated dual federalism as a viable doctrine; but, in effect, it retreated from the arena of economic policy making and left Congress almost unlimited power under the Commerce Clause to regulate and control the national economy.

The Setting

A bit of background will be useful. In October, 1929, the New York stock market crashed, and the Great Depression began. By the end of 1932 industrial production and national income had both fallen below fifty percent of the 1929 level, and unemployment had risen to the thirteen-million mark.[1] It was under these circumstances in early 1933 that President Franklin D. Roosevelt and his Democratically controlled Congress took action to combat the chaos in the economy and to alleviate the human suffering which accompanied it. In the period of a "hundred days" measures were enacted which provided for the federal regulation of almost all aspects of American economic life—agriculture, banking and finance, manufacturing, and labor.

The story of how a number of these statutes were struck down by the Supreme Court prior to 1937 has been told many times and need not be repeated here.[2] Suffice it to say that, after the *Schechter* and *Carter Coal* cases (not to mention *United States v. Butler*[3]) and in view of the landslide election of 1936, Roosevelt determined to curb the Court's power to frustrate New Deal legislation. The result was his famous "Court-Packing Plan" of February 5, 1937, which provided that the President might appoint one additional judge in any federal court for each judge who reached the age of seventy with ten years of service and who did not retire within six months. At the time this would have allowed Roosevelt to appoint six new justices to the Court, whose maximum size was fixed at fifteen.

It seems unnecessary to go into the details of the Court fight which ensued.[4] Several circumstances converged to doom the proposed change. First, the President somewhat disingenuously based his initial attack on the ground that, because of the advanced age of many of the justices and their naturally reduced capacity for work, the Court was unable to keep abreast of its docket of cases.[5] This objection was effectively spiked when, on March 22, Senator Burton K. Wheeler, the leader of the pro-Court forces, released to the Senate Judiciary Committee a letter from Chief Justice Charles Evans Hughes; in it Hughes showed that the Court was handling its work load on time and that an increase in the number of justices "would not promote the efficiency of the Court." Second, in the remaining weeks of the 1936 term the Court handed down several decisions favorable to the New Deal and to the concept of expanded governmental power.[6] Third, on May 18, Justice Willis Van Devanter announced his intention to retire at the end of the term, a move which would allow Roosevelt to appoint a new justice of his own persuasion. Fourth, Senator Joseph T. Robinson, the leader of the anti-Court forces, died in July and left a void which could not be filled. All in all, with many members of Congress opposed to the method of reform and articulated public opinion in general on the side of the Court, the measure had no real chance of passage.

It is beyond the scope of the study here to evaluate the influence which the Court controversy had on the ensuing modification of the constitutional opinions of some of the justices. That it must have had some impact seems indisputable, in spite of official denials to the contrary.[7] It is also true, of course, that the economic and social problems of the 1930's served merely to spotlight the fact that business and industry were organized on a national basis and that every part of the American economy was now dependent upon every other part. Thus regardless of the relative weight given to the economic and political realities of the time, the hard historical fact remains that between 1937 and 1942 the Supreme Court handed down three decisions which, taken together, opted for broad national power over commerce and spelled the end of dual federalism. These cases were *National Labor Relations Board v. Jones & Laughlin Steel Corporation* (1937),[8] *United States v. Darby* (1941),[9] and *Wickard v. Filburn* (1942);[10] they will now be examined in detail to illuminate their significant holdings.

The National Labor Relations Act

On July 5, 1935, Congress passed the National Labor Relations Act,[11] popularly known as the Wagner Labor Act, which imposed extensive and detailed regulations upon labor-management relations in industry. Specifically, the Act created a National Labor Relations Board (NLRB), which was charged with preventing certain "unfair labor practices," principally the interference with employees in their right to form self-organizations and bargain collectively with employers through their own elected representatives. The Board was empowered to investigate charges of unfair labor practices "affecting commerce," to make findings in such cases, and in the event of violations, to petition designated courts to secure the enforcement of its cease-and-desist orders. The Act was based on the finding of Congress that unfair labor practices led to industrial strife—a "burden" or "obstruction" on interstate commerce which Congress could remove under its power to regulate "commerce among the several States." Thus it was limited (at least in theory) to those companies clearly involved in interstate commerce.

One of the first industrial concerns to be investigated was the Jones & Laughlin Steel Corporation of Pittsburgh.[12] The NLRB found that the company had dismissed ten employees because of attempts on their part to organize a local chapter of an independent labor union. The Board ordered the corporation to cease and desist from such coercion, to reinstate the employees with back pay, and for thirty days to post notices that the corporation would not discharge members or prospective members of the union. Jones & Laughlin failed to comply, and the Board petitioned the United States Circuit Court of Appeals for the Fifth Circuit to enforce the order. The Circuit Court denied the petition and based its ruling primarily on the old distinction between production and commerce, which had only recently been reaffirmed in *Carter v. Carter Coal Co.;* the Board appealed the adverse decision.

Arguments in *Jones & Laughlin*

This was an important test case, and both sides knew it. Accordingly, the constitutional arguments of both parties were carefully delineated in the briefs submitted to the Court. The government, on its part, made two main points: (1) the Act was a valid exercise of the preventive power of Congress to protect interstate commerce from the "evils" of industrial strife; and (2) the Act could constitutionally be applied to Jones & Laughlin because the company was engaged in such commerce.[13]

Attorney General Homer S. Cummings and Solicitor General Stanley F. Reed began the defense of the statute by citing statistics and well-known actual occurrences to show the great number of man-hours lost every year due to strikes, work stoppages, and labor-management disputes of all kinds. Such industrial strife had a recurring and deleterious effect on the volume and flow of interstate commerce, a condition which Congress could deal with in two ways: (1) it could enact a statute designed to remove this burden from interstate commerce after it had evidenced itself in a particular case; or (2) it could enact a statute to deal with the causes of the burden in anticipation of their probable effect on commerce. In the first instance, Congress would be using its "control power" over interstate commerce, as it had done in the Sherman Antitrust Act; in the second instance, Congress would be using its preventive power, as it had done in the Packers and Stockyards Act. The Wagner Labor Act was an exercise of the preventive power; and it was specifically directed to elimination of the proscribed unfair labor practices only when they were found to be "affecting commerce," which had been defined in section 2 (7) as "in commerce, or burdening or obstructing commerce or the free flow of commerce, or having led or tending to lead to a labor dispute burdening or obstructing commerce or the free flow of commerce."

Government counsel admitted that the Court had never defined the full extent to which the manufacturing or processing activities of an enterprise extensively engaged in interstate commerce might be brought under congressional control; the Court had held, however, that the preventive power of Congress was applicable to such activities in the event that they were subject to recurring evils which, in their totality, constituted a burden on such commerce. Two precedents in particular, *Stafford v. Wallace* (1922)[14] and *Board of Trade of Chicago v. Olson* (1932),[15] supported this claim for federal power, and the principle clearly extended to the prevention of industrial strife in enterprises engaged in interstate commerce.

Evidence was introduced to show the far-flung and diverse activities of Jones & Laughlin, the fourth largest steel producer in the country. The company was completely integrated from iron ore, coal, and limestone properties to sales offices located nationally and in Canada. It owned and operated steamships, barges, tugboats, and even a railroad. Seventy-five percent of the steel produced at its large Aliquippa plant was shipped outside of Pennsylvania. It was obviously engaged in interstate commerce; and since Congress had found that industrial strife in such enterprises constituted a recurring evil, "the statute may be applied to the individual instances of this recurring burden—that is, to any enterprise which . . . is dependent upon such commerce for the successful conduct of its business."[16]

Finally, Cummings and Reed had to distinguish the two cases of *Schechter Poultry Corporation v. United States* (1935)[17] and *Carter v. Carter Coal Co.* (1936).[18] This was accomplished by arguing that the National Labor Relations Act was concerned with activities which occurred under circumstances closely related to a flow of commerce and which directly affected that flow. It was pointed out that in *Schechter* the flow of chickens had ceased and that in *Carter* the flow of coal had not yet begun. The Labor Act, on the other hand, "deals with matters closely connected with commerce, does not go beyond what is necessary for the protection of commerce, and does not attempt 'a broad regulation of industry within the State.' "[19]

Counsel for Jones & Laughlin were equally sure of the absolute unconstitutionality of the Labor Act. Two main arguments were presented to substantiate this position: (1) the Act was not a true regulation of interstate commerce but a regulation of the labor relations between employer and employees; and (2) Congress had no power to regulate respondent's relations with its production employees because production was not a part of commerce but a local activity which could be regulated only by the states.[20] These two propositions were readily provable by merely looking to the act itself and then to the Constitution and the long line of Supreme Court decisions concerning the commerce power.

Taking up the first point, corporation counsel argued that Article 1, section 8, clause 3 of the Constitution specifically limited Congress to making only bona fide regulations of commerce. It was evident, however, from the legislative history and the language of the present act that it actually constituted a regulation of labor. Congress had been primarily concerned with the establishment and protection of independent labor organizations; this was shown by the fact that the act condemned plant unions, sanctioned "closed shop" agreements, expressly preserved the right to strike, and interfered with the employer's right of hiring and firing employees. Congress had attempted to save the constitutionality of the statute by confining enforcement to those situations "affecting commerce," but the ultimate fact remained that it had enacted a labor law.

Counsel expanded this crucial line of attack. The corporation's relations with its production employees at Aliquippa did not constitute a part of interstate commerce. Even if the interstate activities cited by the NLRB were admitted, the decision in *Hammer v. Dagenhart* (1918)[21] was conclusive of the fact that the respondent's production activities were not thereby subject to congressional control. The jurisdiction of Congress under the Commerce Clause included the power to regulate, restrict, and protect interstate commerce; but it did not include the right to regulate purely local activities which might precede or follow such commerce, and many other Court decisions supported this proposition.[22]

Counsel took up the question of the scope of the preventive power of Congress and carefully distinguished the precedents extending that power to recurring evils which constituted a burden on commerce. *Stafford v. Wallace* and *Board of Trade of Chicago v. Olsen* were inapplicable because stockyards and grain exchanges were themselves instrumentalities of interstate commerce, and the activities in them exerted a direct effect upon the stream of commerce. But neither case supplied any authority for extending the doctrine to production activities which, as here, might only indirectly affect that flow; the distinction between direct and indirect effects on commerce was a viable one, and *Carter v. Carter Coal Co.* clearly controlled the present case. Finally, the old justification for the doctrine of dual federalism was put forward: if the government's argument were accepted, there would be no reason why Congress could not, at some future time, use its power over commerce to stifle and subvert the sovereignty of the states and hence to destroy completely the federal system.

Opinions of the Court

On April 12, 1937, Chief Justice Hughes handed down the bare five-to-four decision in *National Labor Relations Board v. Jones & Laughlin Steel Corporation.*[23] He reviewed briefly the main provisions of the Wagner Act and described in detail the extensive interstate operations of the steel company. Then he came to the first major question: Was the law, in fact, a regulation of interstate commerce? After making a deep bow to the right of the states to regulate their own internal concerns (which will be commented upon later), Hughes asserted that the cardinal principle of judicial statutory construction was to save legislation. He was succinct: "We think it clear that the National Labor Relations Act may be construed so as to operate within the sphere of constitutional authority."[24] The reason was that jurisdiction had been conferred upon the Labor Board to prevent any person (or corporation) from engaging in any unfair labor practice "affecting commerce," and the commerce contemplated was clearly interstate commerce in "the constitutional sense." This was apparent from the definition of "affecting commerce" in section 2 (7), which was one of exclusion as well as inclusion:

> The grant of authority to the Board does not purport to extend to the relationship between all industrial employees and employers. Its terms do not impose collective bargaining upon all industry regardless of effects upon interstate or foreign commerce. It purports to reach only what may be deemed to burden or obstruct that commerce and, thus qualified, it must be construed as contemplating the exercise of control within constitutional bounds. It is a familiar principle that acts which directly burden or obstruct interstate or foreign commerce, or its free flow, are within the reach of the congressional power. Acts having that effect are not rendered immune because they grow out of labor disputes. . . . It is the effect upon commerce, not the source of the injury, which is the criterion.[25]

Whether a particular practice affected commerce in such a "close and intimate" fashion as to be subject to federal control was left to the Board to determine in individual cases, and Hughes examined the various unfair labor practices in section 8 to establish that the statute merely safeguarded the "fundamental" right of employees to self-organization and to selection of their own representatives for collective bargaining. This right had long been recognized, and coercion to prevent its free exercise had been held to be "a proper subject for condemnation" by legislation.[26] But could Congress extend protection to employees engaged in industrial production?

This was the second and crucial question to be answered. The Chief Justice canvassed the opposing arguments and took particular notice of the concept of a "stream of commerce," which had been emphasized by the government and distinguished by the corporation. He found that it was unnecessary to rely upon this principle in the present instance, and he gave sweeping scope to the power of Congress over commerce:

> The congressional authority to protect interstate commerce from burdens and obstructions is not limited to transactions which can be deemed to be an essential part of a "flow" of interstate or foreign commerce. Burdens and obstructions may be due to injurious action springing from other sources. The fundamental principle is that the power to regulate commerce is the power to enact "all appropriate legislation" for its "protection and advancement" . . . ; to adopt measures "to promote its growth and insure its safety" . . . ; "to foster, protect, control, and restrain." . . . That power is plenary and may be exerted to protect interstate commerce "no matter what the source of the dangers which threaten it."[27]

Coming to the more precise matter of regulating production per se, he held that if intrastate activities had "such a close and substantial relation" to interstate commerce that it was essential to control the former in order to protect the latter, "Congress cannot be denied the power to exercise that control."[28] He cited *Stafford v. Wallace* and his own *Shreveport Case* in support of this proposition and concluded: "It is thus apparent that the fact that the employees here concerned were engaged in production is not determinative."[29]

There remained but one final task—to show the effect of the labor practices involved upon interstate commerce. Hughes looked again to the far-flung activities of Jones & Laughlin and had no difficulty in finding that "the stoppage of those operations by industrial strife would have a most serious effect upon interstate commerce",[30] in fact, it was obvious that the effect "would be immediate and might be catastrophic." On this basis, the justices could not be asked to close their eyes on "the plainest facts of our national life and to deal with the question of direct and indirect effects in an intellectual vacuum."[31]

With a "close and intimate" relationship between the steel industry and general commercial activity now established, Hughes asked a rhetorical question, the answer to which was obvious:

> When industries organize themselves on a national scale, making their relation to interstate commerce the dominant factor in their activities, how can it be maintained that their industrial labor relations constitute a forbidden field into which Congress may not enter when it is necessary to protect interstate commerce from the paralyzing consequences of industrial war?[32]

Experience demonstrated that the right of employees to self-organization and free choice of representatives for collective bargaining was often "an essential condition of industrial peace," and Congress clearly possessed "constitutional authority" under the Commerce Clause to safeguard that right. Furthermore, the application of this principle extended to small firms as well as to large manufacturers.[33]

Justice James C. McReynolds delivered a biting opinion for the four dissenters.[34] Citing the "well-established principles" of the *Schechter* and *Carter* cases, he asserted: "Every consideration brought forward to uphold the Act before us was applicable to support the Acts held unconstitutional in causes decided within two years."[35] After a review of the facts, he concluded:

> Any effect on interstate commerce by the discharge of employees shown here, would be indirect and remote in the highest degree. . . .[36]

> . . . Whatever effect any cause of discontent among employees may ultimately have upon commerce is far too indirect to justify Congressional regulation. Almost anything—marriage, birth, death—may in some fashion affect commerce.[37]

> . . . A more remote and indirect interference with interstate commerce or a more definitive invasion of the powers reserved to the states is difficult, if not impossible, to imagine.[38]

Then he invoked the doctrine of dual federalism at its best: "The Constitution still recognizes the existence of states with indestructible powers; the Tenth Amendment was supposed to put them beyond controversy."[39]

Several points of significance stand out in the *Jones & Laughlin* case. The first and foremost is, of course, that the decision broadened the power of Congress under the Commerce Clause to regulate labor-management relations in industry. This represented a clear blow to the doctrine of dual federalism. The fact that Congress could now control certain manufacturing activities, which had heretofore been considered "local" in their nature, meant that the Tenth Amendment did not constitute the severe limitation on the delegated power which had been claimed for it in such cases as *Hammer v. Dagenhart* and *Carter v. Carter Coal Co.* But it must be noted that some undefined degree of restriction on the commerce power still inhered in it. In at least two places in the majority opinion, Hughes was careful to point out that there were limits, however vague, to the federal power. Just before he found the Labor Act to be a regulation of interstate commerce (within the constitutional meaning of the term), he issued this warning:

> The authority of the federal government may not be pushed to such an extreme as to destroy the distinction, which the commerce clause itself establishes, between commerce "among the several States" and the internal concerns of a State. That distinction between what is national and what is local in the activties of commerce is vital to the maintenance of our federal system.[40]

Again, even as he was affirming the proposition that Congress had the power to protect interstate commerce from "burdens and obstructions," he cautioned that the scope of the power "must be considered in the light of our dual system of government" and may not be extended so far as to create "a completely centralized government."[41] Finally, that Hughes did not discard this distinction is shown by the fact that he held the steel company's production activities to have a "close and substantial" effect upon commerce and therefore to be subject to congressional regulation. Thus although he found the "direct-indirect" test to be inapplicable in the present instance, he clearly did not repudiate it completely or irrevocably.

It is beyond the scope of this analysis to reach a conclusion on Hughes' own consistency (or lack of it) in constitutional adjudication of the Commerce Clause. That has been done elsewhere, with varying opinions expressed.[42] What is of central importance here is that his opinion in *Jones & Laughlin* delivered a substantial setback to dual federalism and opted for a considerably more flexible interpretation of national authority over commerce than that which had prevailed in the immediate past. The Court had again, however, reserved for itself the right of being the final censor on federal power and still had at hand a useful (if indeterminate) formula for making its choices in future cases.

The Fair Labor Standards Act

On June 25, 1938, Congress passed the Fair Labor Standards Act,[43] which prescribed an initial minimum wage of twenty-five cents an hour (to rise to forty cents an hour in subsequent stages) and maximum hours of forty-four a week (to be reduced to forty in two years), subject to time-and-a-half for overtime, for all employees engaged in interstate commerce or in the production of goods for that commerce. In addition, the Act made it unlawful to ship, deliver, or sell any goods in interstate commerce which had been produced under substandard labor conditions [section 15(a)(1)] and to violate the provisions on wages and hours if engaged in production for such commerce [section 15(a)(2)]. The statute further called for employers to keep wage-and-hour records on employees, which could be opened for federal inspection. Finally, the law prohibited the shipment in commerce of the products of any firm where child labor had been used in the last thirty days, a virtual reenactment of the Child Labor Act of 1916, invalidated in *Hammer v. Dagenhart* (1918).

The constitutionality of this comprehensive regulation of labor conditions was not long in being tested. Fred W. Darby, owner of a Georgia sawmill which shipped lumber out of state, was indicted for violating the act. The District Court for the Southern District of Georgia quashed the indictment on the ground that Congress was without power to make such regulations of manufacturing within the states, and the government appealed.

Arguments in *Darby*

The case of *United States v. Darby* (1941)[44] presented some old but highly important constitutional questions. The government argued two main points: (1) the Fair Labor Standards Act, in all its provisions, was a valid exercise of the federal commerce power; and (2) the Act did not violate the Tenth Amendment.[45] Solicitor General Francis Biddle and Assistant Attorney General Thurman W. Arnold concentrated on proposition one.[46] The distribution in interstate commerce of goods produced under substandard labor conditions created a national commercial problem which the individual states could not solve independently. Congress had made specific findings in section 2(a) of the statute that low labor standards: (1) were detrimental to the health and efficiency of workers; (2) led to labor disputes which obstructed the free flow of goods in commerce; (3) constituted an unfair method of competition; and (4) were spread and perpetuated by use of the channels of interstate commerce. No state, acting alone, could require labor standards substantially higher than those in effect elsewhere without suffering economic loss; and only an exercise of federal power could correct this condition and the evils attendant upon it. In this connection, the understanding of the framers at the Philadelphia Convention had been that the enumerated powers of Congress (including the commerce power) placed within the jurisdiction of the "general government" control over those problems which were national in scope and thus beyond the competence of the separate states.

Counsel took up the major provisions of the Act one by one. Section 15(a)(1) was clearly a regulation of interstate commerce. Even if the customary dichotomy between "direct" and "indirect" effects were accepted, the existence of substandard labor conditions had a "direct and substantial" effect upon commerce; and the power of Congress to regulate commerce included the power to prohibit it.[47] It made no difference whether the goods were harmful or harmless in themselves; congressional power was no longer limited to proscribing the movement of harmful or deleterious goods.[48] Section 15(a)(2) was a "reasonable and appropriate" means of effectuating the prohibition in section 15(a)(1), that is, of keeping interstate channels free of goods produced under substandard conditions. In other words, section 15(a)(2) was intended to implement the general policy of the statute. It was also designed to prevent labor disputes which might arise out of disagreements over wages and hours; the Labor Board cases had already decided that Congress could meet this evil, and those cases were controlling here.

Biddle and Arnold then turned to that great supposed restriction on national power, the Tenth Amendment. The Fair Labor Standards

Act had been shown to be an exercise of the power granted Congress to regulate commerce, and a reading of the plain words of the amendment disposed of the argument that the statute violated the article:

> Language could not express more clearly that the Amendment does not reserve to the states any part of any power which is "delegated to the United States by the Constitution," nor indicate more plainly that the Amendment does not limit the scope of any power which is delegated to the United States.[49]

History, in the congressional records of the adoption of the amendment, showed that it was simply declaratory of the evident proposition that Congress could not constitutionally exercise powers not granted to it. This stipulation merely acknowledged the fact that the central government was one of enumerated powers.

Counsel for Darby concentrated on one theme with several variations: the Act was an undisguised attempt to regulate conditions in the production of goods throughout the industries of the entire nation and thus could not be sustained as a regulation of interstate commerce within the delegated power of Congress; specifically, it violated the Tenth Amendment.[50] This called for an examination of the origin and the nature of the American constitutional system. The framers had designed the Constitution primarily to correct the weaknesses of the Articles of Confederation; this was the reason that they provided for a national government supreme in its own sphere and free from domination by the states. But the new form of government preserved the sovereignty and individual identity of the several states, and the grant of the enumerated powers was not destructive of this relationship; the Tenth Amendment was passed later expressly to safeguard the sovereignty of the states except as this might be lessened by the delegated powers. What came out of the Convention, then, was a government of dual and independent sovereignties in which the powers of the federal and state governments were mutually exclusive.

Counsel refurbished the familiar argument that manufacturing and production were not ordinarily subjects of commerce and therefore were not within the regulatory control of Congress but subject to the exclusive control of the states. The legislative findings of section 2(a) were merely an attempt to create powers which were not granted to Congress under the Commerce Clause, and it was up to the Court to determine whether certain factual situations "directly affected" interstate commerce. Section 15(a)(1) was an unconstitutional exercise of the commerce power for the reason that a prohibition of shipments in interstate commerce was not permissible under the doctrine of *Hammer v. Dagenhart,* which had invalidated the Child Labor Act. The real basis for that decision was that that act unconstitutionally subjected state policy to national domination. Therefore, regardless of what one thought about the morality of child labor, the decision in *Hammer* had been correct from the point of view of the federal system. Counsel concluded: "The real basis of appellee's argument rests upon a recognition of the established duality of sovereignties under the Constitution."[51] This duality was protected by the Tenth Amendment and could not and should not be altered: "If the Act be sustained, state lines will be of interest in the future solely as historical and geographical markers."[52]

The Darby counsel turned to section 15(a)(2); it, too, was an unconstitutional exercise of the federal commerce power for two reasons. First, the congressional assertion of the necessity for uniform regulation of wages and hours could not bring these purely intrastate subjects within the purview of that power where the result of such regulation was to obscure completely the proper boundaries of national and state power—boundaries which had been carefully marked out in *Schechter* and *Carter Coal.* Second, failure to conform to the statutory standards in manufacturing establishments did not constitute unfair competition and did not affect interstate commerce directly so as to be subject to regulation by Congress. This was shown by the fact that such failure did not interfere with the orderly and fair marketing of goods in commerce; in fact, the Act did not even pretend to regulate interstate markets. The only possible conclusion which could be drawn was that section 15(a)(2) was an impermissible invasion of the reserved powers of the states.

The *Darby* Decision

United States v. Darby was decided on February 3, 1941; Justice Harlan Fiske Stone wrote the unanimous opinion.[53] There were two major questions to be answered: (1) does Congress have constitutional power to prohibit the shipment in interstate commerce of lumber manufactured by employees whose wages are less than a prescribed minimum or whose weekly hours of labor are greater than a prescribed maximum, and (2) does Congress have constitutional power to prohibit the employment of workmen in production of goods for interstate commerce at other than prescribed wages and hours?

Coming to the first question, Stone reasoned:

> While manufacturing is not of itself interstate commerce the shipment of manufactured goods interstate is such commerce and the prohibition of such shipment by Congress is indubitably a regulation of the commerce. The power to regulate commerce is the power "to prescribe the rule by which commerce is to be governed" . . . and extends not only to those regulations which aid, foster and protect the commerce, but embraces those which prohibit it.[54]

He took up the claim that the real purpose of the prohibition was the regulation of wages and hours, control of which was reserved to the states. The language of his answer was blunt and precisely to the point:

> The power of Congress over interstate commerce "is complete in itself, may be exercised to its utmost extent, and acknowledges no limitations, other than are prescribed by the constitution."

> . . . That power can neither be enlarged nor diminished by the exercise or non-exercise of state power. . . . Congress . . . is free to exclude from the commerce articles whose use in the states for which they are destined it may conceive to be injurious to the public health, morals or welfare, even though the state has not sought to regulate their use. . . . Such regulation is not a forbidden invasion of state power merely because either its motive or its consequence is to restrict the use of articles of commerce within the states of destination. . . . It is no objection to the assertion of the power to regulate interstate commerce that its exercise is attended by the same incidents which attend the exercise of the police power of the states.[55]

Stone reiterated the familiar Austinian-Holmesian principle that the courts are given no control over the motives or purpose of legislation. Then he faced his last obstacle, the precedent of *Hammer v. Dagenhart*. He found that it rested on a distinction (harmful versus harmless articles) which had long since been abandoned, and he expressly overruled it. He held that "the power of Congress under the Commerce Clause is plenary to exclude any article from interstate commerce subject only to the specific prohibitions of the Constitution."[56]

Stone turned his attention to the second and, in a sense, tougher question. The validity of the wage-and-hour requirements turned on the question of whether the employment of employees engaged in production for interstate commerce, under other than the prescribed conditions, was so related to the commerce and so affected it as to be within reach of the power of Congress to regulate it. He had no trouble in finding that Darby's business was engaged in "production for commerce," and the remaining problem involved the scope of the commerce power—did it allow restrictions on the conditions of such production? Stone gave broad and penetrative sweep to the delegated power:

> The power of Congress over interstate commerce is not confined to the regulation of commerce among the states. It extends to those activities intrastate which so affect interstate commerce or the exercise of the power of Congress over it as to make regulation of them appropriate means to the attainment of a legitimate end, the exercise of the granted power of Congress to regulate interstate commerce.[57]

> . . . Congress, having by the present Act adopted the policy of excluding from interstate commerce all goods produced for the commerce which do not conform to the specified labor standards, it may choose the means reasonably adapted to the attainment of the permitted end, even though they involve control of intrastate activities.[58]

He looked to the evils which the act sought to control—the spread of substandard labor conditions through the channels of interstate commerce, impairment or destruction of local businesses by unfair competition, and the consequent dislocation of commerce itself—and decided that the means adopted by section 15(a)(2) "for the protection of interstate commerce" were so related to the commerce and so affected it "as to be within the reach of the commerce power." The size of the producer or his volume of shipments made no difference; Congress had "recognized that in present day industry, competition by a small part might affect the whole."[59] To the extent that *Carter v. Carter Coal Co.* was inconsistent with this conclusion, its doctrine was limited by the decisions under the Sherman Antitrust Act and the National Labor Relations Act, which were controlling.[60]

There was one final problem of importance—the claim made in the name of dual federalism that the Tenth Amendment in some fashion imposed a limitation upon the delegated powers of the national government. Stone faced the issue squarely and disposed of it in a now-famous assertion:

> Our conclusion is unaffected by the Tenth Amendment. . . . The amendment states but a truism that all is retained which has not been surrendered. There is nothing in the history of its adoption to suggest that it was more than declaratory of the relationship between the national and state governments as it had been established by the Constitution before the amendment or that its purpose was other than to allay fears that the new national government might seek to exercise powers not granted, and that the states might not be able to exercise fully their reserved powers.

> . . . From the beginning and for many years the amendment has been construed as not depriving the national government of authority to resort to all means for the exercise of a granted power which are appropriate and plainly adapted to the permitted end. . . . Whatever doubts may have arisen of the soundness of that conclusion they have been put at rest by the decisions under the Sherman Act and the National Labor Relations Act which we have cited.[61]

The death knell of dual federalism had been sounded at long last!

Stone very quickly upheld the validity of the record-keeping requirements and dismissed the Fifth-Amendment attack on the authority of *West Coast Hotel Co. v. Parrish* (1937).[62] The Fair Labor Standards Act was an entirely constitutional exercise of power by Congress under the Commerce Clause; and judicial interpretation of that clause now gave Congress the power to control almost every facet of American industry.

Analysis of Stone's Opinion

It is not too much to say that *United States v. Darby* is one of the half-dozen most important cases in the whole 180-year history of American constitutional law. Accordingly, some extended analysis of Stone's opinion is necessary in order to pinpoint its most significant aspects and their far-reaching implications—for national power, for Congress, and, perhaps above all, for the Supreme Court itself. The case raised three major problems which demanded solution by the Court: (1) delineation of the scope of the federal commerce power (which indirectly called for a definition of "commerce"); (2) interpretation of the Tenth Amendment's effect upon the powers delegated to the national government (obviously closely related to problem one); and (3) judicial concern with the motives or purpose of congressional regulations of commerce. Each of these will now be considered separately.

First, there were two clear issues to be decided relative to national power under the Commerce Clause. One was the relatively simple question of whether Congress could bar certain articles from moving in interstate commerce—in this instance, goods produced under substandard conditions of labor. The adjective "simple" is used deliberately because, on any fair reading of the history of the commerce power, Congress had always been allowed extensive leeway to prohibit the movement of articles in commerce, and these included adulterated or misbranded food and drugs, stolen automobiles, convict-made goods, intangibles such as lottery tickets, and even women transported across state lines for immoral purposes.[63] The single exception to this rule had come in the five-to-four decision in *Hammer v. Dagenhart* (1918), which was based on a supposed distinction between goods harmful and harmless in themselves. But the majority reasoning was faulty basically because it denied the plain meaning of the way in which Marshall had defined the power "to regulate" in *Gibbons v. Ogden.* Congress, under Marshall's view, had plenary power to control anything which moved in interstate channels, and the question of whether commodities were harmful or harmless would be irrelevant since the Constitution itself put no such limitation on the delegated power. Ever since *Gibbons* the Court had consistently upheld this interpretation of congressional power to govern commerce "among the several States," and it was not at all difficult for Stone to overrule the *Hammer* deviation and reaffirm what had long been sound constitutional construction of the power of Congress to exclude absolutely from interstate traffic articles of its own choosing.

The other issue was not quite as open and shut. The question of whether Congress could regulate directly the conditions of local production (even though destined for interstate commerce) depended upon two considerations: (1) the definition of "commerce," and (2) the scope of the federal commerce power. Regarding the first element, the Court had held that manufacturing per se was not commerce, and this concept had never been repudiated outright. In regard to the second constitutent, however, it was also clear that Congress could reach any activity which bore a "close and substantial" relation to commerce. But this principle was subject to the

Hughes dictum in *Jones & Laughlin* that the authority of the national government could not be pushed to such an extreme as to destroy the distinction (which was "vital to the maintenance of our federal system") between "commerce among the several states" and the "internal concerns of a state."

In deciding this important question, Stone stayed on firm constitutional ground. He admitted at the outset that "manufacturing is not of itself interstate commerce" and so attempted no new or expanded definition for the term. He looked, instead, to the scope of the power. Relying upon such solid precedents as the *Shreveport Case* and *NLRB v. Jones & Laughlin,* he gave it wide sweep:

> The power of Congress over interstate commerce . . . extends to those activities intrastate which so affect interstate commerce or the exercise of the power of Congress over it as to make regulation of them appropriate means to the attainment cf a legitimate end, the exercise of the granted power. . . .[64]

Then he went on to conclude that the regulation of labor conditions in production was an "appropriate means" of controlling the designated evils of human debasement and unfair business competition which were "so related to" national commerce as to come "within the reach of the commerce power."

Now these statements, on their face, do not appear to go beyond what Hughes had held in *Jones & Laughlin.* But two very important differences must be noted. First, Stone made no mention of "direct" and "indirect" effects. If an activity "affected" commerce, it came within the ambit of congressional power. Thus without saying so explicitly, Stone discarded the vague rule of direct and indirect effects on commerce as a test of the validity of an exercise of national power. Second, he did not repeat the Hughes caveat that federal power could not be extended to the "internal concerns of a state." Under Stone's view, it was "no objection to the assertion of the power to regulate interstate commerce that its exercise is attended by the same incidents which attend the exercise of the police power of the states."[65] In short, Congress could reach the "internal concerns of a state" if control of those internal concerns was necessary to make effective "the attainment of a legitimate end," namely, the plenary authority of Congress to regulate "that commerce which concerns more states than one."

The second problem which *Darby* raised was the effect of the

Tenth Amendment upon the delegated powers of the federal government: did the amendment limit in some fashion the extent to which the enumerated powers could be exercised? Stone emphatically repudiated any such idea and with it the doctrine of dual federalism, a constitutional "heresy" which the Court had accepted only a very few times in its long history of expounding upon the nature and scope of the powers granted to the national government. It is not possible here to make an extensive review of the history of the Tenth Amendment, but a few representative quotations will indicate what has been the generally accepted interpretation of its meaning and purpose. It was proposed by the first Congress and ratified by the states as part of the Bill of Rights, which was added to the original Constitution as the price for ratification of the latter by a number of the states. In the debates in Congress, James Madison viewed the amendment as merely declaratory of what the Constitution already provided:

> I find, from looking into the amendments proposed by the State conventions, that several are particularly anxious that it should be declared in the Constitution, that the powers not therein delegated should be reserved to the several States. Perhaps other words may define this more precisely than the whole of the instrument now does. I admit they may be deemed unnecessary; but there can be no harm in making such a declaration, if gentlemen will allow that the fact is as stated. I am sure I understand it so, and do therefore propose it.[66]

Several of the state conventions ratifying the Constitution had called for an amendment reserving to the states all powers not expressly delegated to the general government.[67] Accordingly, in the congressional debates it was twice moved that the word "expressly" be inserted in the Tenth Amendment; both motions were defeated, with Madison opposed on each occasion.[68] Later, in debating Secretary Hamilton's proposal for a national bank (after nine states had ratified the amendment), Madison commented upon the proper division of power: "Interference with the power of the States was no constitutional criterion of the power of Congress. If the power was not given, Congress could not exercise it; if given, they might exercise it, although it should interfere with the laws, or even the constitution of the States."[69]

In writing his famous *Commentaries on the Constitution,* Justice Joseph Story offered this authoritative interpretation of the Tenth Amendment:

This amendment is a mere affirmation of what, upon any just reasoning, is a necessary rule of interpreting the Constitution.

... It is plain, therefore, that it could not have been the intention of the framers of this amendment to give it effect as an abridgement of any of the powers granted under the Constitution, whether they are express or implied, direct or incidental. Its sole design is to exclude any interpretation by which other powers should be assumed beyond those which are granted. ... The attempts then which have been made from time to time to force upon this language an abridging or restrictive influence are utterly unfounded. ... Stripped of the ingenious disguises in which they are clothed, they are neither more nor less than attempts to foist into the text the word "expressly". ... [70]

Two great chief justices, Marshall and Taney, subscribed to the Madisonian understanding of the Tenth Amendment as a statement which was merely declaratory of a plain reading of the federal Constitution at the time of its framing.[71] In fact, Marshall suggested that the amendment had been adopted solely "for the purpose of quieting the excessive jealousies which had been excited" and that its framers had omitted the word "expressly" in order to avoid "the embarrassments resulting from the insertion of this word in the articles of confederation."[72] Two other eminent justices also concurred with Story's view that the amendment did not abridge any of the powers granted to the national government. In *Champion v. Ames* (1903) the first Justice John Marshall Harlan rejected the argument that the Tenth Amendment forbade a congressional ban on the movement of lottery tickets interstate: "... the answer is that the power to regulate commerce among the States has been expressly delegated to Congress";[73] and in *Missouri v. Holland* (1920) Justice Oliver Wendell Holmes answered a similar argument, this time relating to a federal prohibition on killing wild, migratory birds: "... it is not enough to refer to the Tenth Amendment ... because ... the power to make treaties is delegated expressly."[74]

From all of the foregoing, it appears, then, that Stone was on solid historical and constitutional ground in his reading of the Tenth Amendment and in laying to rest once and for all the dubious, if not pernicious, concepts of dual federalism. Specifically, he was taking Marshall's view that the federal commerce power was "vested in congress as absolutely as it would be in a single government"[75] and that that power was plenary; in Stone's own words, it could "neither be enlarged or diminished by the exercise or non-exercise of state power."[76]

The third and final problem in *Darby* revolved around the question of how the Court should view the motives or purpose of Congress in exercising power under the Commerce Clause. This actually did not present much of an obstacle to Stone, who had long espoused a doctrine of judicial self-restraint when it came to inquiring into legislative findings of the need for, or the wisdom of, economic regulation. He met the issue squarely:

> The motive and purpose of a regulation of interstate commerce are matters for the legislative judgment upon the exercise of which the Constitution places no restriction and over which the courts are given no control. . . . Whatever their motive and purpose, regulations of commerce which do not infringe some constitutional prohibition are within the plenary power conferred on Congress by the Commerce Clause.[77]

Once again, he had substantial underpinnings in precedent for his holding. Marshall had expressed the same general idea in *Gibbons.* After the Chief Justice had defined the power "to regulate" in sweeping terms, he indicated that the only real restraint on the use (or abuse) of the power lay in the electoral process and the responsibility of congressmen to the people at the polls. Likewise, even conservative Chief Justice Taft had preached judicial abstention in the *Stafford* case: "This court will certainly not substitute its judgment for that of Congress in such a matter [as the regulation of constant practices burdening commerce] unless the relation of the subject to interstate commerce and its effect upon it are clearly non-existent."[78] The important point here is that Stone denied the authority of the Supreme Court to look to the motives or purpose of Congress in judging the validity of commercial regulations of the national economy. The Court might still examine the legislative history of a law in order to construe and apply it in particular instances, but there was the strong intimation that the justices would henceforth abide by Austinian principles and concern themselves exclusively with the constitutional power of Congress to regulate commerce. Only time could reveal whether this prophecy would be fulfilled; but the *Darby* opinion challenged the Court to relinquish the prerogative, which it had exercised for almost a half century since *United States v. E.C. Knight Co.,* of acting as final censor on exercises of power by Congress under the Commerce Clause and, in effect, to assume that a coordinate branch of the federal government also possessed "the capacity to govern."

Only a few final comments are needed with respect to the landmark case of *United States v. Darby*. It is obvious from an examination of Stone's opinion that he relied heavily on Marshall's original exposition of the Commerce Clause in *Gibbons v. Ogden*—in the broad and penetrative scope that he gave to the commerce power, in his interpretation of the power as plenary and unconfined except by specific constitutional prohibitions (of which the Tenth Amendment was not one), and in his refusal to look to the motives of Congress in exercising the power. The statement has often been made that in *Darby* the Court returned to the basic Constitution of John Marshall—an instrument of vast national power designed to weld the states into an indivisible Union—and, in the sense of constitutional law, this is true. It is beyond the purview of this analysis to show that Marshall was an economic conservative and a steadfast protector of the rights of private property who might have blanched at many New Deal measures and not have approved of them philosophically. But it is also unfair to transplant "the great Chief Justice" into the twentieth century and to predict his reactions to modern problems. The hard fact remains that Marshall's genius (and that is the correct word) in expounding a constitution designed to endure and to be adaptable to the crises of human affairs provided Harlan Fiske Stone with the constitutional bases necessary to unfetter the power of Congress under the Commerce Clause from the straitjacket of dual federalism and to allow the federal government to deal realistically with a now highly industrialized, highly interdependent national economy. The fact that Stone grasped this opportunity and made the most of it is what makes *Darby* such a highly significant case.

The Agricultural Adjustment Act

On February 16, 1938, Congress passed the second Agricultural Adjustment Act,[79] which provided for a system of marketing quotas for cotton, wheat, corn, tobacco, and rice. It empowered the Secretary of Agriculture, upon a finding that the supply was too large relative to demand, to impose a national marketing quota upon any of these products subject to approval by a referendum of two-thirds of the producers. The Act authorized the Secretary to assign individual quotas to each farm and fixed heavy monetary penalties for marketing quantities in excess of these quotas. The effect of excess supply upon prices and hence the disorderly marketing of agricultural commodities in interstate commerce, and the disruption of that commerce, were cited as the evils to be eliminated by the act;

95

consequently, the regulations were based solely on the federal commerce power.

Mulford v. Smith (1939)

The AAA received its first test of constitutionality in *Mulford v. Smith* (1939).[80] James H. Mulford and other tobacco growers from southern Georgia and northern Florida attempted to market quantities of flue-cured tobacco in excess of their 1938 crop-marketing quotas. Nat Smith and other tobacco warehousemen gave intention of deducting the prescribed penalties from the receipts of the auction sales and paying the money to the Secretary of Agriculture to be put into the United States Treasury. Mulford sought to enjoin Smith from collecting the penalties on the ground that the act was unconstitutional.

It seems unnecessary to go into much detail as to the opposing arguments of counsel. Suffice it to say that these arguments were very similar to those in *NLRB v. Jones & Laughlin,* except that here the question was the extent of federal power over producers of tobacco.[81] Counsel for Mulford contended that the AAA of 1938 was in reality a statutory plan to control agricultural production—a local activity—and hence beyond the power delegated to Congress to regulate interstate commerce. Solicitor General Robert H. Jackson and Assistant Attorney General Thurman W. Arnold (the United States was an intervening defendant along with Smith) argued that the Act only regulated the sale of tobacco in interstate commerce and that even if it were deemed to affect production, it would still be a valid regulation of interstate commerce because such production had a direct effect upon the price and volume of interstate tobacco shipments and therefore a "close and intimate" relationship to such commerce. In short, the arguments in both cases hinged around the same constitutional issues, and the only real difference was that of agriculture versus industry.

Justice Owen J. Roberts delivered the seven-to-two majority opinion which upheld the constitutionality of the Act.[82] He answered the contentions involving the commerce power in three short paragraphs. First, he summarily dismissed the claim that the statute sought to control agricultural production:

> It sets no limit upon the acreage which may be planted or produced and imposes no penalty for the planting and producing of tobacco in excess of the marketing quota. It purports

to be solely a regulation of interstate commerce, which it reaches
reaches and affects at the throat where tobacco enters the
stream of commerce,—the marketing warehouse.[83]

Then, after noting that more than two-thirds of all tobacco produced
in the country moved in interstate commerce, he concluded:

> Any rule, such as that embodied in the Act, which is intended
> to foster, protect and conserve that commerce, or to prevent
> the flow of commerce from working harm to the people of the
> nation, is within the competence of Congress. Within these
> limits the exercise of the power, the grant being unlimited in its
> terms, may lawfully extend to the absolute prohibition of such
> commerce, and *a fortiori* to limitation of the amount of a given
> commodity which may be transported in such commerce.[84]

Finally, Roberts dismissed the motive of Congress as a relevant factor
in determining the validity of the legislation. Thus the Court accepted
the second AAA at face value, acknowledged the power of Congress
to limit in any way it pleased (or even to prohibit) the movement of
agricultural commodities in interstate commerce, and refused to question congressional purpose in passing such regulations. Agriculture,
like industry, had come under the authority of the federal government.

Wickard v. Filburn (1942)

But there was to be a further and more important test of the
Agricultural Adjustment Act of 1938. Congress, in a joint resolution
of May 26, 1941, amended the original act with respect to the quota
and penalty provisions on wheat and corn.[85] Regarding wheat, the
marketing quota became, instead of a percentage of the normal
production of an individual farm's acreage allotment, the actual
production of an individual farm's acreage planted to wheat less the
normal production of any acreage in excess of its allotment. Wheat in
excess of this quota was known as the "farm marketing excess," was
regarded as "available for marketing," and was subject to a penalty
which the amendment raised from fifteen cents to forty-nine cents
per bushel. The only ways in which the penalty could be avoided
were to store the "farm marketing excess" in compliance with the act
or to deliver it to the Secretary of Agriculture. Meanwhile, on May 9,
Secretary Claude R. Wickard proclaimed a national quota for the
marketing year 1941-42; and, on May 31, wheat farmers approved it
overwhelmingly in a referendum.

Roscoe C. Filburn owned and operated a farm in Montgomery County, Ohio. He made a practice of growing winter wheat, some of which he sold, some of which he ground into flour for his own use, some of which he fed to his poultry and livestock, and some of which he kept as seed for the next year. In July, 1940, he had been informed by his County Agricultural Conservation Committee that the allotment for his farm was 11.1 acres and that the normal yield was 20.1 bushels per acre, i.e., 223 bushels in all. But he planted twenty-three acres and in July, 1941, harvested 462 bushels of wheat, a "farm marketing excess" of 239 bushels which, at forty-nine cents per bushel, made him liable for $117.11, which he refused to pay. The government sued to collect.

The arguments of opposing counsel are interesting, but they add nothing to those made in the *Jones & Laughlin* and *Darby* cases.[86] Attorney General Francis Biddle and Solicitor General Charles Fahy argued that the AAA of 1938 (with amendments) was a valid regulation of the marketing of agricultural commodities in interstate commerce. Even if the Act incidentally affected production, it was still valid in that this was necessary for the effective control of the national commerce in agricultural goods, particularly wheat. The government relied, of course, on the Labor Board cases, *United States v. Darby,* and *Mulford v. Smith* to substantiate the constitutionality of the statute. Counsel for Filburn contended that the amendment of May 26 had changed the AAA from a law which validly regulated marketing into a statute which invalidly regulated agricultural production; this was plainly shown by the shift from a flat farm-marketing allotment to a quota based on actual production, minus production in excess of an acreage allotment. Therefore *Mulford v. Smith* was not controlling; and, in fact, *Darby* supported this position from two points of view: (1) Stone had maintained the distinction between manufacturing or production and commerce; and (2) the "excess" wheat which Filburn would retain for his own use could have no possible effect on the interstate market for wheat, and Stone had held that Congress could reach the intrastate activity only if it "affected" interstate commerce. Counsel also argued that the May 26th provision for an increased penalty was retroactive on the 1941 wheat crop and thus deprived Filburn of his property without due process of law in violation of the Fifth Amendment; this argument actually received much more attention than the one which alleged a misuse of the commerce power.

On November 9, 1942, Justice Robert H. Jackson (who had argued the *Darby* and *Mulford* cases for the United States) handed down the unanimous decision in *Wickard v. Filburn,*[87] which sustained the second AAA in all of its provisions. After detailing the facts of the case and reviewing the relevant sections of the Act, he came to the question which the Court obviously deemed most important: Was the May 26th amendment a valid exercise of power by Congress under the Commerce Clause? In view of *Darby,* this issue merited little consideration except for the fact that the AAA extended federal regulation "to production not intended in any part for commerce but wholly for consumption on the farm." He briefly reviewed the opposing arguments, particularly the government's contention that the statute regulated only marketing. The clear reason for this insistence was that some of the Court's decisions had held that "activities such as 'production,' 'manufacturing,' and 'mining' are strictly 'local' and . . . cannot be regulated under the commerce power because their effects upon interstate commerce are, as matter of law, only 'indirect.' "[88] Jackson held that such distinctions were no longer valid:

> We believe that a review of the course of decision under the Commerce Clause will make plain, however, that questions of the power of Congress are not to be decided by reference to any formula which would give controlling force to nomenclature such as "production" and "indirect" and foreclose consideration of the actual effects of the activity in question upon interstate commerce.[89]

To prove this claim, he went back to *Gibbons v. Ogden* to emphasize Marshall's broad definition of the federal commerce power and to point out that Marshall "made emphatic the embracing and penetrating nature of this power by warning that effective restraints on its exercise must proceed from political rather than from judicial processes."[90]

Other precedents, of course, supported the present holding[91] and made the continued mechanical application of abstract legal formulas to commerce cases no longer feasible as grounds for decision:

> Once an economic measure of the reach of the power granted to Congress in the Commerce Clause is accepted, questions of federal power cannot be decided simply by finding the activity in question to be "production" nor can consideration of its economic effects be foreclosed by calling them "indirect."[92]

Therefore it was necessary to reaffirm Stone's view that the commerce power "extends to those activities intrastate which so affect interstate commerce . . . as to make regulation of them appropriate means to the attainment of a legitimate end, the effective execution of the granted power to regulate interstate commerce." Thus the subject of the present regulations was not material for purposes of deciding the instant case. Even if Filburn's activity was local and could not be regarded as commerce per se, "it may still, whatever its nature, be reached by Congress if it exerts a substantial economic effect on interstate commerce and this irrespective of whether such effect is what might at some earlier time have been defined as "direct" or "indirect."[93]

Jackson turned to an examination of the national wheat industry and found that a large percentage of the annual production moved in interstate and foreign channels. The industry had been characterized by declining exports abroad and overproduction at home, and prices were becoming ruinous to American farmers. Furthermore, twenty percent of the average annual crop remained on the farms where it was grown, and this sizable volume of home-consumed wheat had a substantial influence on price-and-market conditions generally in that it competed with wheat sold in commerce. It was obvious that Congress could properly include it in the regulatory scheme designed to stimulate trade at increased prices, and Jackson drew the inevitable conclusion: "That appellee's own contribution to the demand for wheat may be trivial by itself is not enough to remove him from the scope of federal regulation where, as here, his contribution, taken together with that of many others similarly situated, is far from trivial."[94]

This ruling really closed the issue; under the Commerce Clause Congress could reach any individual activity, no matter how insignificant in itself, if, when combined with other similar activities, it exerted a "substantial economic effect" on interstate commerce. In answer to the charge that the May 26th amendment unfairly discriminated against small wheat growers in favor of the large, specialized growers of the Great Plains, Jackson followed Stone in asserting bluntly that the resolution of conflicts of economic interest had been left, under the American governmental system, to Congress; and the Court had nothing to do "with the wisdom, workability, or fairness, of the plan of regulation."[95] Finally, he made short shrift of the Fifth-Amendment claim: "It is hardly lack of due process for the Government to regulate that which it subsidizes."[96]

Wickard v. Filburn is an important case in that it tied up the loose ends which had been left dangling in *United States v. Darby*. First, it completely swept away the old distinction between production and commerce; manufacturing, mining, and agriculture were now considered to be part of commerce and inseparable from it. No longer could there be any constitutional grounds for using the supposed dichotomy as a criterion for the validity of an exercise of the federal commerce power. Second, in plain terms it repudiated once and for all the "direct-indirect" test of the effect of an activity upon interstate commerce. Stone had really done this sub silentio in *Darby*, but now the Court openly abandoned this most indeterminate of standards; in doing so, of course, it further restricted its own authority to pass upon congressional regulations of commerce because the rationale of this test had allowed the Court to scrutinize each instance in which an act of Congress was applied in order to determine its constitutionality. Thus *Wickard* represented a further withdrawal of the Court as a censor of federal economic regulation. Third, in this same connection, Jackson reiterated the determination of the justices not to concern themselves with the motives or wisdom of Congress in legislating national economic policies. Henceforth, if an activity (or the aggregation of a multitude of similar incidents of such activity) could be shown to have a substantial effect upon interstate commerce, Congress could reach and control it by an exercise of its acknowledged plenary power over such commerce, without the fear of judicial intervention or condemnation. In 1942, almost a century and a quarter after *Gibbons v. Ogden,* the Commerce Clause came of age as the vast source and repository of congressional power which Marshall had pre-empted for it so long before.

A few words of summary are in order. From 1937 to 1942 the Supreme Court irrevocably discarded the constitutional doctrine of dual federalism, denied the proposition that the reserved powers of the states in any way limit the delegated powers of the federal government, and gave Congress plenary power under the Commerce Clause to regulate the national economy, free from judicial imposition of abstract or mechanistic legal formulas to decide questions of economic fact and public policy. But if the Court had abandoned its old unrealistic and unduly restrictive methods of judging exercises of national power, it had not renounced its historic function of judicial review over specific applications of that power. In the next quarter of a century the Court would often perform that function in its continuing interpretation of the Commerce Clause.

Notes

1. For graphic descriptions of the depression, see two sources among many: William E. Leuchtenburg, *Franklin D. Roosevelt and the New Deal: 1932-1940* (New York: Harper & Row, Publishers, Inc., 1963), 1-40; Arthur M. Schlesinger, Jr., *The Age of Roosevelt: The Crisis of the Old Order, 1919-1933* (Boston: Houghton Mifflin Company, 1957), 155-76, 248-69, and passim.

2. See, for example, Arthur M. Schlesinger, Jr., *The Age of Roosevelt: The Politics of Upheaval* (Boston: Houghton Mifflin Company, 1960), 252-62, 274-83, and 447-83; Alfred H. Kelly and Winfred A. Harbison, *The American Constitution: Its Origins and Development,* 3rd ed. (New York: W.W. Norton & Company, Inc., 1963), 732-52; Robert H. Jackson, *The Struggle for Judicial Supremacy* (New York: Vintage Books, 1941), 86-175.

3. 297 U.S. 1 (1936). The opinion in this case, which was written by Justice Roberts, invalidated the Agricultural Adjustment Act of 1933, which was based on the national taxing power. Justice Stone, joined by Justices Brandeis and Cardozo, wrote a sharp dissent in which he accused the majority (including Chief Justice Hughes) of adopting "a tortured construction of the Constitution" and of presuming that only the Court properly had "the capacity to govern."

4. For a very detailed, but rather unilluminating, study of this episode, see Leonard Baker, *Back to Back: The Duel between FDR and the Supreme Court* (New York: The Macmillan Company, 1967). A pro-Court view is found in Merlo J. Pusey, *Charles Evans Hughes* (2 vols., New York: The Macmillan Company, 1951), II, 749-65. A more balanced account is in Alpheus Thomas Mason, *Harlan Fiske Stone: Pillar of the Law* (New York: The Viking Press, 1956), 437-64. For a short overview, see Leuchtenburg, *Roosevelt and the New Deal,* 231-39.

5. For the argument that the plan was rationally conceived over a period of time and that it did not represent a last-minute capricious act, see William E. Leuchtenburg, "The Origins of Franklin D. Roosevelt's 'Court-Packing' Plan," in Philip B. Kurland (ed.), *The Supreme Court Review: 1966* (Chicago: The University of Chicago Press, 1966), 347-400.

6. Examples would include: *West Coast Hotel Co. v. Parrish,* 300 U.S. 379 (1937), which upheld a Washington minimum wage law;

Steward Machine Company v. Davis, 301 U.S. 548 (1937), which validated the Social Security Act of 1935; *NLRB v. Jones & Laughlin Steel Corp.,* 301 U.S. 1 (1937), which will be discussed in full in a moment.

7. Chief Justice Hughes commented in his Biographical Notes that the Court plan "had not the slightest effect" on subsequent decisions. See Pusey, *Hughes,* II, 757 and 767-68. The present author thinks that Hughes protested too much.

8. 301 U.S. 1.

9. 312 U.S. 100.

10. 317 U.S. 111.

11. *U.S. Statutes at Large,* XLIX, 449.

12. The background of the case, the investigation of the charges against Jones & Laughlin, the findings and orders of the NLRB, and the briefs of the contending parties are all to be found in the *Records & Briefs of Cases Decided by the Supreme Court of the United States,* Vol. 1, Part 1, U.S. 301 (1-57). These are the official records of Supreme Court cases and contain lower-court decisions, appeal briefs, factual material, and so forth; they will be referred to hereafter as *Records & Briefs.*

13. "Brief for the National Labor Relations Board," *Records & Briefs,* Vol. 1, Part 1, U.S. 301 (1-57), 1-94.

14. 258 U.S. 495.

15. 262 U.S. 1.

16. "Brief for the National Labor Relations Board," *Records & Briefs,* Vol. 1, Part 1, U.S. 301 (1-57), 17.

17. 295 U.S. 495.

18. 298 U.S. 238.

19. "Brief for the National Labor Relations Board," *Records & Briefs,* Vol. 1, Part 1, U.S. 301 (1-57), 18.

20. "Brief for Jones & Laughlin Steel Corporation," *Records & Briefs,* Vol. 1, Part 1, U.S. 301 (1-57), 1-130.

21. 247 U.S. 251.

22. Examples included: *United Mine Workers of America v. Coronado Coal Co.*, 259 U.S. 344 (1922); *Oliver Iron Mining Co. v. Lord*, 262 U.S. 172 (1923); *Industrial Ass'n. of San Francisco v. United States*, 268 U.S. 64 (1925); *Carter v. Carter Coal Co.*, 298 U.S. 238 (1936).

23. For his complete opinion, see 301 U.S. 1, 22-49.

24. Ibid., 30.

25. Ibid., 31-32.

26. On the authority of *Texas & New Orleans Railroad Co. v. Brotherhood of Railway and Steamship Clerks*, 281 U.S. 548 (1930).

27. 301 U.S. 1, 36-37.

28. Ibid., 37.

29. Ibid., 40. (In one short paragraph he disposed of the *Schechter* and *Carter* cases as not controlling; see ibid., 40-41.)

30. Ibid., 41.

31. Ibid., 41.

32. Ibid., 41.

33. On the same day, the Court upheld the Wagner Act in four other cases: *National Labor Relations Board v. Fruehauf Trailer Co.*, 301 U.S. 49; *NLRB v. Friedman-Harry Marks Clothing Co.*, 301 U.S. 58; *Associated Press v. NLRB*, 301 U.S. 103; *Washington, Virginia & Maryland Coach Co. v. NLRB*, 301 U.S. 142.

34. For his complete opinion, see 301 U.S. 1, 76-103. He was joined by Justices Van Devanter, Sutherland, and Butler.

35. Ibid., 77.

36. Ibid., 96-97.

37. Ibid., 99.

38. Ibid., 97.

39. Ibid., 97.

40. Ibid., 30.

41. Ibid., 37.

42. Pusey, *Hughes,* II, 766-72, argues that Hughes was perfectly consistent from *Schechter* to *Jones & Laughlin* and that it was "the vast differences between the situations" which accounted for the change in decision. Pusey also admits that Hughes always held fast to "the distinction between direct and indirect effects upon interstate commerce"; ibid., 767. Samuel Hendel, *Charles Evans Hughes and the Supreme Court* (New York: King's Crown Press, Columbia University, 1951), 258-69, takes the same position as Pusey. Alpheus Thomas Mason, *The Supreme Court: Palladium of Freedom* (Ann Arbor, Mich.: The University of Michigan Press, 1962), 116-48, expresses a harsher, more unfavorable view of the consistency and correctness of Hughes' legal reasoning. See also Mason, *Harlan Fiske Stone,* 457-60.

43. *U.S. Statutes at Large,* LII, 1060.

44. 312 U.S. 100.

45. "Brief for the United States," *Records & Briefs,* Vol. 3, U.S. 312 (96-126), 1-118.

46. Biddle and Attorney General Robert H. Jackson made the oral argument for the appellant before the Court.

47. On the authority of *Champion v. Ames,* 188 U.S. 321 (1903); *Hipolite Egg Company v. United States,* 220 U.S. 45 (1911); *Hoke v. United States,* 227 U.S. 308 (1913); *Brooks v. United States,* 267 U.S. 432 (1925).

48. On the authority of *Brooks v. United States,* 267 U.S. 432 (1925); *Kentucky Whip & Collar Co. v. Illinois Central Railroad Co.,* 299 U.S. 334 (1937); *Mulford v. Smith,* 307 U.S. 38 (1939). *Hammer v. Dagenhart* was characterized as having been weakened to the point that it did not constitute a viable precedent.

49. "Brief for the United States," *Records & Briefs,* Vol. 3, U.S. 312 (96-126), 90.

50. "Brief for Appellee," *Records & Briefs,* Vol. 3, U.S. 312 (96-126), 1-104. It was also contended that the act violated the due-process clause of the Fifth Amendment; see ibid., 85-100.

51. Ibid., 45.

52. Ibid., 48.

53. For his complete opinion, see 312 U.S. 100, 108-26. Undoubted-

ly the only reason for the 8-0 decision was the fact that Justice McReynolds had retired on February 1, two days before.

54. Ibid., 113.

55. Ibid., 114.

56. Ibid., 116.

57. Ibid., 118.

58. Ibid., 121. He cited the *Shreveport Case*, 234 U.S. 342 (1914).

59. Ibid., 123.

60. Ibid., 123. Sherman Act cases: *Northern Securities Company v. United States*, 193 U.S. 197 (1904); *Swift & Company v. United States*, 196 U.S. 375 (1905). Labor Act cases: *NLRB v. Jones & Laughlin*, 301 U.S. 1 (1937); *NLRB v. Fainblatt*, 306 U.S. 601 (1939).

61. Ibid., 123-24.

62. 300 U.S. 379. (See Note 6.)

63. *Hipolite Egg Company v. United States*, 220 U.S. 45 (1911); *Brooks v. United States*, 267 U.S. 432 (1925); *Kentucky Whip & Collar Co. v. Illinois Central Railroad Co.*, 299 U.S. 334 (1937); *Champion v. Ames*, 188 U.S. 321 (1903); *Hoke v. United States*, 227 U.S. 308 (1913).

64. 312 U.S. 100, 118.

65. Ibid., 114.

66. *Annals of Congress*, I, 441.

67. Massachusetts, New Hampshire, South Carolina, and Maryland; New York used the term "clearly delegated." *Elliot's Debates*, I, 322, 326, 325; II, 550; I, 327, respectively.

68. *Annals of Congress*, I, 761, 767-68.

69. *Annals of Congress*, II, 1897.

70. Joseph Story, *Commentaries on the Constitution of the United States*, 4th ed. with notes and additions by Thomas M. Cooley (2 vols., Boston: Little, Brown, and Company, 1873), II (sections 1906-08), 625-27.

71. Marshall: *McCulloch v. Maryland,* 4 Wheaton 316 (1819) at 405-06. Taney: *Gordon v. United States,* 117 U.S. 697 (1864) at 705.

72. Article II read: "Each state retains its sovereignty, freedom and independence, and every Power, Jurisdiction and right, which is not by this confederation expressly delegated to the United States, in Congress assembled."

73. 188 U.S. 321, 357.

74. 252 U.S. 416, 432.

75. *Gibbons v. Ogden,* 9 Wheaton 1, 197.

76. *United States v. Darby,* 312 U.S. 100, 114.

77. Ibid., 115.

78. 258 U.S. 495, 521.

79. *U.S. Statutes at Large,* LII, 31.

80. 307 U.S. 38.

81. *Records & Briefs,* Vol. 2, U.S. 307 (22-61).

82. For his complete opinion, see 307 U.S. 38, 41-51. Justices Butler and McReynolds dissented.

83. Ibid., 47.

84. Ibid., 48.

85. *U.S. Statutes at Large,* LV, 203.

86. *Records & Briefs,* Vol. 317, No. 2 (95-134).

87. 317 U.S. 111. For his complete opinion, see ibid., 114-33.

88. Ibid., 119-20.

89. Ibid., 120.

90. Ibid., 120. He was referring to Marshall's statement in *Gibbons v. Ogden,* 9 Wheaton 1, 197.

91. *Swift & Company v. United States,* 196 U.S. 375 (1905); the *Shreveport Case,* 234 U.S. 342 (1914); *United States v. Wrightwood*

Dairy Co., 315 U.S. 110 (1942).

92. 317 U.S. 111, 123-24.

93. Ibid., 125.

94. Ibid., 127-28.

95. Ibid., 129.

96. Ibid., 131.

Part 2: Present Scope of the Commerce Clause

After 1937 the Supreme Court continued to interpret the Commerce Clause to allow the federal government to exercise far-reaching control over every facet of the American economy. Obviously, only a few areas of national regulation can be covered in any detail here, but those selected are representative of the trend of constitutional adjudication of the commerce power in the last thirty-three years. The study is divided into three sections. Chapter 4 will examine those cases which involve the regulation of labor-management relations in industry and the application of minimum-wage and maximum-hour requirements to the conditions of employment in industry. Chapter 5 will analyze the extension of national supervision to the insurance business and will survey a few miscellaneous cases which involve federal control of food and drugs and corporate combinations; the latter are included merely to demonstrate the long reach of the commerce power in the mid-twentieth century. Chapter 6, finally, will deal with the use of the Commerce Clause first by the Court and then by Congress to guarantee to American minorities freedom from discrimination in the use of public accommodations and facilities. None of these areas are treated exhaustively, but a number of important cases from each are examined closely in order to illuminate the constitutional principles involved and the reasoning of the Court in reaching its decisions. In the process it will become very clear that the Court has invariably resolved questions of power and of statutory construction in favor of the legislative or executive branches; in short, the Court's retreat from the national economic field has been complete and appears now to be irrevocable.

4   Labor-Management Relations

The last chapter analyzed the way in which the Supreme Court opened up American industry to federal regulation under the Commerce Clause. The die was cast, but the real work of the Court had just begun. It faced the difficult problem of marking out the precise limits of the newly emancipated commerce power; that is, it had to put jurisdictional flesh on the constitutional bones of such decisions as *NLRB v. Jones & Laughlin Steel Corp.* and *United States v. Darby.* (*Wickard v. Filburn* rather spoke for itself; no farmer could possibly have thought himself immune henceforth from the dictates of the Secretary of Agriculture.) This chapter, then, will be devoted to the telling of these twin stories.

Early NLRB Cases, 1938-1939

It will be recalled that the National Labor Relations Act of 1935 established the National Labor Relations Board, which was empowered to order companies to cease and desist from certain "unfair labor practices" which were found to "affect" commerce adversely.[1] The Court upheld the validity of the Act, but Chief Justice Charles Evans Hughes was careful to base the exercise of congressional power on a "close and substantial relation" between the proscribed labor practices and their "intimate effect" on commerce. These terms were obviously not self-explanatory, however; they could acquire meaning in a constitutional sense only as the Court explicated them in subsequent case-by-case adjudication.

111

Almost a year later, on March 28, 1938, the Court decided *Santa Cruz Fruit Packing Co. v. National Labor Relations Board.*[2] At Oakland, California, the company operated a plant which canned, packed, and shipped fruits and vegetables grown in California, thirty-seven percent of which went into interstate and foreign commerce by rail, water, and truck. It had attempted to keep its warehousemen from joining a union by locking them out, whereupon they set up a picket line around the plant. This was respected by other union members (teamsters, stevedores, sailors) who refused to move Santa Cruz cargo and thus halted entirely the movement of canned products in commerce. The Labor Board found that the company had been engaged in an unfair labor practice which had led to a labor dispute burdening commerce, and it ordered the company to cease the harassment of its warehouse employees. Santa Cruz contended that its processing activities were "local" and that there was no "flow" of commerce since its raw materials all came from within the state.

Speaking for the five-to-two majority, Chief Justice Hughes had no trouble finding that the company was "directly and largely engaged in interstate and foreign commerce" through its out-of-state sales.[3] The power of Congress extended not only to rules governing those sales "but also to the protection of that interstate commerce from burdens, obstructions, and interruptions, whatever may be their source."[4] He repeated the axiom from *Jones & Laughlin* that a stream of commerce on both sides of the productive activity was not essential to bring federal authority into play.

Hughes was again careful, however, to put limits on the commerce power and to reserve to the Court the role of censor of governmental economic regulation:

It is also clear that where federal control is sought to be exercised over activities which separately considered are intrastate, it must appear that there is a close and substantial relation to interstate commerce in order to justify the federal intervention for its protection.... The subject of federal power is still "commerce," and not all commerce but commerce with foreign nations and among the several states. The expansion of enterprise has vastly increased the interests of interstate commerce, but the constitutional differentiation still obtains.... Whatever terminology is used [direct—indirect, close—remote], the criterion is necessarily one of degree and must be so defined.... In maintaining the balance of the constitutional grants and limitations, it is inevitable that we should define their applications in the gradual process of inclusion and exclusion.[5]

In the present case he found that a "direct relation" had been fully established between the labor practice and the resulting dispute, on the one hand, and the injurious effect upon interstate commerce, on the other. Thus the Board had jurisdiction, and its orders were to be enforced.

Late in the same year, on December 5, 1938, the Court decided *Consolidated Edison Co. v. National Labor Relations Board.*[6] The company was found guilty by the Board of unfair labor practices and ordered to desist from them. Consolidated Edison appealed the order on the ground that it and its affiliates were engaged only in supplying electrical energy, gas, and steam to New York City and Westchester County, solely in the state of New York. The case was complicated by other questions relating to the fairness of the Board's hearing, the sufficiency of the evidence, and so forth; but the matter of real contention related to the jurisdiction of the Board over an admittedly local public utility company.

Chief Justice Hughes again wrote the six-to-two majority opinion which upheld the Board's jurisdiction.[7] He accepted the findings of the Board that Consolidated Edison's operations involved the interests of interstate and foreign commerce in such degree that the federal government was entitled to intervene for their protection. The company supplied electricity to three railroads (including the New York Central), the Port of New York Authority which operated the Holland Tunnel to New Jersey, Western Union, RCA's trans-Atlantic radio service, the Brooklyn air field, United States post offices, the piers of international steamship companies, and lighthouses and beacon lights in New York harbor. The Chief Justice concluded:

> It cannot be doubted that these activities, while conducted within the State, are matters of federal concern. In their totality they rise to such a degree of importance that the fact that they involve but a small part of the entire service rendered by the utilities in their extensive business is immaterial in the consideration of the existence of the federal protective power.[8]

It was, in fact, certain that any interruption of the company's service through industrial strife would be "catastrophic" in its effect on commerce and the instrumentalities thereof, and the federal government clearly had the authority to prevent any such disruption.

There was one further question raised over federal jurisdiction. New York had enacted comprehensive labor legislation of its own; and Consolidated Edison claimed that, as a local public utility, it was subject solely to this exertion of New York's plenary police power. Hughes made short shrift of the company's argument: "It is manifest that enactment of this state law could not override the constitutional authority of the Federal Government. The State could not add to or detract from that authority."[9]

By the end of 1938, then, the authority of the NLRB extended to companies wholly intrastate which shipped goods in interstate commerce or which provided essential services for the instrumentalities of commerce. But more was to come. On April 17, 1939, the Court decided *National Labor Relations Board v. Fainblatt.*[10] Benjamin Fainblatt owned the Somerset Manufacturing Company of Somerville, New Jersey, which processed cloth sent from the Lee Sportswear Company in New York City (or Lee's suppliers) into various types of women's sports garments, which were then delivered to a Lee representative in New Jersey who shipped them on to New York or directly to Lee customers in other states. The Board found Fainblatt guilty of unfair labor practices and petitioned the Third Circuit Court of Appeals to enforce a cease-and-desist order. The Circuit Court denied the petition on the ground that Fainblatt's company was not itself engaged in interstate commerce and had no title or interest in the cloth or finished goods which moved interstate.

Justice Harlan Fiske Stone wrote the seven-to-two majority opinion.[11] He held that an employer might be subject to the Labor Act although not engaged in commerce himself: "The end sought in the enactment of the statute was the prevention of the disturbance to interstate commerce consequent upon strikes and labor disputes induced . . . because of unfair labor practices";[12] such consequences might ensue "from strikes of the employees of manufacturers who are not engaged in interstate commerce where the cessation of manufacture necessarily results in the cessation of the movement of the manufactured product in interstate commerce."[13] In the instant case interstate commerce was involved in the transportation of materials and finished products across state lines, and this was decisive of the Board's jurisdiction: "Transportation alone across state lines is commerce within the constitutional control of the national government and subject to the regulatory power of Congress."[14] The matter of

114

title to the merchandise was immaterial to what might be the end result of a labor dispute—an adverse effect upon commerce.

There was another and more important aspect to the opinion. Fainblatt had argued that the small size of his business (only some 60 employees originally) exempted him from the federal act. Stone thought not: "The power of Congress to regulate interstate commerce is plenary and extends to all such commerce be it great or small."[15] Looking to the language of the statute, he could "perceive no basis for inferring any intention of Congress to make the operation of the Act depend on any particular volume of commerce affected more than that to which courts would apply the maximum *de minimis.*"[16] The test of the Board's jurisdiction was not the volume of commerce affected, "but the existence of a relationship of the employer and his employees to the commerce such that ... unfair labor practices have led or tended to lead 'to a labor dispute burdening or obstructing commerce.'"[17] Since Somerset's products were regularly shipped in interstate commerce, such a relationship existed in the present situation.

Justice James C. McReynolds, joined by Justice Pierce Butler, gave one of his last biting dissents against the new trend in constitutional assessment of the scope of federal power.[18] He was first sarcastic: "If the plant presently employed only one woman who stitched one skirt during each week which the owner regularly accepted and sent to another state, Congressional power would extend to the enterprise, according to the logic of the Court's opinion."[19] Then he was analytical (from the viewpoint of dual federalism): "So construed, the power to regulate interstate commerce brings within the ambit of federal control most if not all activities of the Nation; subjects states to the will of Congress; and permits disruption of our federated system."[20] Finally, he was bitter:

> The resulting curtailment of the independence reserved to the states and the tremendous enlargement of federal power denote the serious impairment of the very foundation of our federated system. Perhaps the change of direction, no longer capable of concealment, will give potency to the efforts of those who apparently hope to end a system of government found inhospitable to their ultimate designs.[21]

NLRB v. Fainblatt proved to be a milestone in constitutional adjudication of the National Labor Relations Act. Not only did it extend federal control of labor-management relations to any firm whose raw materials or finished products moved at any time in commerce, although the firm itself might not be "directly" involved, but it also rejected the criterion of any certain volume of goods as being necessary to the exercise of the NLRB's jurisdiction. Stone's far-reaching grant of regulatory power to the Labor Board under the Commerce Clause effectively closed the question of its jurisdiction from that time up to the present; a review of NLRB cases from 1939 to 1970 reveals no serious contention that the Board lacked authority to investigate charges of unfair labor practices and to issue cease-and-desist orders. After *Fainblatt,* the issues brought before the Court concerned such things as the Board's procedural processes, the adequacy of its evidence, the proper definition of particular unfair labor practice, and so forth, but not the issue of jurisdiction—that is, not the issue of whether the activities of either employer or employees "affected commerce" within the constitutional meaning of section 2(7) of the Labor Act.

In framing his opinion in this crucial case, Stone dispensed with Hughes' "constitutional differentiation" (*Santa Cruz*) between commerce that was interstate and intrastate and overrode the Chief Justice's reluctance to discard the old "direct-indirect" test (even if not by that name) as a measure of the applicability of national power. To Stone the question was simply one of whether the federal commerce power existed in a particular situation; if it did, Congress could regulate the commerce as it saw fit, and the Court's inquiry was at an end. In *Fainblatt* it was the transportation of raw materials and finished products across state lines which was at issue, and such transportation was indisputably commerce "within the constitutional control of the national government and subject to the regulatory power of Congress." Thus two years and five days after the Wagner Act was first held constitutional, the Court, in applying it to a small, wholly intrastate clothing firm, gave its creation, the NLRB, sweeping and virtually unlimited control over American industrial life in terms of labor-management relations, for few would be the companies which at some time would not receive supplies or ship goods in interstate commerce; and the Board's potential authority was made even greater by Stone's flat declaration that the operation of the Act did not depend "on any particular volume of commerce affected."

Solidified Federal Control, 1951-1963

Since 1939 the jurisdiction of the NLRB has been seriously questioned only once—in the case of an insurance company, *Polish Na-*

tional Alliance of the United States v. National Labor Relations Board (1944).[22] This decision will be discussed in full in the next chapter, but it can be noted here that the Board's authority was upheld. Although the scope of the Labor Act has not faced a real challenge in more than twenty-five years, it will be useful to look at some of the cases in this period in which the Supreme Court, in deciding questions of construction of the Act and its amendments, has reaffirmed the broad extent of the NLRB's jurisdiction over industrial operations and economic activities. Three cases decided on June 4, 1951, are illustrative of this breadth. The leading case, *National Labor Relations Board v. Denver Building & Construction Trades Council,*[23] involved the question of a secondary boycott by the Council, an association of unions, against a nonunionized subcontractor working on a commercial building in Denver, Colorado. The principal question was whether the Council had committed an unfair labor practice; the Court held that it had. The point of interest is that the Council had made the ancillary argument, accepted by the District Court, that the activity complained of by the Board did not affect interstate commerce. In his majority opinion Justice Harold H. Burton looked to the Board's findings and found that they were sufficient to give the Board jurisdiction.[24] In 1947 the subcontractor had made raw material purchases of $86,600, of which 65 percent or $55,700 worth came from outside the state; and most of the materials purchased in Colorado had been produced originally in other states. On the building project involved, the subcontractor had used about $350 of materials, which, on the average percentage basis, amounted to $225 of out-of-state supplies. Burton agreed with the Board that "any widespread application of the practices here charged might well result in substantially decreasing the influx of materials into Colorado from outside the State."[25] He concluded that such activities had

> a close, intimate and substantial relation to trade, traffic and commerce among the states and that they tended to lead, and had led, to labor disputes burdening and obstructing commerce and the free flow of commerce. The fact that the instant building, after its completion, might be used only for local purposes does not alter the fact that its construction, as distinguished from its later use, affected interstate commerce.[26]

Citing *NLRB v. Fainblatt,* he drove home the point that "[t]he maxim *de minimis non curat lex* does not require the Board to refuse to take jurisdiction of the instant case."[27]

In another boycott case, *International Brotherhood of Electrical Workers, Local 501, AFL v. National Labor Relations Board* (1951),[28] Burton held that the Board had jurisdiction in a labor dispute involving a nonunionized subcontractor in Port Chester, New York, who had a $325 contract for electrical work on a private dwelling in Greenwich, Connecticut. Movement of materials and services was obviously interstate, but the small amount of these involved shows the extent to which the Court has upheld the Board in enforcing its cease-and-desist orders against mangement and unions alike. Here, as in the *Denver* case, the union's strike to force the general contractor to terminate its agreement with the subcontractor was held to be a secondary boycott in violation of section 8(b)(4)(A) of the Labor Act as amended in 1947 (Taft-Hartley Act).[29]

In the third case, *Local 74, United Brotherhood of Carpenters & Joiners of America, AFL v. National Labor Relations Board* (1951), Burton again upheld a desist order of the Board against the union for committing an unfair labor practice against a specialty wall-and-floor-coverings store in Chattanooga, Tennessee, which hired nonunion installation men. The store was owned by a Rhode Island company which operated 26 or 27 retail stores in seven states, but the Court also relied upon the fact that it purchased one-third of its goods outside the state and that eight percent of its $100,000 annual sales and installation work was done out of state.

These three cases indicate that almost any connection with what would normally be called interstate commerce is sufficient to give the NLRB constitutional authority under the federal commerce power to reach labor-management relations in any facet of the national economy, be it industry, building construction projects, retail trade, or other business activities. The fact should also be noted that because of budgetary and administrative reasons, the Board has set arbitrary limits as a matter of policy on the size of the businesses that it will police.[31] These self-imposed restrictions have always been respected by the Court, and this is the significant point: The Court has left it strictly to the Board to determine the size (usually in terms of annual dollar sales) of the business firms over which it chooses to exercise jurisdiction; a valid conclusion would seem to be that the Court will continue to do this, regardless of how low the Board might set its limits. If a contractor who uses $225 worth of out-of-state materials on a job or who moves $325 worth of materials and labor across a state line can seek and obtain protection of the Board under certain circumstances, it is hard to see where the Court could draw any line excluding the reach of the Board's authority. The fact that the Board has generally set sales limits in terms of six figures or above can not be taken as indicative of the lower range of its constitutionally permissible jurisdiction.

For the sake of completeness, a few more National Labor Relations Act cases will be mentioned briefly in order to show some of the recent instances in which the Court has sustained the application of the statute. In 1953 *Howell Chevrolet Co. v. National Labor Relations Board*[32] held that a retailer of Chevrolet automobiles and parts in Glendale, California, came within the ambit of the Act. Speaking for an eight-to-one majority, Justice Hugo L. Black found that Howell was an "integral part" of General Motors Corporation's national system of distribution.[33] Although the dealer's new cars and parts came from a GM assembly plant and warehouses in California, 43 percent of this merchandise (which totaled $1,000,000 annually) was manufactured outside the state and shipped in for assembly or distribution there; and General Motors exercised very close supervision over Howell's general operations, including its bookkeeping procedures, service facilities, and parts inventory. The unfair labor practices charged to Howell might well lead to a labor dispute which would burden or obstruct commerce, and the Board clearly had authority to issue a cease-and-desist order.

Two cases decided in the late 1950's also merit inclusion here. In *Amalgamated Meat Cutters & Butcher Workmen, Local No. 427, AFL v. Fairlawn Meats, Inc.* (1957)[34] Chief Justice Earl Warren found (contrary to a ruling of the Ohio Court of Appeals) that an Akron retail meat company was in commerce within the scope of the labor law.[35] Of Fairlawn's annual supply purchases of $900,000, one ninth or $100,000 worth came directly from outside the state, and as much or more came indirectly from out of state. Consequently, union picketing of its meat markets was "conduct of which the National Act has taken hold," and the NLRB had jurisdiction. Two years later the Court extended the Act to cover the hotel industry; *Hotel Employees Union, Local No. 255 v. Sax Enterprises, Inc.* (1959),[36] a *per curiam* decision, held that resort hotels in Florida were involved in interstate commerce and thus were subject to national regulation.

Finally, in *National Labor Relations Board v. Reliance Fuel Oil Corporation* (1963),[37] another *per curiam* decision, the Court sustained the Board's jurisdiction in the case of a local New York distributor which purchased in excess of $650,000 worth of fuel oil and related products annually from Gulf Oil Corporation, a supplier concededly in interstate commerce, although the products were stored by Gulf in the state prior to delivery to Reliance. The opinion's summary holding bears quoting at some length:

> This Court has consistently declared that in passing the National Labor Relations Act, Congress intended to and did vest in the Board the fullest jurisdictional breadth constitutionally permissible under the Commerce Clause. . . . The Act establishes a framework within which the Board is to determine "whether proscribed practices would in particular situations adversely affect commerce when judged by the full reach of the constitutional power of Congress. Whether or not practices may be deemed by Congress to affect interstate commerce is not to be determined by confining judgment to the quantitative effect of the activities immediately before the Board. Appropriate for judgment is the fact that the immediate situation is representative of many others throughout the country, the total incidence of which if left unchecked may well become far-reaching in its harm to commerce."
>
> . . . Through the National Labor Relations Act, . . . "Congress has explicitly regulated not merely transactions or goods in interstate commerce but activities which in isolation might be deemed to be merely local but in the interlacings of business across state lines adversely affect such commerce."[38]

It would be difficult to find language more explicit of the proposition that Congress possesses plenary power under the Commerce Clause to regulate labor-management relations which might in any manner affect "that commerce which concerns more states than one."

Employment Standards, 1942–1943

It will be remembered that the Fair Labor Standards Act (FLSA) of 1938[39] prescribed minimum wages and maximum hours for all employees "engaged in commerce or in the production of goods for commerce." Section 15(a)(1) made it unlawful to ship, deliver, or sell any goods produced under substandard labor conditions in interstate commerce; section 15(a)(2) made it unlawful to violate the wage-and-hour provisions for an employee who was so engaged. The Act was upheld in *United States v. Darby* (1941) in which Justice Stone found that the means adopted by section 15(a)(2) for the protection of interstate commerce were so "related to" and so "affected" such commerce as to be a proper exercise of congressional power under the Commerce Clause. The constitutional meaning of this terminology, of course, would have to be spelled out in subsequent applications of the law in concrete cases; and such individual contests were not long in developing.

The scope of the FLSA hinged specifically upon the interpretation of section 3(j) which provided that

> for the purposes of this Act an employee shall be deemed to have been engaged in the production of goods if such employee was employed in producing, manufacturing, handling, transporting, or in any other manner working on such goods, or in any process or occupation necessary to the production thereof, in any State.

It was this language which the Court was called upon to construe in *A.B. Kirschbaum Co. v. Walling,*[40] decided June 1, 1942. Walling, the Administrator of the Wage and Hour Division in the United States Department of Labor, charged Kirschbaum with violating the Act. The latter owned a six-story loft building in Philadelphia which was rented to garment manufacturers who were admittedly producing large quantities of men's and boys' clothing for interstate commerce. Kirschbaum employed 12 maintenance men to produce the heat, hot water, and steam necessary to the manufacturers' operations, to keep the elevators, radiators, fire sprinkler, and light and power systems in working order, and to make necessary repairs and keep the building clean. Since he did not pay them the prescribed minimum wages, the question was whether their activities brought them within the protection of the Act. The Court ruled eight to one in the affirmative.

Justice Felix Frankfurter wrote the majority opinion.[41] He began with a discussion of the changing relationship between federal and state power and noted that "[t]he expansion of our industrial economy has inevitably been reflected in the extension of federal authority over economic enterprise and its absorption of authority previously possessed by the States."[42] This meant that federal legislation had to be construed with regard to the implications for "our dual system" and that the Court could not assume that "when Congress adopts a new scheme for federal industrial regulation, it thereby deals with all situations falling within the general mischief which gave rise to the legislation."[43] The fact was that when the federal government marked out new areas for control, "and thereby radically readjusts the balance of state and national authority, those charged with the duty of legislating are reasonably explicit."[44] Then he reasoned:

> Since the scope of the Act is not coextensive with the limits of the power of Congress over commerce, the question remains whether these employees fall within the statutory definition of employees "engaged in commerce or in the production of goods for commerce," construed as the provision must be in the context of the history of federal absorption of governmental authority over industrial enterprise. . . . Our problem is, of course, one of drawing lines.[45]

Frankfurter turned to a consideration of the facts. He thought that without light, heat, power, and a generally habitable building, the tenants could not engage in production for commerce, that the occupations of the maintenance employees were "necessary to the production" of goods for commerce, and that the "normal and spontaneous meaning of the language" of section 3(j) brought said employees under the coverage of the Act. In answer to Kirschbaum's argument that the building industry in which he was engaged was local, Frankfurter made the very important point that the application of the Act depended expressly upon the character of the employees' activities; to the extent that his employees were engaged in commerce, the employer himself would be considered to be so engaged. There was also no requirement that the employees had to participate in the physical process of making goods before they could be regarded as engaged in production. Such a restrictive construction would, in effect, erase the final clause of the section—"in any process or occupation necessary to the production"—a result which the Court could not sanction. He concluded:

> In our judgment, the work of the employees in these cases [had] such a close and immediate tie with the process of production for commerce, and was therefore so much an essential part of it, that the employees are to be regarded as engaged in an occupation "necessary to the production of goods for commerce."[46]

It seems entirely correct to say that the decision in *Kirschbaum v. Walling* had the same relationship to the scope of the FLSA as the decision in *Fainblatt* had had to that of the National Labor Relations Act; that is, the broad interpretation given to the FLSA furnished the Wage and Hour Administrator with a far-reaching grant of constitutional power to enforce its prescribed conditions of labor against employers in all walks of American economic life. A few brief comments on Frankfurter's important opinion are therefore in order. First, he made the flat assertion that "the scope of the Act is not coextensive with the limits of the power of Congress over commerce"; this could only leave the clear implication that the limits of federal power under the Commerce Clause might well extend even beyond those reached in the instant statute. Second, how far, then, did the Act reach in protecting employees? Frankfurter's answer was: to all employees whose work bore "such a close and immediate tie with the process of production for commerce" that they could be regarded "as engaged in an occupation necessary to the production of goods for commerce," with the extension that this did not require them to "participate in the physical process of the making of the goods." Third and finally, it is obvious that, like Stone's terminology in *Darby,* the language used here—"close and immediate tie" and "necessary occupation"—would have to be more clearly defined by the Court itself in later instances. But this would be done by a judicial assessment of the facts involved and an appraisal of the actual effects generated upon interstate commerce, rather than by reference to the sterile mechanical formulas of pre-1937 days.

Late in the same year, on November 9, 1942, the Court decided *Warren-Bradshaw Drilling Co. v. Hall.*[47] The company contracted with the owners or lessees of Texas oil lands to drill wells to an agreed-upon depth, just short of oil-sand stratum. Two crews worked on each well drilled; a rotary drilling crew prepared the hole; and a cable drilling crew then took over to "bring in" the well or show it to be dry. Hall and other members of the rotary drilling crew claimed that they came within the protection of the FLSA and sued the company for failure to pay overtime wage-rates; their contention was based on the fact that some of the oil produced went into interstate commerce. Warren-Bradshaw argued that it was an independent contractor with no financial interest in the wells and that it had no knowledge that the oil would go into commerce outside Texas.

Speaking for a seven-man majority, Justice Frank Murphy held that the rotary drillers were in "production for commerce."[48] The issue was merely one of statutory delineation, not constitutional power; and, upon a look at the factual conditions and a reading of section 3(j), a "recognition of the obvious" required the conclusion that the employees were engaged in a "process or occupation necessary to the production" of oil and that the connection here was as "close and immediate" as it had been in *Kirschbaum*. Then Murphy went on to substantiate the fact that some of the oil did go into interstate commerce; some of it was owned by companies operating on a national scale, and a large part of the crude oil sent to Texas refineries was shipped out of the state in the form of refined products. The fact that Warren-Bradshaw claimed no knowledge of this was no defense: "Petitioner, closely identified as it is with the business of oil production, cannot escape the impact of the Act by a transparent claim of ignorance of the interstate character of the Texas oil industry."[49]

Although the trend toward a broad construction of the FLSA in favor of extensive federal jurisdiction had been firmly established by the end of 1942, it was to be marred by slight reverses here and there over the succeeding years. These relatively unimportant and infrequent deviations from an almost uniform enlargement of national authority will be noted as they occurred chronologically, since the Supreme Court builds its major constitutional doctrines on a case-by-case basis; and it becomes necessary to know what has gone before in order to understand and analyze correctly any individual decision later. In *Walling v. Jacksonville Paper Co.,*[50] a somewhat complex case decided on January 18, 1943, a unanimous Court held some of the employees of a Florida wholesale distributor to be covered, and some not to be covered, by the Act. The factual situation was this: Jacksonville Paper Company distributed paper products and related articles in a number of southeastern states, the products coming to it from manufacturers and suppliers in other states and foreign countries. It operated 12 branch warehouses, five of which delivered goods to customers in other states and seven of which delivered goods only inside the state. In regard to the seven warehouses, goods moved through them in essentially two ways—they were either ordered in advance in anticipation of the customers' needs and carried in stock or they were ordered in response to a specific request and delivered to the customer upon arrival at the warehouse. There was some evidence that the company's customers constituted a fairly stable group, that their orders were recurrent as to kind and amount of merchandise, and that the branch managers were able to estimate their customers' immediate needs with some degree of precision.

The company did not contend that the employees at the five warehouses shipping interstate were not covered by the Act, but it did argue that those in the seven locations delivering intrastate were exempt; Administrator Walling disagreed and sought to enjoin Jacksonville Paper from violating the Act with respect to the latter. The District Court held that none of the employees in the seven branch houses were subject to the Act. The Fifth Circuit Court of Appeals reversed in part; it held: (1) that employees who were engaged in the procurement or receipt of goods from other states were "engaged in commerce"; and (2) that where the company took an order, filled it outside the state, and the goods were shipped interstate "with the definite intention that those goods be carried at once to that customer, and they are so carried, the whole movement is interstate" and the employees involved, from delivery to final destination, were "engaged in commerce." But only employees in those two types of transactions were protected by the wage-and-hour requirements, and Walling appealed the decision as too restrictive of the Act's scope.

Justice William O. Douglas wrote the opinion which clarified the decision of the Circuit Court.[51] Coming to the Administrator's contention that, under the holding below, any pause at the warehouses would be sufficient to deprive the remainder of the journey of its interstate character, he refuted any such assumption:

> We believe, however, that the adoption of that view would result in too narrow a construction of the Act. It is clear that the purpose of the Act was to extend federal control in this field throughout the farthest reaches of the channels of interstate commerce. There is no indication . . . that, once the goods entered the channels of interstate commerce, Congress stopped short of control over the entire movement of them until their interstate journey was ended. No ritual of placing goods in a warehouse can be allowed to defeat that purpose.[52]

This same line of reasoning would apply to all transactions in which the company ordered goods to meet the needs of specified customers or had the name of a customer printed on the goods at the mill, even though the goods in both cases came into its warehouses and were treated as stock in trade, because such transactions were based on pre-existing contracts or understandings with the customers and hence were "in commerce."

Douglas, having thus construed and, in effect, extended the decision below, took up the Administrator's final claim that, because most of the company's customers formed a fairly stable group and the branch managers could estimate their recurring needs with great accuracy, such business was also "in commerce." Here the justice drew the line. As to this phase of the business, he did not believe that "that practical continuity in transit necessary to keep a movement of goods 'in commerce' within the meaning of the Act"[53] had been established. The evidence did not show 'that the goods in question were different from goods acquired and held by a local merchant for local disposition."[54] In spite of his earlier assertion about the extent of federal control under the Act, Douglas thought that "we cannot be unmindful that Congress in enacting this statute plainly indicated its purpose to leave local business to the protection of the states."[55] Congress had not exercised "the full scope of the commerce power," and the Court could not conclude that "all phases of a wholesale business selling intrastate are covered by the Act solely because it makes its purchases interstate."[56]

Walling v. Jacksonville Paper Co. was an unsatisfactory decision from a number of points of view. While it was clear that all of the wholesaler's employees at its five warehouses shipping interstate came under the protection of the Act, the situation at the seven locations delivering intrastate was muddled. Presumably, all employees at the latter who received or distributed goods ordered specifically for specified customers would be covered, but those employees who distributed goods ordered only in the course of regular, day-by-day operations would not be covered; yet it is difficult to believe that the company could segregate its employees on such an artificial basis. The opinion therefore seems to represent an unrewarding exercise in jurisdictional hair-splitting, rather than a practical solution to the instant problem.

The more important consideration here, however, was that the Court did draw a line (no matter how indefinite of ascertainment) marking the boundary of federal authority under the FLSA; but even this action was marred by Douglas' dictum from the *Kirschbaum* case that, in framing the Act, Congress had not exercised "the full scope of the commerce power." The only observation which can be made with a high degree of certainty is that *Jacksonville Paper* would be a generally weak precedent upon which to base an attack upon the constitutional reach of national power under the Commerce Clause.

Two cases decided within the next five months illustrate the way in which the Court grappled with the continuing problem of how far to extend federal jurisdiction under the Wages and Hours Act. On

February 1, 1943, in *Overstreet v. North Shore Corporation,*[57] it held that employees who maintained and operated a toll road and drawbridge over a navigable waterway were "engaged in commerce." The toll road connected United States Highway 17 with Fort George Island (off the northern coast of Florida) and was much used by persons and vehicles traveling in interstate commerce; the drawbridge had to be raised frequently to permit the passage of boats engaged in interstate traffic on the Intercoastal Waterway (which separated the island from the mainland). Speaking for a six-man majority, Justice Murphy reiterated Douglas' *Jacksonville* contention that the purpose of the Act was "to extend federal control in this field throughout the farthest reaches of the channels of interstate commerce," and he said that the Court would be guided by practical considerations in determining what constituted "commerce" or "engaged in commerce."[58] In the present case, he thought that the test evolved in the cases under the Federal Employers' Liability Act should govern, and he concluded:

> Vehicular roads and bridges are as indispensable to the interstate movement of persons and goods as railroad tracks and bridges. . . .
>
> . . . Those persons who are engaged in maintaining and repairing such facilities should be considered as "engaged in commerce" . . . because without their services these instrumentalities would not be open to the passage of goods and persons across state lines. And the same is true of operational employees whose work is just as closely related to the interstate movement. . . . The work of each petitioner in providing a means of interstate transportation and communication is so intimately related to interstate commerce "as to be in practice and in legal contemplation a part of it". . . .[59]

Four months later, on June 7, 1943, a closely divided Court narrowed somewhat the implied sweep of the *Overstreet* ruling. In *McLeod v. Threlkeld,* Justice Stanley F. Reed held for the five-man majority that a cook, employed by a partnership with a contract to furnish meals to the maintenance men of an interstate railroad, was not "engaged in commerce" under the Act.[60] He was quick to disclaim the Douglas-Murphy proposition with respect to scope: "Congress did not intend that the regulation of hours and wages should extend to the furthest reaches of federal authority."[61] The Act specifically applied only to employees who were "engaged in commerce or in the production of goods for commerce." It was, of course, obvious that McLeod was not engaged "in the production of goods for commerce," and the only question became whether he was "engaged in commerce." To decide this, Reed thought that the test which should be used was whether the employee's activities were "actually in or so closely related to the movement of the commerce as to be a part of it."[62] The answer was no; the furnishing of food to the maintenance-of-way men was too "remote from commerce" to bring the cook within the Act's protection.

Justice Murphy, speaking for Justices Black, Douglas, and Rutledge, dissented.[63] He thought that the Court's construction of the phrase "engaged in commerce" was too restrictive of congressional purpose, which was "to extend the benefits of the Act to employees 'throughout the farthest reaches of the channels of interstate commerce' "[64] McLeod's work was obviously necessary to the operation of the railroad, an instrumentality of interstate commerce, and he should be covered by the Act under the *Overstreet* decision.

Line-Drawing, 1945–1946

Viewed together, the results reached in *Overstreet* and *McLeod* were, of course, somewhat contradictory. It will be shown that the major cases which followed them clearly opted for the sweep of the former and undermined the latter; but two years later, on June 11, 1945, the Court handed down two decisions which again contained conflicting views on the scope of the FLSA. *Borden Company v. Borella*[65] raised the question whether maintenance employees in Borden's central executive office building in New York City came under the Act; the answer was in the affirmative. The company, a large producer of dairy products, was clearly engaged in interstate commerce, but no manufacturing operations took place in the building itself which was 58 percent occupied by Borden. However, as Justice Murphy pointed out for the majority,[66] the building housed Borden's top corporate officers who directed company policies, coordinated production, supervised processing plants and facilities, purchased raw materials, and handled budgeting, financing, legal problems, and labor relations. Referring to the *Kirschbaum* precedent, he could see no economic or statutory significance in the distinction between a building where production was administered, managed, and controlled and a building in which production was carried on physically. Hence such a distinction could not form the basis for concluding that service personnel in the former were not necessary to production for commerce. In an economic sense, production included all activity directed to increasing the amount of scarce economic goods; such "economic production" required planning and control as well as the use of physical labor. Therefore Borden's executive and administrative officers were "actually engaged in the production of goods for commerce," and it followed that the maintenance employees were engaged in occupations "necessary" to that production. In conclusion, Murphy made it clear that the term "production" in the Act was not limited to physical labor on goods and that the Court could not assume "that Congress used the term in other than its ordinary and comprehensive economic sense."[67]

The *Borden* case would require little further comment if it were not for the fact that it was here that Chief Justice Stone drew the line in his interpretation of the scope of the FLSA.[68] Dissenting for himself and Justice Roberts, he argued:

> No doubt there are philosophers who would argue . . . that in a complex modern society there is such interdependence of its members that the activities of most of them are necessary to the activities of most others. But I think that Congress did not make that philosophy the basis of the coverage of the Fair Labor Standards Act. It did not, by a "house-that-Jack-built" chain of causation, bring within the sweep of the statute the ultimate *causa causarum* which result in the production of goods for commerce. Instead it defined production as a physical process.[69]

> . . . The services rendered in this case . . . are too remote from the physical process of production to be said to be, in any practical sense, a part of or necessary to it.[70]

It must be emphasized, however, that Stone's opinion was based on the way he read the literal language of the Act together with the factual situation under review; in other words, he was not saying that this was the point at which congressional power under the Commerce Clause would be completely at an end.[71]

Concurrently, the Court decided *10 East 40th Street Building, Inc. v. Callus*[72] and held that custodial workers in a general office building, 26 percent of whose rentable area was occupied by firms engaged in the production of goods for commerce, were not engaged in occupations "necessary" to production for commerce. Justice Frankfurter, for the bare five-man majority, reiterated his own personal view that Congress had not seen fit to "exhaust its constitutional power over commerce" and added Douglas' view that "Congress in enacting this statute plainly indicated its purpose to leave local business to the protection of the states" (*Jacksonville Paper*).[73] Then he looked to the facts of the situation (building devoted only to office space, over a hundred different tenants) and concluded:

> Renting office space in a building exclusively set aside for an unrestricted variety of office work spontaneously satisfies the common understanding of what is local business and makes the employees of such a building engaged in local business. . . . Running an office building as an entirely independent enterprise is too many steps removed from the physical process of the production of goods. Such remoteness is insulated from the Fair Labor Standards Act by those considerations pertinent to the federal system which led Congress not to sweep predominately local situations within the confines of the Act.[74]

Justice Murphy, joined by Justices Black, Reed, and Rutledge, dissented.[75] He went into some detail to make two points: (1) 26 percent of the building's rentable area was occupied by the executive offices of manufacturing and mining companies engaged in production for commerce; and (2) another six and one-half percent of the area was occupied by concerns engaged in writing and preparing mimeographed, photographic, and printed matter to be shipped in interstate commerce. The combined figure of 32½ percent was substantial enough to bring the building's maintenance employees within the protection of the Act, and he attacked Frankfurter's criterion of "the common understanding of what is local business" as "nebulous" and unrealistic:

> And when Congress said that employees "necessary to the production" of goods for commerce were to be included within the Act, it meant just that, without limitation to those who were necessary only to the physical manufacturing aspects of production. Under such circumstances it is our duty to recognize economic reality in interpreting and applying the mandate of the people.[76]

The Court was still engaged in line-drawing, but within the next year four cases were decided which greatly expanded federal jurisdiction under the FLSA by very broadly construing its crucial terms relating to commerce. On January 28, 1946, in *Roland Electrical Co. v. Walling*,[77] Justice Harold H. Burton held that the employees of a

Baltimore company, engaged in repairing and rebuilding electric motors and installing electrical wiring for commercial and industrial users, most of whom produced goods for interstate were engaged in "the production of goods for commerce."[78] In blunt language he asserted that the definitions in the Act did not require the employees to be directly engaged in commerce or engaged in production of an article which itself went into commerce or even their occupation to be indispensable to production for commerce; it was enough that the occupation be "needed in such production and would, if omitted, handicap the production." Burton concluded that such was the situation in the instant case:

> The necessity to the petitioner's customers, in their productive work, of the sales made and the services supplied to them by the petitioner's employees is the foundation of petitioner's business. The essential need for motors and wiring in the conduct of electrically operated productive process of manufacture is beyond question. . . . Such sales and services must be immediately available to petitioner's customers or their production will stop.[79]

This opinion opened the way for a much enlarged scope of the Act; within two weeks two more decisions extended congressional power over commerce into virtually every nook and cranny of the economy. In *Martino v. Michigan Window Cleaning Co.*,[80] decided February 4, 1946, Justice Burton, again speaking for a unanimous Court, held under the *Roland Electrical* precedent that the employees of an independent service contractor, engaged in cleaning and maintaining windows for industrial plants which produced goods for interstate commerce, were engaged in an occupation "necessary to the production of goods for commerce."[81] In so ruling, he introduced the "substitutability" principle: "If the services rendered in this case had been rendered by employees of respondent's customers engaged in the production of goods for interstate commerce, those employees would have come under the Act."[82]

One week later, on February 11, 1946, the Court handed down *Mabee v. White Plains Publishing Co.*[83] The company published a daily newspaper at White Plains, New York, with a circulation of about 9,000 to 11,000 papers. Forty-five copies, no more than one-half of one percent of the total number printed, were regularly sent to out-of-state subscribers. In a suit brought to force the company to adhere to the requirements of the Act, the New York Court of Appeals had applied the *maxim de minimis* to exclude the publisher from the wage-and-hour provisions. Speaking for a seven-man majority, Justice Douglas went back to *Darby* to find that Congress had made "no distinction as to the volume or amount of shipments in the commerce or of production for commerce."[84] Consequently, with reference to section 15(a)(1), which made it unlawful to ship any goods produced under substandard conditions in commerce, he found that there was "no warrant for assuming that regular shipments in commerce are to be included or excluded dependent on their size."[85] Thus the respondent was engaged in "the production of goods for commerce." But since this answered the sole question immediately before the Court, Douglas made no ruling on whether the employees were protected by the Act; he merely reaffirmed the *Kirschbaum* proposition that applicability was dependent upon the character of the employees' work, such determination to be made on remand to the lower courts.

Justice Murphy, always a strong advocate of a wide sweep for federal power (*McLeod, 10 East 40th Street Bldg.*), dissented. In his opinion, a company producing 99½ percent of its output for local commerce was "essentially and realistically a local business . . . which we have said Congress plainly excluded from this Act."[86]

Finally, on April 29, 1946, *D.A. Schulte, Inc. v. Gangi*[87] was decided. Here the question was whether the Act covered service and maintenance employees of a building in New York City which was occupied by tenants who received, worked on, and returned in intrastate commerce cloth goods belonging to garment makers who subsequently shipped substantial proportions of said products to other states. The answer depended upon whether the tenants could be regarded as producers for interstate commerce, and a five-man majority headed by Justice Reed reasoned in the affirmative:

> Certainly if these tenants had not only manufactured but had also shipped their products interstate, no one would doubt that they were producers for commerce. Mere separation of the economic processes of production for commerce between different industrial units, even without any degree of common ownership, does not destroy the continuity of production for commerce.[88]

These four cases—*Roland Electrical, Martino, Mabee,* and *Schulte*—really closed the question of the scope of the FLSA and, concurrently, the reach of national power under the Commerce Clause. The

Court had now made it clear that Congress could constitutionally regulate any business activity which had any economic connection with interstate commerce, no matter how remote, tenuous, or insubstantial the relationship might be. In fact, it appears that Congress itself thought that the Court had gone somewhat too far; in 1949 it amended the FLSA in an effort to put some limits on its coverage. It will be recalled that section 3(j) provided that "an employee shall be deemed to have been engaged in the production of goods if such employee was employed . . . in any process or occupation necessary to the production thereof, in any State."[89] The last clause of this section was now changed to read: ". . . in any closely related process or occupation directly essential to the production thereof, in any State."[90] This amendment was proposed directly from the floor of the House and was so adopted.[91] Although there was some disagreement between the House and Senate conferees as to the exact effect of the new language, it was clear that both groups sought some restraint on the applicability of the Act.[92] Final interpretation, of course, still rested with the Court.

Present Realities, 1953–1966

In order to round out a complete picture of the decisions under the FLSA, it is necessary to include a last group of five cases which cover the period from 1953 to 1966. Generally speaking, it will be seen that none of these goes beyond the ambit of federal jurisdiction which the Court established for the Act in 1945-1946, but they do indicate the kinds of questions which are still presented for constitutional adjudication under the commerce power. On March 9, 1953, *Alstate Construction Co. v. Durkin*[93] was decided. The facts were these: Alstate was a Pennsylvania company engaged in reconstructing and repairing roads, railways, parkways, and so forth; it also produced "amesite," a bituminous concrete road-surfacing mixture. Eighty-five and one-half percent of the company's work was done for interstate roads and railroads or for Pennsylvania companies producing goods for interstate commerce. The question presented was whether the employees who worked off the roads in the production of the materials (primarily amesite) to repair them were covered by the Act. Justice Black, speaking for a seven-man majority, held that such employees were entitled to protection.[94] He took up Alstate's primary argument that amesite was not produced "for commerce" and dismissed it as being without merit:

> Obviously, acceptance of this contention would require us to read "production of goods for commerce" as though written "production of goods for transportation in commerce"—that is, across state lines. . . . But we could not hold—consistently with *Overstreet v. North Shore Corp.* . . . —that the only way to produce goods "for commerce" is to produce them for transportation across state lines.[95]

The doctrine of *Overstreet* was that employees who repaired roads and railroads—the integrating instrumentalities of the national commercial system—were "in commerce" and that employees who served these instrumentalities also served commerce. *Overstreet* controlled the present case because its principle could be extended one step further: Employees who produced products for "these indispensable and inseparable parts of commerce" necessarily produced "goods for commerce" and came within the protection of the Act.

Justice Douglas, joined by Justice Frankfurter, dissented. He thought that "the circle [of the Act's coverage] gets amazingly large once we say that 'the production of goods for commerce' includes the 'production of goods for those engaged in commerce.' "[96] The history of the Act showed that Congress had intended no such extension of the federal regulatory domain, and an amendment of the Act would be necessary to reach the present conclusion.

Mitchell v. C.W. Vollmer & Co., Inc.[97] was decided on June 6, 1955. The construction firm's employees were engaged in building the Algiers Lock in Louisiana, a unit in the Gulf Intracoastal Waterway, which was designed to relieve traffic congestion and to furnish better passage into and across the Mississippi River than was provided by the old Harvey Lock and Canal. The question was whether they were "engaged in commerce," and the company contended that they were not, since the Algiers Lock was new construction which had not yet become an interstate facility.[98] Justice Douglas, speaking for a majority of six, rejected the argument as out-of-date and inapplicable:

> The question whether an employee is engaged "in commerce" within the meaning of the present Act is determined by practical considerations, not by technical conceptions. . . . The test is whether the work is so directly and vitally related to the functioning of an instrumentality or facility of interstate commerce as to be, in practical effect, a part of it, rather than isolated local activity. . . . Repair of facilities of interstate commerce is activity "in commerce" within the meaning of the Act. . . . And we think the work of improving existing facilities

of interstate commerce, involved in the present case, falls in the same category.

> ... The work on Algiers Lock seems to us to have as intimate a relation to improvement of navigation on the Waterway as the dredging of Harvey Lock would have. It is part of the redesigning of an existing facility of interstate commerce.[99]

While Douglas' position here is sound and realistic, it must be noted that it is also inconsistent with his prior reasoning in *Alstate Construction Co. v. Durkin*. Thus the force of the *Alstate* dissent as a possible future limit on congressional power is blunted.

The decision in *Mitchell v. Lublin, McGaughy & Associates*[100] was handed down on January 12, 1959. This architectural and consulting engineering firm, with offices in Norfolk, Virginia, and Washington, D.C., designed and prepared plans for public, industrial, and residential construction projects. Many of its clients were located outside of Virginia and the District of Columbia, and it did considerable work for the armed services; in many cases, fieldmen were used on the project sites to gather information. The FLSA specifically exempted professional employees such as architects and engineers, but the question was whether the firm's nonprofessional employees—draftsmen, fieldmen, clerks, and stenographers—were "engaged in commerce" and hence covered by the Act. Chief Justice Warren, speaking for a seven-man majority, thought that they were.[101] Using precisely the same "practical test" which had been applied in *Vollmer*, he concluded:

> Coverage in the instant case must be determined by that test for, as the parties stipulated below, the draftsmen, fieldmen, clerks and stenographers all worked intimately with the plans and specifications prepared by respondent for the repair and construction of various interstate instrumentalities and facilities including air bases, roads, turnpikes, bus terminals, and radio and television installations. In our view, such work is directly and vitally related to the functioning of these facilities because, without the preparation of plans for guidance, the construction could not be effected and the facilities could not function as planned. ... Under the circumstances present here, we have no hesitancy in concluding that the employees whose activities were intimately related to such preparation were "engaged in commerce."[102]

Thus far the 1949 amendment to the FLSA had proved to be no

barrier to the extension of federal authority; but on April 4, 1960, the Court was called upon for a specific interpretation of the revised wording in *Mitchell v. H.B. Zachry Company.*[103] This construction contractor had been engaged by the Lower Nueces River Water Supply District to build a dam and impounding facilities on the lower Nueces River in Texas in order to increase tenfold the existing reservoir capacity of the District, which supplied water to local customers in the state, including the city of Corpus Christi. Forty to 50 percent of all the water consumed was accounted for by industrial users, most of whom produced goods for interstate commerce; an unspecified amount also went to facilities and instrumentalities of commerce. The question, of course, was whether the contractor's employees were engaged in the "production of goods for commerce" within the meaning of section 3(j) as amended. The close, five-to-four decision in the negative was written by Justice Frankfurter.[104] He began with the proposition drawn from the Act's general language that "Congress has impliedly left to the States a domain for regulation."[105] He admitted that the amendment of section 3(j) did not alter the basic statutory scheme of the Act's coverage, but it did

> reinforce the requirement that in applying the last clause of the section its position at the periphery of coverage be taken into account as a relevant factor in the determination. In revising coverage Congress turned only to the last clause of the section, which it evidently continued to regard as marking the outer limits of applicability.[106]

With this caveat in mind, the justice turned to the argument of the Secretary of Labor that, since employees were covered who had been engaged in the maintenance and repair of the facilities of a company distributing water for consumption by producers for commerce,[107] the employees engaged here in an essential expansion of similar facilities would also be covered; in other words, the activities of initial construction and subsequent repair and maintenance could not be distinguished in any characteristic made relevant by the new standards of "closely related" and "directly essential" to production. Frankfurter could not agree with this interpretation; the two types of activities were without doubt equally "directly essential" to supplying water for production, but they were not equally "closely related" to the "commerce" for which the production was ultimately intended. He reasoned that although maintenance and repair had a "close

136

relation" to industrial operation, replacement or new construction was "a separate undertaking necessarily prior to operation and therefore more remote from the end result"—the flow of goods in commerce. While this difference might be "difficult to delineate," it was still "a practical distinction to which law must not be indifferent." Then looking to the facts that the Nueces District supplied water "to a miscellany of users throughout its geographical area" and that "somewhat less than half of the consumption is by producers," Frankfurter concluded:

> These are no doubt matters of the nicest degree. They are inevitably so in the scheme and mode of enforcement of this statute. Bearing in mind the cautionary revision in 1949, and that the focal center of coverage is "commerce," the combination of the remoteness of this construction from production, and the absence of a dedication of the completed facilities either exclusively or primarily to production, persuades us that the activity is not "closely related" or "directly essential" to production for commerce.[108]

Justice Douglas, joined by Chief Justice Warren and Justices Black and Brennan, dissented.[109] Looking to the facts of the case, he argued that the "liberal test" which he had applied in *Mitchell v. Vollmer & Co.* (1955) should be controlling; the present project was actually the improvement of an existing water system which supplied water to "instrumentalities of interstate commerce and to various producers of goods for commerce." The work here was at least as close to the process of production as the work of the men producing amesite in the *Alstate Construction Co.* case; and he objected to the fact that "today's decision changes the symmetry of the judicial rulings under the Act, narrows its scope, and impairs its effectiveness."[110] If there was to be a change in the direction of the law, it should be made by Congress and not by mere statutory construction.

The last case is one decided on February 24, 1966—*Idaho Sheet Metal Works, Inc. v. Wirtz.*[111] The company operated a single plant at Burley, Idaho, where it employed 12 workers to fabricate, install, and maintain sheet-metal products, 60 percent of which by number were sold to individuals, farmers, and local merchants—"the general public" as opposed to industrial customers. However, about 83 percent of gross income came from metal work done on equipment used by five potato-processing concerns which dehydrated and froze potatoes for shipment in interstate commerce. The main question presented was whether Idaho Sheet qualified as a "retail or service establishment" under the exemption for such business in section 13(a)(2) of the Wages and Hours Act.

Justice John Marshall Harlan, in a unanimous opinion, held that the company did not meet the exemption requirements.[112] A 1949 amendment to the section stated that a retail or service establishment "shall mean an establishment 75 per centum of whose annual dollar volume of sales of goods or services (or of both) is not for resale and is recognized as retail sales or services in the particular industry," and the precise problem was how to treat the sales in the present case. Harlan looked first to the fact that 83 percent of gross income was received from the sale or servicing of the potato-processing equipment, which transactions could not be called retail, and then to the facts that the equipment was very specialized, was fabricated to meet the individual specifications of a highly limited market, and was without any private or noncommercial utility. He had no difficulty in concluding that with respect to the major part of its business, Idaho Sheet was indistinguishable from "an establishment engaged in the sale and servicing of manufacturing machinery and manufacturing equipment used in the production of goods", Congress had clearly stated that such establishments were not exempt, and the 12 employees came within the protection of the Act.

Conclusions

The foregoing lines of cases under the National Labor Relations Act and the FLSA demonstrate beyond question that in the period since 1937 the Supreme Court has interpreted the Commerce Clause to give Congress broad and far-reaching power to regulate labor-management relations and conditions of employment in all aspects and phases of American business. It seems unnecessary to review these decisions in any detail, but a few summary comments are in order. First, the Court has extended the jurisdiction of the NLRB to reach unfair labor practices in: (1) a wholly intrastate garment manufacturer which processed cloth shipped in interstate commerce (*NLRB v. Fainblatt*); (2) a local construction project wherein a subcontractor used $225 worth of out-of-state materials (*NLRB v. Denver Building & Construction Trades Council*); and (3) a local distributor of petroleum products which purchased from an interstate supplier fuel oil that had been stored in the state prior to delivery to the distributor (*NLRB v. Reliance Fuel Oil Corp.*). On the basis of these decisions, it may be asserted with confidence that federal authority to control economic activities which "affect commerce" is plenary.

Second, the Court has interpreted the key terms of the FLSA— "engaged in commerce," "engaged in the production of goods for commerce," and "engaged in any process or occupation necessary to the production thereof"—to include employees who were engaged in: (1) the maintenance and operation of a loft building where tenants produced goods to be shipped in interstate commerce (*Kirschbaum v. Walling*); (2) the maintenance and operation of an office building over one-half occupied by the executive and administrative personnel of an interstate producer of dairy products (*Borden Co. v. Borella*); (3) the cleaning, painting, and repairing of windows of industrial plants which produced goods for commerce (*Martino v. Michigan Window Cleaning Co.*); and (4) the preparation of plans and specifications for the construction of facilities and instrumentalities of commerce (*Mitchell v. Lublin, McGaughy & Associates*). Finally, a business which sent no more than one-half of one percent of its total output across state lines was held to be "in commerce" under the Act (*Mabee v. White Plains Publishing Co.*). In short, there are now virtually no limits on the constitutional power of Congress under the Commerce Clause to regulate the conditions under which business activities may be conducted. The few cases in which the applicability of the Act was not upheld indicate that there is possibly some kind of quantitative limitation lurking in the background which the Court might be willing to impose at some future time. But the clear thrust of decision is toward widely sweeping and deeply penetrating federal power.

Third, and in support of this last proposition, all but one of the major cases which limited the reach of the Act—*Walling v. Jacksonville Paper Co., McLeod v. Threlkeld, 10 East 40th Street Bldg. v. Callus,* and *Mitchell v. Zachry Company*—found the Court sharply divided in its opinions; the latter three were all decided five to four. Even in these instances the majority was merely construing the language of the Act as it thought consistent with congressional intent; that is, congressional power was not really at stake, and a subsequent act clearly designed to cover the excluded employees would most certainly have been upheld. Thus none of these cases can be given much weight as a counterpoise to the dominant trend of decision outlined above—the nature of which establishes that national authority over the commercial enterprise of the United States is now plenary.

Notes

1. *U.S. Statutes at Large,* XLIX, 449.

2. 303 U.S. 453.

3. Ibid., 463. For his complete opinion, see ibid., 460-69. Justices Cardozo and Reed took no part in the case; Justices Butler and McReynolds dissented.

4. Ibid., 464.

5. Ibid., 466-67.

6. 305 U.S. 197.

7. For his complete opinion, see ibid., 217-39. Justice Cardozo had died, and Justice Frankfurter had not yet been appointed. Justices Butler and McReynolds dissented. Justices Reed and Black concurred on the matter of jurisdiction but dissented from a part of the opinion which went against one of the Board's orders relating to the invalidity of certain employee contracts.

8. Ibid., 221.

9. Ibid., 223.

10. 306 U.S. 601.

11. For his complete opinion, see ibid., 602-09.

12. Ibid., 604.

13. Ibid., 604.

14. Ibid., 606.

15. Ibid., 606.

16. Ibid., 607.

17. Ibid., 608.

18. For his complete opinion, see ibid., 609-14.

19. Ibid., 610.

20. Ibid., 610.

21. Ibid., 614.

22. 322 U.S. 643.

23. 341 U.S. 675.

24. For his complete opinion, see ibid., 677-92.

25. Ibid., 683-84.

26. Ibid., 684.

27. Ibid., 685. The Court was unanimous in this part of the holding; Justices Jackson, Douglas, and Reed dissented from the decision that the unions had been guilty of a secondary boycott as proscribed by section 8(b)(4)(A) of the Act; see ibid., 692-93.

28. 341 U.S. 694.

29. *U.S. Statutes at Large,* LXI, 146.

30. 341 U.S. 707.

31. Up until 1950 the NLRB proceeded on a case-by-case basis; then it began the use of monetary standards. The current standards have been in effect since 1958 and may be found in 23 *NLRB Annual Report* 8 (1958) or in *St. John's Law Review,* XXXIV (May, 1960), 234, footnote 99.

32. 346 U.S. 482.

33. For his complete opinion, see ibid., 482-84. Justice Douglas dissented without opinion.

34. 353 U.S. 20.

35. For his complete opinion, see ibid., 22-25. The case involved other issues which are irrelevant to the present discussion.

36. 358 U.S. 270.

37. 371 U.S. 224.

38. Ibid., 226-27. The quoted portions are from Justice Frankfurter's opinion in *Polish National Alliance v. NLRB,* 322 U.S. 643 (1944) at 648. (See the next chapter.)

39. *U.S. Statutes at Large,* LII, 1060.

40. 316 U.S. 517.

41. For his complete opinion, see ibid., 518-26. Justice Roberts dissented on the ground that the power of Congress could not reach the purely local activities in question; see ibid., 527.

42. Ibid., 520.

43. Ibid., 521.

44. Ibid., 522.

45. Ibid., 523.

46. Ibid., 525-26. Frankfurter said "cases" because he decided *Arsenal Building Corporation v. Walling,* 316 U.S. 517 (1942), at the time and in the same way.

47. 317 U.S. 88.

48. For his complete opinion, see ibid., 89-93. Justice Byrnes had resigned a month earlier; Justice Roberts dissented as in *Kirschbaum.*

49. Ibid., 92-93.

50. 317 U.S. 564. The decision was 8-0; Justice Rutledge had not yet been appointed to replace Justice Byrnes.

51. For his complete opinion, see ibid., 565-72.

52. Ibid., 567-68.

53. Ibid., 570.

54. Ibid., 570.

55. Ibid., 570.

56. Ibid., 571.

57. 318 U.S. 125.

58. For his complete opinion, see ibid., 126-33. Justices Roberts and Jackson dissented without opinion; Justice Rutledge did not come on the Court until February 11, 1943.

59. Ibid., 129-30.

60. 319 U.S. 491. For his complete opinion, see ibid., 492-98.

61. Ibid., 493. Here Reed relied upon the legislative history of the Act; Congress had rejected a proposal to include employees "engaged in commerce in any industry affecting commerce" and had instead chosen language which in his view deliberately and purposefully singled out a "smaller group" for coverage.

62. Ibid., 497.

63. For his complete opinion, see ibid., 498-502.

64. Ibid., 498.

65. 325 U.S. 679.

66. For his complete opinion, see ibid., 680-85. The decision was 7-2; Justice Frankfurter concurred in the result.

67. Ibid., 684.

68. For his complete opinion, see ibid., 685-86.

69. Ibid., 685. Section 3(j) read: " 'Produced' means produced, manufactured, mined, handled, or in any other manner worked on. . . ."

70. Ibid., 686.

71. He cited with approval the *Kirschbaum dictum* that "Congress did not undertake to make the Act applicable to all occupations which affect commerce." Ibid., 685. But it must be noted that Stone's biographer, Alpheus Thomas Mason, hints that the Chief Justice would have liked to have found a dividing line somewhere between "federal power and states' rights." Alpheus T. Mason, *Harlan Fiske Stone: Pillar of the Law* (New York: The Viking Press, 1956), 622, ff. Apparently, however, in actual fact, he never did.

72. 325 U.S. 578.

73. For his complete opinion, see ibid., 579-85.

74. Ibid., 583.

75. For his complete opinion, see ibid., 585-88.

76. Ibid., 588. The Murphy-Frankfurter controversy is reminiscent of the Holmes-Peckham clash in *Lochner v. New York,* 198 U.S. 45 (1905), in which Peckham struck down the state hours law on employ-

ment in bakeries and asserted: "To the common understanding the trade of a baker has never been regarded as an unhealthy one." Holmes objected to the majority thus reading its own predilections into the Constitution and countered: "The 14th Amendment does not enact Mr. Herbert Spencer's Social Statics." Frankfurter's appeal to "common understanding" appears no less objectionable than Peckham's.

77. 326 U.S. 657.

78. For his complete opinion, see ibid., 660-78. The decision was unanimous; Justice Jackson was out of the country and took no part.

79. Ibid., 664. The remainder of the opinion was spent in showing that Roland was not the type of "retail or service establishment" which was exempted by section 13(a)(2).

80. 327 U.S. 173.

81. For his complete opinion, see ibid., 174-78. Justice Jackson took no part.

82. Ibid., 176-77.

83. 327 U.S. 178.

84. For his complete opinion, see ibid., 180-85. The quotation from *United States v. Darby*, 312 U.S. 100 (1941), is at 123. Justice Jackson took no part.

85. Ibid., 181-82. Section 13(a)(8) exempted small weekly or semi-weekly newspapers with under 3,000 circulation, but Douglas found that this did not apply to the daily White Plains paper. Nor did First-Amendment freedom of the press give immunity from congressional regulation of business. [*Associated Press v. National Labor Relations Board*, 301 U.S. 103 (1937).]

86. Ibid., 186.

87. 328 U.S. 108.

88. Ibid., 121. For his complete opinion, see ibid., 109-21. Justices Frankfurter and Burton dissented, but not on the commerce question. Justice Jackson took no part. Chief Justice Stone had died on April 22, 1946.

89. *U.S. Statutes at Large*, LII, 1061.

90. *U.S. Statutes at Large*, LXIII, 911. Wallace Mendelson argues that

this action of Congress "reversed" the decisions in *Roland Electrical Co.* and *Martino*. He makes this point in connection with his larger thesis that Frankfurter is a more impartial and competent judge than Black. See Wallace Mendelson, *Justices Black and Frankfurter: Conflict in the Court* (Chicago: The University of Chicago Press, 1961), 14-30, ff, and the footnotes at 134-38. This same theme is repeated in Wallace Mendelson (ed.), *The Supreme Court: Law and Discretion* (Indianapolis, Ind.: The Bobbs-Merrill Company, Inc., 1967), 33-39 and 439-49. Mendelson abstracts *10 East 40th Street Bldg. v. Callus* (1945) to contend that Frankfurter read congressional intent (as expressed in 1949) more accurately than the "liberal" dissenters—Murphy, Black, Reed, and Rutledge. For the argument that Black is an economic liberal, see John P. Frank, "The New Court and the New Deal," in Stephen Parks Strickland (ed.), *Hugo Black and the Supreme Court: A Symposium* (Indianapolis: The Bobbs-Merrill Company, Inc., 1967), 39-74, particularly 56-67. But see footnote 76 in defense of the Murphy-Black position.

91. *Congressional Record,* XCV, 11000.

92. For example, the House conferees disapproved of the decision in *Martino v. Michigan Window Cleaning Co.* But the Senate conferees stated their conclusion that "employees or employers who produce or supply goods or facilities for customers engaged . . . in the production of other goods for interstate commerce may also be covered." Ibid., 14874, ff. This latter view would still support *Roland Electrical Co. v. Walling,* contrary to Mendelson's reasoning. (See Note 90.)

93. 345 U.S. 13.

94. For his complete opinion, see ibid., 13-17. Concurrently, he extended protection to an employee of a Pennsylvania stone quarry which manufactured cement mixtures for interstate roads, railroads, and airport landing fields. *Thomas v. Hempt Brothers,* 345 U.S. 19 (1953).

95. Ibid., 15.

96. Ibid., 17.

97. 349 U.S. 427.

98. On the authority of *Raymond v. Chicago, Milwaukee, & St. Paul Railway Company,* 243 U.S. 43 (1917).

99. 349 U.S. 427, 429-30. For his complete opinion, see ibid., 428-30. Justices Minton and Frankfurter dissented primarily on the ground that the Court was not observing the principle of *stare decisis* in ignoring the *Raymond* decision. The second Jusitce Harlan took no part.

100. 358 U.S. 207.

101. ,For his complete opinion, see ibid., 208-15. Justices Whittaker and Stewart dissented. Whittaker thought the evidence was insufficient to justify a general injunction; Stewart agreed with the general principles of the opinion, but he reached a different conclusion based on the *McLeod* and *Jacksonville Paper* decisions.

102. Ibid., 212.

103. 362 U.S. 310.

104. For his complete opinion, see ibid., 310-21.

105. Ibid., 314.

106. Ibid., 316-17.

107. On the authority of *Farmers Reservoir & Irrigation Co. v. McComb,* 337 U.S. 755 (1949).

108. 362 U.S. 310, 321.

109. For his complete opinion, see ibid., 321-26.

110. Ibid., 325. By 1960 Douglas had obviously repudiated his *Alstate* dissent of 1953.

111. 383 U.S. 190.

112. For his complete opinion, see ibid., 192-209. At the same time, he gave a similar ruling in *Wirtz v. Steepleton General Tire Company,* 383 U.S. 190 (1966), which extended coverage to about 47 employees of a franchised tire dealer in Memphis, Tennessee, which derived more than half of its gross income from sales and repairs of tires furnished to businesses operating heavy industrial or construction vehicles or fleets of trucks, a sizable portion of which operated in interstate commerce.

5   Insurance and Other Enterprise

By the end of 1942 the Supreme Court had given Congress broad power to regulate economic activities in general industry and agriculture. One prominent aspect of American business, however, had as yet escaped federal control—the insurance industry. That insurance had never come under congressional regulation was due to a unique circumstance of history. After the Civil War the insurance business expanded very rapidly, accompanied by the most unethical practices and flagrant abuses of the public trust. In time the various states, in order to protect their citizens from such chicanery, passed legislation regulating the conduct of the insurance business within their legal jurisdictions. For their part, the insurance companies sought relief from these "hostile state legislatures" and asked Congress to pass a federal incorporation statute which would nullify the local requirements. This Congress refused to do on March 5, 1868.

Meanwhile, in early 1866 Virginia enacted a law which required insurance companies not incorporated in the state to obtain a license before doing business therein. The license could not be obtained until bonds of a certain type (which could be sold to satisfy a company's liabilities) were deposited with the state treasurer. A second act imposed monetary penalties on any person selling insurance for a "foreign"[1] company without a license. In May, 1866, Samuel B. Paul, a Virginia resident, was appointed as an agent for several New York fire insurance companies. He applied for a license but refused to comply with the bond requirement. The license was refused him, but he proceeded to sell insurance without it. He was indicted and convicted for this offense and denied relief by the Supreme Court of Appeals of Virginia. He appealed his case on a writ of error to the United States Supreme Court on the ground that the business of insurance was "commerce" within the meaning of the Constitution and that the Virginia statutes regulated a subject "which must in its nature be exclusively federal." Virginia contented itself with arguing that the license represented a personal tax on Paul, not the foreign insurance companies, and that the latter had no legal existence in the state until they complied with its laws; it cited *Bank of Augusta v. Earle* (1839)[2] as authority for its position.

Justice Stephen J. Field wrote the unanimous opinion for the Court in *Paul v. Virginia* (1869).[3] Coming to Paul's contention that the Commerce Clause nullified the Virginia statutes, he found the argument defective because of the nature of the insurance business:

> Issuing a policy of insurance is not a transaction of commerce. The policies are simple contracts of indemnity against loss by fire, entered into between the corporations and the assured, for a consideration paid by the latter. These contracts are not articles of commerce in any proper meaning of the word. They are not subjects of trade and barter offered in the market. . . . They are like other personal contracts between parties which . . . are not inter-state transactions, though the parties may be domiciled in different States. The policies do not take effect . . . until delivered by the agent in Virginia. They are then, local transactions, and are governed by the local law.[4]

Thus Field decided the case for the state, but he did so on the basis that insurance was not "commerce" within the constitutional meaning of that term. Early nineteenth-century cases on insurance had never invoked the Commerce Clause, and Field had good grounds for his holding. That he could have avoided this flat declaration, however, and upheld state power under the *Cooley* rule seems not to have occurred to him. Or perhaps the Court regarded the burgeoning insurance business as more than "local" in scope and felt that it could not properly apply *Cooley*. But with Congress having refused any uniform legislation, the Court undoubtedly felt obliged to sanction individual state regulations of insurance-company activities.

Insurance Is Commerce

South-Eastern Underwriters (1944)

Subsequent cases invariably reaffirmed the *Paul* ruling that "insurance is not commerce,"[5] and this anomaly became part and parcel of American constitutional law. Meanwhile, of course, the insurance industry grew to gigantic size, until by 1940 it had amassed $37 billion in assets and was collecting $6 billion per year in premium income, while employing over a half-million people. Then it happened. On November 20, 1942, a federal grand jury in Georgia indicted South-Eastern Underwriters Association, an unincorporated association composed of nearly two hundred stock fire insurance companies doing business in six southern states, on two counts of violating the Sherman Antitrust Act by: (1) conspiring to fix and maintain arbitrary and noncompetitive premium rates on fire insurance in restraint of interstate trade and commerce; and (2) conspiring to monopolize trade and commerce in fire insurance and to exclude others from selling it in the six states.[6] South-Eastern filed a demurrer that the indictment stated insufficient grounds for a federal offense since the business of fire insurance was not commerce; and the District Court followed precedent and sustained the demurrer on the ground that under the Sherman Act the conduct restrained must be interstate commerce, and "Supreme Court decisions hold that insurance is not commerce." The United States appealed.

Attorney General Francis Biddle and Solicitor General Charles Fahy had no choice but to appeal to the "prerogative" of the Supreme Court to decide whether to "adhere to prior decisions."[7] Accordingly, the government made two main contentions: (1) the fire-insurance business did constitute interstate commerce within the meaning of the Commerce Clause; and (2) the insurance business was subject to control by the Sherman Act. The argument in support of these propositions was based on present-day realities, upon the Court's decisions in other recent commerce cases, and upon an analysis of the history of congressional antitrust legislation.[8] In regard to the first contention, the size and extent of the modern insurance business was examined in detail; and it was pointed out that it required the continual movement of money, information, and documents across state lines on a large scale and the use of mail, telephone, and express facilities. All of these activities clearly constituted interstate commerce under any reasonable definition of the term, whether now (1944), in 1787, or in 1869.

Government counsel now came to the heart of the first argument. *Paul v. Virginia* and the other insurance cases decided only that the "states have power to regulate or tax the insurance business"; the repeated statement that "insurance is not commerce" arose solely out of the Court's concern that "otherwise the power of the states could not be sustained."[9] These decisions were inconsistent with the broad definition of commerce laid down in *Gibbons v. Ogden* and with the holding on lottery tickets in *Champion v. Ames;* and other decisions had also weakened their value.[10] Finally, the blunt argument was made that fire insurance could be regulated under the federal commerce power because it was necessary to business activity in general, and "Congress has power to regulate and safeguard the availability of an instrumentality so essential to commerce."[11]

Coming to the second contention, Biddle and Fahy sought to show that the insurance business was subject to the restrictions of the Sherman Act. The latter forbade every contract, combination, or conspiracy "in restraint of trade or commerce among the several States"; and since insurance was in commerce, the appellee's conduct was plainly proscribed by "the literal language of the Act." But the fact remained that the Sherman Act had never been thought to cover the insurance industry. Counsel looked to history and found that the congressional reports and debates showed that Congress had not attempted to include insurance because of the Court's decision in *Paul* and not because of any legislative desire to exempt it. This same reason was instrumental in the refusal of Congress to act positively on President Theodore Roosevelt's two proposals in 1904-1905 that insurance companies be subjected to federal regulation; and it was still operative when the Clayton Antitrust Act was framed and passed in 1914.[12] Thus the Court should remove this judicially forged obstruction to the operation of the Sherman Act, in which Congress had intended to exercise its full power under the Commerce Clause.

One final point remained to be argued: If insurance were held to be commerce and subject to federal control, what would happen to the multitude of state regulations which pervaded the field? The government had two answers. One was that the question was irrelevant: constitutional interpretation of the Sherman Act could not depend upon its effect upon state laws, and it was "for Congress not the States to determine the policy by which interstate commerce is to be governed."[13] The other was that this fear was exaggerated: such a decision "would not in itself invalidate the state taxing and regulatory statutes," since the Court had now come to weigh "the competing demands of the state and national interest involved" in accordance with "all the relevant facts and circumstances."[14]

Counsel for South-Eastern defended its actions on three main grounds: (1) fire insurance in and of itself was not interstate commerce;

(2) Congress had not attempted to regulate insurance by the Sherman Act or any later antitrust statutes; and (3) if insurance were held to be commerce, a great deal of state legislation would be invalidated, and the whole regulatory field would become chaotic.[15] Coming to the first point, the fact was stressed that after *Paul v. Virginia* in 1869, the Court had uniformly held that the business of insurance was not commerce.[16] This carefully and deliberately forged line of reasoning had become approved doctrine and should be adhered to in the present case; its validity had seldom been questioned, and its wide acceptance was found most clearly in the history of congressional antitrust legislation.

This led counsel to the second argument—that Congress had not included insurance in the Sherman Act. A plain reading of the congressional reports and debates at the time showed that the bill's sponsors and backers did not think that insurance companies would come within its provisions. Congress had repeatedly refused thereafter to approve any federal legislation applying to insurance; in fact, on three occasions (1914, 1915, and 1933) it rejected constitutional amendments which would have given it the power to regulate the insurance business.[17] Thus the positions argued by the government that Congress could regulate insurance and that the Sherman Act could apply to it were straw issues; Congress had not attempted to regulate the industry, and the Sherman Act had not been framed to include it.

The third contention emphasized by counsel was that if the Court held insurance to be commerce within the meaning of the Sherman Act, many state regulatory statutes would be invalidated, and chaos would be the order of the day. The first result would occur because "present day State regulation follows a comprehensive pattern curtailing competition and encouraging uniformity of rates in direct contrast to the unrestricted competitive demands of the Sherman Act."[18] Since all of this state legislation would be "diametrically opposed" to the federal law, it would have to fall. The second result would follow because insurance companies would not know what state regulations were valid or invalid and therefore would not know whether to abide by the Sherman Act and face revocation of their state licenses to do business or comply with the state laws and face the criminal penalties of the Sherman Act. In the latter case, the penalties would be retroactive, and the language of the Sherman Act itself might be rendered unconstitutionally vague. In any event, the dislocations would be sweeping, widespread, and unsettling to the industry and to the states.

Opinions of the Court

On June 5, 1944, Justice Hugo L. Black handed down the close, four-to-three opinion in *United States v. South-Eastern Underwriters Association.*[19] The record of the case presented two questions:

> (1) Was the Sherman Act intended to prohibit conduct of fire insurance companies which restrains or monopolizes the interstate fire insurance trade? (2) If so, do fire insurance transactions which stretch across state lines constitute "Commerce among the several States" so as to make them subject to regulation by Congress under the Commerce Clause?[20]

Since the second question was the really crucial one, Black took it up first and answered it in the affirmative. He began with a finding that the word "commerce" in 1787 included at least trade—business in which persons bought and sold, bargained and contracted; thus the word "commerce" in the Constitution would have to be read at least this broadly and would necessarily include insurance.

Black then took pains to show the obvious interstate nature of the modern insurance business.[21] He cited the relevant figures as to the vast size and scope of the industry, its constant use of interstate channels to carry on its business activities, and its great economic effect on people all over the nation. He had no difficulty in showing the undoubted interstate character of the 196 companies which were combined in South-Eastern Underwriters.

Black was now squarely face-to-face with the Court's previous decisions holding that "insurance is not commerce." In all of these cases, he noted, "attention was focused on the validity of state statutes—the extent to which the Commerce Clause automatically deprived states of the power to regulate the insurance business."[22] Since Congress had never attempted to regulate insurance, invalidation of the state statutes would have left the industry with no legal restraints on the abuses which had attended it from the first, and this circumstance the Court had consistently been unwilling to permit. But now the justices were asked to apply this same doctrine "to strike down an Act of Congress which was intended to regulate certain aspects of the methods by which interstate insurance companies do business."[23] This would have the effect of narrowing the scope of federal power to regulate the activities of a great interstate business, and other decisions of the Court had emphasized that "legal formulae devised to uphold state power cannot uncritically be accepted as trustworthy guides to determine Congressional power under the Commerce Clause."[24] Upon closer inspection, he found that the reasons given to support the decisions in the insurance cases were inconsistent with the reasoning in many other decisions which had upheld federal power over commerce; thus the insurance precedents could not be controlling in the present case.

Black thought that the real answer to the question was to be found "in the Commerce Clause itself and in some of the great cases which interpret it."[25] First, he looked to the many types of activities which had been held to be interstate commerce—the transportation across state lines of lottery tickets, prostitutes, stolen automobiles, and even electrical impulses.[26] Then he cited Marshall's definition of commerce as intercourse and as being interstate when it "concerns more states than one." The commerce power had been designed to secure the "maintenance of harmony and proper intercourse among the States" and to allow Congress to negate any state regulations of commerce which might be deemed "inimical to the national interest." This positive grant encompassed the power "to legislate concerning transactions which, reaching across state boundaries, affect the people of more states than one"; and it included the power "to govern affairs which the individual states, with their limited territorial jurisdictions, are not fully capable of governing."[27]

Finally, Black came to the crux of his first point:

> Our basic responsibility in interpreting the Commerce Clause is to make certain that the power to govern intercourse among the states remains where the Constitution placed it. That power, as held by this Court from the beginning, is vested in the Congress, available to be exercised for the national welfare as Congress shall deem necessary. No commercial enterprise of any kind which conducts its activities across state lines has been held to be wholly beyond the regulatory power of Congress under the Commerce Clause. We cannot make an exception of the business of insurance.[28]

The second question concerned the application of the Sherman Act to the insurance industry, and Black held that the Act was applicable. He thought that the sweeping language of sections 1 and 2 afforded no basis for the contention that Congress had intended to exclude interstate insurance companies, nor did any congressional reports or debates reveal a specific purpose to exempt them. The fact that Congress, at the time, might have known that the states were already regulating the insurance business did not now justify the Court in reading an exemption into the Act; the same applied to the fact that later Congresses had refused to enact legislation providing for federal regulation of insurance. Black was distinctly unimpressed with the historical evidence presented by the appellees and thought it largely irrelevant to the present issue; the mere lack of congressional action was not sufficient to show that "any Congress has held the view that insurance alone, of all businesses, should be permitted to enter into combinations for the purpose of destroying competition by coercive and intimidatory practices."[29] In conclusion, he reasserted the Court's newly solidified position with respect to economic policy: "Whether competition is a good thing for the insurance business is not for us to consider. Having power to enact the Sherman Act, Congress did so; if exceptions are to be written into the Act, they must come from the Congress, not this Court."[30]

There was one final point to be disposed of—the effect of the holding on state regulation of insurance, and Black made short shrift of it. He thought it an exaggeration to say that the Sherman Act would necessarily invalidate many state laws; few states allowed insurance companies to agree upon and fix rates privately without any official supervision, and no states authorized the kind of coercive and intimidatory practices which had been alleged against South-Eastern Underwriters. Accordingly, the federal law could not be denied full applicability to the field.

Chief Justice Harlan Fiske Stone wrote the leading dissenting opinion.[31] He did not deny that transactions across state lines were subject to federal regulation or that many aspects of the insurance business had "such interstate manifestations and such effects on the interstate commerce" as to subject it to the "appropriate exercise of federal power." Congress could, of course, regulate the facilities of commerce. However:

> The Congressional power to regulate does not extend to the formation and performance of insurance contracts save only as the latter may affect communication and transportation which are interstate commerce or may otherwise be found by Congress to affect transactions of interstate commerce. And even then, such effects on the commerce as do not involve restraints in competition in the marketing of goods and services are not within the reach of the Sherman Act.[32]

Expanding upon this last statement, Stone admitted that if insurance contracts were in fact made instruments of restraint in such marketing, they would come within the purview of the Sherman Act; but he thought that since trade in articles of commerce was not the subject matter of such contracts, there would be little scope for their use in restraining competition in interstate commerce. Thus the conclusion seemed inescapable that "the formation of insurance contracts, like many others, and the business of so doing, is not, without more, commerce within the protection of the commerce clause of the Constitution."[33]

Second, it followed logically from this that "agreements to fix premium rates, or other restraints on competition in entering into such contracts are not violations of the Sherman Act."[34] This rather startling statement was buttressed with an appeal to the historical fact that nothing in the legislative history of the Act suggested that it had been intended to apply to the insurance industry; the sponsors and supporters of the antitrust law had been primarily concerned with removing restraints of competition in the marketing of goods and commodities sold in national commerce and had disclaimed any attempt to invade the legislative authority of the states (which were, of course, regulating the insurance business). Furthermore, Congress had not changed its mind since then.

Finally, the Chief Justice came to the heart of the whole matter as he saw it, and he stated his position bluntly:

> This Court has never committed itself to any rule or policy that it will not "bow to the lessons of experience and the force of better reasoning" by overruling a mistaken precedent.
>
> . . . But the rule of *stare decisis* embodies a wise policy because it is often more important that a rule of law be settled than that it be settled right. This is especially so where, as here, Congress is not without regulatory power.[35]

With regard to the last statement, Stone was careful to note that the Court's insurance decisions had placed no field of activity beyond the control of both national and state governments as *Hammer v. Dagenhart* had done. He pointed to the extensive and effective systems of regulation which the states had developed over the years, and he disagreed with Black as to the constitutional consequences of the new holding; the immediate and practical effect of the decision would be "to withdraw from the states, in large measure, the regulation of insurance and to confer it on the national government." In short, the action of the bare four-man majority

> cannot fail to be the occasion for loosing a flood of litigation and
> of legislation, state and national, in order to establish a new
> boundary between state and national power, raising questions
> which cannot be answered for years to come, during which a
> great business and the regulatory officers of every state must be
> harassed by all the doubts and difficulties inseparable from a
> realignment of the distribution of power in our federal system.[36]

Justice Felix Frankfurter joined in the opinion of the Chief Justice.[37]
Justice Robert H. Jackson dissented in part.[38] Jackson agreed with the
majority that as a matter of fact insurance was commerce and that
Congress could regulate it as it chose, comprehensively or partially. But
Congress had not acted; and until it did, the Court should adhere to the
present constitutional fiction which sustained the traditional regulation
and taxation of insurance companies by the states. Then Jackson came
to the crux of his dissent which was, in effect, a plea for judicial
self-restraint: "To force the hand of Congress is no more the proper
function of the judiciary than to tie the hands of Congress."[39]

Analysis of South-Eastern

Several items of significance stand out in regard to the *South-Eastern
Underwriters* case. The first is, of course, that the Court reversed 75
years of precedent to hold that the business of insurance per se is
commerce within the constitutional meaning of that term and hence
subject to control by Congress under the Commerce Clause. Two things
are important here: (1) Black stressed the factual circumstances involved, which make it plain that the modern insurance industry is
dependent upon interstate commerce for its very existence, regardless
of whether its business is seen as a "flow of commerce" or as only have
a "close and intimate" relationship to commerce; and (2) he made it
clear that in view of the great national economic importance of
insurance, the Court in 1944 would not deny the federal government
power to regulate the industry and to prosecute it for antitrust
violations. In essence, these two considerations—one of fact and one of
policy—were responsible for this very controversial ruling on an important constitutional issue by less than a majority of the nine
justices.[40]

Second, the logical result of the holding is that insurance companies
are now subject to the terms of the Sherman Act and to all other
federal regulatory measures. The interesting thing here is that Black

looked not to the uncontroverted historical fact that Congress had never attempted to include insurance under federal regulation but to some sparse evidence that certain members of Congress would have liked to include it, if it had not been for the *Paul* decision. At its best, this is a rather novel way to determine the "intent" of Congress; at its worst, it is a clear misuse of the often legitimate recourse to history to decide matters of legislative purpose. But the point is at least arguable; and given the scope of federal power by 1944, perhaps the intention of Congress in 1890 or 1914 was really irrelevant to the immediate question. In fact, Black denigrated the historical evidence pro and con and rested his opinion squarely on the broad language of Marshall in *Gibbons v. Ogden* and, by implication, on the admonition in *McCulloch v. Maryland*: "we must never forget that it is a constitution we are expounding." If Black's course of action were not the most advisable or the most proper under the circumstances, his decision at least reflected the economic realities of the middle twentieth century and did not perpetuate a constitutional myth. As Alfred H. Kelly and Winfred A. Harbison have pointed out in its defense:

> Criticism of the majority opinion in the South-Eastern Under-writers case tended to obscure the significant fact that the justices had been unanimous in the conviction that the business of insurance, if not in itself commerce, nonetheless substantially affected commerce and so was subject to federal regulation insofar as it had such effect.[41]

Third, and this point is in a way the most important, Black dismissed the threat of the holding to state regulation as "exaggerated." This problem had two facets: (1) the effect of the federal antitrust laws on state statutes, and (2) the effect of the Commerce Clause per se on state regulation and taxation. With respect to the former, it is clear (and Black made no attempt to disguise the fact) that the federal antitrust regulations would have to take precedence and that any state laws found to be in direct conflict with them would automatically be invalid; fortunately, there were very few state acts which would fall into this category. But the second facet of the problem was really of crucial concern because many a state regulation of interstate commerce had been struck down under the inherent force of the Commerce Clause to protect such commerce from undue burdens, discriminations, and so forth; even Stone's more liberal "balancing-of-interests" formula had not saved all such state acts from invalidation.

The precise point here is that Black's decision was carefully worded to avoid the implication of any wholesale attack upon state regulation and taxation of the insurance business; in arguing that the Court could no longer accept the proposition that "insurance is not commerce," he took vigorous exception to the contention that if insurance were treated as commerce, then all control over it would be taken away from the states. Without qualification, that broad conclusion was inconsistent with many decisions, including *Cooley v. The Board of Wardens* (1852) and *Parker v. Brown* (1943). Black thought that for constitutional purposes, certain activities of a business might be intrastate and subject to state control, while other activities might be interstate and subject to federal regulation. Furthermore, recent commerce cases had established this rule of decision:

> In marking out these activities the primary test applied by the Court is not the mechanical one of whether the particular activity affected by the state regulation is part of interstate commerce, but rather whether, in each case, the competing demands of the state and national interests involved can be accommodated.[42]

In short, and in line with his thinking generally,[43] Black did not see his opinion as a weapon with which to invalidate state legislation; clear and gross would have to be state discrimination against interstate insurance companies in favor of local ones before the Court could or should strike it down as repugnant to the Commerce Clause. It seems accurate then, in the words of Alpheus Thomas Mason and William M. Beaney, to characterize Black's opinion as "the first since Marshall's day to give the Commerce Clause an all-embracing yet state-power-saving construction."[44]

Fourth, and this final point is the reverse side of the coin, the dissents of Stone and Jackson really both hinge upon the fear (not shared by Black) that the decision would invalidate, wholesale, state regulation and taxation of the insurance business and force Congress to assume complete control over it. This was because they believed that the Commerce Clause is a two-edged sword which operates affirmatively to uphold federal power, but negatively to deny any exercise of state power which would unduly "burden," "obstruct," or "discriminate against" interstate commerce.[45] Stone would take a very pragmatic look at the actual economic "effects" of any state statute and would apply his realistic "balancing-of-interests" formula to determine the boundary between national and state power; thus much, but not all, state legislation would be saved. Jackson, on the other hand, would take a harder position that historically the Commerce Clause had been framed with the intention to create in the United States a great free-trade area, free from virtually any local restrictions; thus very little state regulation of interstate commercial activities could be allowed to stand. In addition, both men were firm believers in judicial self-restraint; this view is expressed with particular clarity and force by Jackson, who thought that the justices had no business upsetting long and well-established precedents in the absence of any positive legislative action on the subject.

On the same day the Court applied the National Labor Relations Act to the insurance industry. In *Polish National Alliance of the United States of North America v. National Labor Relations Board* (1944)[46] Justice Frankfurter concluded that in view of the Alliance's obviously interstate activities, the Labor Board was justified in its finding that the unfair labor practices of the Alliance would "affect commerce" and hence came within the scope of the federal statute.[47] To the question of whether Congress had exceeded its power to regulate commerce in proscribing such conduct on the part of an insurance company, Frankfurter bowed to the judgment of the legislature:

> [T]his Court is concerned with the bounds of legal power and not with the bounds of wisdom in its exercise by Congress. When the conduct of an enterprise affects commerce among the States is a matter of practical judgment, not to be determined by abstract notions. . . . To hold that Congress could not deem the activities here in question to affect what men of practical affairs would call commerce, and to deem them related to such commerce merely by gossamer threads and not by solid ties, would be to disrespect the judgment that is open to men who have the constitutional power and responsibility to legislate for the Nation.[48]

Thus Frankfurter avoided a flat declaration that "insurance is commerce" and massed a unanimous Court.[49] Justice Black, joined by Justices Douglas and Murphy, wrote a very short concurring opinion in which he added bluntly that the business of insurance was commerce under the authority of the *South-Eastern* decision and that on this basis the Alliance's activities were subject to federal regulation.[50] The insurance industry, like agriculture and manufacturing, was now within the ambit of national authority under the Commerce Clause.

Congress Acts and the Court Responds

Prudential Insurance Co. (1946)

But the final chapter of the story had not yet been written. On February 27, 1945, Congress passed the McCarran-Ferguson Act,[51] which, in effect, left regulation of insurance to the states. Section 1 declared that this was in the public interest and that silence on the part of Congress should not be construed to impose any barrier to the regulation or taxation of such business by the states. Section 2(a) stated directly that insurance, and everyone engaged therein, should be subject to the laws of the several states; section 2(b) stated that no act of Congress should be construed to "invalidate, impair, or supersede" any state law, unless such congressional act specifically related to insurance: provided that, after January 1, 1948, the federal antitrust laws should be applicable to the business of insurance "to the extent that such business is not regulated by state law." Even this frank expression of the will of Congress, however, could not deter the insurance companies from attempting to capitalize on the negative implications of the *South-Eastern* decision; the target selected for the constitutional attack was South Carolina. Accordingly, The Prudential Insurance Company of America sued in the South Carolina Supreme Court to enjoin the state from collecting a premium license tax levied against "foreign" insurance companies by sections 7948 and 7949 of the South Carolina Code of 1942, upon the ground that the tax contravened the Commerce Clause. The state court denied relief, and Prudential appealed.

The issues presented to the United States Supreme Court were not complex; they were for the most part a rehash of those from the *South-Eastern* case, with the added problem of the effect of the McCarren-Ferguson Act. South Carolina made essentially three main arguments: (1) the premium tax did not "regulate" or "discriminate against" interstate commerce; (2) the decision in *South-Eastern Underwriters* did not invalidate the tax; and (3) the McCarran-Ferguson Act specifically protected the right of the state to regulate and tax the business of insurance.[52] Coming to the first point, South Carolina argued that Prudential could not conduct its intrastate business without state permission and that the premium tax .was an appropriate condition imposed for the privilege of doing business within its borders. It stressed the fact that the activity which measured the tax (the collection of premium income from state policyholders) was the result of a number of local transactions, which ranged from medical examinations to final delivery of the policies; and the size of Prudential and its effect on commerce did not alter the fundamental nature of these transactions. Furthermore, Prudential had paid the tax without any protest for 35 years and had grown and prospered in the state, which proved that the exaction exerted no "undue burden" on the conduct of interstate commerce.

Second, South Carolina urged the proposition that nothing in *South-Eastern* invalidated the tax. In analyzing the Court's opinion, it picked up Black's remarks that some activities of a business might be interstate and subject to federal regulation, while other activities might be intrastate and subject to state control and that the Court would look to practical considerations, rather than mechanical tests, to resolve the competing demands of state and nation, particularly where there had been a long absence of any federal regulation. This was enough to convince the state that until Congress found that the premium tax had "such an effect on interstate commerce as to place it in conflict with a Federal statute, that tax is a lawful fee for the privilege of doing business within the state."[53]

Third, South Carolina, naturally enough, relied heavily on the McCarran Act to sustain the validity of its tax. Pointing out that *Cooley* had made a distinction between "those aspects of interstate commerce which require national uniformity of regulation and those local in nature which do not," it asserted:

> In the McCarran-Ferguson Act Congress has legislated in both of these fields. As to those aspects of the insurance business requiring uniform national regulation it has rebutted the presumption [that Congress intended no state regulation] by saying that its silence is not to be construed as prohibiting state regulation. As to those aspects of the insurance business which comprise matters local in nature the Congress has given specific permission to the states to continue as heretofore in regulation and taxation.[54]

Thus it was clear that the McCarran Act had been intended to end any doubts about the right of the states to continue to regulate and tax the business of insurance; Congress had undoubted power "to redefine the distribution of power over interstate commerce" and could allow the states to regulate such commerce "in a manner which would otherwise not be permissible."[55] The premium tax was a valid exercise of the state's taxing power and was in complete harmony with the commerce power of the federal government.

The Prudential Insurance Company countered with three main contentions of its own: (1) the insurance business in which it was engaged, including its business in South Carolina, was interstate in character; (2) the South Carolina taxing statutes unconstitutionally discriminated against interstate commerce and were invalid; and (3) the McCarran-Ferguson Act was not intended to permit, nor could it validly permit, such discriminatory taxation of interstate commerce.[56] Regarding the first point, there could be no doubt as to the accuracy of the claim: Prudential operated in all 48 states, the District of Columbia, Hawaii, and Canada; it had almost $6 billion in assets, almost $23 billion of insurance in force, and 34 million policies issued, covering 23 million people. All applications for insurance had to be approved at the home office in Newark, New Jersey, and all policies were issued from there. Extensive and continuous use was made of mail, telephone, telegraph, and express services.[57]

Prudential then came to what it termed the "sole issue" before the Court—the contention that the premium tax unduly discriminated against interstate insurance companies in favor of domestic ones. The taxing statutes "on their face" subjected foreign companies to a "very real and substantial discrimination" in the form of "a protective tariff which the several states have been prohibited by the Commerce Clause from imposing on foreign companies engaging in interstate commerce."[58] To support this claim Prudential argued that the premium tax had to be treated as general operating expense, which had the effect in a mutual company of raising the cost of insurance; thus "South Carolina, by discriminating as she has, therefore increases the cost of insurance to all policyholders, wherever resident . . . who place their insurance with an out-of-state company."[59] Such discrimination was clearly invalid under the Commerce Clause, which had been inserted in the Constitution to remedy commercial rivalry among the states.[60]

Finally, Prudential took up the matter of the McCarran-Ferguson Act. On a plain reading of its provisions the company failed to see "any intention on the part of Congress, either expressed or implied, to validate, authorize, or sanction state statutes which discriminate against interstate commerce."[61] The purpose of the Act had been two-fold: (1) to permit the states to continue such regulation and taxation of insurance as was constitutional and not discriminatory, and (2) to remove any question of the validity of such measures as might be deemed invalid under the so-called "silence-of-Congress" doctrine. Point one represented the crux of Prudential's argument: the McCarran

Act only permitted continued state control of the interstate insurance business which was nondiscriminatory, that term, of course, to be defined by the Court; and if the McCarren Act could be construed as sanctioning discriminatory state legislation, it would be invalid because even Congress did not have the power to consent to state discrimination against commerce.[62]

Rutledge's Opinion

On June 3, 1946, Justice Wiley B. Rutledge handed down the unanimous decision in *Prudential Insurance Co. v. Benjamin*,[63] which upheld the validity of the two South Carolina statutes and, more importantly, the constitutionality of the McCarran-Ferguson Act. His opinion was divided into four major parts, each of which will be analyzed in some detail, since the Court's holdings are a landmark in the extent to which it has allowed Congress and the states joint regulation of an area of economic activity. The plenary nature of the federal commerce power is also again brought into sharp focus and reaffirmed without reservation.

In part one Rutledge faced the problem of "the continuing necessity in our federal system for accommodating the two great basic powers it comprehends," that is, "the paramount national authority over commerce" and the "appropriate exercise of the states' reserved powers touching the same or related subject matter."[64] He noted that historically there had been shifts in the general balance of authority between the two centers of power but that the situation had been particularly anomalous with respect to insurance; thus the states took over exclusive regulation of the industry and "inevitably exerted their powers to limits and in ways not sought generally to be applied to other business held to be within the reach of the Commerce Clause's implied prohibition."[65] Now on the basis of the *South-Eastern* decision, these state statutes were challenged on the ground that the Commerce Clause was a "two-edged instrument" which, in this instance, required the striking down of much state legislation. But Rutledge denied the appellant's sweeping claims:

> Prudential's misconception relates . . . to the nature and scope of the negative function of the commerce clause. It is not the simple, clean-cutting tool supposed. . . . For cleanly as the commerce clause has worked affirmatively on the whole, its implied negative operation on state power has been uneven, at times highly variable.

... That the clause imposes some restraint upon state power has never been doubted. For otherwise the grant of power to Congress would be wholly ineffective. But the limitation not only is implied. It is open to different implications of meaning. And this accounts largely for variations in this field continuing almost from the beginning until now.[66]

With respect to the present, the trend of decision ran decidedly toward sustaining state regulation and taxation of commerce by putting judicial emphasis on "facts and practical considerations rather than dogmatic logistic."

Having discussed these general propositions, Rutledge took up the insurance company's specific contention that state regulation discriminating against interstate commerce could not stand. First, he dismissed the precedents relied upon as irrelevant because in each case "the question of the validity of the state taxing statute arose when Congress' power lay dormant"; then he considered and rejected the constitutional effect which Prudential's argument would produce:

[I]t maintains that the commerce clause "of its own force" and without reference to any action by Congress, whether through its silence or otherwise, forbids discriminatory state taxation of interstate commerce. This is to say, in effect, that neither Congress acting affirmatively nor Congress and the states thus acting coordinately can validly impose any regulation which the Court has found or would find to be forbidden by the commerce clause, if laid only by state action taken while Congress' power lies dormant. In this view the limits of state power to regulate commerce in the absence of affirmative action by Congress are also the limits of Congress' permissible action in this respect, whether taken alone or in coordination with state legislation.

... So conceived, Congress' power over commerce would be nullified to a very large extent. For in all the variations of commerce clause theory it has never been the law that what the states may do in the regulation of commerce, Congress being silent, is the full measure of its power. Much less has this boundary been thought to confine what Congress and the states acting together may accomplish.

... The commerce clause is in no sense a limitation upon the power of Congress over interstate and foreign commerce. On the contrary, it is ... a grant to Congress of plenary and supreme authority over those subjects. The only limitation it places upon Congress' power is in respect to what constitutes commerce, including whatever rightly may be found to affect it. . . . This

164

limitation, of course, is entirely distinct from the implied prohibition of the commerce clause. The one is concerned with defining commerce, with fixing the outer boundary of the field over which the authority granted shall govern. The other relates only to matters within the field of commerce, . . . including whatever may fall within the "affectation" doctrine. The one limitation bounds the power of Congress. The other confines only the powers of the states. And the two areas are not coextensive.[67]

Second, Rutledge held that the precedents which were relevant were those where the silence of Congress had been judicially interpreted as forbidding state action and where Congress had later disclaimed the prohibition or undertaken to nullify it.[68] He found that in such cases the Court had never "held such a disclaimer invalid or that state action supported by it could not stand"; true, the Court had never conceded to Congress the power "to make conclusive its own mandate concerning what is commerce," but it had, nevertheless, always "accommodated its previous judgment to Congress' expressed approval" of such local action.[69] But these precedents did not automatically decide the present case because Prudential had further asserted that the McCarran Act had not been intended to accede to any discriminatory state regulation or taxation of interstate commerce; in short, even a declaration of Congress would not affect the Commerce Clause's inherent ban on such action. This claim, of course, raised questions concerning the validity of the congressional expression of policy and whether the policy extended to the kind of state legislation which was immediately in issue.

Part three of the opinion, then, was devoted to an analysis of the McCarran-Ferguson Act. Briefly, Rutledge found that its purpose was "to give support to the existing and future state systems for regulating and taxing the business of insurance."[70] He also thought that two conclusions could be drawn from its language: (1) Congress had declared "that uniformity of regulation, and of state taxation, are not required in reference to the business of insurance by the national public interest"; and (2) Congress had determined "that state taxes, which in its silence might be held invalid as discriminatory, do not place on interstate insurance business a burden which it is unable generally to bear or should not bear in the competition with local business."[71] It was these clear policy judgments of the national legislature which, Prudential argued, could not be given constitutional effect under the Commerce Clause.

Rutledge was now ready to decide the case. He thought that in view of what had been said, the Court would be "going very far to rule that South Carolina no longer may collect her tax. To do so would flout the expressly declared policies of both Congress and the state."[72] The real answer was to be found in the nature of the authority and discretion granted by the Commerce Clause itself:

> The power of Congress over commerce exercised entirely without reference to coordinated action of the states is not restricted, except as the Constitution expressly provides, by any limitation which forbids it to discriminate against interstate commerce and in favor of local trade. Its plenary scope enables Congress not only to promote but also to prohibit interstate commerce, as it has done frequently and for a great variety of reasons.

> ... This broad authority Congress may exercise alone ... or in conjunction with coordinated action by the states, in which case limitations imposed [on Congress] for the preservation of their [the states'] powers become inoperative and only those designed to forbid action altogether by any power or combination of powers in our governmental system remain effective. Here both Congress and South Carolina have acted, and in complete co-ordination, to sustain the tax. It is therefore reinforced by the exercise of all the power of government residing in our scheme. Clear and gross must the evil which would nullify such an exertion. ...

> ... No conceivable violation of the commerce clause, in letter or spirit, is presented. Nor is contravention of any other limitation.[73]

Thus the mere fact of a constitutional division of legislative power "into the respective spheres of federal and state authority" did not forbid cooperation between the two centers to achieve certain public policies, particularly in the field of the regulation and taxation of interstate commerce.

Analysis of *Prudential*

There are a number of facets to this really profound opinion which might well warrant some extended examination, but only two of Rutledge's conclusions will be commented upon here. First, it is important to note what he had to say with respect to the negative effect of the Commerce Clause on state power. He not only recognized the great variability of the Court's past decisions in sustaining or striking down attempted state control of interstate commerce—the high susceptibility of the whole process to different implications drawn largely from judicial interpretation of the commerce power, but he also emphasized the present leniency of the Court toward the states in this area—the clear trend of current decision to uphold exercises of state power which admittedly impinged upon commerce. In other words, he rejected the view that the Commerce Clause operated automatically to invalidate any state action which might mechanistically be said to "burden," "obstruct," or "regulate" interstate commerce; rather the Court would now look to the "facts and practical considerations" of the matter to decide the validity of state legislation attacked under the federal grant. Second and of equal significance, he stressed the plenary nature of national power over commerce and anything "affecting" commerce; this reaffirmation contained at least two principles, both well known and long established but reasserted by Rutledge in a most straight-forward way: (1) the power of Congress over commerce was in no sense limited to the measure of what the states might do in its silence; to put it a little differently, the Commerce Clause was a grant of "supreme authority" to Congress and in itself represented no limitation on congressional control over the subjects of commerce; and (2) federal power was not restricted to merely promoting or protecting commerce; Congress could, if it wished, absolutely prohibit commerce or even "discriminate against interstate commerce and in favor of local trade." In summary, *Prudential Insurance Co. v. Benjamin,* like the decision in *South-Eastern Underwriters,* opted for essentially "an all-embracing yet state-power-saving" construction of the Commerce Clause.

On the same day as the *Prudential* case, the Court decided *Robertson v. California* (1946),[74] which upheld the conviction of the petitioner under two state statutes regulating the actions of insurance agents. Section 703(a) of the California Insurance Code made it a misdemeanor (except for a "surplus line broker") to act as an agent for a nonadmitted insurer in the transaction of insurance business in the state; section 1642 made it a misdemeanor to act as an agent, broker, or solicitor for any insurance company until a license was obtained from the insurance commissioner authorizing such action. The undisputed evidence showed that Robertson, acting for an Arizona mutual insurance company which was not admitted to do business in California, had violated both sections of the code.

Justice Rutledge, speaking for a six-man majority,[75] affirmed the conviction and upheld both provisions against the general contention that they were regulations of interstate commerce which were forbidden by the Commerce Clause. Without relying on the McCarran-Ferguson Act, which was passed after the date of Robertson's acts and hence would be an *ex post facto* law if applied to him, Rutledge took up the code provisions one at a time. Section 1642 applied to all insurance agents, whatever company they represented, and was not discriminatory or exclusory in character; rather, it was merely "designed and reasonably adapted to protect the public from fraud, misrepresentation, incompetence and sharp practice which falls short of minimum standards of decency in the selling of insurance by personal solicitation and salesmanship."[76] Section 703(a) also applied to all agents, but it was complicated by two facts: (1) there were both monetary and moral requirements to be met in becoming a "surplus line broker" (section 1765 of the code); and (2) there were certain capital and reserve requirements to be met in becoming an admitted insurer in the state (section 10510). Taken together, Robertson argued that these requirements discriminated against out-of-state insurers and in favor of domestic ones; and as a result of the *South-Eastern* decision, California could no longer require foreign insurance companies to comply with section 10510 in order to do business there. Rutledge quickly found the discrimination argument to be without substance because the requirements were the same for all surplus-line brokers and both domestic and foreign companies; the crucial contention was the state's supposed inability to exclude any company. But he had no trouble in concluding that California's reserve requirements were not excessive for the protection of its citizens and that they were not designed to exclude foreign insurers.

With this holding in favor of state power, the Court closed its consideration of the constitutional issues arising out of *United States v. South-Eastern Underwriters*. In that case, it had endowed Congress with power under the Commerce Clause to regulate the American insurance industry—wholly, or in such aspects of its business as Congress might choose. Congress had responded with passage of the McCarran—Ferguson Act, which left regulation and taxation of the industry to the states. In *Prudential Insurance Co. v. Benjamin* the Court unqualifiedly accepted this legislative judgment and allowed Congress, in effect, to delegate its commerce power to the states in a show of complete cooperation between the two centers of power.[77] Finally, the *Robertson* case was an example of the now very large extent to which the Court would uphold state power over "foreign" corporations, even in the absence of positive and complementary action by Congress.[78]

Enough has been written to show that by the end of 1946 the Supreme Court had interpreted the Commerce Clause to be, in the words of Robert L. Stern, "a grant of authority permitting Congress to allow interstate commerce to take place on whatever terms it may consider in the interest of the national well-being."[79] Three cases decided in the late 1940's serve to underscore the accuracy of this conclusion and to add support for the generalization that, constitutionally speaking, there are virtually no limits on the federal commerce power.

Miscellaneous Regulation

The Beet-Sugar Industry

The first case is *Mandeville Island Farms, Inc. v. American Crystal Sugar Co.* (1948),[80] which concerned the application of the Sherman Antitrust Act. Mandeville Farms accused American Crystal Sugar of conspiring with two other northern California sugar refiners (all of whom sold sugar in interstate commerce) to restrain trade by fixing and maintaining a uniform price for sugar beets and thereby to create and maintain a monopoly in trade and commerce; the sugar company denied that its actions brought it within the reach of the federal statute.[81] The facts were as follows: from 1939 to 1941, the three refiners entered into an agreement to pay uniform prices for sugar beets by adopting identical form contracts and computing beet prices on the basis of their average net return per one hundred pounds of sugar sold. The beet growers had the choice of signing the form contract or quitting production. Mandeville sued for treble damages under the antitrust law, but the District Court held that "products of the farm which are subsequently manufactured or processed into articles of commerce are beyond the reach of said Act." The Ninth Circuit Court of Appeals affirmed the judgment, and Mandeville appealed to the Supreme Court.

The opposing arguments in the case (particularly those of the respondent) are interesting, coming as they do as late as 1948, and each one will be reviewed briefly. Counsel for the farm corporation argued that the price-fixing combination among the refiners clearly came within the ban of the Sherman Act. This was true for two main reasons: (1) the price to the growers was based on the sugar content of the beets and was fixed by the returns secured by the refiners in the interstate sale of the processed sugar; hence interstate commerce was involved in the entire transaction, and this brought the local supply contracts within the reach of the Act; and (2) if the refiners themselves had grown the beets, each step would have been part of interstate commerce; this "stream" had not been broken because the independent growers performed some of the steps. In sum, the conspiracy on the part of the three refiners to fix sugar-beet prices to the growers involved interstate commerce and was a manifest violation of the federal antitrust law.

In reply, counsel for the sugar company contended that Mandeville's complaint was insufficient to state a claim under the Sherman Act. Two arguments in particular supported this view. First, the activities complained of were not in interstate commerce. The intrastate planting, growing, harvesting, selling, and manufacturing of farm products into a commodity for interstate shipment was not in itself commerce. The only commodity moving interstate was refined sugar, and the grower had merely alleged price fixing of raw sugar beets, an entirely different and separate product which never moved in commerce at all.

Second, price fixing was illegal only where it had a substantial, adverse effect upon interstate commerce; but Mandeville Farms had not shown that there was any effect upon either the price or the supply of sugar—the interstate commodity. The simple and unamended Sherman Act merely forbade any restraint of trade or commerce; and since American Crystal's activities had had no such effect upon commerce, they did not come within the prohibitions of the Act. In short, the petitioner really had no case.

Mandeville Island Farms v. American Crystal Sugar Co. was decided May 10, 1948; Justice Rutledge wrote the seven-to-two majority opinion which held that the uniform price-fixing agreements of the refiners were unlawful under the antitrust law.[82] Actually, for the purposes of this chapter, the specific holding, turning as it did on certain facts and assumptions, is somewhat immaterial. What is of prime importance is Rutledge's analysis of the history of the Commerce Clause and his reaffirmation of the plenary power which it bestows upon Congress to regulate economic activity; in this respect, his opinion must be compared to the one he wrote in *Prudential Insurance Co. v. Benjamin* (1946).

After detailing the facts of the case, Rutledge reviewed the opposing arguments, particularly that of American Crystal Sugar. He pointed out the emphasis laid upon the separation of the sequence of activities between the growing, selling, and refining of the sugar beets and the

170

later marketing of sugar; the first three stages were "purely local" in nature, while only the marketing of the refined sugar involved interstate commerce. He cited the company's added contention that "since the restraints precede the interstate marketing of the sugar and immediately affect only the local marketing of the beets, they have no restrictive effect upon the trade and commerce in sugar."[83] He also noted the flat denial that the price fixing of the beets came within the reach of the Sherman Act. Finally, Rutledge rejected American Crystal's general argument:

> The artificial and mechanical separation of "production" and "manufacturing" from "commerce," without regard to their economic continuity, the effects of the former two upon the latter, and the varying methods by which the several processes are organized, related and carried on in different industries or indeed within a single industry, no longer suffices to put either production or manufacturing and refining processes beyond reach of Congress' authority or of the [federal antitrust] statute.[84]

The justice turned to the history of the commerce power to prove his point. He admitted that in the first decision under the Sherman Act, *United States v. E.C. Knight Co.* (1895), the Court had applied these artificial distinctions to nullify the effects of coverage both of the Act and of the federal grant upon which it was based. But the evolving nature of American industrialism foredoomed the *Knight* precedent to reversal; and the *Shreveport Case* (1914) marked "a great turning point in the construction of the Commerce Clause," since it broke the "bonds confining Congress' power and made it an effective instrument for fulfilling its purpose."[85] In fact, because of *Shreveport* and its "affectation" approach,

> it was necessary no longer to search for some sharp point or line where interstate commerce ends and intrastate commerce begins, in order to decide whether Congress' commands were effective. For the essence of the affectation doctrine was that the exact location of this line made no difference, if the forbidden effects flowed across it to the injury of interstate commerce or to the hindrance or defeat of congressional policy regarding it.
>
> ... The *Shreveport* doctrine cut Congress loose from the haltering labels of "production" and "manufacturing" and gave it rein to reach those processes when they were used to defy its purpose regarding interstate trade and commerce.[86]

Rutledge conceded that the judicial transition to this approach was neither smooth nor immediate, but it was more and more used by the Court until the climax of the late 1930's established its compelte dominance. Now in view of this evolution, and given a restraint of the type forbidden by the Sherman Act, and a showing of an actual or threatened effect upon commerce, the only question became "whether the effect is sufficiently substantial and adverse to Congress' paramount policy declared in the Act's terms to constitute a forbidden consequence" because:

> The *Shreveport* doctrine did not contemplate that restraints or burdens become or remain immune merely because they take place as events prior to the point in time when interstate commerce begins. Exactly the contrary is comprehended, for it is the effect upon that commerce, not the moment when its cause arises, which the doctrine was fashioned to reach.[87]

Obviously, the criteria urged by the respondent were wholly inapplicable; and at this late date the Court was not prepared to take the long backward step to *E.C. Knight Co.*

Having structured the framework in which the case was to be decided, Rutledge turned to the questions of whether the complaint showed monopolistic practices of the type outlawed by the Sherman Act and, if so, whether those acts produced the forbidden effects upon commerce. He thought, first, that it was clear that the price-fixing agreement was the sort of combination condemned by the Act, since the means used to monopolize the local business of beet-growing was the interstate marketing of the refined sugar. The Act extended its protection to "all who are made victims of the forbidden practices," which included sellers or suppliers; and the amount of the national sugar industry which the three California refiners controlled was irrelevant, "so long as control is exercised effecitvely in the area concerned," because:

> Congress' power to keep the interstate market free of goods produced under conditions inimical to the general welfare . . . may be exercised in individual cases without showing any specific effect upon interstate commerce . . . ; it is enough that the individual activity when multiplied into a general practice is subject to federal control . . . or that it contains a threat to the interstate economy that requires preventive regulation.[88]

Second, there was the matter of the actual effect of the price agreements on commerce, and Rutledge concluded that "there can be no question that their restrictive consequences were projected substantially into the interstate distribution of the sugar."[89] The tie-in between "the price paid for beets with the price received for sugar" showed very clearly the "interdependence and inextricable relationship between the interstate and the intrastate effects of the combination" among the refiners—effects which not only "deprived the beet growers of any competitive opportunity for disposing of their crops," but also "tended to increase control over the quantity of sugar sold interstate."[90] Such restrictive and monopolistic effects fell "squarely within the Sherman Act's prohibitions" and created injuries for which relief could be afforded.[91]

Only two brief comments about *Mandeville Farms v. American Crystal Sugar* are in order. First, the opinion in the case is important not only because of Rutledge's remarks concerning the history of the Commerce Clause in general and his emphasis on the *Shreveport Case* and its "affectation" doctrine in particular, but also because of his strong assertion of congressional power in the present—a power that might be "exercised in individual cases without showing any specific effect upon interstate commerce," as long as the individual activity "when multiplied into a general practice" would be subject to federal control. In other words, in *Mandeville Farms* the Court reiterated and reemphasized the proposition accepted in *Wickard v. Filburn* and *Polish National Alliance v. NLRB* that, in respect to an exercise of power by Congress under the Commerce Clause, "[a]ppropriate for judgment is the fact that the immediate situation is representative of many others throughout the country, the total incidence of which if left unchecked may well become far-reaching in its harm to commerce." Second, the decision stands in stark contrast to the one handed down in *United States v. E.C. Knight Co.* over 50 years before. In the latter, the Court refused to apply the newly passed Sherman Antitrust Act to a group of five sugar companies who controlled over 95 percent of all the sugar refined in the United States; in *Mandeville Farms,* the Court was quick to invoke the prohibitions of the same, unamended statute against three sugar-beet processors who controlled the refining of sugar in only one part of one state of the Union (and who had no interest at all in cane sugar). No better illustration could attest to the now permanent change which has taken place in the reach of the federal commerce power under the Supreme Court's current interpretation of its constitutional scope.

The second case, which was also decided under the Sherman Act, is *United States v. Women's Sportswear Manufacturers Association* (1949).[92] The facts here were these: Women's Sportswear Manufacturers was an unincorporated trade association of independent stitching contractors in Boston, Massachusetts, who did work for jobbers in the women's sportswear industry. The jobbers maintained sales offices in New York City and solicited orders nation-wide. Upon receiving an order, the jobber bought the proper fabric, cut it to the customer's specifications, and sent it to the contractor who stitched the garments, put on accessories such as buttons, bows, and so forth, and returned it to the jobber who, in turn, shipped it to the original customer. In 1948-49 the Boston area ranked fifth in the national production of women's sportswear, and about 80 percent of the cloth used came from out-of-state sources, while a similar percent of the finished goods was shipped outside the state. The Association, whose member contractors handled at least one-half of the sportswear produced in Boston, forced 21 jobbers, who merchandised a substantial portion of the Boston output, to sign a contract requiring each jobber: (1) to employ only stitchers who were members of the Association, (2) to refrain from dealing with nonmembers, (3) to accept no secret price rebates, and (4) to divide its work "as equally and equitably as possible" among the Association contractors engaged by it. The federal government brought suit to enjoin the Association from restraining trade and commerce in sportswear under the antitrust law. The District Court dismissed the case chiefly on the ground that the Association and its members were not themselves engaged in interstate commerce. The government appealed this ruling.

On March 28, 1949, the Supreme Court reversed the lower court's decision; Justice Robert H. Jackson wrote the unanimous opinion.[93] Based on the facts, he found that "the intent and effect of the agreement is substantially to restrict competition and to control prices and markets."[94] The contract provided the members of the Association with a virtual monopoly over the jobbers' work and thus constituted a restraint of trade which was in clear violation of the Sherman Act. Then Jackson came to the important part of the opinion—his answer to the District Court. He thought that in determining application of the federal antitrust statute, the exact nature of the accused's operations was irrelevant; and he concluded:

Restraints, to be effective, do not have to be applied all along the line of movement of interstate commerce. The source of the restraint may be intrastate, as the making of a contract or combination usually is; the application of the restraint may be intrastate, as it often is; but neither matters if the necessary effect is to stifle or restrain commerce among the states. If it is interstate commerce that feels the pinch, it does not matter how local the operation which applies the squeeze.[95]

A more succinct or forceful description of the federal commerce power would be difficult to frame.

The Drug Industry

The third case arose under the Federal Food, Drug, and Cosmetic Act of 1938.[96] This statute amended the Pure Food and Drug Act of 1906 and added section 301(k) which prohibited

The alteration, mutilation, destruction, obliteration, or removal of the whole or any part of the labeling of, or the doing of any other act with respect to, a food, drug, device, or cosmetic, if such act is done while such article is held for sale after shipment in interstate commerce and results in such article being misbranded.

Section 502(f) declared a drug to be misbranded unless its labeling bore "(1) adequate directions for use; and (2) such adequate warnings against use . . . dangerous to health, or against unsafe dosage . . . as are necessary for the protection of users."

Jordan J. Sullivan, a retail druggist in Columbus, Georgia, bought a properly labeled bottle of 1000 sulfathiazole tablets from an Atlanta consignee who six months previously had received an interstate shipment of several such bottles from a drug laboratory in Chicago, Illinois. The large bottle was labeled in part as follows: "Caution.—To be used only by or on the prescription of a physician. Warning.—In some individuals Sulfathiazole may cause severe toxic reactions." On two separate occasions about three months later, Sullivan sold a pill box containing 12 tablets, each of which was labeled simply "sulfathiazole." The government charged him with two violations of section 301(k) of the federal Act and secured his conviction in the District Court. He appealed, and the Fifth Circuit Court of Appeals reversed the conviction on the ground that the Act should be held "to apply only to the holding for the first sale by the importer after interstate shipment"; otherwise, its application would result in too far-reaching an inroad upon the customary control by local authorities of traditionally local activities. This time the government appealed.

On January 19, 1948, the Supreme Court decided *United States v. Sullivan.*[97] Justice Black handed down the five-man majority opinion which upheld the conviction.[98] It seems unnecessary to detail his answers to certain technical questions with respect to the effects of various interpretations of the law, except to say that he thought the Court should neither depart from the "clear meaning" of a statute nor judicially narrow the scope of an offense by "envisioning extreme possible applications" of its provisions. Coming to the central questions, he found no ambiguity in the misbranding language or in the requirement that misbranding occur "while such article is held for sale after shipment in interstate commerce." In the first instance, it was clear that misbranding occurred unless the label contained both adequate directions and warnings; and obviously, such label had to be on the consumer's box because the chief purpose of proper labeling was to inform and protect the ultimate user. In the second instance, section 301(k) was equally clear and applicable:

> He [Sullivan] held the drugs for sale after they had been shipped in interstate commerce from Chicago to Atlanta. It is true that respondent bought them over six months after the interstate shipment had been completed by their delivery to another consignee. But the language used by Congress broadly and unqualifiedly prohibits misbranding articles held for sale after shipment in interstate commerce, without regard to how long after the shipment the misbranding occurred, how many intrastate sales had intervened, or who had received the articles at the end of the interstate shipment.[99]

Thus Sullivan's conduct came within the literal language of that section's prohibitions. Finally, to the contention that the statute as so construed was beyond the authority of Congress in that it invaded the reserved powers of the states, Black merely cited *McDermott v. Wisconsin* (1913).[100] This had upheld the Pure Food and Drug Act of 1906 against a similar challenge, *United States v. Darby* (1941), and *Wickard v. Filburn* (1942) as controlling.

The results of these three cases may be summarized very briefly. In the years 1948 and 1949 the Supreme Court reaffirmed and reinforced the plenary nature of national power under the Commerce Clause. Specifically, Congress can now exercise that power without regard to: (1) a showing of any specific effect on interstate commerce in an

176

individual instance, as long as a multiplication of such instances would produce an ascertainable effect on the commerce; (2) the character of the activity—no matter how "local"—as long as it creates a restraining or adverse effect on trade or commerce; and (3) the length of time involved, or the number of transactions removed, or the number of intermediate actors participating, between the regulated activity and the channels of interstate commerce. These cases, then, merely serve to substantiate further the broad generalizations which have already been made regarding the federal commerce power. In short, that power—in the words of John Marshall—"is complete in itself, may be exercised to its utmost extent, and acknowledges no limitations, other than are prescribed in the constitution."[101]

The Question of Limits

The question which must now be asked is this: Are there any limitations prescribed in the Constitution which the Supreme Court might be willing to invoke against an exercise of congressional power? The answer hinges upon an assessment of two cases—*American Communications Ass'n., CIO v. Douds* (1950) and *United States v. Brown* (1965). It will be seen immediately that these are very complex cases which involve the difficult problem of national security versus individual liberty in an era of cold war and which therefore go quite beyond mere economic matters. Accordingly, no attempt will be made to report or analyze them in depth; instead, the central holding in each will be noted briefly in order to provide, at best, a rather speculative answer to the above-posed question.

First, Congress, by the Labor-Management Relations Act of 1947,[102] amended the National Labor Relations Act of 1935, and in order to protect the free flow of national commerce from so-called "political strikes," it changed section 9(h) to read in part as follows:

> No investigation shall be made by the [National Labor Relations] Board of any question affecting commerce concerning the representation of employees, raised by a labor organization . . . unless there is on file with the Board an affidavit executed contemporaneously or within the preceding 12-month period by each officer of such labor organization . . . that he is not a member of the Communist Party or affiliated with such party, and that he does not believe in . . . the overthrow of the United States Government by force or by any illegal or unconstitutional methods.

The constitutionality of this "non-Communist affidavit provision" was soon questioned; two unions contended that it violated fundamental rights guaranteed by the First Amendment, that it was constitutionally vague, and that it was a proscribed bill of attainder. In *American Communications Ass'n. v. Douds,* handed down May 8, 1950, Chief Justice Fred M. Vinson held that Congress had not exceeded its power under the Commerce Clause in enacting the amended section 9(h).[103] Although most of the Chief Justice's opinion—joined in full by only Justices Reed and Burton—discussed First-Amendment issues, in the end he balanced freedom of speech and assembly against the continuing threat of substantial harm to interstate commerce and found that the latter would have to take precedence:

> There can be no doubt that Congress may, under its constitutional power to regulate commerce among the several States, attempt to prevent political strikes and other kinds of direct action designed to burden and interrupt the free flow of commerce. We think it is clear, in addition, that the remedy provided by [section] 9(h) bears reasonable relation to the evil which the statute was designed to reach.[104]

Justices Frankfurter and Jackson concurred in the Court's decision, with the exception that they thought the second half of the oath, which required a statement of non-belief in violent change, went beyond congressional constitutional authority.[105] Justice Black wrote a brilliant and bitter dissenting opinion.[106] For present purposes; however, two main points emerge: (1) the Court upheld the commerce-based statute in the face of First-Amendment and bill-of-attainder objections; but (2) the six participating justices were badly divided over the outcome, which prejudices the value of the decision as a future precedent.

Second, Congress, by the Labor-Management Reporting and Disclosure Act of 1959,[107] undertook to accomplish the same purpose as section 9(h)—that is, to protect the national economy by minimizing the danger of "political strikes"—in section 504, but in a more direct and effective way:

> (a) No person who is or has been a member of the Communist Party . . . shall serve—
> (1) as an officer, director, trustee, member of any executive board or similar governing body, business agent, manager, organizer, or other employee . . . of any labor organization . . . during or for five years after the termination of his membership in the Communist Party.

Archie Brown, an open and avowed Communist, was elected to three one-year terms on the Executive Board of Local 10 of the International Longshoremen's and Warehousemen's Union in San Francisco from 1959 to 1961. The federal government indicted him for willful violation of section 504 and secured his conviction in the District Court. On appeal, the Ninth Circuit Court of Appeals set aside the conviction and dismissed the indictment on the grounds that section 504 violated both the First and Fifth Amendments. The government appealed the decision; before the Supreme Court, Brown's counsel also urged that section 504 was an unconstitutional bill of attainder.

On June 7, 1965, *United States v. Brown* was decided. Chief Justice Earl Warren, speaking for a bare, five-man majority, held that section 504 was in point of law a bill of attainder which violated Article I, section 9, clause 3 of the Constitution.[108] The opinion, of course, was primarily concerned with the history of the bill-of-attainder clause and the way in which the Court had interpreted its prohibition previously. Here, Warren thought, the legislature had gone too far:

> Congress undoubtedly possesses power under the Commerce Clause to enact legislation designed to keep from positions affecting interstate commerce persons who may use such positions to bring about political strikes. In [section] 504, however, Congress has exceeded the authority granted it by the Constitution. The statute does not set forth a generally applicable rule decreeing that any person who commits certain acts or possesses certain characteristics (acts and characteristics which, in Congress' view, make them likely to initiate political strikes) shall not hold union office, and leave to courts and juries the job of deciding what persons have committed the specified acts or possess the specified characteristics. Instead, it designates in no uncertain terms the persons who possess the feared characteristics and therefore cannot hold union office without incurring criminal liability—members of the Communist Party.[109]

The Chief Justice admitted that the legislature could use an equivalent, shorthand phrase to summarize the characteristics of persons with whose activities it was concerned, but this it had not done:

> Even assuming that Congress had reason to conclude that some Communists would use union positions to bring about political strikes, "it cannot automatically be inferred that all members shar[e] their evil purposes or participat[e] in their illegal conduct." . . . In utilizing the term "members of the Communist Party" to designate those persons who are likely to incite political strikes, it plainly is not the case that Congress has merely

179

substituted a convenient shorthand term for a list of the characteristics it was trying to reach.[110]

Again for present purposes, only two major points are relevant: (1) the Court struck down a congressional statute which was based squarely on the commerce power; but (2) the justices were split five to four on the decision, which impairs its usefulness as an enduring guide to future judicial holdings on acts with a similar thrust.

To the original question as to whether there are any limitations specified in the Constitution which the Supreme Court would invoke to invalidate an exercise of congressional power under the Commerce Clause, the answer can only be a tentative yes. To amplify this a bit, several comments are in order. First, ground may be cleared by stating unequivocally that the Court would no longer use either the Fifth Amendment's prohibition on deprivation of property without due process of law or the Tenth Amendment's reserved powers of the states to strike down an act of Congress (*United States v. Darby*). Second, the only constitutional limitations which would apply at all would be the civil-liberty guarantees in the Bill of Rights (primarily First-Amendment freedoms) and other specific guarantees of individual rights, such as the protection against bills of attainder and *ex post facto* laws. But even here no flat statement can be made with certainty about what the Court might do with respect to an attempt on the part of Congress to limit freedom of speech or assembly by an act based on the Commerce Clause, except to surmise that the spirit of protection of the individual as evinced in *Brown* might prevail. For, it will be remembered, only three justices in *Douds* thought that both of the oath requirements in section 9(h) were within the authority of Congress.

Third, and finally, it is precisely because of the sharp divisions on the Court in both *Douds* and *Brown* that the situation today remains speculative, with no firm generalization possible. But, perhaps, one proposition can be ventured: If Congress should seek to attaint certain persons because of their beliefs and prohibit them from holding certain positions in the economy by use of the commerce power, it will be treading on the outermost perimeter of its constitutional authority, even under that vast, specifically delegated power. Thus if Congress makes such an attempt and expects to be successful, it had better do its homework thoroughly (by showing a causal relationship between abstract beliefs and concrete action having an adverse effect upon commerce) and frame its legislation carefully (by avoiding prior indictments of specific persons or groups). The present Court has, it is true, renounced entirely its role as a perpetual censor on federal economic regulation; but it has, at the same time, become a staunch defender of individual rights and liberties.

The hard fact remains, however, that the Supreme Court in its interpretation of the Commerce Clause over the past 33 years has given Congress plenary power to work its will in the regulation of any activity which has any relationship to "that commerce which concerns more states than one." The weight of the evidence in support of this generalization or "law" of constitutional adjudication of the federal commerce power is overwhelming.[111] Even the possibility of limits just discussed and the caveat noted do not really detract from its validity. For with one minor exception,[112] *United States v. Brown* is the only instance of judicial negation which a careful survey of the time period under consideration reveals. In spite of this clear and irreversible trend, certain political and social events of the 1960's led to an equally clear and determined challenge against the use of this power to effect certain national goals—the elimination of racial segregation in public accommodations and facilities "affecting" commerce and the guarantee of "equal access" to these by all Americans; and this recent, explosive issue requires some individual attention.

Notes

1. The adjective "foreign" here means "out-of-state." This will uniformly be its meaning throughout this discussion unless specifically designated otherwise.

2. 13 Peters 519. In this case, one of the three *Alabama Bank Cases,* Chief Justice Taney held that a state had the power to prevent an out-of-state corporation from doing business within its jurisdiction but that under the principle of comity it would be assumed that the corporation could do business in a state unless the latter expressly forbade such activity; that is, state consent to "foreign" business was implied in the absence of a clear intention to exclude it. For more details on the case, see Carl Brent Swisher, *American Constitutional Development,* 2nd ed. (Cambridge, Mass.: Houghton Mifflin Company, 1954), 221-25. For a more extended discussion, see Maurice G. Baxter, *Daniel Webster & the Supreme Court* (Amherst, Mass.: The University of Massachusetts Press, 1966), 185-94.

3. 8 Wallace 168, 75 U.S. 357.

4. 75 U.S. 357, 361.

5. Examples would include: *Hooper v. California*, 155 U.S. 648 (1895); *New York Life Insurance Company v. Deer Lodge County*, 231 U.S. 495 (1913); *Colgate v. Harvey*, 296 U.S. 404 (1935), in *dictum* at 432.

6. The Sherman Antitrust Act, *U.S. Statutes at Large*, XXVI, 209 (1890), by sections 1 and 2 made such actions illegal.

7. The record of the case and the opposing briefs are to be found in *Records and Briefs of Cases Decided by the Supreme Court of the United States*, Vol. 322, No. 5 (471-708). This source will be referred to hereafter as *Records and Briefs*.

8. "Brief for the United States," *Records and Briefs*, Vol. 322, No. 5 (471-708), 1-133.

9. Ibid., 7. Based on a statement from *New York Life Insurance Co. v. Deer Lodge County*, 231 U.S. 495 at 509: "... if insurance is commerce ... then all control over it is taken from the States."

10. These included: *Thames & Mersey Marine Insurance Company v. United States*, 237 U.S. 19 (1915); *American Medical Ass'n. v. United States*, 317 U.S. 519 (1943).

11. "Brief for the United States," *Records and Briefs*, Vol. 322, No. 5 (471-708), 9. *Darby* and *Wickard* were cited.

12. Ibid., 82-99.

13. Ibid., 123.

14. Three cases were cited to support this generalization: *South Carolina State Highway Department v. Barnwell Bros.*, 303 U.S. 177 (1938); *McGoldrick v. Berwind-White Coal Mining Co.*, 309 U.S. 33 (1940); *Parker v. Brown*, 317 U.S. 341 (1943).

15. "Brief for Appellees," *Records and Briefs*, Vol. 322, No. 5 (471-708), 1-86.

16. See Note 5 for the appropriate citations.

17. "Brief for Appellees," *Records and Briefs*, Vol. 322, No. 5 (471-708), 23-33.

18. Ibid., 34. South-Eastern's counsel used almost half of the brief to show that in regulating insurance the states had generally curtailed competition on the theory that unrestricted competition was not in the public interest. Counsel agreed with this theory but pointed out its

great variance with the principles of the Sherman Act; see ibid., 33-73.

19. 322 U.S. 533. For his complete opinion, see ibid., 534-62. With him were Justices Douglas, Murphy, and Rutledge. Justices Roberts and Reed took no part in the case.

20. Ibid., 538-39.

21. Ibid., 539-43.

22. Ibid., 544.

23. Ibid., 545.

24. Ibid., 545. Here Black cited *Swift & Company v. United States,* 196 U.S. 375 (1905); *Stafford v. Wallace,* 258 U.S. 495 (1922); *Wickard v. Filburn,* 317 U.S. 111 (1942).

25. Ibid., 549.

26. *Champion v. Ames,* 188 U.S. 321 (1903); *Hoke v. United States,* 227 U.S. 308 (1913); *Brooks v. United States,* 267 U.S. 432 (1925); *Pensacola Telegraph Co. v. Western Union Telegraph Co.,* 96 U.S. 1 (1877).

27. 322 U.S. 533, 552.

28. Ibid., 552-53.

29. Ibid., 561.

30. Ibid., 561.

31. For his complete opinion, see ibid., 562-83.

32. Ibid., 568.

33. Ibid., 571.

34. Ibid., 572.

35. Ibid., 579.

36. Ibid., 583.

37. For his complete opinion, see ibid., 583-84.

38. For his complete opinion, see ibid., 584-95.

39. Ibid., 594-95.

40. The *South-Eastern* decision stirred up a storm of criticism. See, for example, *The New York Times,* June 8, 1944; Thomas Reed Powell, "Our High Court Analyses," *The New York Times Magazine,* June 18, 1944. But most of it was based on the fact that the Court had refused to follow precedent. For a behind-the-scenes look at the disagreements among the justices, see Alpheus Thomas Mason, *Harlan Fiske Stone: Pillar of the Law* (New York: The Viking Press, 1956), 617-27. For the view that Justice Black has always disliked monopolies in any form, see John P. Frank, "The New Court and the New Deal," in Stephen Parks Strickland (ed.), *Hugo Black and the Supreme Court: A Symposium* (Indianapolis, Ind.: The Bobbs-Merrill Company, Inc., 1967), 39, 56-67. This may have been one reason why Black was determined to decide the case and was unwilling to join in a proposed *per curiam* compromise (see Mason) which would have affirmed the decision of the District Court but reserved judgment on the constitutional issues to another day.

41. Alfred H. Kelly and Winfred A. Harbison, *The American Constitution: Its Origins and Development,* 3rd ed. (New York: W.W. Norton & Company, Inc., 1963), 777.

42. 322 U.S. 533, 548.

43. For a more extended analysis of Black's views on the Commerce Clause in relation to state power, see the discussion in Chapter 8.

44. Alpheus Thomas Mason and William M. Beaney, *American Constitutional Law: Introductory Essays and Selected Cases,* 4th ed. (Englewood Cliffs, N.J.: Prentice-Hall, Inc., 1968), 166.

45. The specific views of Stone and Jackson on this subject will be analyzed in more detail in Chapter 7. (See Note 43.)

46. 322 U.S. 643.

47. For his complete opinion, see ibid., 643-51. The Alliance operated in 27 states, the District of Columbia, and Canada and engaged in extensive advertising and financing activities across state lines from its headquarters in Chicago, Illinois.

48. Ibid., 650-51.

49. The decision was 8-0; Justice Roberts took no part in the case.

50. For his complete opinion, see 322 U.S. 643, 651-53.

51. *U.S. Statutes at Large*, LIX, 34.

52. "Brief for Appellee," *Records and Briefs*, Vol. 328, No. 8 (395-494), 1-18.

53. Ibid., 13.

54. Ibid., 15.

55. Ibid., 18.

56. "Brief for Appellant," *Records and Briefs*, Vol. 328, No. 8 (395-494), 1-59.

57. Ibid., 3-6 and 14-18. It is interesting to observe the totally different pictures painted of the insurance business by Prudential and South-Eastern Underwriters, due, of course, to the Court's holding that insurance is commerce. The companies, however, were being perfectly consistent in both cases; they wanted to escape governmental regulation, national or state, as much as possible.

58. Ibid., 21.

59. Ibid., 23.

60. Ibid., 23-24, ff. Prudential cited several precedents for its position: *Baldwin v. G.A.F. Seelig, Inc.*, 294 U.S. 511 (1935); *Hale v. Bimco Trading Inc.*, 306 U.S. 375 (1939); *Best & Co. v. Maxwell*, 311 U.S. 454 (1940).

61. Ibid., 42.

62. Prudential's main authority was a statement of Stone's in *South Carolina State Highway Department v. Barnwell Bros.*, 303 U.S. 177 (1938) at 185: "The commerce clause, by its own force, prohibits discrimination against interstate commerce, whatever its form or method." (The case, incidentally, upheld the right of the state to regulate the weight and width of trucks used on its highways.) See Note 68.

63. 328 U.S. 408. The decision was 7-0. Justice Black concurred in the result; Justice Jackson took no part in the case; Chief Justice Stone had died in April. For Rutledge's complete opinion, see ibid., 410-40.

64. Ibid., 412-413.

65. Ibid., 417.

66. Ibid., 418-19.

67. Ibid., 422-23.

68. Ibid., 423-24, Examples included: *Pennsylvania v. Wheeling & Belmont Bridge Co.*, 18 Howard 421 (1856), which upheld an act of Congress declaring that a bridge over the Ohio River, which the Court had ruled earlier obstructed interstate river navigation, was a lawful structure; *In re Rahrer*, 140 U.S. 545 (1891), which upheld the Wilson Act, which provided that intoxicating liquor "upon arrival" in a state was to be subject to the laws of that state; *Clark Distilling Company v. Western Maryland Railway Co.*, 242 U.S. 311 (1917), which upheld the Webb-Kenyon Act, which prohibited the shipment of intoxicating liquor into a state in violation of any law of that state. (For details of the latter two cases, see Chapter 2.)

69. Ibid., 424-25.

70. Ibid., 429.

71. Ibid., 431, for both quotations.

72. Ibid., 433.

73. Ibid., 434-36.

74. 328 U.S. 440.

75. For his complete opinion, see ibid., 443-62. Justice Douglas dissented in part; Justice Jackson took no part; Chief Justice Stone had died.

76. Ibid., 447.

77. There was nothing novel about such a procedure. See the cases in Note 68. Furthermore, the decision in *Panama Refining Co. v. Ryan*, 293 U.S. 388 (1935), had been put to rest by Stone in *Opp Cotton Mills, Inc., v. Administrator*, 312 U.S. 126 (1941). Finally, speaking directly to the subject of divided power, Rutledge had refuted Prudential's claim of unconstitutional delegation of power thus: "Such a conception would reduce the joint exercise of power by Congress and the states to achieve common ends in the regulation of our society below the effective range of either power separately exerted, without basis in specific constitutional limitation or otherwise than in the division itself. We know of no grounding, in either constitutional experience or spirit, for such a restriction." (328 U.S. 408, 439.)

78. The whole question of the extent of state power under the

Commerce Clause will be examined in detail in Chapters 7 and 8.

79. Robert L. Stern, "The Commerce Clause and the National Economy, 1933-1946," *Selected Essays on Constitutional Law: 1938-1962*, compiled and edited by a committee of the Association of American Law Schools (St. Paul, Minn.: West Publishing Co., 1963), 218-79, 278. See ibid., 264-77, for a discussion of federal regulation of utility holding companies, a topic which is not covered in this study.

80. 334 U.S. 219.

81. The record of the case and the opposing briefs are to be found in *Records and Briefs,* Vol. 334, No. 7 (182-249).

82. For his complete opinion, see 334 U.S. 219, 221-46. Justice Jackson, joined by Justice Frankfurter, dissented.

83. Ibid., 228.

84. Ibid., 229.

85. Ibid., 232.

86. Ibid., 232-33.

87. Ibid., 234. (For both quotations.)

88. Ibid., 236.

89. Ibid., 238.

90. Ibid., 241-42.

91. Ibid., 242-43. In the rest of the opinion, Rutledge rejected the technical argument that Mandeville Farms, because it amended its complaint and deleted the allegation that the refiners had conspired to restrain commerce "in sugar," had failed to state a cause of action under the Sherman Act. It was on this point that Jackson dissented; see ibid., 246-49. But he did not question Rutledge's extended analysis of the nature and scope of the federal commerce power, which was the most significant feature of the case.

92. 336 U.S. 460.

93. For his complete opinion, see ibid., 461-65.

94. Ibid., 463.

95. Ibid., 464.

96. *U.S. Statutes at Large,* LII, 1042.

97. 332 U.S. 689.

98. For his complete opinion, see ibid., 690-98. The decision was 6-3. Justice Rutledge wrote a concurring opinion; see ibid., 698-705. Justices Frankfurter, Reed, and Jackson dissented primarily on the ground that the scope of the statute as framed was not clear enough to permit Sullivan's conviction to stand under it; see ibid., 705-07.

99. Ibid., 696.

100. 228 U.S. 115. The Court held that a Wisconsin law, which required certain commodities to bear a state label and no other, could not be applied to articles which had been labeled in accordance with the federal statute.

101. See Robert L. Stern, "The Scope of the Phrase Interstate Commerce," *Selected Essays on Constitutional Law: 1938-1962,* 298-309, for the similar argument that the modern Court is back to Marshall's original interpretation of the commerce power and that therefore that power is now "commensurate with the national needs."

102. *U.S. Statutes at Large,* LXI, 146.

103. 339 U.S. 382. For his complete opinion, see ibid., 385-415. The decision was 5-1. Justices Douglas, Clark, and Minton took no part; Justice Black dissented. Decided at the same time was *United Steelworkers of America v. National Labor Relations Board,* 339 U.S. 382 (1950).

104. Ibid., 390-91.

105. Frankfurter: ibid., 415-22; Jackson: ibid., 422-45. (See the latter for some interesting views on the nature of the Communist Party as different from ordinary political parties.)

106. For his complete opinion, see ibid., 445-53. He dissented wholly on the basis of an infringement of First-Amendment freedoms.

107. *U.S. Statutes at Large,* LXXIII, 536.

108. 381 U.S. 437. For his complete opinion, see ibid., 438-62. Because of this holding, he found it unnecessary to consider the arguments under the First and Fifth Amendments. Justices White, Clark, Harlan, and Stewart dissented; see ibid., 462-78.

109. Ibid., 449-50.

110. Ibid., 456.

111. See Robert L. Stern, "The Problems of Yesteryear—Commerce and Due Process," in Robert G. McCloskey (ed.), *Essays in Constituional Law* (New York: Vintage Books, 1957), 150-80, for added proof of this proposition.

112. *United States v. Five Gambling Devices,* 346 U.S. 441 (1953), in which a congressional act of January 2, 1951 (*U.S. Statutes at Large,* LXIV, 1134), which prohibited the shipment of gambling machines in interstate commerce (except where state law provided for gambling) and required manufacturers and dealers to register with the Attorney General and report their monthly sales and deliveries to him, was delcared unconstitutional for vagueness. Even this decision was 5-4, with Chief Justice Warren among the dissenters.

6   Civil Rights

The era since the Supreme Court's landmark decision in *Brown v. Board of Education of Topeka* (1954)[1] has been very aptly described as that of "the Negro Revolution." From the time of their legal (even if not de facto) emancipation from segregated schooling to the present moment, Negro Americans have sought with increasing vigor to claim for themselves the liberties and privileges of United States citizenship which they have all too often been denied (particularly in certain sections of the country), and which white Americans take for granted. In fact, it is probably not too much to assert that America's most pressing domestic problem is that of granting equal civil rights and equal economic opportunity to its minority groups, whether they be Negro, Mexican, Puerto Rican, or native Indian. But the first-named group is, of course, the most numerous and is the one which occupies the center of the national stage in the drive for personal equality. Consequently, this chapter will examine closely the ways in which the Commerce Clause of the federal Constitution has been utilized by both the Supreme Court and Congress to further the cause of Negro rights.

At first glance, it may seem incongruous to associate the Commerce Clause and its clear relation to economic regulation with the current struggle for human dignity and individual rights. But the fact is that the Commerce Clause has played a major role over the past quarter century in the efforts of the federal government to secure "equal justice under law" for American minority groups in general and Negroes in particular. The history of the use of the clause to this end falls very nicely for purposes of analysis into two main sections.

The first part of the chronicle deals with the Supreme Court alone; in the period from 1941 to 1963 it interpreted the Commerce Clause to forbid state infringements of the individual right to unembarrassed interstate movement and to uphold state guarantees of individual freedom from racial discrimination in situations closely connected with interstate commerce. The Court thus took an early lead in advancing Negro rights via its traditional role as final arbiter of national-state powers in commercial matters.[2] The second and really more important part of the story concerns congressional action and the Court's response to it; in the Civil Rights Act of 1964,[3] Title II, Congress prohibited racial discrimination in the use of public accommodations and public places of amusement based upon its power under the Commerce Clause and under sections 1 and 5 of the Fourteenth Amendment. It seems fair to say that this action was taken because a majority of the American people approved of it and felt that it was time (or past time) to end second-class citizenship in the United States after a century of neglect. However, the issue was not this cut and dried; the provisions of Title II evoked strenuous and determined attack from many quarters—both in and out of Congress, and it was inevitable that its constitutionality would be tested before the Supreme Court. How the Court responded to this recent positive action of Congress and the objections raised against it, then, will form the major part of the analysis to be made here.

Early Decisions, 1941–1948

The Supreme Court was the branch of the federal government which took the lead in using the Commerce Clause as a legal weapon against racial discrimination. A bit of historical background will show how this came about. In his decision in *Gibbons v. Ogden* (1824) John Marshall defined commerce to include the transportation of passengers for hire. This holding that the movement of persons was a part of commerce became the generally accepted rule[4] and was reaffirmed early in this century in *Hoke v. United States* (1913),[5] which upheld the federal Mann Act prohibiting the transportation of women across state lines for immoral purposes. The next commerce case involving persons was *Edwards v. California* (1941).[6] The state had passed a law which made it a misdemeanor for any person to bring, or assist in bringing, into the state any nonresident of the state, knowing him to be an indigent person, i.e., a person "so destitute of means" for the support of himself and his family "as to be dependent on public aid." The Act was designed to protect California from an influx of people from the Great Plains who had been made poor by the dust bowl conditions and depressed farm prices of the 1930's and who were seeking the comfort of the state's mild climate and liberal welfare programs. This naturally created large social and economic problems for even the "Golden State." Edwards brought his brother-in-law into California, knowing he was indigent, and was tried and convicted of the misdemeanor. He appealed his conviction.

The opposing arguments before the Supreme Court were simple and straightforward.[7] Counsel for Edwards argued that the state statute imposed a definite, arbitrary burden on interstate commerce in that it impeded the free movement of employables across state lines and imposed a barrier against the competition of the labor of nonresidents; thus it unconstitutionally invaded the power of the national government over such commerce. California contended that the law was merely a valid exercise of the state's police power, designed to protect its own citizens from the staggering problems of higher taxes due to swollen public relief rolls, epidemics of disease resulting from malnutrition and lack of sanitation among the migrants, and a tremendous increase in the incidence of local crime; the Act was clearly sustainable under the holding in *New York v. Miln* (1837) that a state could exclude paupers even though this might have an incidental effect on commerce.

By a vote of nine to nothing the Court struck down the California exclusion policy. Justice James F. Byrnes wrote the majority opinion which held that the statute was "an unconstitutional barrier to interstate commerce."[8] He began with the flat statement that the transportation of persons is "commerce" within the constitutional meaning of that term. He next admitted that the justices were well aware of the "grave and perplexing" problems faced by the state and that it was not their function to pass upon "the wisdom, need, or appropriateness" of state legislative efforts to solve such problems. Then he explained the Court's reasoning in invalidating the Act:

> But this does not mean that there are no boundaries to the permissible area of State legislative activity. There are. And none is more certain than the prohibition against attempts on the part of any single State to isolate itself from difficulties common to all of them by restraining the transportation of persons and property across its borders. It is frequently the case that a State might gain a momentary respite from the pressure of events by the simple expedient of shutting its gates to the outside world. But, in the

words of Justice Cardozo: "The Constitution was framed under the dominion of a political philosophy less parochial in range. It was framed upon the theory that the peoples of the several states must sink or swim together, and that in the long run prosperity and salvation are in union and not division."

...It is difficult to conceive of a statute more squarely in conflict with this theory than the Section challenged here. Its express purpose and inevitable effect is to prohibit the transportation of indigent persons across the California border. The burden upon interstate commerce is intended and immediate; it is the plain and sole function of the statute.[9]

This settled the case, but Byrnes went on to point out that public relief was no longer solely the responsibility of local government, that it had now become the common responsibility of the nation, and that the social phenomenon of large-scale interstate migration was a matter of national concern which did not admit of diverse treatment by the states; in other words, the subject clearly fell within that class of subjects which were of such a nature as to demand that their regulation must be prescribed by a single authority. Finally, he simply dismissed the precedent of *New York v. Miln* as no longer controlling; poverty could not be considered synonymous with "moral pestilence," and the California law could not be accepted as a legitimate exercise of the state's police power.

The decision stood for the general proposition that the Commerce Clause conferred upon all persons the right to move freely from state to state; the Court had, in effect, used the federal commerce power to "create" an individual or personal constitutional guarantee, and it was not long before the opportunity arose to use this federally protected right as a club to strike at discriminatory state laws affecting interstate transportation. A Virginia statute of 1930 (updated in 1942) required all passenger motor-vehicle carriers, both interstate and intrastate, to separate the white and colored passengers in their motor buses so that contiguous seats would not be occupied by persons of different races at the same time; a violation of this requirement was a misdemeanor by the carrier and by the operator. On an interstate bus trip from Gloucester County, Virginia, through the District of Columbia to Baltimore, Maryland, Irene Morgan, a Negro, refused to change seats as requested. The operator caused her to be arrested; she was then tried and convicted for a violation of the Virginia code. She appealed her conviction (and was represented by Thurgood Marshall, among others) to the Supreme Court on the ground that the state statute was a burden on commerce and thus repugnant to the Commerce Clause. Virginia argued that the law was a legitimate exercise of the state's police power; it had been designed to prevent unnecessary friction between the two races and so to promote civil peace and order.

On June 3, 1946, the case of *Morgan v. Virginia*[10] was decided. Justice Stanley F. Reed delivered the majority opinion which invalidated the state statute.[11] He admitted that the "precise degree" of restriction on state authority "cannot be fixed generally," but he asserted that there was "a recognized abstract principle . . . for testing whether particular state legislation in the absence of action by Congress is beyond state power."[12] The principle, though abstract in nature and requiring case-by-case application, could be thus formulated: "[S]tate legislation is invalid if it unduly burdens that commerce in matters where uniformity is necessary—necessary in the constitutional sense of useful in accomplishing a permitted purpose. Where uniformity is essential for the functioning of commerce, a state may not interpose its local regulation."[13]

Reed then turned his attention to the Virginia law and held that it had the effect of requiring interstate bus passengers "to order their movements on the vehicle in accordance with local rather than national requirements."[14] Thus such passengers could be made to change seats at any time during a trip, an obviously disturbing factor on the new large buses with their reclining seats designed for convenient rest. Also pertinent was the fact that the states had different regulations; 18 states prohibited any racial separation on public carriers, but 10 states specifically required it; the result was a confusion of transportation rules which only exacerbated the difficulties of interstate travel in an era when the volume of such travel was on the increase. It was clear that the state regulation represented an actual obstruction to commerce and that under the Court's ruling in *Hall v. DeCuir* (1878)[15] it could not be allowed to stand. In the final analysis, the issue turned on a "balance between the exercise of the local police power and the need for national uniformity in the regulations for interstate travel," and Reed concluded that "seating arrangements for the different races in interstate motor travel require a single, uniform rule to promote and protect national travel."[16]

This holding rendered the state statute null and void. Justice Harold H. Burton dissented;[17] he believed that the appellant simply had not produced the facts and findings essential to demonstrate a "serious and major burden" on interstate commerce. He recognized the different conditions which existed in the country as evidenced by the very diversity of state legislation and reasoned that this, together with the absence of any positive action by Congress, undermined the Court's assumption that a "single uniform national rule" was required. But whatever the practical merits of his argument, it was obviously unacceptable to the majority; by 1946 the Commerce Clause was being fashioned into an instrument for protecting minority rights in matters in any way associated with commerce among the states or with foreign nations. *Morgan v. Virginia* illustrated the interstate application; a 1948 case related to foreign commerce.

The State of Michigan had on its books an anti-discrimination law which forbade the operators of "public conveyances" from refusing service to anyone because of race, creed, or color. The Bob-Lo Excursion Company was a Michigan corporation which was engaged chiefly in the round-trip transportation of passengers from Detroit to Bois Blanc Island, Canada. The company owned almost all of the island and operated it as a place of amusement for Detroit people; it excluded anyone who was disorderly or who was colored. A group from Commerce High School made arrangements with the company to take an outing to the island; all of the members of the class were allowed to go except for a Negro girl who was refused passage. The company was subjected to criminal prosecution and found guilty; it appealed its conviction to the United States Supreme Court mainly on the grounds that since it was engaged in foreign commerce (with the Canadian island), the Commerce Clause prohibited this particular application of the state's civil rights legislation.

The case of *Bob-Lo Excursion Co. v. Michigan*[18] was decided on February 2, 1948. Justice Wiley B. Rutledge wrote the majority opinion which upheld the Michigan statute.[19] He first noted that the appellant's transportation of its patrons to the island was foreign commerce and that the Court needed to be "watchful of state intrusion into intercourse between this country and one of its neighbors."[20] But this was a unique situation. There were no regular means of communication from the Canadian side to the island, and the company's business was insulated from "all commercial or social intercourse and traffic with the people of another country usually characteristic of foreign commerce."[21] Thus it appeared that the *Cooley* rule was applicable:

> It would be hard to find a substantial business touching foreign soil of more highly local concern. . . . [T]he island is economi-

cally and socially, though not politically, an amusement adjunct of the city of Detroit. . . . As now conducted, . . . the business is of greater concern to Detroit and the State of Michigan than to Dominion or Ontario interests or to those of the United States in regulating our foreign commerce.[22]

By the same token (that is, the distinctly local nature of the commerce), the precedents of *Hall v. DeCuir* and *Morgan v. Virginia* could not be considered as controlling. Rutledge drove home the point regarding Michigan's dominant interest:

It is difficult to imagine what national interest or policy, whether of securing uniformity in regulating commerce affecting relations with foreign nations or otherwise, could reasonably be found to be adversely affected by applying Michigan's statute to these facts or to outweigh her interest in doing so. . . . [T] he ruling would be strange indeed, to come from this Court, that Michigan could not apply her long-settled policy against racial and creedal discrimination to this segment of foreign commerce, so peculiarly and almost exclusively affecting her people and institutions.[23]

The state requirement imposed no undue burden on the appellant in its business in foreign commerce and so had to stand.

Bob-Lo Excursion Co. v. Michigan was a prime example of the Court refusing to use the Commerce Clause to strike down state legislation directed against racial discrimination, even though that legislation might incidentally affect interstate or foreign commerce. But again the decision was too much for all of the Court's members. Justice Robert H. Jackson dissented;[24] he thought first that the majority opinion failed to lay down any fixed standards by which to judge "when foreign commerce is foreign enough to become free of local regulation." Then he took his usual hard line toward state regulation of that commerce which the Constitution had committed to the national government: "I believe that once it is conceded, as it is in this case, that the commerce involved is foreign commerce, that fact alone should be enough to prevent a state from controlling what may, or what must, move in the stream of that commerce."[25] However, like Burton, Jackson was fighting a losing battle. The federal Commerce Clause was now a constitutional weapon which could be employed either affirmatively or negatively by the Court to serve the ends of promoting racial justice and prohibiting discrimination in areas connected with commercial intercourse.

Later Precedents, 1960–1963

As shown previously, the years from the late 1940's until the early 1960's saw a new trend in Supreme Court expansion and protection of basic American civil rights for minority groups as the Court developed the equal-protection clause of the Fourteenth Amendment into a major vehicle for invalidating discriminatory state legislation. The advent of the 1960's, however, brought with it a return to Commerce-Clause adjudication. The first case of major importance was *Boynton v. Commonwealth of Virginia*,[26] decided on December 5, 1960. Boynton, a Negro, purchased a Trailways Bus Company ticket from Washington, D.C., to Montgomery, Alabama. On a stopover at Richmond, Virginia, he went into the Trailways Bus Terminal and found a segregated restaurant where he sought service on the "white" side and was denied. He was asked to move to the "colored" part, but he refused and was arrested, tried, and convicted for unlawfully remaining on the premises after having been forbidden to do so by the assistant manager of the restaurant. Represented by Thurgood Marshall, he appealed his conviction to the Supreme Court on the ground that he had "a federal right as an interstate passenger of Trailways to be served without discrimination by this restaurant used by the bus carrier for the accommodation of its interstate passengers"[27] and so was on the premises lawfully. Discrimination here (and state enforcement of it) would be an unconstitutional burden on commerce under the Commerce Clause and a violation of the due-process and equal-protection clauses of the Fourteenth Amendment. Virginia countered with the argument that the conviction for trespass represented a valid application of the state's police power.

By a vote of seven to two the Court upheld Boynton's claim and reversed his conviction. Justice Hugo L. Black, author of the majority opinion, first admitted that two constitutional questions involving the Commerce Clause and the Fourteenth Amendment had been posed, but he declined to reach them since he thought that the case could be decided on the basis of a conflict between federal and state law in which the former would, of course, have to prevail.[28] To understand Black's reasoning it is necessary to digress for a moment and look at the interpretation of a federal statute in two earlier cases.

Section 3 (1) of the Interstate Commerce Act[29] made it unlawful for an interstate carrier "to subject any particular person . . . to any undue or unreasonable prejudice or disadvantage in any respect whatsoever." In *Mitchell v. United States* (1941)[30] Chief Justice Hughes held that the Act prohibited an interstate railroad from refusing first-class accommodations to a Negro (and a member of the United States House of Representatives) who was willing to pay for them. Such action, Hughes said, "was manifestly a discrimination against him in the course of his interstate journey [from Memphis, Tennessee, to Hot Springs, Arkansas] and admittedly that discrimination was based solely upon the fact that he was a Negro."[31] The denial of equal accommodations because of race was "essentially unjust" and a violation of the federal act which specifically safeguarded the "fundamental right of equality of treatment." Almost a decade later in *Henderson v. United States* (1950) the Court again used the act to forbid the Southern Railway Company from dividing its dining cars by means of a curtain, allotting 10 tables exclusively to white passengers and one table exclusively to Negroes, and forcing the latter to wait their turn even if space were available at the "white" tables. Justice Burton based his unanimous (8-0) opinion very largely upon the *Mitchell* precedent.[32]

Based upon the decisions in *Mitchell* and *Henderson,* the question in the *Boynton* case then became whether the application of the Virginia law in this particular instance violated the Interstate Commerce Act. Black thought it was clear that interstate buses could not supply discriminatory dining service "in transit" or "in terminals and terminal restaurants owned or operated or controlled by interstate carriers."[33] But the record showed that the Trailways Bus Company neither owned nor actively operated nor directly controlled either the bus terminal or the restaurant in it. In answer to this factual circumstance, Black took the last one-third of his opinion to show the close connection between the operation of the restaurant and the transportation of interstate travelers. He pointed to the indisputable facts that the terminal building "constituted one project for a single purpose"—to serve passengers of bus companies, that all the various activities within the terminal "were geared to the service of bus companies and their passengers," and that here was "a well-coordinated and smoothly functioning plan for continuous cooperative transportation services between the terminal, the restaurant and buses like Trailways."[34] The inescapable conclusion had to be drawn:

> This bus terminal plainly was just as essential and necessary, and as available for that matter, to passengers and carriers like Trailways that used it, as though such carriers had legal title and complete control over all of its activities. Interstate passengers have to eat. . . . Such passengers . . . had a right to expect that this essential transportation food service . . . would be rendered without discrimination prohibited by the Interstate Commerce Act.[35]

Thus Boynton had "a federal right" under the federal law to remain in the "white" part of the restaurant, and the state conviction for trespass could not stand. Obviously, the Court was willing to apply the act to a "local" restaurant on the ground that its operations were so closely intertwined with interstate commerce that it could not escape the federal demand of nondiscriminatory treatment of interstate travelers. But Black carefully limited the scope of the statute's reach: "We are not holding that every time a bus stops at a wholly independent roadside restaurant the Interstate Commerce Act requires that restaurant service be supplied in harmony with the provisions of that Act."[36]

A second case of importance was *Colorado Anti-Discrimination Commission v. Continental Air Lines, Inc.* (1963).[37] The Colorado Anti-Discrimination Act of 1957 prohibited employers from discriminating against job applicants because of race, creed, color, national origin, or ancestry. The state Commission charged with enforcement of the Act found that Continental Air Lines, an interstate air carrier, had refused to hire a pilot because he was a Negro; it ordered the airline to cease and desist from such illegal practices. Continental appealed the ruling, and the Supreme Court of Colorado dismissed the order on the ground that under the *Cooley* rule the state law imposed an undue burden on interstate commerce. The Commission in turn appealed this decision.

On April 22, 1963, the United States Supreme Court reversed the state court. Justice Black wrote the unanimous opinion which upheld the Colorado statute.[38] He began with the premise that the line "separating the powers of a State from the exclusive power of Congress is not always distinctly marked"; therefore, it was necessary to make a case-by-case analysis "to determine whether the dangers and hardships of diverse regulation justify foreclosing a State from the exercise of its traditional powers."[39] This was what the Court had done in *Morgan v. Virginia* and *Bob-Lo Excursion Co. v. Michigan.* On this basis he thought that requiring Continental Air Lines to refrain from discriminatory hiring practices would not unduly burden the operation of commercial air travel: "Not only is the hiring within a State of an employee, even for an interstate job, a much more localized matter than the transporting of passengers from State to State but more significantly the threat of diverse and conflicting regulation of hiring practices is virtually nonexistent."[40] While it might be possible for states to impose such "onerous, harassing, and conflicting conditions" on hiring that transportation service could be impaired, such was not the case here. The Colorado statute did not impose "a constitutionally prohibited burden upon interstate commerce," nor was it in conflict with any relevant federal laws. Black's decision was in perfect harmony with the decisions in *Morgan* and *Bob-Lo Excursion Co.;* the Court would use the Commerce Clause only to prevent or strike down racial discrimination.

The Civil Rights Act of 1964

The scene of major civil rights action now shifted from the judicial department to the legislative branch of the federal government. As the 1960's wore on, the demands of Negro Americans and their allies for equality of treatment and opportunity grew more insistent and became less amenable to pleas for delay and time to adjust. "Sit-ins" and other kinds of peaceful demonstrations became more and more frequent; then violence of various types erupted here and there on both sides; and finally, actual riots took place in a number of cities—North and South. To deal with the increasing racial unrest, President John F. Kennedy on June 19, 1963, submitted a bill to Congress calling for a wholesale attack upon the problems of civil rights. Among other things he asked for legislation to help guarantee Negroes the right to vote, to provide for equal access to privately owned places of public accommodation, to authorize the Justice Department to sue to desegrate public schools and other facilities, to require most companies and labor unions to grant equal employment opportunity, to extend the life of the Civil Rights Commission for four years and give it new powers, to establish a Community Relations Service to help work out civil rights problems at the local level, and to require the Census Bureau to gather voting statistics by race in order to determine where deprivation of the ballot might be occurring. In preface to this omnibus request, the President said in a nation-wide television address on June 11: "We are confronted primarily with a moral issue"; and it was in this spirit that a good many Congressmen took up their legislative cudgels to do battle for what would become the Civil Rights Act of 1964.

Most of the proposals in the omnibus bill were merely extensions of protections which had been incorporated into the prior Civil Rights Acts of 1957 and 1960. But the "symbolic heart" of the new statute was the positive guarantee of the right of free and equal access to privately owned public accommodations, such as hotels, motels, restaurants, and places of amusement. It was this "radical and revolutionary" proposal which, more than any other, created the most violent opposition and the most determined defense, both inside and outside of Congress.

The recommendations began their long and torturous journey through the legislative mill. In the House of Representatives, Subcommittee No. 5 of the Committee on the Judiciary, chaired by Emanuel Cellar (D.–N.Y.), held extensive hearings on the whole bill, reported out a stronger version than that asked by the Administration, and then hammered out a compromise package with the Administration and the Republican minority on the Committee. In the Senate the public-accommodations section was introduced as a separate measure (S. 1732) and sent to the Committee on Commerce for action. Under the chairmanship of Senator Warren G. Magnuson (D.–Wash.), hearings were held from July 1 to August 2, 1963, and forty witnesses were called and allowed to testify; in addition, opinions were sought and received from law school deans and professors, private lawyers, state governors, state attorney-generals, and various governmental agencies. In short, the most thorough consideration was given to the profound legal, constitutional, and policy questions which were at issue.

The Commerce Committee delivered its official report on February 10, 1964, and recommended the adoption of S. 1732.[41] As it turned out, S. 1732 was set aside in favor of the omnibus bill passed by the House, Title II of which contained the same basic public-accommodations provisions.[42] In the final draft of the legislation which was passed and signed by President Lyndon B. Johnson on July 2, 1964, Title II provided that: "All persons shall be entitled to the full and equal enjoyment of the goods, services, facilities, privileges, advantages, and accommodations of any place of public accommodation . . . without discrimination or segregation on the ground of race, color, religion, or national origin."[43] The Act went on to list four classes of business establishments designated as places of public accommodation and the circumstances under which they would "affect commerce" and hence be covered: (1) any inn, hotel, motel, or other establishment which provided lodging to transient guests (unless it had five rooms or less for rent and was actually occupied by the proprietor) affected commerce per se; (2) any restaurant, cafeteria, lunchroom, lunch counter, soda fountain, or other facility "principally engaged in selling food for consumption on the premises" affected commerce if it served or offered to serve interstate travelers or if a substantial portion of the food or other products sold had "moved in commerce," and any gasoline station; (3) any motion picture house, theater, concert hall, sports arena, stadium, or other place of exhibition or entertainment affected commerce if it customarily presented films, performances, or athletic teams which moved in commerce; and (4) any establishment which was "physically located within the premises of any establishment otherwise covered" and which held itself out "as serving patrons of such covered establishment" affected commerce. Bona fide private clubs were specifically exempted. Remedies were provided for violations of the Act, but they were limited to civil actions for preventive relief. The Attorney General was given authority to intervene in behalf of aggrieved persons, and United States district courts were vested with jurisdiction.

Such were the far-reaching provisions of Title II; and in incorporating them into the Civil Rights Act of 1964, Congress confidently rested their constitutionality squarely upon the Commerce Clause and sections 1 and 5 of the Fourteenth Amendment. Although both bases were relied upon, only the arguments arising under the use of the Commerce Clause are of concern here for two reasons: (1) It is quite beyond the range of this study to analyze the numerous and involved issues pertaining to the scope of congressional power under the Fourteenth Amendment; and (2) when the constitutionality of Title II was questioned before the Supreme Court, the Court looked only to Commerce-Clause considerations to determine the outcome and specifically declined to discuss Fourteenth-Amendment questions. Consequently, the present discussion will be limited to the scope of congressional power under the Commerce Clause.

Constitutional Arguments

The legal test of Title II was not long in coming. From Georgia and Alabama suits were brought to determine the constitutionality of the public-accommodations sections. The Heart of Atlanta Motel, a large enterprise with most of its guests from out of state, refused to accept Negro travelers and was sued by the government for violation of the Act. The District Court upheld the Act, and the motel owner appealed the decision to the Supreme Court. Similarly, in Birmingham, Ollie's Barbecue, a family-owned restaurant buying large quantities of meat which had moved interstate, refused to serve Negroes and sought an injunction against application of the Act to its "local" business. (Ollie McClung, the owner, wanted to test the law before it was applied to a national chain of restaurants such as Howard Johnson's, which most surely would be covered.) The District Court held that the Act could not be applied to Ollie's because "there was no demonstrable connection between food purchased in interstate commerce ... and the conclusion of Congress that discrimination in the restaurant would affect that commerce." The Attorney General appealed this adverse decision, and the case was decided simultaneously with the one involving the motel.

Under the Commerce Clause

The opposing arguments fall rather nicely into two main categories: (1) the scope of the commerce power per se and its effect upon the American federal system, and (2) Fifth-Amendment limitations on governmental regulation of private property and free entrepreneurial choice. These arguments will be taken mostly from the hearings conducted before the Senate Committee on Commerce, from the debates in Congress, and from the opposing law briefs filed with the Supreme Court in the two major cases which challenged the constitutionality of Title II. These three primary sources have been chosen because they furnish samples of the ablest and most lucid contentions made on both sides and because they fairly represent all shades of opinion.

Supporters of Title II very often began their defense of it by stressing the moral problem which the statute sought to solve—the daily humiliation, degradation, and affront to human dignity caused by racial discrimination in places of public accommodation throughout the nation. But they always turned to the economic aspects of this widespread practice, its deleterious effects upon the national economy, and the appropriateness of using the Commerce Clause as a basis for outlawing such discrimination. In regard to the latter, the arguments were numerous and substantial. First, it was a recognized principle of long-standing that the delegated power of Congress to regulate commerce among the states authorized "all appropriate legislation" for the protection, advancement, or control of interstate or foreign commerce and that Congress had utilized this power on numerous occasions to regulate monopolies and combinations in restraint of trade, to strike at price fixing and other unfair competitive business practices, to prohibit unfair labor practices, to determine the wage-and-hour standards under which labor could be employed, to set limits on agricultural production, to protect the public from impure food and drugs and from unsafe appliances, to outlaw interstate gambling and prostitution, and to forbid the transportation of stolen vehicles across state lines. In testifying in favor of S. 1732, Attorney General Robert F. Kennedy drew the obvious analogy; he reasoned that since Congress controlled the method of serving oleomargarine in every restaurant, "surely it can insure our nonwhite citizens access to those restaurants," and since Congress specified the labeling for every bottle of aspirin in every drug store, "surely it is no deprivation of anyone's liberty to permit Negroes to shop and to eat there."[44] This same point was made by Paul A. Freund, a law professor at Harvard University, in a brief attached to Magnuson's report. Freund noted that discrimination of one kind or another had been a common target of congressional legislation under the Commerce Clause—antiunion discrimination in the hiring and discharging of employees and discrimination in the pricing of goods to purchasers, to cite only two examples.[45]

Second, the principle was equally well established that this power included the power to regulate local activities which might have a substantial and harmful effect upon interstate commerce. The classic example here, of course, was the Supreme Court's decision in *National Labor Relations Board v. Jones & Laughlin Steel Corporation* (1937). The argument was amplified again by Freund, who pointed out that the increasingly great mobility of persons and goods in American society had transformed many problems, "otherwise local," into issues of national concern. Congress had developed two major legislative techniques to deal with such problems: One was to regulate practices "local in themselves" that substantially affected commerce (National Labor Relations Act); the second was to prohibit the use of the channels of interstate commerce in instances in which such use facilitated an evil or abuse (Fair Labor Standards Act).[46] S. 1732 followed the first pattern, and Freund thought that its findings were well within the mold of pervious legislation which rested upon the effects of local practices on "commerce among the States." In short, the power was there; the matter was one of policy:

> The question is whether the same power that has been used in the interest of preventing deception, disease, and immorality, as well as discrimination against members of unions and against small business, shall be utilized in the interest of preventing discrimination among patrons of establishments whose practices have repercussions throughout the land and which take advantage of the facilities of our national commercial market for their patronage or their supplies or both.[47]

Erwin N. Griswold, Dean of Harvard University Law School, agreed with this position. In testimony before the Senate Commerce Committee, he was direct and forceful: "In my judgment, Congress has authority under the Constitution to provide a complete remedy for the discriminatory denial of access to places of public accommodations. This power can be exercised pursuant to the Commerce Clause."[48] Citing the many uses that Congress had made of the commerce power, Dean Griswold stressed the point about its reach to local activities:

> It is equally clear that when Congress is dealing with a subject appropriate for legislation it has plenary authority to achieve its objectives. Congressional authority is not limited to the regulation of commerce among the States. It extends, as the Supreme Court said in United States v. Darby: "to those activities intrastate which so affect interstate commerce or the exercise of power of the Congress over it as to make regulation of them appropriate means to the attainment of a legitimate end, the exercise of the granted power of Congress to regulate interstate commerce." In practice this has meant the regulation of intrastate transactions when they are—"so comingled with or related to interstate commerce that all must be regulated if interstate commerce is to be effectively controlled."[49]

Third, proponents of Title II emphasized the fact that the constitutional test of the act in any given case would not turn upon the effect of the individual practices of a particular establishment on interstate commerce, but upon the aggregate or cumulative effect that such discriminatory practices in many establishments similarly situated throughout the country would have upon the commerce. The leading precedent in support of this proposition was *Wickard v. Filburn* (1942). Freund in his brief also referred to *Polish National Alliance v. National Labor Relations Board* (1944), and another precedent frequently mentioned was the *per curiam* decision in *National Labor Relations Board v. Reliance Fuel Oil Corporation* (1963).[50] Perhaps a report filed with Subcommittee No. 5 of the House Judiciary Committee by the Bar Association of New York City summed up this facet of the argument in the most sweeping language:

> Even if an activity or transaction considered in isolation is both intrastate in character and insubstantial in its impact on interstate commerce, Congress may legislate with regard to the aggregate impact or burden on interstate commerce of all such activities or transactions. The power reaches not only activities which are purely "commercial" in nature, but, in furtherance of particular public policies, can be, and has been, used to reach noncommercial activities.[51]

206

Fourth, the motives and purpose of Congress in passing the public-accommodations bill were irrelevant to its validity. Or to put it another way, the fact that Congress was seeking to deal with a moral and social—rather than a strictly economic—problem did not impair or diminish its authority under the Commerce Clause. Many precedents supported this principle: *Champion v. Ames* (1903), *Hoke v. United States* (1913), *Brooks v. United States* (1925), and the more recent cases involving application of the Interstate Commerce Act, namely, *Mitchell v. United States* (1941) and *Henderson v. United States* (1950). Writing to Senators Hubert H. Humphrey (D.—Minn.) and Thomas H. Kuchel (R.—Calif.), floor managers for the bill, Harrison Tweed of New York City and Bernard G. Segal of Philadelphia spoke to this contention. They were joined by an illustrious group: three former United States Attorney Generals—Francis Biddle, Herbert Brownell, and William P. Rogers and four law school deans—Erwin N. Griswold (Harvard University), William B. Lockhart (University of Minnesota), Eugene V. Rostow (Yale University), and John W. Wade (Vanderbilt University), among others. Countering the argument that Congress was not attempting to correct a primarily economic problem and hence was using its commerce power improperly, they said:

> Although racial discrimination may or may not have the same commercial motivation as the economic restrictions involved in antitrust and similar violations, a legislative judgment of the adverse effect of such discrimination on the freedom or volume of the interstate movement of people and goods cannot, under the decided cases, be subject to serious doubt. Whatever its nature, a practice which has a detrimental or limiting effect on commerce may be reached by the Congress under the commerce clause.[52]

The preceding four principles were the ones upon which the supporters of Title II (and the government) rested the case for its constitutionality. Only one point remained: to show the actual economic burden of discrimination in public accommodations upon commerce. Before the Senate Commerce Committee three witnesses in particular—Attorney General Kennedy, Secretary of Labor W. Willard Wirtz, and Undersecretary of Commerce Franklin D. Roosevelt, Jr.—stressed the factual connections. Roosevelt's testimony was full, detailed, and impressive. He began with the straightforward assertion that "segregation imposes unnatural limitations in the conduct of business which are injurious to the free flow of commerce."[53] Then the Undersecretary listed six specific detrimental effects attributable to the practice:

(1) obstacles to interstate travel; (2) distortions in the pattern of expenditures by Negroes because of limited access to places of public accommodations; (3) limitations on the ability of organizations to hold national and regional conventions in convenient places; (4) adverse effects in the entertainment field; (5) disruptions in trade resulting from demonstrations protesting discrimination in retail establishments; and (6) numerous other hurdles to the normal conduct of business—for example, difficulties in recruiting professional and skilled personnel and rejection of otherwise desirable plant locations.[54]

Concrete examples and statistical surveys were presented to substantiate the burden in each case upon the national economy.

Roosevelt took up the points one-by-one. With respect to travel, he produced a booklet entitled *GO-Guide to Pleasant Motoring,* published for Negroes, which listed motels, hotels, and other facilities open to anyone, to show the relative scarcity of places serving Negroes and to demonstrate the frequency of the long distances between places of decent accommodations for them. He thought it obvious that the resulting physical discomfort and personal humiliation could not help but reduce the amount of interstate travel by Negroes. Similarly, he produced statistics to show that at the same income level, Negroes in the North spent more than Southern Negroes for entertainment admissions, food eaten away from home, and automobile operations, whereas again at the same income level, Southern whites spent more than Northern whites in all three categories—the clear implication being that segregated facilities discouraged such discretionary spending by Southern Negroes.

The story was the same in other ways. Instances were cited of national organizations such as the American Legion transferring their convention sites from one city to another because of lack of facilities for their Negro members. Although one city's lost tourist business might be another's gain, this still represented an artificial barrier to free economic choice. It extended to the entertainment field where companies such as the Metropolitan Opera might cancel engagements rather than perform for segregated audiences and thus deprive entire areas of a variety of cultural advantages. Finally, evidence was introduced to show the adverse effects of discrimination upon business in general and business location and expansion in particular. Statistics confirmed the sharp drop in industrial investment in Arkansas after the Little Rock episode of 1957 and the decline in retail sales in Birmingham, Alabama, following the spring demonstrations of 1963; and news stories from

The Wall Street Journal illustrated the difficulties of business in getting qualified professional people and skilled technicians to work in areas where segregation was practiced. The burdens upon commerce were "close and substantial."

Despite all of the carefully marshalled principles of constitutional law and the masses of economic evidence available to support the validity of Title II, the opponents of the bill maintained that it exceeded congressional power under the Commerce Clause. The basic reason was simple: This use of the commerce power distorted its traditional scope; that is, its application here went far beyond any previously established boundary line of federal control. In his "individual views" in the Senate Report on S. 1732 J. Strom Turmond of South Carolina explained the point in full:

> This measure constitutes a radical departure from previous areas of regulation which Congress has seen fit to authorize under the commerce clause. S. 1732 does not regulate the means of transportation, the goods which are transported, nor the methods under which the goods are either manufactured or produced. It would regulate the very method of operation which an individual businessman, of his own free will and accord, has elected to follow. Such an attempt does violence to the intent of the commerce power and would pave the way for further encroachments upon private business.[55]

To show the extent of the perversion, the Southerners discussed the original intention of the Constitution's framers regarding the Commerce Clause. Senator Thurmond noted that during the first two months of the Philadelphia Convention almost all of the delegates' references to the power to regulate commerce was to the power to pass "navigation acts." From this circumstance he thought that one conclusion was plain: "Neither in the Constitutional Convention or in any of the ratifying conventions was there anything said or even hinted at which indicated that the power to regulate commerce might be perverted into the power to regulate the use of purely private property at rest within the confines of any particular State."[56] Furthermore, it could not be overemphasized or repeated often enough that the most fundamental principle of the Constitution was the "separation of powers" between the states and the national government. This doctrine was basic to the American federal system and reflected the belief of the "Founding Fathers" that local self-government was preferable for the large majority of governmental functions.

Moreton Rolleston, Jr., who was the owner of the Heart of Atlanta Motel and who acted as his own counsel, agreed with Thurmond. He argued that the genius of the Constitution was that it had created a federal republic whose "singular strength" lay in its "balance of powers and the various restrictions placed upon each segment." If Congress were able to establish its complete supremacy in any field of legislation merely by "saying that such field has a relationship to interstate commerce"—for example, commerce includes the movement of people interstate; people use motels for sleeping purposes; therefore, all motels are engaged in interstate commerce—then there would be "no logical or foreseeable end to the extension of the power of Congress under the Commerce Clause." Thus the "delicate balance" so carefully invented by the framers would be irreparably smashed:

> There will be no area left for the exclusive jurisdiction of state legislatures because the Congress can appropriate any field of law, since all areas of the law and all principles of law affect those same people that Congress would like to say are part of interstate commerce. Such an unwarranted extension of the power of Congress, based on an unlimited interpretation of the Commerce Clause would in effect destroy our Republican and Federal form of government.[57]

This he hoped the Supreme Court would not allow to happen.

Along this same line, Senator A. Willis Robertson (D.—Va.) turned to one of James Madison's famous statements for aid and comfort. Writing to Joseph C. Cabell in 1829, Madison commented on the proper significance to be attributed to the delegated power "to regulate commerce among the several States":

> I always foresaw that difficulties might be started in relation to that power which could not be fully explained without recurring to views of it, which, however just, might give birth to specious though unsound objections. Being in the same terms with the power over foreign commerce, the same extent, if taken literally, would belong to it. Yet it is very certain that it grew out of the abuse of the power by the importing States in taxing the non-importing, and was intended as a negative and preventive provision against injustice among the States themselves, rather than as a power to be used for the positive purposes of the General Government, in which alone, however, the remedial power could be lodged.[58]

Robertson admitted that the commerce power had become extremely broad during the last fifty years and that now Congress was dealing with "an awesome power indeed." But this power was not without limits, and the aspect of the power involved here was "the affirmative power of Congress to regulate private activities in the field of commerce."[59] Looking to the relevant precedents, he emphasized Chief Justice Hughes' caveat in *NLRB v. Jones & Laughlin* about obliterating the distinction between what is national and what is local, and he emphasized the size of the home-consumed wheat crop (one fifth of the total national production) in *Wickard v. Filburn*. In the present situation, on the other hand, there was simply a lack of evidence to show "a substantial and burdensome indirect effect" upon commerce; Undersecretary Roosevelt's testimony was "puny and nebulous," and many of his figures were stale or irrelevant.

James J. Kilpatrick, editor of the *Richmond News Leader* and vice-chairman of the Virginia Commission on Constitutional Government, charged that the Commerce Clause was being "deceptively adapted" to social reform. Testifying before Magnuson's committee, he said:

> When the Congress first began to regulate "commerce among the several States," the object was to regulate the carriers in which the goods were hauled. In time, a second area of regulation developed, as the nature of the goods themselves came into the congressional power. Then a third area developed, as Congress sought to regulate the conditions under which the goods themselves were manufactured. In this bill, a fourth area is opened up. It is as wide as the world. Here the Congress proposes to impose a *requirement to serve....* Here Clancy's Grill and Mrs. Murphy's Hat Shoppe are equated with A.T.&T. The neighborhood drugstore is treated as the gas company: *It must serve.* Within the realm of section 202, the owner has no option, no right of choice.[60]

Like Robertson, Kilpatrick thought that this perversion of the commerce power was not based upon any substantial evidence of a burden, and he asked the rhetorical question whether there was a "Federal right" under the Constitution to adequate lodging accommodations. Obviously, the answer was no.

Senator John Stennis (D.–Miss.) was another who argued that evidence was lacking to show any harm to commerce. In debate he drew a conclusion which was echoed again and again by those opposed to the legislation:

I submit that there is not one shred of evidence to support the hypothesis in title II that there are existing burdens obstructing and impeding commerce as a result of the absence of a Federal public accommodation law that require and demand the exercise by the Congress of its constitutional power over commerce. Certainly no evidence to this effect has been presented to the Senate.[61]

This lack of proof, of course, was fatal to the constitutionality of the act; and Congress should reject it for this reason alone.

But there were other facts which militated against the validity of this use of the commerce power. Three court cases in particular contained statements contrary to the Civil Rights Act of 1964. The first and most important was the *Civil Rights Cases* (1883).[62] At stake in those cases was the constitutionality of the Civil Rights Act of 1875, which made it a misdemeanor to deny any person equal rights and privileges in places of public accommodation, regardless of color or previous condition of servitude—an almost exact parallel to the new statute except that Congress had grounded the old Act solely on the Thirteenth and Fourteenth Amendments. The Supreme Court invalidated the 1875 Act. In narrowing the field of inquiry, Justice Joseph P. Bradley had commented: "Of course, no one will contend that the power to pass it was contained in the Constitution before the adoption of the last three amendments."[63] The inference was plain: the Commerce Clause had been a part of the Constitution from the first; the Supreme Court had summarily dismissed it as a basis for the legislation then under review. What was the supreme law of the land in 1883 still had to be respected in 1964.

The second case relied upon was *Williams v. Howard Johnson's Restaurant* (1950).[64] Williams, a Negro and an interstate traveler, sued the restaurant for refusing to serve him and claimed that the Commerce Clause of its own force prohibited such discrimination. The lower federal court dismissed the plaintiff's suit. It held: "[W]e do not find that a restaurant is engaged in interstate commerce merely because in the course of its business of furnishing accommodations to the general public it serves persons who are traveling from State to State." Finally, there was Justice Black's cautionary remark from *Boynton v. Virginia* (1960): "We are not holding that every time a bus stops at a wholly independent roadside restaurant the Interstate Commerce Act requires that restaurant service be supplied in harmony with the provisions of that Act." These two disclaimers undermined any reliance upon the Commerce Clause to sustain the present bill.

212

Under the Fifth Amendment

The preceding arguments, by and large, summed up the contentions of both sides with respect to the scope of the commerce power per se. The second major exchange came over the extent to which the Fifth Amendment limited congressional regulation of the use of private property. In a very real sense an appeal to the guarantees of the due-process clause lay at the heart of the opposition to Title II. Repeatedly the accusation was made that the statute would deprive owners of their liberty and property without due process (in forcing them to serve all comers) and, in effect, would take their property for public use without just compensation. Senator Thurmond put it succinctly: "This proposal is no more than an attempt to regulate the use of private property which is entirely within the borders of one State, and to infringe upon the right of persons engaged in the operation of public accommodations to select their own customers."[65] Rolleston equated the right to use his property as he saw fit with ownership of the property; to restrict his right of choice in its use was to lessen its value to him or to take the property from him. Since Title II provided that any motel serving transient guests was covered per se, there was a denial of any of the usual due-process protections of a judicial hearing and a "responsible" finding; and since no monetary indemnification was provided for the loss of his right to choose whom he would serve, there was a "taking" of his property without proper compensation.[66]

This, of course, was the crux of the issue. The opponents of the bill protested the imposition of a nation-wide ban upon individual freedom in the choice of customers for the owners and operators of businesses open to the public. And the reason that was advanced was not always the obvious one of defending the practice of racial segregation and discrimination. James Kilpatrick expressed the problem in basic philosophical terms and contended that every citizen possessed the right to discriminate:

> This right is vital to the American system. If this be destroyed, the whole basis of individual liberty is destroyed. The American system does not rest upon some "right to be right" as some legislative majority may define what is "right." It rests solidly upon the individual's right to be wrong—upon his right in his personal life to be capricious, arbitrary, prejudiced, biased, opinionated, unreasonable—upon his right to act as a freeman in a free society.[67]

This theme in many variations was put forward countless times.

Those in favor of Title II had a standard reply. The Act did not, in fact, take private property and did not place any more onerous restrictions upon property owners than many other kinds of laws—both federal and state. Zoning laws were pointed to as imposing much more severe controls on the use to which property might be put, and such laws had always been accepted as legitimate regulations of business. In this same connection, 32 states already had public-accommodations statutes on their books, and these had consistently been sustained by the courts against due-process objections. Then there was the doctrine of a "business affected with a public interest" which had first been recognized in *Munn v. Illinois* (1877).[68] In that case Chief Justice Morrison R. Waite wrote into American jurisprudence an axiom expressed by Lord Chief Justice Hale, an English jurist of the 17th century:

> Property does become clothed with a public interest when used in a manner to make it of public consequence and to affect the community at large. When, therefore, one devotes his property to a use in which the public has an interest, he, in effect, grants to the public an interest in the use, and must submit to be controlled by the public for the common good, to the extent of the interest he has thus created. He may withdraw his grant by discontinuing the use; but, so long as he maintains the use, he must submit to the control.[69]

This principle had become a fixed rule of constitutional law with the death of economic "substantive due process" in *Nebbia v. New York* (1934)[70] and *West Coast Hotel Co. v. Parrish* (1937).[71]

To the charge that Title II would become a precedent for any type of congressional control over private property and over personal liberty in the operation of that property, Dean Griswold (who was appointed United States Solicitor General on October 12, 1967) made reply. Questioned by Senator Norris Cotton (R.—N.H.) as to whether Congress could also require restaurants to have fish available on Friday and kosher food on hand at all times, he went directly to the heart of the whole acrimonious controversy. In language strongly reminiscent of John Marshall in *Gibbons v. Ogden,* Griswold answered:

> I think I would like to add, with respect to these other things, too, Senator, that I don't think that we have to defend against every conceivable bill that Congress might some time have to consider. One of the reasons we have the Congress is to make

decisions. And I assume that Congress will not pass bills which are foolish or improper or go too far. There is obviously a question of judgment here.[72]

In the Supreme Court

Heart of Atlanta Motel (1964)

While the foregoing arguments pro and con represent only a tiny fraction of the verbal exchanges engendered by the Civil Rights Act of 1964 in Congress and before the Supreme Court, they do highlight the principal constitutional issues involved and set the stage for the decisions made by the Court. On December 14, 1964, the twin cases of *Heart of Atlanta Motel v. United States*[73] and *Katzenbach v. Mc Clung*[74] were decided. Justice Tom C. Clark wrote both majority opinions which affirmed the validity of Title II.[75] In the first case Clark recited the pertinent facts: Heart of Atlanta Motel (so-named because of its location) had 216 rooms; it solicited patronage from outside of Georgia through various national advertising media and maintained over 50 billboards and signs within the state; and it accepted convention trade, with about 75 percent of all its guests coming from out of state. He detailed the various provisions of Title II and noted that the motel admitted to coverage under section 201 (a). The sole question involved the constitutionality of the Act under the Commerce Clause.

Clark narrowed the scope of the inquiry. It was unnecessary to consider "the other grounds relied upon"—namely, the Fourteenth Amendment. But he still felt it essential to consider the *Civil Rights Cases*. The decision there was "inapposite, and without precedential value" in the present case. First, the Civil Rights Act of 1875 had broadly proscribed discrimination in public accommodations, while Title II was carefully limited to enterprises affecting commerce. Times had changed, the American people had become much more mobile, and this "sheer increase in volume of interstate traffic alone would give discriminatory practices which inhibit travel a far larger impact upon the Nation's commerce than such practices had on the economy of another day."[76] Second, in the old cases the government had not relied upon the commerce power; and Justice Bradley's oft-repeated quotation could not be read as disposing of the Commerce-Clause argument, particularly in view of a later statement in which he has asserted bluntly:

Of course, these remarks do not apply to those cases in which congress is clothed with direct and plenary powers of legislation over the whole subject, accompanied with an express or implied denial of such power to the states, as in the regulation of commerce . . . among the several states. . . . In these cases congress has power to pass laws for regulating the subjects specified, in every detail, and the conduct and transactions of individuals in respect thereof.[77]

This disposed of the opinion as carrying any current authority.

Clark turned to the basis for congressional action. He admitted that the Act itself carried no findings of fact, but he pointed out that the legislative record of hearings and debates was "replete with evidence of the burdens that discrimination by race or color places upon interstate commerce." He did not spend long in repeating some of the evidence—most of it from the testimony of Undersecretary of Commerce Roosevelt. Then he took up analysis of the power of Congress over interstate travel, which he held depended "on the meaning of the Commerce Clause." Clark went straight back to Marshall's opinion in *Gibbons v. Ogden* for the answer and quoted all the familiar statements regarding "commerce," "among the several States," and "the power to regulate." He concluded: "In short, the determinative test of the exercise of power by the Congress under the Commerce Clause is simply whether the activity sought to be regulated is 'commerce which concerns more States than one' and has a real and substantial relation to the national interest."[78]

It was time to look at the specifics. Commerce clearly included the movement of people interstate.[79] Congress had used its commerce power in many and varied ways and had had its enactments upheld.[80] It made no difference that Congress was attempting to reach and rectify a moral wrong; that fact did not "detract from the overwhelming evidence of the disruptive effect that racial discrimination has had on commercial intercourse." Similarly, it was immaterial that the motel claimed its activities were local. Clark quoted the late Justice Jackson: "If it is interstate commerce that feels the pinch, it does not matter how local the operation which applies the squeeze."[81] Finally, he summed up his decision:

Thus the power of Congress to promote interstate commerce also includes the power to regulate the local incidents thereof, including local activities in both the States of origin and destination, which might have a substantial and harmful effect upon that commerce. One need only examine the evidence . . . to see that Congress may—as it has—prohibit racial discrimination by motels serving travelers, however "local" their operations may appear.[82]

It remained only to answer the subsidiary contentions. In two short pages Clark dismissed the arguments under the Fifth Amendment. He held that since Congress had a rational basis for finding that racial discrimination affected commerce and since the means selected to eliminate the evil were reasonable and appropriate, the appellant had no "right" to select its guests as it saw fit, "free from governmental regulation." He referred to the fact that similar laws had been upheld in 32 states against due-process demurrers and observed that such legislation had never been held to interfere with personal liberty or to constitute a taking of property without just compensation.

Katzenbach v. McClung (1964)

In the second case Clark again began by surveying the relevant facts: Ollie's Barbecue, a family-owned restaurant in Birmingham, with a seating capacity of 220, specialized in barbecued meats and home-made pies; it purchased locally approximately $150,000 worth of food annually, $69,700 or 46 percent of which was meat which came from outside of the state; but it did no advertising, even in the local papers, and made no effort to attract transient customers. The restaurant admitted that it came under the provisions of Title II, but it denied their applicability.

Counsel for McClung made the ingenious (though not necessarily ingenuous) claim that the Act could not be applied because it contained no statutory requirement that there be a connection between interstate commerce and the racial policy of a particular restaurant. Congress had legislated "a conclusive presumption" that the operations of a restaurant affected commerce if it served interstate travelers or if a substantial portion of the food which it served had moved in commerce, but the magic words "affect commerce" were keyed to the "operations" of the restaurant generally and not to its method of choosing its clientele.[83] The District Court had accepted the argument!

In Clark's view, however, the question was whether Congress had an adequate basis for finding that racial discrimination at restaurants covered by Title II imposed "a burden of national magnitude" upon interstate commerce. He briefly restated some of the main items of evidence brought out in the hearings before the Senate Commerce Committee pertaining to the restrictive effect upon interstate travel by

Negroes, the reluctance of new business to locate in areas of segregation, and a general reduction in the amount of goods moving interstate which resulted from an artificial limiting of the market to white customers. The fact that the volume of food purchased by Ollie's Barbecue was an insignificant part of the total made no difference; Justice Jackson had settled that point in *Wickard v. Filburn.*[84] Here Congress had found that discrimination was of nation-wide scope and had appropriately moved to combat it before it became "far-reaching in its harm to commerce."[85]

Then Clark considered the power of Congress to regulate local activities. He cited with approval Stone's conclusions in *United States v. Darby* and again relied heavily upon Jackson's opinion in *Wickard v. Filburn* to conclude: "Much is said about a restaurant business being local but 'even if appellee's activity be local and though it may not be regarded as commerce, it may still, whatever its nature, be reached by Congress if it exerts a substantial economic effect on interstate commerce.' "[86] Turning to the "conclusive presumption" argument— the fact that in the Act Congress had not provided for an independent case-by-case inquiry into whether the policy of a particular business "affected commerce," he gave it short shrift:

> Here . . . Congress has determined for itself that refusals of service to Negroes have imposed burdens both upon the interstate flow of food and upon the movement of products generally. Of course, the mere fact that Congress has said when particular activity shall be deemed to affect commerce does not preclude further examination by this Court. But where we find that the legislators, in light of the facts and testimony before them, have a rational basis for finding a chosen regulatory scheme necessary to the protection of commerce, our investigation is at an end.[87]

Since the restaurant admittedly served food, a substantial portion of which had moved in interstate commerce, it was subject to the Act; and Clark went on to emphasize that the absence of direct evidence "connecting discriminatory restaurant service with the flow of interstate food" was not "a crucial matter." Finally, he summed up the Court's attitude toward congressional use of the Commerce Clause: "The power of Congress in this field is broad and sweeping; where it keeps within its sphere and violates no express constitutional limitation it has been the rule of this Court, going back almost to the founding days of the Republic, not to interfere."[88] Title II of the Civil Rights Act of 1964 had been vindicated!

Justice Black wrote his own concurring opinion.[89] He thought first that it required "no novel or strained interpretation of the Commerce Clause" to sustain the Act, and he referred to Marshall's broad rendering of the power "to regulate commerce among the States." But there was a second consideration of crucial importance:

> Furthermore, it has long been held that the Necessary and Proper Clause . . . adds to the commerce power of Congress the power to regulate local instrumentalities operating within a single State if their activities burden the flow of commerce among the States. Thus in the *Shreveport Case* . . . this Court recognized that Congress could not fully carry out its responsibility to protect interstate commerce were its constitutional power to regulate that commerce to be strictly limited to prescribing the rules for controlling the things actually moving in such commerce or the contracts, transactions, and other activities, immediately concerning them. . . . And since the *Shreveport Case* this Court has steadfastly followed, and indeed has emphasized time and time again, that Congress has ample power to protect interstate commerce from activities adversely and injuriously affecting it, which but for this adverse effect on interstate commerce would be beyond the power of Congress to regulate.[90]

Black took up the provisions of the Act and reviewed the salient facts about the Heart of Atlanta Motel and Ollie's Barbecue; under the circumstances, he agreed that Title II was a valid exercise of congressional power as applied to both of them, especially in view of the aggregate effect of a great number of discriminatory acts upon interstate commerce. But, like Stone before him, he thought that there must (or should) be a line somewhere between state and federal power and, consequently, a point beyond which even the broad and plenary commerce power could not extend:

> I recognize that every remote, possible, speculative effect on commerce should not be accepted as an adequate constitutional ground to uproot and throw into the discard all our traditional distinctions between what is purely local, and therefore controlled by state laws, and what affects the national interest and is therefore subject to control by federal laws. I recognize too that some isolated and remote lunchroom which sells only to local people and buys almost all its supplies in the locality may possibly be beyond the reach of the power of Congress to regulate commerce. . . .[91]

Black proceeded very quickly to reject the Fifth Amendment and *Civil*

Rights Cases as constitutional barriers to the statute. He adopted the position of the majority that it was unnecessary to consider the adequacy of the Fourteenth Amendment to sustain the Act; and finally, he reemphasized the validity of the legislation under the combination of the Commerce Clause and the necessary and proper clause. He was obviously unwilling to rest his concurrence on the force of the federal commerce power in and of itself, even in conjunction with an act of Congress.

Justice William O. Douglas and Justice Arthur J. Goldberg added their individual interpretations in separate concurrences.[92] Douglas joined the Court's opinion in both cases, but he preferred to rest the outcome on section 5 of the Fourteenth Amendment; Goldberg thought that Title II of the Act was valid under the Commerce Clause and under sections 1 and 5 of the Fourteenth Amendment. The Douglas-Goldberg position is interesting and is perhaps a harbinger of the future. It holds that the Fourteenth Amendment per se forbids racial discrimination in public accommodations or businesses.[93] Thus the amendment gives Congress power to pass positive legislation in this area. Furthermore, it is a preferable basis for guaranteeing civil rights. As Douglas put it here:

> A decision based on the Fourteenth Amendment would have a more settling effect, making unnecessary litigation over whether a particular restaurant or inn is within the commerce definitions of the Act or whether a particular customer is an interstate traveler. Under my construction, the Act would apply to all customers in all the enumerated places of public accommodation. And that construction would put an end to all obstructionist strategies and finally close one door on a bitter chapter in American history.[94]

But a majority of the justices chose to rest the decisions only on the Commerce Clause and not go to the Douglas stand based on the Civil War amendments.[95]

Conclusions

In a sense, the decisions in *Heart of Atlanta Motel v. United States* and *Katzenbach v. McClung* were anticlimactic. The constitutionality of Title II had been so thoroughly analyzed and debated from all sides that Clark's rather prosaic opinions did nothing more than put the official seal of judicial approval upon this particular exertion of congressional power. All of the relevant legal precedents ran in favor of the Act, and the factual evidence of an immense economic burden on national commerce was clear and indisputable to anyone who cared to look; the Court could not possibly have invalidated the statute without at the same time repudiating everything it had done over the last quarter of a century.[96]

It seems unnecessary, therefore, to spend much time in a dissection of these two cases. Only a few points warrant any extended comment. First, it is interesting to note the sources most cited by Clark. There were primarily three: John Marshall in *Gibbons v. Ogden;* Harlan Fiske Stone in *United States v. Darby;* and Robert H. Jackson in *Wickard v. Filburn.* Clark took from Marshall the broad definitions originally laid out for the Commerce Clause which by now need no repetition. From Stone he derived two major propositions: (1) the federal commerce power extends to intrastate or "local" activities if control of these is necessary to the effective regulation of any facet of interstate commerce; and (2) the motives and purpose of Congress are beyond the competence of the Court to judge and hence are irrelevant to the constitutionality of a law. Jackson provided Clark with the final consideration which was necessary to uphold the application of the Act to the motel and to the restaurant: appropriate for judicial notice is the aggregate effect upon commerce of the prohibited practice by many establishments similarly situated and not the effect of the two businesses in isolation. These long-established rules of Commerce-Clause adjudication, combined with the well-documented evidence of a burden "of national magnitude" on the economy, could lead to only one conclusion—that Title II was clearly constitutional.

Second, notice must be taken of Justice Black's reluctance to find in the Commerce Clause alone the power for Congress to forbid racial discrimination in privately owned places of public accommodation. Only when coupled with the necessary and proper clause does the commerce power become adequate for this task, and even then there may be a point beyond which federal jurisdiction does not extend. Black, like Stone before him, appears to be searching for some line between state and federal power.[97] Stone never found that dividing line; and, indeed, he once expressed a principle which makes it impossible to locate: in *Darby* he said that it was "no objection to the assertion of the power to regulate interstate commerce that its exercise is attended by the same incidents which attend the exercise of the police power of the states."[98] In other words, Stone held that a regulation of commerce enacted by Congress under its delegated power could not be negated simply because it might coincide in character with a local regulation passed under the inherent police power of the states; the former would have to take precedence over the latter. Furthermore, as Alpheus Thomas Mason and William M. Beaney in commenting upon the decisions in *Heart of Atlanta Motel* and *McClung* have put it: "[I]t may be asked whether, in spite of Justice Black's disclaimer, there is now any commercial activity beyond the reach of congressional power?"[99] The short answer is that there is not, and Black will have as great difficulty as Stone in marking out any fixed boundary to federal power under the Commerce Clause.

But all of this leads inevitably to a final consideration. If Congress can reach the practice here proscribed, that is, tell the private business-man whom he must serve, does not this make the national government all-powerful, obliterate any distinction between state and federal jurisdiction, and, in effect, render the federal system created by the Constitution meaningless? The answer to this question lies in an analysis of the basic premises underlying the assertion, and these will now be examined briefly.

An initial observation is in order. Although it is incontestable that the framers of the Constitution meant to establish a federal republic, it is equally undeniable that they intended for the newly created national government to operate directly upon the people, without reference to the state governments. The fact is that the federal government was given (via the delegated powers) the constitutional authority to regulate in many ways the individual activities of its citizens. But the argument is advanced that Congress still has no power to restrict the right of a private businessman to choose his clientele. Aside from the fact that Congress has been allowed to override his choice in other areas—the reasons he can use to hire and fire employees, the wage-and-hour standards he must meet, and so forth, the real fallacy here lies in the use of the word "private." Opponents of Title II constantly attacked what they called an infringement on private property and private control of business. But the simple fact is that a businessman does not engage in "private" activities. Once he opens up his business to the public, it becomes, as Chief Justice Waite said, "affected with a public interest." In other words, in offering to serve the general public, the proprietor voluntarily agrees to meet whatever requirements the public through its government thinks are necessary concomitants of the privilege of doing business. For example, it is the case in most states that if the mythical Clancy wants to open a grill, he must maintain certain standards of cleanliness in the preparation of his food to protect the health of his customers, and in all states if he wants to serve oleomargarine he must post a large sign to this effect and serve the oleo in triangular patties. What is any different about telling him that he cannot discriminate against potential customers because of their race, creed, or national ancestry—attributes which are totally unrelated to their ability to pay or to the way in which they are likely to behave while on the premises?

To come at this question from the philosophical point of view, it is worth repeating what Kilpatrick said about the American system: "It rests solidly upon the individual's right to be wrong—upon his right in his personal life to be capricious, arbitrary, prejudiced, biased, opinionated, unreasonable—upon his right to act as a freeman in a free society." Although there might be those who would disagree with this on moral grounds, it does in fact reflect one of the basic tenets of the American heritage—the right of the individual to think what he pleases, say what he pleases, and associate with whom he pleases. But note the all-important qualifying words—"in his personal life." This is precisely the point. For where the individual acts as a businessman and opens his business to the public, he is no longer acting in a personal and private capacity; he has become engaged in a public undertaking which is subject to public regulation and control.

Finally, what is the effect on the American federal system? It is not destroyed. In *Hammer v. Dagenhart*,[100] decided a half century ago, the Supreme Court refused to allow Congress to tell the "private" manufacturer that if he wanted to ship his products in interstate commerce, he could not "choose" to hire child labor. The reasoning of the five-man majority was that if the Child Labor Act of 1916 were upheld, "all freedom of commerce will be at an end, and the power of the States over local matters may be eliminated, and thus our system of government be practically destroyed." Justice Oliver Wendell Holmes in one of his most famous and brilliant dissents countered this dire prediction:

> The act does not meddle with anything belonging to the states. They may regulate their internal affairs and their domestic commerce as they like. But when they seek to send their products across the state line they are no longer within their rights. If there were no Constitution and no Congress their power to cross the line would depend upon their neighbors. Under the Constitution such commerce belongs not to the states, but to Congress to regulate. It may carry out its views of public policy whatever indirect effect they may have upon the activities of the states.[101]

This is exactly what Congress did in Title II; it made it the public policy of the United States that places of public accommodation should be open to all. The powers of the states are in no way reduced or impaired. But, more pertinently, as Dean Griswold put it: "It has been said long ago that the Commerce Clause is the cement of the Nation. The Commerce Clause is the thing that makes us a nation. This is something on which we ought to be a nation, it seems to me."[102] If the objection is raised that the door is now open for Congress to do anything it sees fit in regulating private businesses which have any conceivable connection with interstate commerce, the sufficient rejoinder is that in all representative political systems really effective restraint upon the abuse of governmental power lies in the wisdom and discretion of the legislators, "their identity with the people, and the influence which their constituents possess at elections," which is merely another way of saying that the United States is a democratic—as well as federal—republic.

Notes

1. 347 U.S. 483. The final decree of the Court was fashioned in *Brown v. Board of Education of Topeka,* 349 U.S. 294 (1955).

2. Beginning in the late 1940's and early 1950's and accelerating after the two *Brown* cases, the Court turned principally to the equal-protection clause of the Fourteenth Amendment to secure Negro rights. Thus it has used that clause to strike down racial segregation in the following areas: public beaches and bathhouses, *Mayor of Baltimore City v. Dawson,* 350 U.S. 877 (1955); municipal golf courses, *Holmes v. City of Atlanta,* 350 U.S. 879 (1955); intrastate buses, *Gayle v. Browder,* 352 U.S. 903 (1956); public athletic contests, *State Athletic Commission v. Dorsey,* 359 U.S. 533 (1959); municipal airport restaurants, *Turner v. City of Memphis,* 369 U.S. 350 (1962); seating in courtrooms, *Johnson v. Virginia,* 373 U.S. 61 (1963); municipal auditorium facilities, *Schiro v. Bynum,* 375 U.S. 395 (1964); marriage, *Loving v. Commonwealth of Virginia,* 388 U.S. 1 (1967). However, this is an entirely separate study which is quite beyond the scope of the present analysis.

3. *U.S. Statutes at Large,* LXXVIII, 241.

4. In *New York v. Miln,* 11 Peters 102 (1837), Justice Philip P. Barbour, supposedly speaking for five of seven justices, made the statement that persons were not properly "subjects of commerce." Two of the five, James M. Wayne and Henry Baldwin, did not concur with that specific holding but could do nothing about it because Barbour delivered the opinion on the last day of the term. See three sources:

Maurice G. Baxter, *Daniel Webster & The Supreme Court* (Amherst, Mass.: The University of Massachusetts Press, 1966), 223, footnote 124; Alpheus Thomas Mason and William M. Beaney (eds.), *American Constitutional Law: Introductory Essays and Selected Cases,* 4th ed. (Englewood Cliffs, N.J.: Prentice-Hall, Inc., 1968), 160; Carl Brent Swisher, *American Constitutional Development,* 2nd ed. (Cambridge, Mass.: Houghton Mifflin Company, 1954), 197.

5. 227 U.S. 308.

6. 314 U.S. 160.

7. For a brief summary of them, see ibid., 161-70.

8. For his complete opinion, see ibid., 170-77. Justice Douglas, joined by Justices Black and Murphy, concurred in the result, refused to express an opinion on the Commerce-Clause question, and stated that the state statute ran afoul of the privileges and immunities clause of the Fourteenth Amendment; see ibid., 177-81. Justice Jackson agreed with the result, even on Commerce-Clause grounds; but he preferred to base the decision on the same privileges and immunities clause, which would be a more comprehensive ground; see ibid., 181-86. Both Douglas and Jackson regarded the right to move freely from state to state as a privilege of national citizenship, which was "protected from state abridgement," and which should not be dependent upon "a man's mere property status" or the effect on commerce of limiting the movement of persons.

9. Ibid., 173-74.

10. 328 U.S. 373.

11. For his complete opinion, see ibid., 374-86. The decision was 6-1. Chief Justice Stone had died in April, and Justice Jackson took no part. Justice Rutledge concurred in the result. Justice Black "acquiesced" reluctantly; he was still unhappy with the "undue-burden-on-commerce" formula which had gained acceptance the year before in *Southern Pacific Co. v. Arizona,* 325 U.S. 761 (1945). Justice Frankfurter concurred, largely on the basis of *Hall v. DeCuir,* 95 U.S. 485 (1878). Only Justice Burton dissented.

12. Ibid., 377.

13. Ibid., 377. He cited *Cooley v. The Board of Wardens* and *Southern Pacific Co. v. Arizona* in support of this proposition.

14. Ibid., 380-81.

15. 95 U.S. 485. Ironically enough, this was a case in which Chief Justice Waite struck down a Louisiana statute which required that all persons be given equal rights and privileges in all parts of public conveyances, without discrimination as to race or color.

16. 328 U.S. 373, 386.

17. For his complete opinion, see ibid., 389-94.

18. 333 U.S. 28.

19. For his complete opinion, see ibid., 29-40. The decision was 7-2. Justice Douglas wrote a concurring opinion. Justice Jackson, joined by Chief Justice Vinson, dissented.

20. Ibid., 35.

21. Ibid., 36.

22. Ibid., 35-36.

23. Ibid., 40.

24. For his complete opinion, see ibid., 43-45.

25. Ibid., 45. See Jackson's majority opinion in *H.P. Hood & Sons v. DuMond*, 336 U.S. 525, 526-45 (1949), in which he amplified his views; see Chapter 7.

26. 364 U.S. 454.

27. Ibid., 456.

28. See the supremacy clause in Article VI of the Constitution. For his complete opinion, see 364 U.S. 454, 455-64. It must be noted that this case marks a departure from those which precede and follow it. In *Morgan v. Virginia*, 328 U.S. 373 (1946), the Court invalidated a state segregation statute as an "undue burden" on commerce; in *Colorado Anti-Discrimination Comm'n. v. Continental Air Lines*, 372 U.S. 714 (1963), it held that a state nondiscrimination statute did not "unduly burden" commerce. But in *Boynton* the Court declined to go to the constitutional issues under the Commerce Clause per se and the Fourteenth Amendment; instead, it used the finding of a violation of the Interstate Commerce Act to decide the case. The reasons for this apparent deviation are open only to speculation. Remember that Black wrote the Court's opinion. He is not fond of the "burden-on-commerce" doctrine and would undoubtedly prefer not to perpetuate it. (He could use it in the 1963 case because there it supported state

power.) Black also does not believe that the Fourteenth Amendment in and of itself prohibits a policy of discrimination in a privately owned business, absent state action; see his dissenting opinion in *Bell v. Maryland,* 378 U.S. 226, 318-46 (1964). (He was joined by Justices Harland and White. Justices Douglas and Goldberg, joined by Chief Justice Warren, asserted flatly that the Fourteenth Amendment alone extends the right of access to places of public accommodation to all American citizens; see 378 U.S. 226, 242-60 and 286-318.) Add to this the fact (which will be discussed more fully later) that Black found it requisite to drag in the necessary and proper clause to help the Commerce Clause in sustaining the Civil Rights Act of 1964, and it becomes a good guess that the factious majority in *Boynton* was happy to escape on the construction of the Interstate Commerce Act and thus avoid reaching the constitutional issues.

29. *U.S. Statutes at Large,* LIV, 902.

30. 313 U.S. 80.

31. Ibid., 94.

32. 339 U.S. 816.

33. 364 U.S. 454, 459.

34. Ibid., 462.

35. Ibid., 462-63.

36. Ibid., 463. Even so, the decision was too much for Justice Whittaker, who, joined by Justice Clark, dissented primarily on the ground that there was no evidence either that the bus company had volunteered to make restaurant services available to its passengers or that the proprietor of the restaurant had ever agreed to such an undertaking; see ibid., 464-70.

37. 372 U.S. 714.

38. For his complete opinion, see ibid., 716-25.

39. Ibid., 719, for both quotations in the sentence.

40. Ibid., 721.

41. *Senate Report No. 872, 88th Congress, 2nd Session,* 1-24.

42. For a good overview of the sequence of events from the proposal of the omnibus bill to its final passage, see the booklet, *Revolution in*

Civil Rights, 3rd ed. (Washington, D.C.: Congressional Quarterly Inc., 1967), 50-78.

43. *U.S. Statutes at Large,* LXXVIII, 241.

44. *Hearings Before the Committee on Commerce, United States Sentate, 88th Congress, 1st Session, on S. 1732,* Part 1, Serial 26, 19.

45. *Senate Report No. 872, 88th Congress, 2nd Session,* 82.

46. Ibid., 83.

47. Ibid., 87.

48. *Hearings Before the Committee on Commerce, United States Senate, 88th Congress, 1st Session, on S. 1732,* Part 2, Serial 26, 770.

49. Ibid., 771.

50. These two NLRB cases were reviewed in Chapter 4.

51. *Hearings Before Subcommittee No. 5 of the Committee on the Judiciary, House of Representatives, 88th Congress, 1st Session, on H.R. 7152,* 2490. Quotation taken from a "Report on Proposed Federal Civil Rights Laws Relating to Public Accommodations," ibid., 2489-2500, The Association of the Bar of the City of New York, Committee on Federal Legislation, August 19, 1963.

52. *Congressional Record, Proceedings and Debates of the 88th Congress, 2nd Session* (Washington, D.C.: U.S. Government Printing Office, 1964), Vol. 110, 7053.

53. *Hearings Before the Committee on Commerce, United States Senate, 88th Congress, 1st Session,* Part 2, Serial 26, 691.

54. Ibid., 691-92.

55. *Senate Report No. 872, 88th Congress, 2nd Session,* 62.

56. Ibid., 55.

57. "Brief for Appellant," *Records and Briefs of Cases Decided by the Supreme Court of the United States,* Vol. 379, 41. These arguments are to be found in full in ibid., 14-16 and 38-45.

58. *Congressional Record,* Vol. 110, 13361. The quotation is somewhat more complete than that given by Robertson and is taken from "James Madison to J.C. Cabell," February 13, 1829, in Max Farrand

(ed.), *The Records of the Federal Convention of 1787* (4 vols., New Haven, Conn.: Yale University Press, 1911), III, 478. It must be remembered that Madison was more states' rights in 1829 than in 1787. (See the discussion of the origins of dual federalism in Chapter 2.)

59. Ibid., 13362.

60. *Hearings Before the Committee on Commerce, United States Senate, 88th Congress, 1st Session*, Part 1, Serial 26, 404.

61. *Congressional Record*, Vol. 110, 4827.

62. 109 U.S. 3.

63. The amendments referred to are, of course, the Thirteenth, Fourteenth, and Fifteenth—the Civil War amendments which were designed to protect the rights of the newly freed Negroes.

64. 268 F. 2d 845 (C.A.4).

65. *Senate Report No. 872, 88th Congress, 2nd Session*, 62.

66. "Brief for Appellant," *Records and Briefs*, Vol. 379, 51-54.

67. *Hearings Before the Committee on Commerce, United States Senate, 88th Congress, 1st Session*, Part 1, Serial 26, 404.

68. 94 U.S. 113.

69. Ibid., 126.

70. 291 U.S. 502.

71. 300 U.S. 379.

72. *Hearings Before the Committee on Commerce, United States Senate, 88th Congress, 1st Session*, Part 2, Serial 26, 780-81.

73. 379 U.S. 241.

74. 379 U.S. 294.

75. For his complete opinions, see 379 U.S. 241, 242-62 and 379 U.S. 294, 295-305. The two decisions were unanimous.

76. 379 U.S. 241, 251.

77. Ibid., 251-52. Quoted from 109 U.S. 3, 18 (1883).

78. Ibid., 255.

79. Clark cited the *Passenger Cases,* 7 Howard 283 (1849); *Hoke v. United States,* 227 U.S. 308 (1913); *Morgan v. Virginia,* 328 U.S. 373 (1946).

80. Examples included: *Champion v. Ames,* 188 U.S. 321 (1903); *Brooks v. United States,* 267 U.S. 432 (1925); *NLRB v. Jones & Laughlin Steel Corp.,* 301 U.S. 1 (1937); *United States v. Darby,* 312 U.S. 100 (1941); *Wickard v. Filburn,* 317 U.S. 111 (1942).

81. 379 U.S. 241, 258. Quoted from *United States v. Women's Sportswear Manufacturers Ass'n.,* 336 U.S. 460, 464 (1949).

82. Ibid., 258.

83. "Brief for Appellees," *Records and Briefs,* Vol. 379, 5-7 and 18-27.

84. 379 U.S. 294, 300-01. Clark was referring to statements made in *Wickard v. Filburn,* 317 U.S. 111, 127-28.

85. Ibid., 301. Clark was quoting from Frankfurter's opinion in *Polish National Alliance v. NLRB,* 322 U.S. 643, 648 (1944).

86. Ibid., 302. The part quoted was from Jackson's opinion in *Wickard v. Filburn,* 317 U.S. 111, 125.

87. Ibid., 303-04.

88. Ibid., 305.

89. For his complete opinion, see 379 U.S. 241, 268-79.

90. Ibid., 271-72.

91. Ibid., 275.

92. For their complete opinions, see 379 U.S. 241, 279-86 and 291-93, respectively.

93. See Note 28 and see Douglas in *Lombard v. Louisiana,* 373 U.S. 267, 274-83 (1963).

94. 379 U.S. 241, 280.

95. That the Court may be edging toward this last position, however, is seen in the 1968 case of *Jones v. Alfred H. Mayer Co.,* 392 U.S. 409, in which Justice Stewart, speaking for a majority of six with Douglas

concurring, held that the Civil Rights Act of 1866 "bars all racial discrimination, private as well as public, in the sale or rental of property, and that the statute, thus construed, is a valid exercise of the power of Congress to enforce the Thirteenth Amendment." It is open only to speculation whether the Court will now turn to the Thirteenth Amendment to take over much of the area previously protected by the Fourteenth Amendment (see Note 2) or whether it will finally overrule the *Civil Rights Cases* and extend a broad-form protection under section 5 of the Fourteenth Amendment. In either of these events, the Commerce Clause would become a less "preferable" (and, in fact, an unnecessary) basis for upholding civil rights. But if and when the Civil War amendments come into their own as shields against public or private deprivations of fundamental human rights, let it be remembered that the Commerce Clause formed the initial cutting edge in judicial action against discrimination.

96. See the discussions in Chapter 3, 4, and 5.

97. See Stone's dissenting opinion in *Borden Company v. Borella*, 325 U.S. 679, 685-86 (1945).

98. 312 U.S. 100, 114.

99. Mason and Beaney (eds.), *American Constitutional Law*, 4th ed., 227.

100. 247 U.S. 251 (1918).

101. Ibid., 281.

102. *Hearings Before the Committee on Commerce, United States Senate, 88th Congress, 1st Session,* Part 2, Serial 26, 775-76.

Part 3: State Power under the Commerce Clause

The preceding three chapters were concerned entirely with the nature and scope of the federal commerce power. The following three chapters will consider the extent of state power over interstate commerce. This is a vast and exceedingly diverse area of constitutional law; in the past thirty-three years the Supreme Court has decided literally hundreds of commerce cases involving state power. Consequently, it would be impossible to review even a small fraction of the Court's output, and no attempt will be made to do so. Instead, the focus of the present study is four-fold. Chapter 7 will expound in some detail the three constitutional philosophies of state commerce power which have vied for acceptance on the Court since the "constitutional revolution" of 1937. Then, as a separate but related part of the subject, the present permissible range of state regulation in the absence of congressional action will be delineated by reference to a few leading cases.

Chapter 8 will examine a group of cases in which there is alleged conflict between state and federal legislation. With steadily increased congressional regulation of the national economy, the opportunity for such conflict has risen sharply; in fact, this is now a critical testing ground of American federalism and as such demands close and extensive analysis. Finally, in order to round out the picture on state power, Chapter 9 will provide a somewhat cursory look at the important but broad and highly technical field of state taxation. Here the trend of increasing leniency toward the states on the part of the Court and the recent entry of Congress into the area will be noted. A study of these four major topics will show the difficulties involved in umpiring the federal system and the virtual impossibility of making any very firm generalizations about the future. It will also demonstrate something else: the very wide discretion of the Court in establishing and maintaining the delicate balance between national and state power over commerce.

7   State Power: Theories and Application

Chapter 2 developed the thesis that in *Cooley v. The Board of Wardens* (1852) the Supreme Court reserved to itself the prerogative to decide questions of state power and developed various formulas or tests to facilitate its task. This chapter will elucidate the updating of these tests over the last third of a century by examining rather carefully the conflicting views of three very influential justices—Chief Justice Harlan Fiske Stone, Justice Hugo L. Black, and Justice Robert H. Jackson—on the scope of state power over commerce. Following a short analysis of each of these, it will be argued that the Stone position is the one to be "preferred" from the standpoint of maintaining equity and harmony in the American federal system. Finally, some of the more current cases which involve questions of state power will be analyzed in order to show where the law stands today.

The Stone View

Commerce and Common Sense, 1938-1940

While the various doctrines or rules which grew out of the *Cooley* decision were generally applied with wisdom and restraint, more conservative justices sometimes abused their use in the interest of protecting business from any regulation, state or national. For example, Justice Pierce Butler's majority opinion in *DiSanto v. Pennsylvania* (1927)[1] is a classic illustration of the misuse of a legal formula; without any reasoning or analysis at all he struck down the state license requirement as a "direct burden" on foreign commerce.[2] This form of judicial decision making was attacked in trenchant fashion by Justice Stone, who, soon after his appointment to the Court, began to articulate an essentially common-sense approach to the perennially vexatious problem of the negative effect of the Commerce Clause upon state power. The basic elements of the Stone position can best be elaborated by an examination of a few of his important commerce decisions.

The *Cooley* case, in finally opting for Daniel Webster's selective exclusive theory, stood for the proposition that the Commerce Clause per se did not deprive the states of all power over interstate commerce. The crucial question is: what precisely does the Commerce Clause by its own force prohibit the states from doing? Stone assayed a beginning answer in his *DiSanto* dissent when he asserted that "the purpose of the Commerce Clause was not to preclude all state regulation of commerce crossing state lines, but to prevent discrimination and the erection of barriers or obstacles to the free flow of commerce, interstate or foreign."[3] In utilizing the Clause, however, the Court should make its decision in each case on "a consideration of all the facts and circumstances, such as the nature of the regulation, its function, the character of the business involved, and the actual effect on the flow of commerce."[4] This substitution of factual analysis and pragmatic reasoning for the mere incantation of a legal formula was the hallmark of Stone's approach.

The 1930's brought the Great Depression which curtailed state tax receipts, but which increased public pressure for greater governmental activity and spending. At the same time the economic system continued its drive toward greater interdependence and interweaving of the national and local processes of production and distribution. The result was that many state legislatures began to enact measures regulating and/or taxing various aspects of interstate commerce. These measures were often challenged before the Supreme Court, and this gave Stone an excellent opportunity to press his position. Two cases in particular illustrate his method of decision.

South Carolina State Highway Department v. Barnwell Brothers, Inc. (1938)[5] furnished the occasion for a full exposition on state regulation. In 1933 the South Carolina legislature passed a statute which prohibited the use on the state's highways of motor trucks and semi-trailer trucks whose width exceeded ninety inches and whose weight loaded exceeded 20,000 pounds. Speaking for a unanimous Court (7-0), Stone

236

upheld the state restrictions over the objection of interstate truckers and the Interstate Commerce Commission that they imposed an unconstitutional burden upon commerce. He began with a general statement of constitutional doctrine:

> The commerce clause, by its own force, prohibits discrimination against interstate commerce, whatever its form or method, and the decisions of this Court have recognized that there is scope for its like operation when state legislation nominally of local concern is in point of fact aimed at interstate commerce, or by its necessary operation is a means of gaining a local benefit by throwing the attendant burdens on those without the state. . . . It was to end these practices that the commerce clause was adopted.[6]

In a footnote he defended his second point by an appeal to political theory. "Underlying the state rule," he said,

> has been the thought, often expressed in judicial opinion, that when the regulation is of such a character that its burden falls principally upon those without the state, legislative action is not likely to be subjected to those political restraints which are normally exerted on legislation where it affects adversely some interests within the state.[7]

Stone then went into an exhaustive examination of all the factors involved. He recognized that a large amount of interstate truck traffic passed over South Carolina's highways, that most trucks were ninety-six inches wide and weighed more than ten tons when fully loaded, that most state highways were built to sustain greater weights without injury, that the state had used some federal money in improving its highway system, and that, as the District Court had found, "compliance with the weight and width limitations demanded by the South Carolina Act would seriously impede motor truck traffic passing to and through the state and increase its cost."[8]

On the other hand, it was undeniable that South Carolina had "built its highways and owns and maintains them"; few subjects were "so peculiarly of local concern" as the use of state highways. Much of the controversy centered around the relative merits of using a gross-weight limitation (as per the legislature) as against an axle or wheel weight limitation. Although some technical evidence indicated that the actual stresses on roads were determined by wheel weights, the gross-weight standard was more adaptable to official enforcement. There was the added fact that over one half of South Carolina's highways had been built without the usual longitudinal center joint which imparted added strength and durability to a road. Finally, as to the width limitation, it was admitted that increasing the width of a vehicle increased the hazards attendant upon its operation.

Under the circumstances the state legislature had acted "within its province," and its judgment was not without a "rational basis." Congress had not attempted to regulate the weight and width of vehicles, and Stone held that "a state may impose non-discriminatory restrictions with respect to the character of motor vehicles moving in interstate commerce as a safety measure and as a means of securing the economical use of its highways."[9] The fact that the South Carolina regulations affected large numbers of shippers "within as well as without the state" was a "safeguard against their abuse," and they did not result in a constitutionally forbidden burden on interstate commerce.

With the ink barely dry on this important opinion Stone spoke for the Court in *Western Live Stock v. Bureau of Revenue* (1938)[10] and again announced important principles with respect to state power. In 1934 New Mexico levied a privilege tax of two percent on all gross receipts derived from the sale of advertising space by any person engaged in the publication of newspapers and magazines. *Western Live Stock* was a monthly livestock trade journal which was prepared, edited, and published wholly within the state, but which had a circulation in states other than New Mexico. It also carried advertisements from out-of-state advertisers, payment for which was remitted interstate after the circulation of the magazine. The publishers challenged the tax on two grounds: (1) The gross income received under the advertising contracts was immune because the contracts were consummated by interstate commerce; and (2) "performance" of the contracts depended upon interstate circulation. By a vote of six to two the state tax was upheld.[11]

Stone dismissed the first contention in short order. He held that "the mere formation of a contract between persons in different states is not within the protection of the Commerce Clause ... unless the performance is within its protection."[12] This latter consideration presented the crucial question. To answer it he began by asserting basic principles:

> It was not the purpose of the commerce clause to relieve those engaged in interstate commerce from their just share of state tax

238

burden even though it increases the cost of doing the business. "Even interstate business must pay its way," . . . and the bare fact that one is carrying on interstate commerce does not relieve him from many forms of state taxation which add to the cost of his business.[13]

Various types of state taxes, all of which added to the expense of carrying on interstate business, had been sustained by the Court. However, taxes measured by gross receipts from interstate commerce had often failed and for good reason:

> The vice characteristic of those which have been held invalid is that they have placed on the commerce burdens of such a nature as to be capable, in point of substance, of being imposed . . . with equal right by every state which the commerce touches, merely because interstate commerce is being done, so that without the protection of the commerce clause it would bear cumulative burdens not imposed on local commerce. . . .The multiplication of state taxes measured by the gross receipts from interstate transactions would spell the destruction of interstate commerce and renew the barriers to interstate trade which it was the object of the commerce clause to remove.[14]

Stone then turned his attention to the New Mexico tax which he characterized as "an excise conditioned on the carrying on of a local business," and which was measured by the receipts from advertising only. The business of preparing, printing, and publishing magazine advertising was "peculiarly local and distinct from its circulation," and a tax upon it was not invalid merely because "the value is enhanced by appellant's circulation of their journal interstate." The events upon which the tax was conditioned occurred "in New Mexico and not elsewhere"; thus the tax could not "in form or substance" be duplicated by other states "in such manner as to lay an added burden on the interstate distribution of the magazine,"[15] and the danger of multiple taxation was absent.

The *Barnwell* and *Western Live Stock* cases deserve a few summary comments. In *Barnwell* Stone laid down two cardinal principles of Commerce-Clause adjudication. First, he held unequivocally that that constitutional provision by its own force "prohibits discrimination against interstate commerce." He buttressed this canon not only with an accurate appeal to history[16] but also with the sound contemporary argument that judicial intervention was justified when a state regulation fell principally upon those without the state and so was not subject "to those political restraints which are normally exerted on legislation where it affects adversely some interests within the state." Thus he accented the negative cutting edge of the Commerce Clause and made no apologies for the Court's use of it to protect the national interest "in maintaining untrammeled the freedom of commerce across state lines." Second, he emphasized the need to examine carefully all of the relevant facts and circumstances in any given case in order to arrive at a reasoned decision. That is, the justices were required to engage in some hard analysis, to weigh competing demands, to determine the actual economic effect on commerce, and only then to arrive at a final judgment. In short, a "balance" was to be struck between the state and national interests involved.

In the *Western Live Stock* case Stone brought to fruition his idea of a practical test for state taxation of interstate commerce. Recognizing the legitimate needs of the states for revenue, and subscribing to the proposition that "interstate business must pay its way," he enunciated the multiple-taxation theory as a guide to decision. The essence of the doctrine was that if a challenged tax could be levied "with equal right" by other states, this would impose "cumulative burdens" on the commerce which could not be allowed to stand; however, if the tax could not be duplicated elsewhere, no barrier to interstate trade would result and the exaction could be sustained. The concept itself was a relatively simple one, and yet it was designed to give the Court help in an exceedingly complex area. Furthermore, it was consistent with Stone's view of the Court's function. As Alpheus Thomas Mason has commented: "The multiple burden test was in effect an application in the tax field of the principle enunciated in the Barnwell decision. As in the former case, it justified judicial intervention to protect interstate commerce from locally imposed, politically irremediable burdens."[17]

A 1939 case, *Gwin, White & Prince, Inc. v. Henneford*,[18] proved that the multiple-taxation doctrine could cut both ways. Gwin, White & Prince was a marketing agent for fruit growers and growers' cooperative associations in Washington and Oregon. Through numerous representatives it sold fruit (apples and pears) in other states and foreign countries, arranged transportation, collected and accounted for the proceeds, and deducted a fee for each box sold. Washington sought to levy a business-activities tax of one-half of one percent on the gross receipts of the marketer as measured by the amount of fruit shipped from that state (about seventy-five percent of the total). The company protested imposition of such an exaction and appealed its case to the Supreme Court.

240

Stone spoke for the seven-to-one majority.[19] He held that since the basic service of the business was in aid of the sale and shipment of the fruit out of state, the tax reached "the entire interstate commerce service rendered both within and without the state and burdens the commerce in direct proportion to its volume."[20] Consequently, the applicable principles were clear and needed no elaboration. He came directly to the point:

> [I]t is enough for present purposes that under the commerce clause, in the absence of Congressional action, state taxation, whatever its form, is precluded if it discriminates against interstate commerce or undertakes to lay a privilege tax measured by gross receipts derived from activities in such commerce which extend beyond the territorial limits of the taxing state. Such a tax, at least when not apportioned to the activities carried on within the state . . . burdens the commerce in the same manner and to the same extent as if the exaction were for the privilege of engaging in interstate commerce and would, if sustained, expose it to multiple tax burdens, each measured by the entire amount of the commerce, to which local commerce is not subject.[21]

Here the tax was not apportioned, and there was the danger of multiple taxation. This was enough to invalidate the tax, and Stone bluntly rejected the idea that an actual burden had to be shown: "Unlawfulness of the burden depends upon its nature, measured in terms of its capacity to obstruct interstate commerce, and not on the contingency that some other state may first have subjected the commerce to a like burden."[22]

A year later Stone again reviewed local taxation. The case was *McGoldrick v. Berwind-White Coal Mining Co.* (1940).[23] New York City laid a two-percent sales tax upon consuming purchasers of tangible personal property.[24] It was conditioned upon events occurring within the state, either transfer of title or taking possession of the purchased property, or an agreement for transfer or possession. Berwind-White was a Pennsylvania corporation which mined coal in that state, shipped it through Jersey City, and sold it to customers in New York. It resisted the tax primarily on the ground that it was levied on the total gross receipts from the interstate sales of coal without apportionment to the activities carried on within New York. Since Pennsylvania and New Jersey could also tax the coal shipments, the commerce might be exposed to the type of multiple tax burden which had been condemned in the *Western Live Stock* and *Gwin, White & Prince* cases. By a vote of six to three the Court rejected this argument and sustained the tax.

In writing the majority opinion Stone made his usual careful analysis of the law and the facts.[25] He admitted that state taxation which tended to prohibit commerce or to place it at a disadvantage as compared with local trade was prohibited. But he also stressed the point that "it was not the purpose of the Commerce Clause to relieve those engaged in interstate commerce of their just share of state tax burdens, merely because an incidental or consequential effect of the tax is an increase in the cost of doing the business."[26] State taxes which the Court had invalidated had fallen because they imposed a burden on the commerce which intrastate commerce did not bear.

Taking this last criterion as controlling, Stone examined the New York tax and found that it bore no such vice:

> Equality is its theme .... It does not aim at or discriminate against interstate commerce. It is laid upon every purchaser, within the state, of goods for consumption, regardless of whether they have been transported in interstate commerce. Its only relation to the commerce arises from the fact that immediately preceding transfer of possession to the purchaser within the state, which is the taxable event regardless of the time and place of passing title, the merchandise has been transported in interstate commerce and brought to its journey's end.[27]

Then, beginning with *Woodruff v. Parham* (1869), he cited case after case in which state sales taxes had been upheld. The present case was no different, and validation of the New York tax had ample support in precedent. It also reflected "a due regard for the just balance between national and state power."[28] This line of reasoning constituted Stone's main defense of the tax. He sidestepped the question of a possible multiple burden by merely asserting that the exaction was conditioned "upon a local activity, delivery of goods within the state upon their purchase for consumption. It is an activity which ... is subject to the state taxing power."[29]

Conflicting views have been expressed on Stone's opinion in the *Berwind-White* case. Alpheus Thomas Mason sees it as perfectly consistent with his earlier decisions and refers to it as the "climax in the evolution of Stone's theory."[30] But Samuel J. Konefsky characterizes it as an "unexpected development ... at variance with his earlier views."[31] Perhaps Thomas Reed Powell resolves the controversy as acceptably as possible. He says, "Mr. Justice Stone for the majority was somewhat happier in supporting the wisdom of the result than in finding it warranted by previous decisions."[32] This would indicate that

242

the *Berwind-White* decision was not wholly consistent with Stone's general objections to multiple taxation; and, in fact, he skirted this issue in his opinion. But Powell adds another statement which helps to explain Stone's decision. He comments: "One would have to be unduly myopic not to perceive the undoubted need of the state of the market for protection from the competition of untaxed deliveries of goods from sister states."[33] Here is probably the point. Stone devised the multiple-taxation theory as a practical guide to reconciling the competing constitutional demands "that commerce between the states shall not be unduly impeded by state action, and that the power to lay taxes for the support of state government shall not be unduly curtailed."[34] But he was never wedded to any judicial formula, even one of his own making; and since he always insisted upon a consideration of all the facts in a case, and was not at all myopic, he undoubtedly felt that the result in *Berwind-White* represented a wise and workable solution to a difficult problem[35]

Balancing-of-Interests, 1943-1945

Two further cases demonstrate Stone's dedication to the pragmatic approach in deciding questions of state power. The first is *Parker v. Brown* (1943).[36] At stake was the validity of an agricultural-marketing program, established under the California Agricultural Prorate Act of 1933, a measure designed to bring stability to the state's important raisin industry by controlling the volume and price of raisins. At the time almost all of the raisins consumed in the United States and nearly one-half of the world crop were grown in California, and thus over ninety percent of the state's output ultimately moved in interstate or foreign commerce. The proration program for the 1940 raisin crop was challenged on three grounds: (1) It violated the Sherman Antitrust Act; (2) it conflicted with the federal Agricultural Marketing Agreement Act of 1937; and (3) it was repugnant to the Commerce Clause.

Speaking for a unanimous Court (8-0), Stone upheld the California regulations against all objections. First, the Sherman Act, on the basis of its language and legislative history, was applicable only to "persons," including business corporations, and gave no hint "that it was intended to restrain state action or official action directed by a state."[37] Second, an examination of the Agricultural Marketing Agreement Act showed that it contemplated "the existence of state programs at least until such time as the Secretary shall establish a federal marketing program,"[38] and this the Secretary had not done. In fact, federal officials had collaborated with California officials in drafting the program, and the Commodity Credit Corporation had loaned the state money to carry it into effect. To Stone this indicated that "the Secretary has reason to believe that the state act will tend to effectuate the policies of the federal act so as not to require the issuance of an order under the latter."[39] Then he turned to the Commerce-Clause question.

The state program undeniably had a substantial impact on the volume and price of raisins shipped in interstate commerce. But the Court had repeatedly held that "the grant of power to Congress by the Commerce Clause did not wholly withdraw from the states the authority to regulate the commerce with respect to matters of local concern, on which Congress has not spoken."[40] Stone proposed two tests of state power in the present situation. The first was the old mechanical test which had held that "manufacture" was not a part of commerce. Under this test, the California regulations applied only to the disposition of raisins "before they are processed and packed preparatory to interstate sale and shipment"—transactions wholly intrastate.[41] The second and more genuine test was Stone's famous "balancing-of-interests" doctrine, which may be seen in his earlier cases, but which he now articulated expressly:

> When Congress has not exerted its power under the Commerce Clause, and state regulation of matters of local concern is so related to interstate commerce that it also operates as a regulation of that commerce, the reconciliation of the power thus granted with that reserved to the state is to be attained by the accommodation of the competing demands of the state and national interests involved. . . . Such regulations by the state . . . are to be upheld because upon a consideration of all the relevant facts and circumstances it appears that the matter is one which may appropriately be regulated in the interest of the safety, health and well-being of local communities, and which, because of its local character and the practical difficulties involved, may never be adequately dealt with by Congress.[42]

The balancing-of-interests test was a practical one, and Stone devoted four pages to analyzing the California raisin industry and its need for economic protection from overproduction and disastrous price cutting. His conclusions were that preservation of the industry depended upon a workable stabilization policy and that the state marketing program was an appropriate means to that end. Furthermore, the effect of the prorate program coincided with and complemented national policy to alleviate the generally distressed condition of agricultural production. In short, the state regulation had to stand.

244

Parker v. Brown was an important case. At the time and for at least twenty years thereafter[43] it represented the outer limits of state power under the Commerce Clause. Here the state was allowed to regulate an entire agricultural industry, most of whose product moved in interstate and foreign commerce. But the local restraints were justified; if they had not been upheld, there might soon have been no raisins produced and shipped at all. Bankrupt growers do not make efficient producers—a fact which Stone grasped with admirable insight. This was his great strength; he was always able to cut through legal formalism to the facts and then allow the Constitution to perform its proper function in the American federal system, that is, to empower government at one level or the other to meet in adequate fashion the pressing needs of the times.

The second case is *Southern Pacific Co. v. Arizona ex rel. Sullivan* (1945),[44] which marked the high point in the use of Stone's balancing method. In 1912 the Arizona state legislature enacted a train-limit law which prohibited railroads from operating a train of more than fourteen passenger cars or seventy freight cars; each violation was subject to a fine. In 1940 Arizona sued Southern Pacific to collect penalties assessed for operating trains above the statutory limits. The railroad admitted the illegal operations, but it contended that the state law offended the Commerce Clause. The state defended it as a legitimate exercise of its police power to secure the safety of its railroad-employed citizens.

Stone wrote the seven-to-two majority opinion which struck down the state act.[45] The principal controversy centered on the Commerce-Clause contention, and he explored its ramifications at length. He recognized that there was "a residuum of power in the state to make laws governing matters of local concern which nevertheless in some measure affect interstate commerce or even, to some extent, regulate it."[46] But it was also established that the states could not control "those phases of the national commerce which, because of the need of national uniformity, demand that their regulation, if any, be prescribed by a single authority."[47] The reconciliation of conflicting claims was to be attained "only by some appraisal and accommodation of the competing demands of the state and national interests involved,"[48] and he made it crystal clear to whom this task was entrusted:

> For a hundred years it has been accepted constitutional doctrine that the commerce clause, without the aid of Congressional legislation, thus affords some protection from state legislation inimical to the national commerce, and that in such cases, where Congress has not acted, *this Court,* and not the state legislature, is

under the commerce clause the final arbiter of the competing demands of state and national interests.[49]

Stone then set about weighing all the relevant factors. He noted that it was standard practice to operate long trains over main lines, and that more than ninety percent of the freight and passenger traffic in Arizona was interstate. A definite relationship existed between economy of operation and train length; as length increased, operating costs were reduced. Furthermore, the enforced breaking up and remaking of trains resulted in a loss of through-service time. In short, the Arizona law imposed a "serious burden" on rail transportation.

The nub of the matter then became a question of safety. "Slack action," or the total amount of free movement between loosely coupled railroad cars, increased with the number of cars and affected the severity of shock in train movements. This whiplash effect created a hazard to operating rail personnel; and, as the length of a train increased, the greater was the likelihood of injury to these employees. On the other hand, the number of typical railway accidents increased with the number of trains operated and the injuries to workers from these accidents were generally of a more serious nature than those due to slack action. All in all, the safety arguments were relative and inconclusive.

This last circumstance tipped the scales for Stone, and he concluded that "the total effect of the law as a safety measure in reducing accidents and casualties is so slight or problematical as not to outweigh the national interest in keeping interstate commerce free from interferences which seriously impede it."[50] The subject of train lengths demanded uniform regulation, which "Congress alone can prescribe," and even an apposite state interest had to be subordinated to the larger interest of the nation in maintaining "an adequate, economical and efficient railway transportation service."

The Black Position

The *Southern Pacific* decision rested squarely upon the balancing-of-interests doctrine and threw into bold relief the broad discretion of the Court in such cases. A second view of state power—the one espoused by Justice Black—is opposed to that doctrine precisely because it does provide wide latitude for judicial choice. The Black position is that in the absence of congressional legislation the Commerce Clause by its own force merely prohibits the states from patently discriminating against interstate commerce in favor of local trade, and he would limit judicial review of state economic policy to this single inquiry. In fact, John P. Frank, one of Black's former law clerks, argues that:

> Black is the strongest supporter of the power of the states of the Union to regulate the economic affairs of men and concerns within their borders that the Court has had in more than a hundred years. Indeed, fair argument can be made that he is the most complete and consistent supporter of state power of all the Justices in the history of the Court.[51]

While this appraisal may be somewhat exaggerated, Black's reluctance to interfere with state power is well established, as his opinions in a few cases demonstrate.

Shortly after Stone had enunciated his "multiple-taxation" doctrine in *Western Live Stock v. Bureau of Revenue,* the Court was faced with the validity of the Indiana Gross Income Tax Act of 1933 as it applied to an in-state manufacturer of road machinery and equipment which sold eighty percent of its products outside the state. Indiana had attempted to tax all of the company's gross receipts, but in *J.D. Adams Manufacturing Co. v. Storen* (1938)[52] Justice Owen J. Roberts invoked the Stone doctrine to disallow the tax on the company's interstate sales.

Black dissented vigorously.[53] He noted that the Indiana gross income tax fell uniformly upon all income "whether derived from interstate or intrastate business" and that there had been no contention that the statute "was inspired by any spirit of antagonism or hostility to interstate commerce or that it discriminates against interstate commerce in amount or method of application."[54] To his mind the real question was whether "the Commerce Clause, of itself, prohibits *all* such state taxes, as 'regulations' of interstate commerce, even though general, uniform and nondiscriminatory."[55] The answer was clearly "no"; such a construction of the clause would actually serve "to impose an unfair and discriminatory burden upon local intrastate business" because the latter would have to bear the entire cost of supporting state government while interstate commerce would be absolved of any similar financial duty.

Black then focused his attack on the multiple-taxation doctrine as a judically contrived test of state power and argued that only Congress

> has the power to formulate rules, regulations and laws to protect interstate commerce from *merely possible future unfair burdens.*

Here the record does not indicate any charge or proof of an existing extraordinary, unfair or multiple tax burden on appellant. . . . The control of future conduct, the prevention of future injuries and the formulation of regulatory rules in the fields of commerce and taxation, all present legislative problems.[56]

If any general rule on state taxation were to be promulgated, it should be "considered and determined by Congress" under that body's supreme power to regulate interstate commerce.

Black took the same position eight months later in his dissent in *Gwin, White, & Prince, Inc. v. Henneford* (1939),[57] this time in direct opposition to Stone. The Washington gross receipts tax should be sustained (even as to sales made out of state) in order to prevent "discrimination against Washington intra-state businesses." Congress had not acted to prohibit such state taxes on gross income from interstate commerce, and until it did they should be allowed to stand. Black drew his own line between what was and what was not proper conduct on the part of the federal judiciary:

While there are strong logical grounds upon which this Court has based its invalidation of state laws actually imposing unjust, unfair, and discriminatory burdens against interstate commerce as such, the same grounds do not support a judicial regulation designed to protect commerce from validly enacted non-discriminatory state taxes which do not—but may sometime—prove burdensome.[58]

This was a direct thrust at Stone's strong assertion that the unconstitutionality of a state tax "depends upon its nature, measured in terms of its capacity to obstruct interstate commerce, and not on the contingency that some other state may first have subjected the commerce to a like burden";[59] and Black went on to question the propriety of Stone's suggestion that an apportioned tax might be valid. No scheme of tax apportionment could be accomplished "without national inquiry and national action," and for the Court to approve any state formula would be

to transfer the constitutional power to regulate such commerce from Congress to the States and federal courts to which the Constitution gives no such power. The Constitution contemplates that Congress alone shall provide for necessary national uniformity in rules governing foreign and interstate commerce.[60]

The job of policing state taxation of commerce was strictly a matter of public policy to be left to the national legislative will, and the Court should not intervene "except for state acts designed to impose discriminatory burdens on interstate commerce because it *is* interstate."[61]

Black's leniency toward state economic action carried over from taxation to outright state regulation of interstate commerce, and he found himself again opposed to Stone in *Southern Pacific Co. v. Arizona* (1945).[62] He pointed to the circumstance that there was factual evidence to support both sides of the safety argument, bluntly accused the Court of acting as a "super-legislature," and denounced its action:

> [T]he determination of whether it is in the interest of society for the length of trains to be governmentally regulated is a matter of public policy. Someone must fix that policy—either the Congress, or the state, or the courts. A century and a half of constitutional history and government admonishes this Court to leave that choice to the elected legislative representatives of the people themselves, where it properly belongs both on democratic principles and the requirements of efficient government.[63]

To the contention that there was a need for uniformity in interstate rail transportation, Black answered that Congress knew about the Arizona regulation and could have legislated upon the subject if it had chosen to do so. The Court was simply writing into law its own belief that "both the legislature of Arizona and the Congress made wrong policy decisions in permitting a law to stand which limits the length of railroad trains."[64] Furthermore, the alleged "burden" on commerce reduced itself to one of "mere cost," and he thought that it was reprehensible to favor "an economical national railroad system" at the expense of "the personal safety of railway employees." Resolution of such an issue was much more properly a subject for "legislative consideration" than for "judicial determination."

A review of these dissenting opinions serves to show clearly Justice Black's position on state power over commerce. Briefly put, he would allow very wide scope for state action and, in the absence of congressional legislation, would frustrate state taxation or regulation only in a clear-cut case of deliberate and malicious discrimination against interstate business simply because it is interstate. More extended comment on the implications of this theory will be reserved to later.

The Jackson Hard Line

A third view of state power, at odds with both the Stone and Black positions, is one which was advocated by Justice Jackson. A former

Solicitor General and Attorney General, Jackson possessed some well-defined and strongly articulated notions about the extent of state power. He held that the Commerce Clause created in the United States a great free-trade area and thus prohibited state restraints upon the free movement of goods and services nationally. He took what might be termed a "hard line" toward exercises of state power, and his disposition would be to scrutinize state acts with a suspicious eye, ready to strike down almost any obstruction to the freedom of commerce. And, as he saw it, it was preeminently the responsibility of the Supreme Court to protect this commerce from the states. Two of his opinions serve to illuminate this line of reasoning.

Two months after Jackson came on the Court at the beginning of the 1941 term, the routine case of *Duckworth v. Arkansas*[65] was decided. At stake was the validity of an Arkansas statute which required a permit for the transportation of intoxicating liquor through the state. The stated purpose of the permit, which was obtainable upon application and payment of a small fee, was to identify those engaged in such transportation and thus to enable local officials to prevent diversion or dumping of liquor in the state. Chief Justice Stone wrote the main opinion which held that the state requirement did not unduly encroach upon national power and so was valid under the *Cooley* rule.[66] Since the act was not repugnant to the Commerce Clause, there was no need to decide whether it derived support from the Twenty-first Amendment.

Jackson wrote his own concurring opinion.[67] He thought that the controversy should have been determined "by guidance from the liquor clauses of the Constitution" because the Twenty-first Amendment created "an important distinction between state power over the liquor traffic and state power over commerce in general";[68] thus the state statute might well be sustainable under a liberal interpretation of that amendment.

Then Jackson voiced in some detail his objections to the use of the Commerce Clause to decide the case. He admitted that the problem of reviewing state legislation was vexatious; but it was one the Court had to face, and he deplored the recent judicial tendency to sustain state laws

> on the ground that Congress has power to supersede them with regulation of its own. It is a tempting escape from a difficult question to pass to Congress the responsibility for continued

existence of local restraints and obstructions to national commerce. But these restraints are individually too petty, too diversified, and too local to get the attention of a Congress hard pressed with more urgent matters. The practical result is that in default of action by us they will go on suffocating and retarding and Balkanizing American commerce, trade and industry.[69]

He relied upon his experience as an administrative official to press his plea for increased judicial control:

The sluggishness of government, the multitude of matters that clamor for attention, and the relative ease with which men are persuaded to postpone troublesome decisions, all make inertia one of the most decisive powers in determining the course of our affairs .... Because that is so, I am reluctant to see any new local systems for restraining our national commerce get the prestige and power of established institutions. The Court's present opinion and tendency would allow the states to establish the restraints and let commerce struggle for Congressional action to make it free.[70]

Jackson, of course, was acutely aware of the events leading up to the "constitutional revolution" of 1937, but he cautioned his brothers that in reacting against "excessive judicial interference with legislative action," they should not "merely rush to other extremes." There was an essential difference between using the due-process clause to invalidate state regulation of internal state affairs and invoking the Commerce Clause "to keep the many states from fastening their several concepts of local 'well-being' onto the national commerce."[71] True, Congress could act to prevent such a "strangling effect," but meanwhile the Court had a positive duty to protect the commerce because:

[T]o let each locality conjure up its own dangers and be the judge of the remedial restraints to be clamped onto interstate trade inevitably retards our national economy and disintegrates our national society. It is the movement and exchange of goods that sustain living standards, both of him who produces and of him who consumes. This vital national interest in free commerce among the states must not be jeopardized.[72]

Jackson wanted no part in an opinion upholding the Arkansas regulation under sanction of the Commerce Clause.

The high point in influence of Jackson's philosophy came in *H.P. Hood & Sons v. DuMond* (1949).[73] A New York law forbade any dealer to buy milk from in-state producers unless licensed to do so by the state Commissioner of Agriculture and Markets. Receipt of a license depended upon the fulfillment of certain requirements, financial and otherwise; in addition the Commissioner had to be satisfied that issuance of the license "will not tend to a destructive competition in a market already adequately served." Hood, a Massachusetts corporation engaged in distributing milk and milk products in the Boston area, operated three milk receiving plants in New York. It applied for a license to establish a fourth plant, but was turned down by Commissioner DuMond on the ground that there had been a shortage of milk in that area and that another plant would create destructive competition among dealers. Hood appealed this ruling.

In a close, five-to-four decision the Court struck down the New York statute. Jackson spoke for the majority.[74] He admitted that the production and distribution of milk were intimately related to local public health and welfare; the question was what limitations the Commerce Clause placed on the power of the state to protect these. To answer this he looked to past cases which dealt with state control of milk. Most relevant to the present case, wherein the volume of interstate milk was curtailed, was *Baldwin v. G.A.F. Seelig, Inc.* (1935)[75] in which the Court had struck down an attempt by New York to exclude milk from Vermont because the price paid to Vermont producers was below the minimum price paid to New York producers. There Justice Benjamin N. Cardozo had distinguished between the legitimate power of a state to protect the health, safety, and general welfare of its citizens and the forbidden power to retard, burden, or constrict the flow of interstate commerce for its purely economic advantage. He had held that a state could not establish "an economic barrier against competition with the products of another state or the labor of its residents";[76] and he had made the now-famous assertion that the Constitution "was framed upon the theory that the peoples of the several states must sink or swim together, and that in the long run prosperity and salvation are in union and not division."[77]

These views were in perfect harmony with Jackson's own thought, and he took six pages of his opinion to show that the history of the Philadelphia Convention and subsequent legal precedents fully supported Cardozo's interpretation of the delegated power. Furthermore, the Court's steadfast adherence to that interpretation had·resulted in a "federal free trade unit" which had brought to the inhabitants of the states the most impressive material success "in the history of commerce."

This economic interdependence of the states, however, only emphasized "the necessity of protecting interstate movement of goods against local burdens and repressions."[78] What would happen, Jackson asked rhetorically, if those states specializing in a particular manufactured product of those blessed with some scarce natural resource should decree that home users had first priority? Think of the "fantastic rivalries and dislocations and reprisals" that would surely ensue. It was just such a contingency which the Constitution forbade:

> Our system, fostered by the Commerce Clause, is that every farmer and every craftsman shall be encouraged to produce by the certainty that he will have free access to every market in the Nation, that no home embargoes will withhold his exports, and no foreign state will by customs duties or regulations exclude them. Likewise, every consumer may look to the free competition from every producing area in the Nation to protect him from exploitation by any. Such was the vision of the Founders; such has been the doctrine of this Court which has given it reality.[79]

With this sweeping declaration as a guide, Jackson very quickly disposed of the state's two principal contentions. First, the fact that Hood already operated three plants, which were not limited as to the quantities of milk they might purchase, did not prove that commerce was unrestricted; a buyer had to buy "where there is a willing seller," and the milk business necessitated locating plants near producers. Second, the argument of destructive competition was ineffective, because its use would be "equally effective to exclude an entirely new foreign handler from coming into the State to purchase,"[80] a result precluded by the Commerce Clause. In sum, the state statute as applied was repugnant to the national commerce power and thus was invalid.

Justice Black registered his strong dissent.[81] The crux of his detailed, eight-part opinion was that the Court had set up "a new constitutional formula for invalidation of state laws regulating local phases of interstate commerce" which was more hazardous to state power than any previous test and which would "leave a large area of local business activity free from state regulation." Like Jackson he used history and precedent to prove his point. He discussed the Taney view that the commerce power was concurrent and that "this Court was without power to strike down state regulations unless they conflicted with a valid federal law."[82] He admitted that the *Cooley* case had rejected this in part; but he argued that the *Cooley* rule at least required a careful weighing of conflicting interests, and he found that implicit in the rule was "a determined purpose not to leave areas in which interstate activities could be insulated from any regulation at all."[83]

This was the vice of the present decision; the Court had abandoned "the *Cooley* balancing-of-interests rule" and had killed the New York statute "by a mere automatic application of a new mechanistic formula."[84] In a pointed thrust Black charged that the only support for the result reached was "the philosophy of the *Duckworth* concurring opinion." Thus meaningful judicial appraisals under the *Cooley* rule were gently laid to rest, and "bad local business practices are now judicially immunized from state regulation."[85]

Finally Black looked to the facts. Commissioner DuMond's finding of destructive competition had not been refuted. The state statute was not on its face discriminatory against out-of-state milk dealers, and there was no evidence that it had been administered "with a hostile eye." The state's "fair attempt to protect the healthful milk supply of consumers" should not be forbidden by the Court acting as a superlegislature; and he concluded, "I would leave New York's law alone."[86]

Ratiocinations

These three conflicting theories of state power over commerce may now be summarized and commented upon briefly. The never-ending judicial argument has been over the extent to which state economic action could be sanctioned constitutionally in order to create and maintain a fair and workable balance between state and national interests.[87] Of the modern judges it may be argued that Chief Justice Stone stood out with his pragmatic approach to the problem. With a distrust of mechanical formulas, a deference for legislative judgments, a sense of judicial self-restraint, a clear-headed appreciation of the complexities of the federal system, and a corresponding sympathy for the legitimate needs of the states, Stone perfected his balancing-of-interests doctrine into a highly workable device for drawing the line between state and national power. But he recognized that in a federal system final authority must reside somewhere, and he was firm in his belief that it rested in the Supreme Court. In a 1945 letter to Noel T. Dowling, Stone asserted:

> [H]ow we could have settled all the questions arising out of distribution of power between the state and national governments without the arbitrament of a supreme court or some other body with corresponding functions, I do not know. The only other alternative in many cases might well be resort to force. The

Constitution, read as a whole and in the light of its background and purposes, plainly contemplated that the Supreme Court should do just that, not only in connection with the commerce clause but with other clauses whose meaning and application necessarily determine the rights of litigants.[88]

The Court, too, was "an instrument of government" which had been invested with the "power to govern."

To Stone's "right" stood Justice Jackson, tough-minded advocate of a federal free-trade unit upon which the states could encroach but little before running afoul of the sharp cutting edge of the Commerce Clause.[89] That he never deviated from his restrictive concept of state power is seen in some thoughts he expressed just before his death in October, 1954. In preparing a series of Harvard lectures, Jackson wrote:

> There can be no doubt that in the original Constitution the states surrendered to the Federal Government the power to regulate interstate commerce, or commerce among the states. They did so in the light of a disastrous experience in which commerce and prosperity were reduced to the vanishing point by states discriminating against each other through devices of regulation, taxation and exclusion. It is more important today than it was then that we remain one commercial and economic unit and not a collection of parasitic states preying upon each other's commerce. I make no concealment of and offer no apology for my philosophy that the federal interstate commerce power should be strongly supported and that the impingement of the states upon that commerce which moves among them should be restricted to narrow limits.[90]

That there is a strong patriotic appeal in this position is undeniable, but noble ideas do not necessarily make good or safe guides to judicial decision making. On balance the Jackson view would probably limit exercises of state power too severely, and the states would not retain enough flexibility of action to supervise effectively commercial activities of an essentially local and diverse nature.

At the opposite end of the judicial spectrum is Justice Black, who holds that the mere grant of the commerce power to Congress did not ipso facto displace state power except to the extent that no state can discriminate against interstate commerce in order to further its own economic advantage. On the surface this "liberal" view of state power appears to be designed to give the states wide latitude in the management of their own affairs and to allow them an enhanced and vigorous role in the federal system. But there are problems here which militate against uncritical acceptance of the Black philosophy. One relates to his conception of the role of the Court; the other concerns the practical politics of American government. Noel T. Dowling has pinpointed these flaws so incisively that he requires quoting at some length:

[1.] It is difficult to understand how Mr. Justice Black finds authority in the Constitution for the Court to negative discriminatory measures, but no power to overturn less flagrant infringements upon the national concern in the free course of commerce, for the Constitution is no more cognizant of "discrimination" than it is of "competitive disadvantage." Nor is this the sole difficulty in his position. Discrimination is a delusively simple term. How overreaching must a state measure be to merit condemnation as discriminatory? It seems apparent that in answering this question the Court must make the same sort of value judgment that it has been making in performing its broader protective function. Discrimination exists or not, depending upon whether there is an economic justification for the difference in treatment which the state accords interstate commerce. Only by an evaluation of all the facts and circumstances can such an issue be decided by the Court.[91]

[2.] There is no assurance that the commerce problem would be as well handled by Congress alone as where both Congress and the courts participate in its solution. I say "would," drawing a distinction between what seems likely and what is theoretically possible. Congress is a big and heavy machine to set in motion, and its progress is sometimes impeded even when national interests of the highest order are at stake. Meanwhile much damage to interstate commerce, to say nothing of the otherwise amicable relationships among the states, might be caused by unrestrained state action.[92]

Dowling has exposed the major weaknesses of the Black position. What superficially appears to be the ultimate in judicial self-restraint is in reality the same judicial discretion exercised by Stone and Jackson but biased toward the states. Furthermore, seemingly forgotten or ignored by ex-Senator Black is the way in which Congress operates. Combine the committee and seniority system in both houses with the two-thirds cloture rule in the Senate, both of which work to the advantage of Southern, states' rights Congressmen and Middle-Western, rural conservatives, and the chances of persuading Congress to undo regulations by the "sovereign" states affecting adversely the national commerce become almost nonexistent.[93]

There is one further consideration. As Stone noted, the American federal system with its two levels of government invites and indeed makes inevitable clashes between those two centers of power. In order to have a smoothly functioning system, someone, somewhere, must adjudicate those clashes. In Articles III and VI of the Constitution, in Section 25 of the Judiciary Act of 1789, and in *Cohens v. Virginia* (1821) the decision was hammered out that the Supreme Court was to be that someone. Given this fact the real question becomes: how should the Court discharge its constitutional responsibility to decide questions of national and state power? If it is admitted that such a herculean task necessarily carries with it very broad judicial discretion, then this inquiry reduces itself to a consideration of what guidelines or what forms of reasoning are most appropriate to, and will result in the most widely acceptable resolutions of, the whole complex problem. Without intending to disparage invidiously either Justice Jackson or Justice Black, the thrust of the argument to this point is that the best answer lies in the kinds of fair-minded, intellectually tenable analyses proposed and executed by Chief Justice Stone.

Leading State Cases, 1944-1964

The foregoing theories have been canvassed in some detail because they represent, broadly speaking, "ideal types" of the various judicial approaches to solution of the state-power problem. But at any given time the Supreme Court is composed of nine men, each of whom has his own individual attitudes, beliefs, predilections, and capacity for decision; and the fact is that commerce cases are not often decided by use of one of the theories alone. More frequently the decisions rest upon a combination of ideas blended together in a fashion which is agreeable to the opinion-writer and which can command a majority of the justices. Indeed, a look at the cases of the recent period will demonstrate that while the Court has become more sophisticated in its handling of state questions, it continues to speak in many of the old familiar terms or formulas which were outlined in Chapter 2. The hands of judgment may be those of Black or Clark or White, but the voice is often that of Bradley or Field or Waite. A survey of a few of the more important cases of state regulation will bring this part of the present study up-to-date.

That *Hood v. DuMond* did not wholly settle the problem of local milk laws is seen in two later cases. The first is *Dean Milk Co. v. City of Madison* (1951).[94] An ordinance of Madison, Wisconsin, forbade the sale of milk unless it had been pasteurized and bottled at an approved plant within five miles of the center of the city; a second provision also prohibited the sale of milk unless it came from a source of supply which had been inspected by city health officials, and said officials were expressly relieved of any duty to inspect farms located beyond a radius of twenty-five miles from the city. Dean Milk, and Illinois corporation whose suppliers and pasteurization plants were located outside of the specified area, challenged the statute. By a vote of six to three the Court invalidated it.

Justice Tom C. Clark spoke for the majority.[95] He noted that Dean's plants and producers were inspected by Chicago public health authorities and that its milk was labeled "Grade A" under standards recommended by the United States Public Health Service; the reason for the denial of a selling license in Madison was solely geographical. Clark admitted that in some particulars the Madison sanitation standards were more rigorous than those of Chicago, but he held that "the ordinance imposes an undue burden on interstate commerce."[96] The practical effect of the regulation was to exclude from Madison "wholesome milk produced and pasteurized in Illinois." He continued:

> In thus erecting an economic barrier protecting a major local industry against competition from without the State, Madison plainly discriminates against interstate commerce. This it cannot do, even in the exercise of its unquestioned power to protect the health and safety of its people, if reasonable nondiscriminatory alternatives, adequate to conserve legitimate local interests, are available.[97]

The question then became whether "reasonable and adequate alternatives" were available, and Clark found in the affirmative. Madison could (1) use its own inspectors in Dean's plants and charge "the actual and reasonable cost of such inspection," or (2) have the United States Public Health Service spot-check the accuracy of safety ratings in the Chicago area to be sure that sanitation standards there were being properly enforced. Under these circumstances the ordinance was "not essential for the protection of local health interests," invited "a multiplication of preferential trade areas destructive of the very purpose of the Commerce Clause," and necessarily had to yield to the *Baldwin* principle that "one state in its dealings with another may not place itself in a position of economic isolation."[98]

Predictably, Justice Black dissented.[99] He denied that the Madison regulation excluded "wholesome milk coming from Illinois or anywhere else." It was merely Dean's "personal preference" not to pasteurize its

258

milk "within the defined geographical area" which kept its milk out. The city's "bona fide health law" should not be invalidated merely because "alternative milk-inspection methods might insure the cleanliness and healthfulness" of Dean's milk; to use this ground was to elevate "the right to traffic in commerce for profit above the power of the people to guard the purity of their daily diet of milk."[100] Because the sanitation standards prescribed locally were more demanding than the United States Public Health Service's "minimum" requirements, the Court could not be "satisfied beyond a reasonable doubt that the substitutes it proposes would not lower health standards";[101] therefore, it should allow the law to stand.

The second milk case is *Polar Ice Cream & Creamery Co. v. Andrews* (1964).[102] The Florida Milk Commission imposed a complex set of regulations upon producer-distributor dealings in the Pensacola Milk Marketing Area which had the effect of forcing any distributor to (1) pay a minimum price of sixty-one cents per gallon for all milk purchased from local producers and sold as Class I milk,[103] (2) allocate all Class I milk requirements to local producers first, and (3) accept as much milk as these producers might offer. Polar, a Pensacola processor and distributor, sold fluid milk and milk products in Florida in competition with Alabama distributors.[104] Prior to the Milk Commission regulations, it purchased up to seventy percent of its milk from out-of-state producers or brokers. The price of this milk varied, but some was purchased for as low as thirty to thirty-five cents per gallon. Polar opposed the new three-pronged regulatory structure on the ground that it imposed an undue burden on interstate commerce in milk. By a unanimous vote (9-0) the Supreme Court agreed.

Justice Byron R. White explained the vice of the state scheme.[105] Under its provisions Polar was required to buy from local producers an amount of raw milk equal to its Class I sales and could turn to outside sources only after the local supply was exhausted. Since the Pensacola producers could at times cover Polar's entire Class I needs, "an Alabama dairy farmer could not become one of Polar's regular producers and sell all of his milk to that company."[106] Thus the case was controlled primarily by the principles of *Baldwin v. Seelig* (1935), which were "as sound today as they were when announced." White elaborated:

The Florida controls preempt for the Florida producers a large share of the Florida market, especially the most lucrative fluid milk market. Out-of-state milk may not partitipate in this part of the Florida market, unless local production is inadequate, and given the exclusive domain of the Florida producers over Class I sales, out-of-state milk may not profitably serve the remainder of the Florida market, since it is relegated to the surplus market alone. These barriers are precisely the kind of hindrance to the introduction of milk from other States which *Baldwin* condemned as an "unreasonable clog upon the mobility of commerce. They set up what is equivalent to a rampart of customs duties designed to neutralize advantages belonging to the place of origin. They are thus hostile in conception as well as burdensome in result."[107]

The Court brushed aside the Florida contention that Polar merely wished to buy outside milk at distress prices with the flat assertion that "the State may not, in the sole interest of promoting the economic welfare of its dairy farmers, insulate the Florida milk industry from competition from other States."[108] Nor was the fact that Florida allowed competition on the distributor level sufficient to justify its actions. White was succinct: "The burden on commerce and the embargo on out-of-state milk remain."[109]

If the states have not fared well in their attempts to curtail the free flow of milk across their borders, they have had a good deal more success in denying "foreign" corporations access to their courts. Two cases substantiate this point. The first is *Union Brokerage Co. v. Jensen* (1944).[110] Union, a North Dakota corporation, conducted a customhouse brokerage business at Noyes, Minnesota. Its function was to represent American importers of Canadian goods in declaring the contents and value of shipments, in estimating the tariff charges due, and in advancing payment so that the goods might be cleared. This is a very demanding occupation, and the United States Treasury Department, under congressional authorization, has prescribed elaborate rules and regulations for the licensing of such brokers. Union, so licensed, sued Jensen, a former employee, for breach of certain fiduciary obligations in relation to its business. Jensen defended on the ground that Union could not resort to the Minnesota courts because it had not complied with the Minnesota Foreign Corporation Act, which required a certificate of any foreign corporation doing business in the state as a prerequisite for maintaining an action in a state court. The Supreme Court of Minnesota sustained this defense, and Union appealed.

The United States Supreme Court upheld the lower state court. Justice Felix Frankfurter wrote the seven-to-two majority opinion.[111] The case presented two questions: Did enforcement of the Minnesota law in this situation run counter to the federal licensing provisions, and was its enforcement barred by the Commerce Clause? Frankfurter had no trouble in answering both in the negative. He held first that "the limited and defined control which federal authority has thus far seen fit to assert over customhouse brokers does not deny to Minnesota the power to subject Union to the same demand which it makes of all other foreign corporations";[112] the reason was that the federal and state requirements could "move freely within the orbits of their respective purposes without impinging upon one another."[113] The federal regulations were concerned solely with Union's financial activities in relation to the United States and to importers and exporters; the state was interested only in the protection of its citizens who might have other types of financial dealings with Union.

The second objection to the state act was equally easy to override. Acquisition of a certificate required a filing fee of five dollars and an initial license fee of fifty dollars. The foreign corporation then had to file annual reports on the basis of which an annual fee was assessed, but the measure of this fee was substantially the same as for domestic corporations. Frankfurter found this license requirement to be "a conventional means of assuring responsibility and fair dealing on the part of foreign corporations coming into a State."[114] Although Union was clearly engaged in foreign commerce, its activities went beyond its services "at the port of entry" to include "a wide variety of dealings with the people in the community." Thus it had localized its business and had given Minnesota a special interest in supervising it. The concomitant fee system did not offend the Commerce Clause:

> By its own force that Clause does not imply relief to those engaged in interstate or foreign commerce from the duty of paying an appropriate share for the maintenance of the various state governments. Nor does it preclude a State from giving needful protection to its citizens in the course of their contacts with businesses conducted by outsiders when the legislation by which this is accomplished is general in its scope, is not aimed at interstate or foreign commerce, and involves merely burdens incident to effective administration.[115]

Union was denied access to Minnesota's courts.

The second case is *Eli Lilly & Co. v. Sav-On-Drugs, Inc.* (1961).[116] Lilly, an Indiana pharmaceutical corporation, brought action to enjoin Sav-On-Drugs from selling Lilly products in New Jersey at prices lower than those fixed in minimum retail price contracts which Lilly had signed with a number of New Jersey drug retailers. (Under the New

Jersey Fair Trade Act such negotiated prices became obligatory on nonsigning retailers.) Sav-On-Drugs moved to dismiss the complaint under a New Jersey law which denied a foreign corporation access to the state courts unless it had obtained a certificate authorizing it to do business in the state. Lilly opposed the motion to dismiss on the ground that its business in New Jersey was entirely in interstate commerce and that any attempt to require it to obtain a certificate would be forbidden by the Commerce Clause. The trial court found that Lilly was in fact engaged in local business and granted the motion to dismiss; this judgment was affirmed above, and Lilly appealed.

The real question before the Supreme Court was the extent of Lilly's activities within New Jersey, that is, whether Lilly was conducting an intrastate (as well as an interstate) business. By a vote of five to four the Court held that it was. Justice Black, speaking for four justices, looked to the facts to justify this conclusion.[117] Lilly sold its products to New Jersey wholesalers who then resold them to retailers, hospitals, and physicians within the state. Lilly maintained a marketing office in Newark and employed eighteen detailmen on a regular basis to visit retail druggists, doctors, and hospitals throughout the state and acquaint them with Lilly's products. The detailmen provided free advertising and promotional material to these outlets and, on occasion, received a purchase order for transmittal to a wholesaler. Under these circumstances the finding of the trial court that Lilly was engaged in intrastate business activities had to be sustained.[118] That the detailmen were not engaged in the systematic solicitation of retail orders did not alter the fact that Lilly was conducting "a domestic business—inducing one local merchant to buy a particular class of goods from another."[119] Under *Union Brokerage Co. v. Jensen,* therefore, New Jersey could require Lilly to obtain a certificate. Since the company had neglected to do so, it was barred from use of the state's courts.

Justice William O. Douglas dissented.[120] The precise issue was "whether a State can require a license for the doing of an interstate business"; and he argued:

> The power to license the exercise of a federal right, like the power to tax it, is "the power to control or suppress its enjoyment." . . . Soliciting interstate business has up to this day been on the same basis as doing an interstate business, so far as the protection of the Commerce Clause is concerned.[121]

Douglas could not see that the activities of Lilly's employees were materially different from those of a drummer for any interstate business, and he could see no distinction between inducing sales and soliciting them.[122] The Court's holding repudiated "the whole line" of drummer cases beginning with *Robbins v. Shelby County Taxing District* (1887) and set up a new formula whereby "a State can stand over the channels of interstate commerce in a way that promises to do great harm to the national market that heretofore the Commerce Clause has protected."[123] But the Black-Harlan position that Lilly's promotional activities constituted a "local business" prevailed.

Interestingly enough, it has been in the Commerce-Clause area that Black and Douglas, who have stood together on so many issues for so long a time, have evidenced a tendency to disagree. One case, pertinent to the present survey, further illustrates this parting of the ways. A second case demonstrates essential agreement, but with Douglas' reasoning in the ascendancy.

The clash came in *Lloyd A. Fry Roofing Co. v. Wood* (1952).[124] The company manufactured asphalt roofing products in Memphis, Tennessee, and shipped them in trucks to customers in nearby states. Some of the trucks were driven by their owners who had supposedly leased them to Fry and become company employees. Five of these driver-owners were arrested in Arkansas for failing to obtain a permit for interstate carriage as required of all "contract carriers" by section 11 of the Arkansas Motor Act. Fry sought on both state and federal grounds to enjoin the state Public Service Commission from further molestation of the drivers. First, the state law exempted "private carriers," and Fry argued that it fell into this class since it carried its own products in its own leased trucks operated by its own *bona fide* driver-employees. Second, Fry argued that the permit requirement unduly burdened interstate commerce and invaded a field of regulation preempted by the Federal Motor Carrier Act. The Commission responded that the truck leases were mere pretenses, a subterfuge to escape the provisions of section 11. This latter argument prevailed at the state level. The federal contentions likewise were rejected, and Fry appealed.

In a close, five-to-four decision the Supreme Court upheld the Arkansas statute. Justice Black wrote the majority opinion.[125] On the state question he admitted that there was factual evidence to support both sides; but since there were no "exceptional circumstances" involved, the findings of the state supreme court should be accepted. He then turned to the federal questions. The granting of a permit under section 11 was dependent upon a number of factors, including a consideration of the adequacy of transportation services already being performed by other types of carriers. Just such a proviso had been held to be an unconstitutional obstruction of interstate commerce in *Buck v. Kuykendall*, 267 U.S. 307 (1925), but here Arkansas had not claimed any discretionary right to refuse to grant permits.

Black emphasized this last point heavily. The state had asked the driver-owners "to do nothing except apply for a permit as contract carriers are required to do" and had asserted no power "to require the drivers to do more than register with the appropriate agency."[126] No showing had been made that the state Commission had attempted or would attempt "to attach any burdensome conditions to the grant of a permit, or conditions that would in any manner conflict with the National Motor Carrier Act or any Interstate Commerce Commission regulations issued thereunder."[127] He concluded:

> In this situation our prior cases make clear that a state can regulate so long as no undue burden is imposed on interstate commerce, and that a mere requirement for a permit is not such a burden. It will be time enough to consider apprehended burdensome conditions when and if the state attempts to impose and enforce them. At present we hold only that Arkansas is not powerless to require interstate motor carriers to identify themselves as users of that state's highways.[128]

Justice Douglas dissented.[129] Whether the driver-owners were contract or private carriers was immaterial to the crucial federal question of "whether Arkansas can require a person engaged exclusively in the interstate transportation of goods by motor carrier to obtain a certificate of necessity and convenience from Arkansas."[130] The label of "Certificate of Necessity and Convenience" was far more accurate than "permit" because the state conditioned its grant of permission on a review of several factors such as the reliability and financial condition of the applicant, the effect of the proposed service upon the existing transportation service, the likelihood of the service being permanent throughout the year, and so forth. Douglas was blunt in his condemnation of the Arkansas Motor Act:

> This statute is a regulation of interstate commerce, not a regulation of the use of Arkansas' highways. It is precisely the kind of control which the State of Washington tried to exercise over motor carriers and which was denied her by *Buck v. Kuykendall* .... As Mr. Justice Brandeis, speaking for the Court

in that case, said, the effect of this kind of state regulation is "not merely to burden, but to obstruct" interstate commerce.

. . . The certificate or permit exacted here is one authorizing an interstate contract carrier "to engage in such business." Until today no state could impose any such condition on one engaged exclusively in interstate commerce. Until today such a certificate was the concern solely of the Interstate Commerce Commission.[131]

Congress had preempted the field, had left no phase of interstate motor transportation untouched, and had effectively precluded "both inconsistent and overlapping state regulations." It was up to the ICC alone to regulate Fry's leasing operation.

A 1959 case shows the persistent problem faced by the Court to "balance" state and national needs. *Bibb v. Navajo Freight Lines, Inc.* involved the validity of an Illinois statute which required the use of specially contoured mudguards on all trucks and trailers operated on the state's highways. Justice Douglas spoke for a unanimous Court in stricking down the Illinois regulation.[133] He admitted, citing *South Carolina Highway Dept. v. Barnwell Bros.,* that the power of a state over its highways was "broad and pervasive." The facts, then, became of paramount importance.

Navajo Freight Lines had presented evidence, unrebutted by the state, to show a "heavy burden" on interstate commerce.[134] With two possible exceptions the mudguards required in other states would not meet the Illinois standards. Since an interstate carrier could not know which of its equipment might be used in a particular area at a particular time, any carrier operating into or through Illinois would have to install the contour mudguards on all of its equipment. This alone entailed a sizable dollar cost. But worse still, the new regulation seriously interfered with the "interline" operations of a carrier, that is, the practice of interchanging trailers between carriers not serving the same areas in order to provide speedy through-service by eliminating the need to unload and reload cargo. An originating carrier which never operated in Illinois would not be expected to use the special mudguards, and yet its equipment could not be operated in that state without them. In effect, this simply meant an end to interlining, which comprised a substantial portion of the appellee's interstate operations.

Illinois countered with the argument that the statute was a legitimate exercise of its police power to enact safety measures. The mudguards "prevented the throwing of debris into the faces of drivers of passing cars and into the windshields of a following vehicle." But other evidence showed that the contour mud flap posessed "no advantages over the conventional or straight mud flap previously required in Illinois and presently required in most of the states"; in fact, the contour guards created new highway hazards in two ways: (1) They caused an accumulation of heat in the brake drum which decreased the effectiveness of brakes; and (2) they were frequently bumped and knocked off onto the highway which created obstacles to traffic flow.

Under all of these circumstances Douglas reasoned that *Southern Pacific Co. v. Arizona* and *Morgan v. Virginia* were the cases which most accurately delimited the dimensions of the Court's present problem. The outcome was inevitable:

> This is one of those cases—few in number—where local safety measures that are nondiscriminatory place an unconstitutional burden on interstate commerce. This conclusion is especially underlined by the deleterious effect which the Illinois law will have on the "interline" operation of interstate motor carriers. . . . A State which insists on a design out of line with the requirements of almost all the other States may sometimes place a great burden of delay and inconvenience on those interstate motor carriers entering or crossing its territory. Such a new safety device . . . may be so compelling that the innovating State need not be the one to give way. But the present showing—balanced against the clear burden on commerce—is far too inconclusive to make this mudguard meet that test.[135]

Even Justice Black joined the Douglas opinion, which clearly utilized and sanctioned Stone's durable balancing-of-interests doctrine.

The preceding discussion illustrates the perplexing problems which confront the Supreme Court in its role as arbiter of the American federal system. The very nature of that system, however, demands that there be a final authority capable of settling the disputes and conflicts of interest which will inevitably arise therein, and the process of historical decision has laid that task primarily upon the Court.[136] Given this fact, wide judicial discretion is admittedly a necessity, and the crucial question relates only to the way in which it is to be exercised. It is the argument here that Stone's balancing-of-interests formula provides the best answer. If the teachings of the *Cooley* case are accepted and used as a starting point, then it appears that Stone was not only true to the real meaning of the *Cooley* rule, but that he also added significantly to its updating in terms of the judicial process of applying it in concrete circumstances. The foregoing cases show the continuing usefulness of the doctrine and indicate the present constitutionally permissible limits of state authority over interstate commerce in the absence of federal legislation—limits which have expanded considerably from pre-1937 days under the pragmatic, realistic Stone approach to drawing the boundary line between national and state power.

Notes

1. 273 U.S. 34.

2. See Chapter 2 for details of the case.

3. 273 U.S. 34, 43-44.

4. Ibid., 44. The following year he repeated and expanded this view in a speech. See Harlan F. Stone, "Fifty Years' Work of the United States Supreme Court," *American Bar Association Journal,* LIII (Aug.-Sept., 1928), 259.

5. 303 U.S. 177. For Stone's complete opinion, see ibid., 180-96. Justices Cardozo and Reed took no part in the case.

6. Ibid., 185-86.

7. Ibid., 185, footnote 2. Stone liked to put novel ideas in footnotes. See his famous footnote 4 in *United States v. Carolene Products Co.,* 304 U.S. 144, 152-53 (1938), in which he intimated that there might be "narrower scope for operation of the presumption of constitutionality when legislation appears on its face to be within a specific prohibition of the Constitution, such as those of the first ten amendments"—an inference that the judiciary has a special responsibility to protect individual liberties from governmental encroachment. See Alpheus Thomas Mason, *Harlan Fiske Stone: Pillar of the Law* (New York: The Viking Press, 1956), 512-15.

8. Ibid., 183.

9. Ibid., 190. Stone compared such regulations with local regulations of rivers, harbors, docks, and quarantine regulations, and he used a whole page of citations to support the case for state power; see ibid., 188, footnote 5. He included *Willson* and *Cooley.*

10. 303 U.S. 250. This case was decided exactly two weeks after *South Carolina Highway Dept. v. Barnwell Bros.* For his complete opinion, see ibid., 251-61.

11. Justices McReynolds and Butler dissented without opinion; Justice Cardozo was ill and took no part.

12. 303 U.S. 250, 253. Here he relied mainly on the insurance cases, beginning with *Paul v. Virginia,* 8 Wallace 168. (See Chapter 5.)

13. Ibid., 254.

14. Ibid., 255-56.

15. Ibid., 260.

16. Stone cited such sources as Farrand, *Records of the Federal Convention,* Vol. II, 308, and Vol. III, 478, 548, 574; *The Federalist,* No. XLII (to which the present author would add Nos. XI and XXII); Curtis, *History of the Constitution,* Vol. I, 502; and Story, *Commentaries on the Constitution of the United States,* section 259. See 303 U.S. 177 at 186 for this listing. Here, as in his *Darby* discussion of the Tenth Amendment, Stone was on solid historical grounds. (See the analysis of the *Darby* case in Chapter 3.)

17. Mason, *Harlan Fiske Stone,* 493. See pages 490-94 for a discussion of the *Barnwell* and *Western Live Stock* cases.

18. 305 U.S. 434.

19. For his complete opinion, see ibid., 435-41. Justice Butler, joined by Justice McReynolds, wrote an opinion concurring in the result. Justice Cardozo had died and had not been replaced. Justice Black's dissenting opinion will be considered later.

20. Ibid., 438.

21. Ibid., 438-39.

22. Ibid., 440.

23. 309 U.S. 33.

24. The burden of the tax fell on the seller, however, if he did not collect it and remit it to the city.

25. For his complete opinion, see 309 U.S. 33, 41-59.

26. Ibid., 46.

27. Ibid., 48-49.

28. Ibid., 51.

29. Ibid., 58. It was here that Chief Justice Hughes, joined by Justices McReynolds and Roberts, dissented on the ground that the tax was a "direct burden" on commerce which could be duplicated by Pennsylvania and New Jersey; see ibid., 59-70.

30. Mason, *Harlan Fiske Stone,* 493.

31. Samuel J. Konefsky, *Chief Justice Stone and the Supreme Court* (New York: The Macmillan Company, 1945), 88. For a very good treatment of Stone's views on state power, see Chapter 2. "The Commerce Clause and State Power," 48-97.

32. Thomas Reed Powell, *Vagaries and Varieties in Constitutional Interpretation* (New York: Columbia University Press, 1956), 189.

33. Ibid., 189. For an excellent overview of state power through 1954, see Chapters 5 and 6, 142-215.

34. 309 U.S. 33, 47.

35. That he did not abandon his multiple-taxation theory, however, is shown by his later dissent in *Northwest Airlines v. Minnesota,* 322 U.S. 292 (1944), in which he protested the imposition of a personal property tax on the entire fleet of airplanes owned by an interstate airline with its home port in St. Paul; see ibid., 308-26. For a fairly comprehensive discussion of state taxation up to 1951, see Edward L. Barrett, Jr., "State Taxation of Interstate Commerce—'Direct Burdens,' 'Multiple Burdens' or What Have You?" in *Selected Essays on Constitutional Law: 1938-1962,* compiled and edited by a committee of the Association of American Law Schools (St. Paul, Minn.: West Publishing Co., 1963), 324-55.

36. 317 U.S. 341. For Stone's complete opinion, see ibid., 344-68.

37. Ibid., 351. Stone noted that Congress could prohibit such a stabilization program under the commerce power and that a state could not immunize private violators of the Sherman Act, but these were moot points here.

38. Ibid., 354.

39. Ibid., 356.

40. Ibid., 360.

41. Ibid., 361. Remember that *Darby* and *Wickard* had been only

recently decided and that Stone was dealing with a matter of state power in the absence of any conflicting federal legislation.

42. Ibid., 362-63.

43. *Florida Lime & Avocado Growers, Inc. v. Paul*, 373 U.S. 132 (1963), which will be discussed in full in Chapter 8, is even more lenient toward state power in the view of the present author.

44. 325 U.S. 761.

45. For his complete opinion, see ibid., 763-84. Justice Rutledge concurred in the result. Justices Black and Douglas wrote separate dissenting opinions.

46. Ibid., 767.

47. Ibid., 767.

48. Ibid., 769.

49. Ibid., 769. Stone cited the *Cooley* case in support of this proposition. It should be noted that, of course, the Court from time to time shares the role of arbiter with Congress. See, for example, *Prudential Insurance Co. v. Benjamin*, 328 U.S. 408 (1946), which was discussed in full in Chapter 5. In fact, Stone admitted here that "Congress has undoubted power to redefine the distribution of power over interstate commerce"; and he cited *In re Rahrer*, 140 U.S. 545 (1891), and *Clark Distilling Company v. Western Maryland Railway Co.*, 242 U.S. 311 (1917), as proof. See 325 U.S. 761, 769.

50. Ibid., 775-76.

51. John P. Frank, *Mr. Justice Black: The Man and His Opinions* (New York: Alfred A. Knopf, Inc., 1948), 154. See also pages 109-14, wherein Frank attributes to Black the original position of Chief Justice Taney that "the commerce clause by itself should never be considered as ousting the states from the power to tax or regulate." Ibid., 113. For a very similar view of Black, see Charlotte Williams, *Hugo L. Black: A Study in the Judicial Process* (Baltimore: The Johns Hopkins Press, 1950), 85-103. For a somewhat different view of Black, see Wallace Mendelson, *Justices Black and Frankfurter: Conflict in the Court* (Chicago: The University of Chicago Press, 1961), 98-111.

52. 304 U.S. 307.

53. For his complete opinion, see ibid., 316-33.

54. Ibid., 317.

55. Ibid., 320.

56. Ibid., 328.

57. 305 U.S. 434, 442-55.

58. Ibid., 444-45.

59. Ibid., 440.

60. Ibid., 450.

61. Ibid., 455.

62. 325 U.S. 761, 784-95.

63. Ibid., 789.

64. Ibid., 792.

65. 314 U.S. 390.

66. For his complete opinion, see ibid., 391-97. The decision was unanimous, 9-0.

67. For his complete opinion, see ibid., 397-402.

68. Ibid., 398.

69. Ibid., 400.

70. Ibid., 400-01.

71. Ibid., 401.

72. Ibid., 401.

73. 336 U.S. 525.

74. For his complete opinion, see ibid., 526-45. Justice Black, joined by Justice Murphy, dissented in an opinion which will be reviewed later. Justice Frankfurter, joined by Justice Rutledge, dissented basically on the ground that the Court did not have enough information at the time upon which to base an intelligent "balancing" process; see ibid., 564-76.

75. 294 U.S. 511.

76. Ibid., 527.

77. Ibid., 523.

78. 336 U.S. 525, 538.

79. Ibid., 539.

80. Ibid., 540.

81. For his complete opinion, see ibid., 545-64.

82. Ibid., 550. The words are Black's.

83. Ibid., 552.

84. Ibid., 554.

85. Ibid., 555.

86. Ibid., 564.

87. For a variety of opinions on the proper distribution of power between the national and state governments, see, for example, William A. Anderson, *The Nation and the States: Rivals or Partners?* (Minneapolis: The University of Minnesota Press, 1955); James J. Kilpatrick, *The Sovereign States: Notes of a Citizen of Virginia* (Chicago: Henry Regnery Company, 1957); Robert A. Goldwin (ed.), *A Nation of States: Essays on the American Federal System* (Chicago: Rand McNally & Company, 1963).

88. Stone to Dowling, October 19, 1945. Quoted in Mason, *Harlan Fiske Stone,* 786.

89. Besides the cases studied here, see Jackson's opinions in *United States v. South-Eastern Underwriters Association,* 322 U.S. 533 (1944); and *Bob-Lo Excursion Co. v. Michigan,* 333 U.S. 28 (1948).

90. Robert H. Jackson, *The Supreme Court in the American System of Government* (New York: Harper & Row, Publishers, Inc., 1963), 66-67.

91. Noel T. Dowling, "Interstate Commerce and State Power—Revised Version," *Selected Essays on Constitutional Law: 1938-1962,* 280, 290.

92. Ibid., 294-95. Dowling was writing in 1940, but the present author

272

would argue that his analysis is as accurate and pertinent now as then. The discussions in Chapters 8 and 9 clearly support the current relevancy of the Dowling thesis.

93. The recent (1962-1964) reapportionment decisions of the Supreme Court may in time alter the validity of this admittedly greatly oversimplified analysis of the national legislative process, but the author will stick by his guns until proof of any real change is presented. For example, anyone who followed the Civil Rights Act of 1964 through to enactment knows the formidable obstacles which can be raised against any law allegedly designed to curtail states' rights prerogatives. (See the last chapter.)

94. 340 U.S. 349.

95. For his complete opinion, see ibid., 350-57.

96. Ibid., 353.

97. Ibid., 354.

98. Ibid., 356. Here Clark was quoting Cardozo in *Baldwin v. Seelig*, 294 U.S. 511, 527 (1935).

99. For his complete opinion, see ibid., 357-60. He was joined by Justices Douglas and Minton.

100. Ibid., 358-59. Black has a tendency to attribute crass financial motives to his colleagues when they do not agree with him that state legislation should be sustained. See also *Southern Pacific Co. v. Arizona,* 325 U.S. 761, 794 (1945). Presumably, of course, the thought never entered the minds of Madison's city fathers that their health regulations "incidentally" protected the Wisconsin dairy industry. Perish any such aspersions on their motives.

101. Ibid., 359.

102. 375 U.S. 361.

103. Milk is designated Class I, II, III, and IV depending upon its end use. Class I is fluid milk or milk products sold in fluid form and commands the highest price.

104. It also supplied large quantities of milk to United States military installations, both within and without Florida.

105. For his complete opinion, see 375 U.S. 361, 362-83.

106. Ibid., 376.

107. Ibid., 376-77.

108. Ibid., 377.

109. Ibid., 378. A less important aspect of the case is omitted. Florida levied a tax of 0.15¢ per gallon on all milk handled, regardless of where purchased or to whom sold. Polar challenged the tax on its "military" milk because of the federal government's exclusive jurisdiction over its installations. The Court upheld the tax because it was "upon the activity of processing or bottling milk in a plant located within Florida, and not upon work performed on a federal enclave or upon the sale and delivery of milk occurring within the boundaries of federal property." Ibid., 382.

110. 322 U.S. 202.

111. For his complete opinion, see ibid., 202-12. Justices Jackson and Rutledge dissented without opinion.

112. Ibid., 207.

113. Ibid., 207.

114. Ibid., 210.

115. Ibid., 212. It must be noted that historically the states have always exercised some power over "foreign" corporations. In fact, in *Bank of Augusta v. Earle,* 13 Peters 519 (1839), Taney held that a state could prevent a corporation of another state from doing business within its legal jurisdiction, if the state enacted positive regulatory legislation. (See Note 2 in Chapter 5 and the sources cited.) Although the Court later materially altered the Taney doctrine and found protections for business in the Fourteenth Amendment (ratified in 1868) and in the Commerce Clause (under the *Cooley* rule), a state can still impose some conditions on an out-of-state corporation seeking to do business within its borders. See Norman J. Small (ed.), *The Constitution of the United States of America: Analysis and Interpretation* (Washington, D.C.: Senate Document No. 39, 88th Congress, 1st Session; U.S. Government Printing Office, 1964), 232 and 270-71.

116. 366 U.S. 276.

117. For his complete opinion, see ibid., 276-84. He was joined by Chief Justice Warren and Justices Clark and Brennan. Justice Harlan wrote his own concurring opinion; see ibid., 284-88.

118. He relied on *Cheney Brothers Co. v. Massachusetts,* 246 U.S. 147 (1918). In that case the Court had held that Northwestern Consolidated Milling Company of Minnesota was engaged in intrastate commerce when a group of its salesmen traveled the state and promoted the sale of flour by Massachusetts wholesalers to Massachusetts retailers. The salesmen also solicited orders to be turned over to the nearest wholesaler.

119. 366 U.S. 276, 281-82. Quoted from 246 U.S. 147, 155. Black could see no difference between the *Cheney* case and the present one.

120. For his complete opinion, see ibid., 288-92. He was joined by Justices Frankfurter, Whittaker, and Stewart.

121. Ibid., 290.

122. The *Cheney* precedent was inapposite. There the entire activity was "the direct solicitation of orders for local wholesalers"; here the predominant activity was nothing more than "advertising and public relations." Ibid., 292.

123. Ibid., 292.

124. 344 U.S. 157.

125. For his complete opinion, see ibid., 158-63. With him were Justices Reed, Frankfurter, Jackson, and Clark.

126. Ibid., 161.

127. Ibid., 161-62.

128. Ibid., 162-63.

129. For his complete opinion, see ibid., 163-66. He was joined by Chief Justice Vinson and Justices Burton and Minton.

130. Ibid., 163.

131. Ibid., 165.

132. 359 U.S. 520.

133. For his complete opinion, see ibid., 521-30. Justice Harlan, joined by Justice Stewart, wrote a one paragraph concurring opinion. Ibid., 530.

134. For Douglas' review of all the facts, see ibid., 524-28.

135. Ibid., 529-30.

136. See Charles L. Black, Jr., *Perspectives in Constitutional Law* (Englewood Cliffs, N.J.: Prentice-Hall, Inc., 1963), 32-38, for the argument that Congress could lighten the Court's load with respect to judicial review of state commercial legislation. Congress obviously has power to pass comprehensive statutes to regulate various aspects of interstate commerce and to authorize existing or newly created administrative commissions to assume supervision of certain fields. Black has a point; and it is true that the federal regulatory agencies could take over much of the subject. The ICC, for example, is competent to make uniform rules for truck mudguards. But even if these legislative and administrative changes were to take place, government officials (federal and state), private entrepreneurs, and other interested parties would seek a final judgment; and, while the scope of decision might be narrowed, the need for the Court to continue as arbiter of the federal system would remain.

8   Conflict in State and Federal Legislation

Extensive federal regulation of American economic life is now a commonplace. In the field of constitutional law this means that the Supreme Court has had increasingly frequent occasion to pass upon the validity of state enactments which impinge upon corresponding congressional legislation. In order to uphold the command of Article VI of the Constitution that "the Laws of the United States . . . shall be the supreme Law of the Land . . . any Thing in the Constitution or Laws of any State to the Contrary notwithstanding," the Court has continued to exercise its historic role as final arbiter of state and national power. In the performance of this function, it has framed its decisions primarily in terms of the theory of pre-emption.[1] Simply stated, this doctrine holds that when Congress has legislated comprehensively on a given subject, it is presumed to have "occupied the field" to the exclusion of all incompatible state legislation on the same subject. In view of the supremacy clause, then, the latter must fall.

The argument may be advanced, however, that the pre-emption doctrine is in reality merely a refined or sophisticated adaptation of the familiar balancing-of-interests test, which was elucidated in the last chapter; a little analysis will show this to be true. In *Florida Lime & Avocado Growers, Inc. v. Paul* (1963)[2] Justice William J. Brennan, Jr. summarized the crucial features of pre-emption. He held that at the heart of the doctrine lie two inquiries: With respect to the federal legislation, does either the "nature of the subject matter" or an "explicit declaration of congressional design" operate to supersede state regulation in the same area?[3] Both of these tests call, of course, for independent judgments on the part of the Supreme Court. To answer the first question, it must make a determination precisely like one of those demanded under the *Cooley* rule, that is, whether the subject is national and needs uniform regulation or local and admits of diverse control. To meet the second standard, the Court must ascertain "the intent of Congress"—either from the language of the federal act, or its legislative history, or a combination of the two.

In regard to this last matter, however, the fact is that in the great majority of instances Congress does not make its intent clear,[4] and the Court is forced to draw upon its own wisdom to determine that "intent." Thus in *Rice v. Santa Fe Elevator Corp.* (1947)[5] Justice William O. Douglas spelled out the ways in which the Court might identify a congressional purpose to displace or pre-empt state power:[6]

1. The scheme of federal regulation may be so pervasive as to make reasonable the inference that Congress left no room for the States to supplement it.

2. Or the Act of Congress may touch a field in which the federal interest is so dominant that the federal system will be assumed to preclude enforcement of state laws on the same subject.

3. Likewise, the object sought to be obtained by the federal law and the character of obligations imposed by it may reveal the same purpose.

4. Or the state policy may produce a result inconsistent with the objective of the federal statute.

But it is obvious that in order to apply these criteria the Court must decide, in each particular case, what constitutes a proper "balance" between national and state power, again almost exactly in the manner in which it would employ the *Cooley* rule. That the thrust of this argument is correct and that the Court has continued to adhere fundamentally to the balancing-of-interests doctrine to determine the scope of state power permissible under the Commerce Clause will appear from an examination of the leading cases which involve "conflict" between federal and state legislation.

Pre-Emption Takes Shape, 1942–1949

Cloverleaf Butter Co. v. Patterson (1942)[7] concerned the validity of an Alabama food and drug law which authorized state officials to inspect and seize packing stock butter, an ingredient used in the manufacture of process or renovated butter. Cloverleaf, a Birmingham producer of renovated butter, obtained 75 percent of this unprocessed material from outside the state and shipped 90 percent of the finished product in interstate commerce. It sought an injunction against repeated factory seizures of its packing stock butter on the ground that federal regulations relating to the manufacturing of renovated butter excluded such state action. Alabama invoked the authority of its police power to protect the health of its citizens and argued that Congress had not "exclusively occupied the field."

Justice Stanley F. Reed wrote the five-to-four opinion which struck down the state statute.[8] He admitted that "it must be clear that the federal provisions are inconsistent with those of the state to justify the thwarting of state regulations."[9] This called for a perusal of the federal act in point. Sections 2320 to 2327 of the Internal Revenue Code[10] provided for taxation of and control over the production and distribution of renovated butter. Section 2325 explicitly required the Secretary of Agriculture to make "rigid" sanitary inspections of plants producing renovated butter for shipment in interstate commerce and authorized him to seize any of the finished product found to contain any deleterious or unwholesome materials. (Intermediate materials—such as packing stock butter—were subject to inspection only and could not be confiscated.) Pursuant to this authorization, the Department of Agriculture had established detailed sanitation standards to be followed in the manufacturing process.

The precise question was whether the state's claim of power "to condemn packing stock butter held for renovation" interfered or conflicted with "the purpose or provisions of the federal legislation," and Reed held that it did:

> The manufacture and distribution in interstate and foreign commerce of process and renovated butter is a substantial industry which, because of its multi-state activity, cannot be effectively regulated by isolated competing states. . . . Science made possible the utilization of large quantities of packing stock butter which fell below the standards of public demand and Congress undertook to regulate the production in order that the resulting commodity might be free of ingredients deleterious to health. It left the states free to act on the packing stock supplies prior to the time of their delivery into the hands of the manufacturer and to regulate sales of the finished product within their borders. But, once the material was definitely marked for commerce by acquisition of the manufacturer, it passed into the domain of federal control.[11]

... To uphold the power of the State of Alabama to condemn the material in the factory, while it was under federal observation and while federal enforcement deemed it wholesome, would not only hamper the administration of the federal act but would be inconsistent with its requirements. ... Since there was federal regulation of the materials and composition of the manufactured article, there could not be similar state regulation of the same subject.[12]

Chief Justice Harlan Fiske Stone filed a strong dissent.[13] He thought that the Alabama statute in providing for the seizure of packing stock butter, "an article which is a notorious menace to health," merely aided and supplemented the federal regulation. There was a "complete want of conflict between the two statutes and their administration"; if the state seized unfit packing stock, then the federal authorities were relieved "of the necessity of detecting it and of seizing the renovated product which it contaminates."[14] The record showed an "active and sympathetic cooperation between state and federal agencies in effecting a common purpose, prevention of the consumption of unfit butter,"[15] and the sole result of the majority opinion was "to condemn a working, harmonious federal-state relationship for the sake of a sterile and harmful insistence on exclusive federal power."[16] He found it "ironical" that while judicial construction of the federal Pure Food and Drug Act did not preclude state seizure of the packing stock, Cloverleaf had discovered "an avenue of escape by appeal to the Renovated Butter Act which does not authorize federal seizure of the ingredient."[17]

Finally, Stone issued a strong caveat against inordinate interpretations of the effect of congressional legislation upon the ordinary powers of the states:

It is one thing for courts in interpreting an Act of Congress regulating matters beyond state control to construe its language with a view to carrying into effect a general though unexpressed congressional purpose. It is quite another to infer a purpose, which Congress has not expressed, to deprive the states of authority which otherwise constitutionally belongs to them, over a subject which Congress has not undertaken to control. Due regard for the maintenance of our dual system of government demands that the courts do not diminish state power by extravagant inferences regarding what Congress might have intended if it had considered the matter, or by reference to their own conceptions of a policy which Congress has not expressed and is not plainly to be inferred from the legislation which it has enacted.[18]

Once more, the Chief Justice was true to Austinian principles; in complete agreement Justice Felix Frankfurter added that the decision amounted to "destructive legislation—the Court takes power away from the states but is, of course, unable to transfer it to the federal government."[19]

Two comments seem appropriate to the *Cloverleaf* case. First, for the majority Reed emphasized the fact that the production and distribution of renovated butter constituted a substantial "multi-state" industry rather than a primarily "local" activity. Furthermore, the state had attempted to regulate the manufacturing process in the factory—the precise point at which the federal sanitation standards took hold of the subject; thus the state regulation had the same purpose as the federal requirements and was inconsistent with them in providing for seizure of any deleterious material before processing occurred. These are both quite clearly *Cooley* types of considerations which would be pertinent to a balancing process.

Second, Stone was on solid ground when he pointed out that the invalidated state statute merely supplemented the Renovated Butter Act and actually furthered the federal objective of protecting consumers from impure butter; there was no necessary conflict between the two regulatory schemes, extant federal-state cooperation in the area was abruptly terminated, and private business practices were accorded an immunity previously unavailable under another equally relevant federal act. In short, Stone's admonition against judicial extravagance in the interpretation of congressional intent in relation to state authority demonstrated again his hard-headed, pragmatic approach to resolving the problems of power-distribution which are inherent in a federal system. It seems fair to say that Reed wrung a "tortured" conclusion from the federal provisions—one which was not warranted by a due consideration of all the "facts and circumstances" of the case.

The *Cloverleaf* case demonstrated the need for care in deciding conflicts between state and federal statutes, and a more careful approach was taken in *Rice v. Santa Fe Elevator Corp.* (1947),[20] a case which involved the application of the Illinois Public Utilities Act to a warehouse firm licensed under the United States Warehouse Act. Rice, a partnership dealing in grain, filed a complaint with the Illinois Commerce Commission in which it charged Santa Fe with a long list of violations of both acts; these included: (1) charging unjust and unreasonable rates for grain storage, (2) discriminating against the public by granting prohibited preferential rates to the federal government and its agencies, (3) maintaining the dual position of storing and dealing in its own grain while storing grain for the public, (4) mixing high-quality public grain with its own inferior grain, (5) providing unsafe and inadequate warehouse facilities and service, and (6) operating without a state license. Santa Fe argued that since these specific subjects were covered by the federal act, they could not be regulated in any way by the Illinois Commission. Rice contended that "since the area taken over by the Federal Government is limited, the rest may be occupied by the States."[21] By a vote of seven to two the Court agreed with Santa Fe.

Justice Douglas spoke for the majority.[22] He first took up the complaints one-by-one and compared the provisions of the state Public Utilities Act, which were generally more rigorous, with those of the federal Warehouse Act.[23] For example, the state Commission was authorized to fix reasonable warehousing rates while the Secretary of Agriculture could only disallow any unjust rates; similarly, the state law prohibited the practice of holding the dual position of warehouseman and dealer, but the federal statute merely required the disclosure of such a position. Douglas admitted that the field was one traditionally subject to local control (*Munn v. Illinois*) and that state power was not to be displaced unless "that was the clear and manifest purpose of Congress."[24] He then looked to the language and circumstances of the federal legislation in order to discover the congressional purpose.

Douglas pointed out that the original Warehouse Act of 1916[25] made federal regulation "subservient to state regulation." Section 29 provided that there should be no conflict between the federal statute and state laws; section 6 required warehousemen to obtain a bond, issuance of which was to be conditioned upon their compliance with state requirements. But in 1931 Congress amended the Act.[26] Section 29 was changed to provide that "the power, jurisdiction, and authority conferred upon the Secretary of Agriculture under this Act shall be exclusive with respect to all persons securing a license hereunder"; section 6 omitted entirely the requirement that procurement of a bond be conditioned on compliance with state regulations. He found further help in the congressional committee reports. The Senate Report stated that if a warehouseman secured a federal license, he would be "authorized to operate without regard to State acts and be solely responsible to the Federal act"; the House Report expressed a purpose to make the Act "independent of any State legislation on the subject."

Douglas thought that this was "strong language" which said in plain terms that "the matters regulated by the Federal Act cannot be regulated by the States."[27] Congress had clearly intended to eliminate "dual regulation" of warehousemen and had sought to achieve "uniform business practices":

> The test, therefore, is whether the matter on which the State asserts the right to act is in any way regulated by the Federal Act. If it is, the federal scheme prevails though it is a more modest, less pervasive regulatory plan that that of the State. By that test each of the nine matters we have listed is beyond the reach of the Illinois Commission, since on each one Congress has declared its policy in the Warehouse Act. The provisions of Illinois law on those subjects must therefore give way by virtue of the Supremacy Clause.[28]

Thus the test of coincidence of regulation resulted in a holding that federal control superseded the jurisdiction of the state regulatory body.

Justice Frankfurter, supported by Justice Wiley B. Rutledge, dissented in the same manner as in *Cloverleaf*.[29] He first accused the Court of uprooting "a vast body of State enactments which in themselves do not collide with the licensing powers of the Secretary of Agriculture."[30] Then he admonished his colleagues that a "due regard" for the federal system favored survival of state authority over matters of intimate local concern unless "Congress has clearly swept the boards of all State authority, or the State's claim is in unmistakable conflict with what Congress has ordered."[31] Finally, he argued that neither the language nor the history of the 1931 amendments demanded the drastic interpretation that their purpose was "to displace all State regulation of warehousing." The federal license was optional, and a minimum of regulation accompanied it. That Congress intended no fundamental change in federal-state relations was shown by the fact that appropriations for the administration of the Act were not increased significantly after its passage. The sole effect of the Court's decision was to introduce "*laissez faire* outside the very narrow scope of the Secretary's powers" by displacing "settled and fruitful State authority."[32]

The clash between Douglas and Frankfurter was more apparent than real; neither would exclude the states entirely from the field of warehouse regulation. In spite of his emphasis on the "strong language" of Congress, from which pre-emption could be inferred, Douglas was unwilling to rule on those subjects of complaint which were not specifically included in the federal statute. Thus the difference between the majority and the minority actually lay in where to draw the line excluding state power; Douglas would merely draw it sooner than

Frankfurter. Such exercises in line-drawing are, of course, one of the components in an application of the balancing-of-interests doctrine. This is what both justices were engaged in; it happened that they arrived at slightly different conclusions.

The *Rice* case was important primarily for Douglas' delineation of the four pre-emption tests, although it must be admitted that these were enunciated rather casually. But two years later the Court denigrated the coincidence test as an independently applicable part of the formula. *California v. Zook* (1949)[33] involved the validity of a state statute which prohibited the sale or arrangement of any transportation over California's public highways unless the carrier held a permit from the Interstate Commerce Commission. This provision was substantially the same as one in the Federal Motor Carrier Act. Zook operated a travel bureau in Los Angeles which arranged "share-expense" passenger transportation in automobiles; many of the trips crossed state lines. Zook was prosecuted for violation of the state act; he admitted his unlawful activity, but his defense was that the state regulation entered "an exclusive congressional domain." In a five-to-four decision the Supreme Court sustained the California regulation.

Justice Frank Murphy wrote the majority opinion.[34] He began with a review of basic Commerce-Clause principles. In the absence of specific congressional action, the Court would adhere to "the *Cooley* case's broad delineation of the areas of state and national power over interstate commerce."[35] This involved the familiar test of "uniformity versus locality" or, more accurately, the question of "whether the state interest is outweighed by a national interest in the unhampered operation of interstate commerce."[36] He admitted, citing *Prudential Insurance Co. v. Benjamin* (1946), that Congress could "redefine the areas of local and national predominance" and that when it so acted, "we try to discover to what extent it intended to exercise its power of redefinition."[37] He summarized:

> But whether Congress has or has not expressed itself, the fundamental inquiry, broadly stated, is the same: does the state action conflict with national policy? The *Cooley* rule and its later application, *Southern Pacific Co. v. Arizona,* . . . the question of congressional "occupation of the field," and the search for conflict in the very terms of state and federal statutes are but three separate particularizations of this initial principle.[38]

Murphy found it necessary to "restate the familiar" because Zook was urging the adoption of a fourth rule: "that when Congress has made specified activity unlawful, 'coincidence is as ineffective as opposition,' and state laws 'aiding' enforcement are invalid."[39] But this argument could not be accepted for two reasons: (1) It just assumed—rather than proved—the stated premise "that Congress has 'taken the particular subject-matter in hand,' to the exclusion of state laws";[40] and (2) it was too mechanical a rule to apply in determining congressional intent, that is, coincidence was only one factor "in a complicated pattern" of such discovery. In short, the mere showing of identity did not compel "the automatic invalidity of state measures," and the question of supersession could be answered only by "a judgment upon the particular case."[41]

To make this judgment Murphy turned to a scrutiny of the facts. The business of share-expense transportation involved a number of recognized dangers: (1) abandonment of passengers before they reached their destination, (2) personal injuries caused by irresponsible driving, (3) crowded riding conditions due to excessive numbers of passengers, and (4) mental anxiety or fright induced by reckless driving and/or the poor mechanical condition of vehicles. Such evils were among "the oldest within the ambit of the police power: protection against fraud and physical harm to a state's residents."[42] Furthermore, there was no conflict in the provisions of the state and national acts, "and no possibility of such conflict, for the state statute makes federal law its own in this particular."[43]

Additional considerations supported California's action. Since only two or three states were regulating such transportation when the ICC activated the federal regulation in 1941, the logical inference was that Congress intended "to fill a void rather than nationalize a single rule."[44] The fact that the state law provided a more serious penalty than the federal act could be justified on the grounds that the problem was more prevalent in California than elsewhere and that the ICC had recognized these differences in magnitude. Finally, not even the possibility of double punishment established an intent to displace local laws, and Murphy summed up his defense of the state action:

> This is not a hypothetical case on "normal Congressional intent." It is California's attempt to deal with a real danger to its residents. . . . In this case the factors indicating exclusion of state laws are of no consequence in the light of the small number of local regulations and the state's normal power to enforce safety and good-faith requirements for the use of its own highways. . . . So far as casual, occasional, or reciprocal transportation of passengers for hire is concerned, the State may punish as it has

in the present case for the safety and welfare of its inhabitants; the nation may punish for the safety and welfare of interstate commerce. There is no conflict.[45]

Justice Harold H. Burton dissented vehemently.[46] In a long and detailed opinion, he argued that "Congress has exercised its power of regulation of this precise form of interstate commerce to the exclusion of the states and in conflict with the regulation attempted here by the State of California."[47] He began with a thrust at Murphy's injunction to judge each pre-emption case on its own merits. The real principle to be drawn from past cases was this:

> Once Congress has lawfully exercised its legislative supremacy in one of its allotted fields and has not accompanied that exercise with an indication of its consent to share it with the states, the burden of overcoming the supremacy of the federal law in that field is upon any state seeking to do so.[48]

Armed with this restrictive concept of state power, Burton turned to the case in hand. He took 20 pages to review the legislative, administrative, and judicial history which had preceded, included, and followed "the taking of complete jurisdiction by Congress." All of the events showed clearly that Congress had "*expressly vested in the Interstate Commerce Commission the regulation of the transportation of passengers by motor carriers engaged in interstate commerce.*"[49] Under the authority the ICC in 1941 had taken over positive supervision of share-expense transportation and thus had deliberately substituted federal for state regulation—"the very opposite of a procedure permissive of joint or duplicating federal and state control."[50]

Finally, Burton emphasized the divergence in penalties between the federal and state statutes and the possibility of double punishment as illustrative of the conflict between the two regulatory schemes; and he contended: "We cannot readily assume congressional consent to state legislation that makes an expressly stated congressional 'maximum' penalty no longer a maximum penalty."[51] In conclusion, he predicted direly that to the extent that California was permitted so to share the exclusive jurisdiction of Congress, "federal law will have lost its constitutional supremacy over state law."[52]

California v. Zook is perhaps the best example of the Court's use of the pre-emption format to cover what was at bottom an exercise in balancing state and national interests. Although Murphy couched his

majority opinion in pre-emption language, he went to a good deal of trouble to show that the business of share-expense transportation was fraught with evils which came "within the ambit of the police power"—in other words, the subject was primarily local; and he upheld the state regulation on the basis of a perfectly expressed balancing test: "In this case the factors indicating exclusion of state laws are of no consequence in the light of . . . the state's normal power to enforce safety and good-faith requirements for the use of its own highways."[53]
In dissent Burton and Frankfurter both attacked the conflicting state penalties which attached to the federally proscribed conduct; this would indicate more concern with the elimination of inconsistent state provisions than with the absolute exclusion of regulations—again, a principal consideration in balancing national and state power.

Pre-Emption In Transportation, 1954–1967

State regulation of interstate transportation has provided continuing problems for the Court.[54] Three cases spread over more than a decade well illustrate this fact. The first is *Castle v. Hayes Freight Lines, Inc.* (1954),[55] which questioned the validity of an Illinois statute, a measure which limited the weight of freight carried in a commercial truck over the state's highways and which required a balanced distribution of the weight on the truck's axles; repeated violations of these provisions were made punishable by total suspension of the carrier's right of operation for periods of 90 days and one year. Hayes Freight Lines, an interstate motor carrier licensed under the Federal Motor Carrier Act, was prosecuted as a repeated violator of the Illinois law. It resisted punishment on the ground that state suspension of interstate transportation would conflict with the federal law.

Justice Hugo L. Black spoke for a unanimous Court (8-0) in striking down the state act.[56] He wasted no time in bluntly asserting federal supremacy in the matter:

Congress in the Motor Carrier Act adopted a comprehensive plan for regulating the carriage of goods by motor truck in interstate commerce. The federal plan of control was so all-embracing that former power of states over interstate motor carriers was greatly reduced. No power at all was left in states to determine what carriers could or could not operate in interstate commerce. . . . Under these circumstances [ICC licensing of carriers], it would be odd if a state could take action amounting to a suspension or revocation of an interstate carrier's commission-granted right to operate.[57]

He went on to point out that Hayes used Illinois highways not only "to transport interstate goods to and from that State" but also "as connecting links to points in other states"; if Hayes' operations were suspended, "the carriage of interstate goods into Illinois and other states would be seriously disrupted."[58]

Finally, Black faced the claim that if the state could not impose punishment by suspension, it would have no appropriate remedy against recalcitrant carriers. He was not persuaded that "conventional forms of punishment" were inadequate to secure enforcement of such weight regulations; furthermore, an appeal for help could always be made to the ICC, which did have the power to protect fully any legitimate interest of the state in the use of its highways. But Illinois alone could not block or impede the transportation of goods interstate.

The second case is *City of Chicago v. Atchison, Topeka & Santa Fe Railway Co.* (1958).[59] For many years interstate railroads operating into and out of Chicago had provided for the transfer of through passengers from one station to another by means of a systematically organized, independent motor carrier service. In 1955 the railroads decided to terminate this long-standing arrangement with Parmelee Transportation Company and engage Railroad Transfer Service, a new company organized specifically for that purpose. At the time Chicago had in effect a detailed licensing plan for public passenger vehicles. It thereupon amended its code to provide that no license for a transfer vehicle could be issued unless the City Commissioner of Licenses first determined that "public convenience and necessity" required the additional service. Such determination depended upon "due consideration" of a number of factors: public demand for transfer service, public safety, economic feasibility, and "any other facts which the commissioner may deem relevant." Railroad Transfer Service refused to apply for a certificate of convenience and necessity, primarily on the ground that the city requirement was inconsistent with the federal Interstate Commerce Act; it and the railroads then sought to have the Chicago statute declared invalid.

Justice Black wrote the six-to-three opinion which denied Chicago the power "to decide whether a motor carrier may transport passengers from one station to another."[60] He based his reasoning squarely upon conflict between the city ordinance and federal law. Sections 1(4) and 3(4) of the Interstate Commerce Act[61] authorized, indeed required, all common rail carriers to establish "reasonable through routes with other such carriers" and to provide "all reasonable, proper, and equal facilities for the interchange of traffic between their respective lines and connecting lines." In addition, section 302(c) of the Act provided that motor vehicle transportation between terminals should be regarded as railroad transportation and should be regulated "in the same manner." Black had no difficulty in drawing the obvious conclusions:

> The various provisions set forth above manifest a congressional policy to provide for the smooth, continuous and efficient flow of railroad traffic from State to State subject to federal regulation. In our view it would be inconsistent with this policy if local authorities retained the power to decide whether the railroads or their agents could engage in the interterminal transfer of interstate passengers. We believe the Act authorizes the railroads to engage in this transfer operation themselves or to select such agents as they see fit for that purpose without leave from local authorities.[62]

Black admitted that "use of local streets is involved." The city retained the power to enforce general traffic regulations, exact reasonable use fees, and so forth. But Congress had put interstate railroad transportation under national control and had granted it "freedom from local restraints"; Chicago could not interdict that freedom.

The third case is a follow-up of the second. Chicago continued its harassment of Railroad Transfer Service. Although it repealed the section of its code which was invalidated in the *Atchison* case, the city added some new provisions and amended others to require, *inter alia,* that the company: (1) obtain annual licenses for its vehicles, (2) pay an annual license fee of 40 dollars for each terminal vehicle, (3) hire only Chicago residents as drivers, (4) maintain its principal place of business in Chicago, and (5) file annually a detailed written application complete with financial reports. The ordinance made licenses revocable upon a number of widely discretionary grounds and provided for a fine of 100 dollars per day for each violation of any of its provisions. The company challenged the regulations "as unconstitutional burdens on interstate commerce and unconstitutional attempts to regulate in an area preempted by the Interstate Commerce Act."

In *Railroad Transfer Service, Inc. v. City of Chicago* (1967)[63] the Supreme Court again frustrated local interference with the free flow of interstate rail traffic. Justice Black relied entirely upon his previous opinion to conclude:

> The rationale of *Atchison* compels our holding that the provisions of the ordinance now challenged by Transfer cannot be validly

applied to it. . . . The [Interstate Commerce] Act, as we said in *Atchison,* gives the railroads, not the city, the "discretion to determine who may transfer interstate passengers and baggage between railroad terminals." . . . That power, that discretion, is precisely what the comprehensive licensing scheme of the amended ordinance purports to reserve to the city. It matters not that the city no longer seeks to exercise that power by requiring a showing of public convenience and necessity. The total effect of the current ordinance on Transfer's operations and the burdens it places on interstate commerce are the same.[64]

The Chicago ordinance was constitutionally invalid.

Pre-Emption Full Blown, 1960-1963

Air-Pollution Standards

The 1960's brought a new round of important cases which involved state regulation in the face of federal action; and, generally speaking, the states fared very well. *Huron Portland Cement Company v. City of Detroit* (1960)[65] is a good example of the Supreme Court's increasing leniency toward exercises of state power. Huron, a Michigan corporation engaged in the manufacturing of cement, maintained a fleet of five vessels (licensed by the United States Coast Guard) which it used to transport cement from its Michigan mill to distributing plants in various states bordering on the Great Lakes. Two of its ships were equipped with hand-fired Scotch marine boilers which, when used in port to operate the deck machinery, emitted smoke which exceeded the maximum standards of the Detroit Smoke Abatement Code. The city brought criminal proceedings against Huron and the officers of its two vessels; the company challenged the prosecution on two grounds: (1) Since the vessels and their equipment had been inspected, approved, and licensed under "a comprehensive system of regulation enacted by Congress," Detroit could not impose additional standards; and (2) the municipal ordinance materially affected interstate commerce "in matters where uniformity is necessary." By a vote of seven to two the Court rejected both of Huron's contentions.

Justice Potter Stewart wrote the majority opinion.[66] He directed almost all of his discussion toward the pre-emption issue. An intent to supersede state action was not to be implied "unless the act of Congress, fairly interpreted, is in actual conflict with the law of the state."[67] He admitted that Congress for many years had maintained "an extensive and comprehensive set of controls over ships and shipping" and that those controls included various inspection requirements. But the purpose of the federal regulations was "to insure the seagoing safety of vessels subject to inspection"; on the other hand, the manifest aim of the Detroit ordinance was "the elimination of air pollution to protect the health and enhance the cleanliness of the local community"[68] —a clear exercise of traditional police power. This difference in purpose was enough for the majority, and he asserted flatly: "We conclude that there is no overlap between the scope of the federal ship inspection laws and that of the municipal ordinance here involved. For this reason we cannot find that the federal inspection legislation has pre-empted local action."[69]

Stewart then turned to the additional argument that the licensed vessels had been given "a dominant federal right to the use of the navigable waters of the United States," free from any local impediment. He recognized the *Gibbons* precedent that a state could not exclude a federally licensed ship from its waters, but he relied on *Cooley* to hold that the mere possession of a federal license "does not immunize a ship from the operation of the normal incidents of local police power, not constituting a direct regulation of commerce."[70] The city ordinance required no more than "compliance with an orderly and reasonable scheme of community regulation" and did not invalidly burden the federal license.

This reasoning really settled the second contention about the need for uniformity of commerce, but Stewart went ahead to answer it in abbreviated and perfunctory terms: the regulation applied to "any person, firm or corporation" within the city and thus did not discriminate against interstate commerce; no competing or conflicting regulations of other local governments were in evidence; therefore, the ordinance imposed no constitutionally impermissible burden on commerce.

Justice Douglas, joined by Justice Frankfurter, dissented.[71] He emphasized the fact that the current controversy was not merely "an inspection case"; rather, it was "a criminal prosecution against a shipowner and officers of two of its vessels for using the very equipment on these vessels which the Federal Government says may be used."[72] He reviewed the provisions of the federal inspection statutes and the Detroit smoke ordinance to show that they were "squarely in conflict"; equipment approved and licensed by the Coast Guard for use on the navigable waters of the United States could not "pass muster under local law." Douglas was blunt in his rejection of the Court's emphasis on disparate purposes:

> The fact that the Federal Government in certifying equipment applies standards of safety for seagoing vessels, while Detroit applies standards of air pollution seems immaterial. Federal preemption occurs when the boilers and fuel to be used in the vessels are specified in the certificate. No state authority can, in my view, change those specifications. Yet that is in effect what is allowed here.[73]

The principal issue in the case came to this: "by what authority can a local government fine people or send them to jail for using in interstate commerce the precise equipment which the federal regulatory agency has certified and approved?"[74] The application of such criminal sanctions could only have a crippling effect on the utility of the federal certificate, and Douglas protested the decision bitterly:

> Never before, I believe, have we recognized the right of local law to make the use of an unquestionably legal federal license a criminal offense. . . . The variety of requirements for equipment which the States may provide in order to meet their air pollution needs underlines the importance of letting the Coast Guard license serve as authority for the vessel to use, in all our ports, the equipment which it certifies.[75]

Several comments on the *Huron* case are appropriate. First, Stewart structured his opinion quite rigidly in terms of the pre-emption question, but he rested his negative answer primarily upon the fact that the purposes of the federal Shipping Act and the local Smoke Abatement Code were different. The latter was a health measure enacted under the police power, and even the possession of a federal navigation license did not immunize Huron's ships from the operation of that power; to support this conclusion, Stewart relied specifically on *Cooley v. The Board of Wardens*. The fact that he referred obliquely to the Detroit ordinance as an indirect regulation of commerce also indicates that his opinion was based squarely upon the modern reinterpretation of the *Cooley* rule—that is, the balancing-of-interests doctrine.

Second, there are varying views of the soundness of the decision. Jon D. Hartman argues quite correctly that the importance of the case lies "in its reflection of the Court's present willingness to let state legislation stand, when with equally sound reasoning and precedent it could have found that the federal law had occupied the field."[76] He finds the approach of the majority to be "commendable," and he supports his position with this reasoning:

> If, in close questions where Congress is silent, the Court allows state laws to stand, Congress may still legislate to forbid state action if it so desires, while in the interim the evil recognized by the state law is controlled. To find conflict where none exists creates gaps in needed regulation, a no-man's land where a local evil, easily recognized and cured by state action, goes unchecked. If state laws are kept in effect until actual conflict arises, the states are encouraged to assume their responsibilities over local matters without fear of interference from an implied but ineffective federal power over commerce, while at the same time plenary power remains, as it should, with Congress.[77]

Two other legal commentators, however, disagree with the decision. One, writing in the *Harvard Law Review,* puts his objection in this fashion:

> The ordinance in the present case sets a maximum standard for the density and duration of smoke. In this respect it is analogous to the regulation of train lengths which was invalidated in *Southern Pac. Co. v. Arizona.* In terms of that decision, the burden of the Detroit enactment may not be sufficiently mitigated by a showing by the state of substantial effect on the evil the ordinance was designed to alleviate.... Because Detroit in the present case failed to show that the ordinance, as applied to interstate shipping, had a substantial effect on the health or comfort of its citizens as compared with the cost to the carrier, the ordinance should, it seems, have been deemed to impose an unduly severe—and hence unconstitutional—burden.[78]

And Bernard Schwartz attacks the Court's ruling from a slightly different aspect of the same precedent:

> The implication is that for the *Southern Pacific* holding to apply, it must be shown that there are actually conflicting state regulations in existence. One wonders whether this is not to misread both *Southern Pacific* and the test of *Cooley v. Board of Wardens of the Port of Philadelphia* upon which it was based. In *Southern Pacific* itself, there was no showing that states other than Arizona had imposed train-limit requirements. Yet that did not deter the Court from ruling that the Arizona law was invalid. It was the possibility, not the actuality, of a "crazy-quilt" of train-limit requirements that made a uniform regulatory system essential. The variety of requirements for equipment pollution needs underscores the argument that the same considerations

should apply in a case like *Huron Portland Cement Co. v. City of Detroit.*[79]

Hartman takes essentially the Black position on exercises of state power—let them stand unless and until Congress acts specifically to override them. The Harvard reviewer and Schwartz are both closer to the Stone position. In particular, the principle underlying Schwartz' criticism of *Huron* is not only to be found in *Southern Pacific;* it is also part of the rationale behind Stone's multipletaxation doctrine—the mere possibility of multiple or conflicting local burdens on interstate commerce is reason enough to void such state taxation or regulation of a subject.

Third, in view of the foregoing, Douglas was on solid ground in arguing that the Coast Guard license should "serve as authority" for a ship to use all the ports of the United States. If Detroit can set its own smoke standards and force a federally licensed vessel to comply with them, why may not Chicago and Cleveland each set still different standards and enforce them against the same vessel? But what happens then to the utility of the federal license and to the efficiency of transportation on the Great Lakes? Does the Court have to wait until a "crazy quilt" of local regulations have been fastened onto interlake commerce before it can decree that such commerce is to be "free and untrammeled?" Long ago, Chief Justice John Marshall answered a similar question in favor of the "freedom of commerce";[80] in dissenting Douglas put himself squarely in the Marshall-Stone tradition of Commerce-Clause interpretation, a position which is hard to fault.

Tobacco Labeling

The only recent case annulling state power is *Campbell v. Hussey* (1961).[81] In the late 1950's Type 14 flue-cured tobacco, grown principally in southern Georgia and to some extent in Florida and Alabama, developed a reputation as the best American tobacco and commanded a premium price. Growers from areas outside of the three states took advantage of the fact that all types of flue-cured tobacco are similar in appearance to bring into Georgia inferior tobacco to be sold as Type 14. In 1960 the Georgia legislature responded to this threat by passing a law which required warehousemen within the state to place a white tag on Type 14 and a blue tag on all other types. The amount of out-of-state tobacco sold at auction declined markedly, and Georgia warehousemen brought suit to enjoin enforcement of the act on the ground that it regulated a field pre-empted by the federal Tobacco Inspection Act of 1935.

Justice Douglas spoke for five justices in voiding the state statute.[82] He began with the obvious: "Sales at these warehouses are sales within the competence of Congress to regulate."[83] Then he took up the Tobacco Inspection Act,[84] which provided for *"uniform standards* of classification and inspection" of tobacco according to type, grade, and other characteristics which affected its selling price. Section 511b authorized the Secretary of Agriculture "to establish standards for tobacco by which its type, grade, size, condition, or other characteristics may be determined, which standards shall be *the official standards of the United States."* Pursuant to this authorization, the Secretary had prescribed detailed standards of classification; with respect to "type," the regulations stated: "Tobacco which has the same characteristics and corresponding qualities, colors, and lengths shall be treated as one type, *regardless of any factors of* historical or *geographical nature* which cannot be determined by an examination of the tobacco."[85]

The question was whether, in view of the foregoing, the federal regulatory scheme left room for the Georgia identification requirements, and Douglas found in the negative. He rejected summarily the argument that the state regulation merely supplemented the federal plan and declared:

> We do not have here the question whether Georgia's law conflicts with the federal law. Rather we have the question of pre-emption. Under the federal law there can be but one "official" standard— one that is "uniform" and that eliminates all confusion by classifying tobacco not by geographical origin but by its characteristics. In other words, our view is that Congress, in legislating concerning the types of tobacco sold at auction, pre-empted the field and left no room for any supplementary state regulation concerning those same types.[86]

He buttressed this conclusion by referring to the legislative history of the federal Act; in the floor debates in the House the speakers had emphasized again and again the imperative need to establish "standard grades" for tobacco sold at auction.

In a footnote Douglas cited a finding of the District Court which he evidently thought clinched the case. The lower court had stated that since the Georgia statute defined Type 14 tobacco solely on the basis of geographical origin, tobacco grown just across the Savannah River in South Carolina "would not be Type 14 and would be given a blue tag";

the effect of making such a distinction was "to create a wide disparity of price between the two groups of tobacco, the Carolina growers receiving a much lower amount."[87] But according to Douglas' reading of the federal standards, tobacco was included in Type 14, "regardless of where it may have been grown, provided it meets the specifications of that type"; and he concluded:

> We have then a case where the federal law excludes local regulation, even though the latter does no more than supplement the former. Under the definition of types or grades of tobacco and the labeling which the Federal Government has adopted, complementary state regulation is as fatal as state regulations which conflict with the federal scheme.[88]

Justice Black found himself again opposed to Douglas.[89] He noted two important facts: (1) The federal Act required tobacco sold at auction to be labeled as to its official grade, but not as to its official type; and (2) the Department of Agriculture had designated as Type 14 tobacco "only flue-cured tobacco grown in Georgia, Florida, and Alabama."[90] Black then summarized his disagreement with the majority position in such cogent fashion that his statement is worth quoting at some length:

> The Court is therefore compelled to decide this case . . . on the premise that the Georgia definition of Type 14 tobacco is not in conflict with, but rather is precisely the same as, the federal definition. Consequently, the Court must accept as an undoubted fact that the full effect of the Georgia law is simply to assure that bidders at Georgia auction markets located in the Type 14 area will be able to distinguish between officially classified Type 14 tobacco, grown only in Georgia, Florida and Alabama, and other types of tobacco grown in other States. Since the conceded basic purpose of the Federal Act itself was to assure that tobacco growers and buyers would have as much information as possible about the commercial qualities of tobacco sold on auction markets, the Court must also admit that this Georgia law is designed to and does help to effectuate the Federal Act and to secure all of the benefits of that Act's official tobacco type classifications. At least as early in the history of this country as 1619, when Virginia passed its first tobacco inspection act, the States have sought to protect honest sellers of tobacco from those who were willing for a profit to damage the integrity of the product. Yet the Court now holds that Congress, by passing the Federal Tobacco Inspection Act, intended to cover the entire field of tobacco regulation, even to the extent of compelling States to abandon historic laws that are not only completely in

harmony with federal type classifications, but are actually necessary to give them full effect.[91]

He justified his last statement by an appeal to both history and logic. When Congress passed the Act, it omitted the requirement of a "type" label because in 1935 tobacco was marketed locally in the "type area" in which it was grown, and "no two types of tobacco were sold on the same market."[92] But tobacco marketing had changed radically by 1959; in that year over 22 million pounds of non-Type 14 tobacco were taken into Georgia to be sold as native tobacco. Thus the Georgia statute, in seeking to protect the market for Type 14 tobacco from fraud, attempted "to do no more than prevent a partial frustration through changing commercial practices of the very objective Congress itself sought to attain by the enactment of the Tobacco Inspection Act."[93] Black was sharp in his criticism of Douglas' reasoning:

[T]he Court proceeds from the bare fact of congressional legislation to the conclusion of federal pre-emption by application of a mechanistic formula which operates independently of congressional intent. That formula, as stated by the Court, is that "complementary state regulation is as fatal as state regulations which conflict with the federal scheme." I know of no case in which this formula has previously been applied by this Court.[94]

In defense of his position he added pointedly that *Rice v. Santa Fe Elevator Corp.* (1947) did not support the decision here; rather, the opinion in that case (which had been written by Douglas) contained "a very clear statement" of the proper rule to be invoked in pre-emption cases—"the rule that pre-emption of the historic police powers of the States can be found only where 'that was the clear and manifest purpose of Congress.' "[95] By that test the Georgia law could not be invalidated.

For once Black had the better argument. Douglas looked to the language of the Tobacco Inspection Act and found that it provided for "uniform standards" and an "official" federal system of grading tobacco; from this—and without much more—he concluded that the Act excluded all state regulations which attempted to define and label types of tobacco. But as Black pointed out, such a holding really negated the basic purpose of the Act—the protection of growers and buyers from deception as to the quality and price of the product. Times and the traditional method of marketing tobacco had changed, and a type label of the kind prescribed by Georgia was actually necessary to effectuate fully the original aims of Congress.

Thomas W. Christopher labels the decision in *Campbell v. Hussey* as "contentious pre-emption."[96] He argues that the Court misconstrued the facts and failed to perceive that Type 14 tobacco was one and the same product under both federal and state definitions; thus there was no real conflict between the two statutes. Then he contends that the Court stretched the pre-emption doctrine "to undue lengths" because realistically speaking, there was "no substantial interference with federal enforcement or with commerce."[97] Christopher concludes that apparently the "red flag" in the case was "the special ticket required to be attached to the product of three states," that is, the requirement of additional information to supplement the federal label, and he criticizes the majority for basing its finding of pre-emption upon this circumstance; such pre-emption is contentious and unjustified.

Although Christopher's basic position is sound, it appears from a critical scrutiny of Douglas' brief opinion that the Court struck down the state regulation, not because of the extra tag requirement, but because of the finding of the District Court that the Georgia law "discriminated against" South Carolina tobacco growers. To rest the holding on this latter premise, of course, is to invoke one of the *Cooley* formulas which is used in the balancing-of-interests process; in fact, Christopher himself sees the fundamental nature of pre-emption quite clearly. In the course of castigating the *Campbell* decision as unrealistic, partly because the Court failed to perceive that geography is a factor in tobacco type, he makes this revealing admission: "The doctrine of pre-emption, properly used in a situation such as this, involves the striking of a balance between federal and state interests."[98]

Avocado Maturity Tests

The case which accorded the greatest scope to state power since *Parker v. Brown* (1943) is *Florida Lime & Avocado Growers, Inc. v. Paul* (1963).[99] At stake was the validity of section 792 of California's Agricultural Code of 1925 which gauged the maturity of avocados by oil content and which prohibited the transportation or sale in California of avocados which contained "less than eight percent of oil, by weight . . . excluding the skin and seed." In 1954 the Secretary of Agriculture, acting under amendments made to the Agricultural Adjustment Act in 1935, promulgated marketing orders for avocados grown in South Florida; the maturity test was based upon a schedule of picking dates, sizes, and weights and did not include an oil-content requirement. Almost all commercial avocados are grown in southern California and Florida. The California varieties are of Mexican ancestry and usually contain at least eight percent oil when mature; most Florida varieties are of Guatemalan ancestry and reach maturity before they attain an eight-percent oil content, although they may reach that figure while they are still prime.

The effect of the state statute was to exclude on an annual average more than six percent of Florida's avocados from the California market. The Florida growers attacked the California maturity standard on three grounds: (1) In the face of the federal standards for maturity, it could not stand under the force of the supremacy clause; (2) it denied the out-of-state producers equal protection of the laws in violation of the Fourteenth Amendment; and (3) it unreasonably burdened or discriminated against the interstate marketing of avocados in repugnance to the Commerce Clause. California argued that its regulation was designed merely to prevent the deception of its consumers—a legitimate police measure which was supported by the fact that avocados which are picked prematurely do not ripen properly, tend to decay or shrivel up and become rubbery and unpalatable, and are difficult for even experienced grocerymen to identify on the basis of physical characteristics alone.

In a close, five-to-four decision the Court upheld the state law. Justice Brennan handed down the majority opinion.[100] His main focus was on the pre-emption or supremacy-clause issue. The principle established by past decisions and applicable here was that "federal regulation of a field of commerce should not be deemed pre-emptive of state regulatory power in the absence of persuasive reasons—either that the nature of the regulated subject matter permits no other conclusion, or that the Congress has unmistakably so ordained."[101]

With respect to the first test, Brennan argued that the maturity of avocados was not a subject which demanded "exclusive federal regulation in order to achieve uniformity vital to national interests"; rather, it was a subject which fell squarely within the traditional scope of state control: "Specifically, the supervision of the readying of foodstuffs for market has always been deemed a matter of peculiarly local concern."[102] He emphasized that the decision in *Cloverleaf Butter Co. v. Patterson* (1942) did nothing to undercut this proposition, and he continued:

Federal regulation by means of minimum standards of the picking, processing, and transportation of agricultural commodities, however comprehensive *for those purposes* that regulation may be, does not of itself import displacement of state control over the distribution and retail sale of those commodities in the interests of the *consumers* of the commodities within the State. . . . Congressional regulation of one end of the stream of commerce does not, *ipso facto,* oust all state regulation at the other end. Such a displacement may not be inferred automatically from the fact that Congress has regulated production and packing of commodities for the interstate market.[103]

Here it was clear that the subject matter fell "well within the scope of California's police powers" to prevent the deception of its avocado-consuming public.

Brennan then took up the issue of congressional purpose. A mandate to bar state regulation had to be "clear and manifest"; but an examination of the Agricultural Adjustment Act of 1935[104] revealed no such legislative intent. First, the AAA, unlike the Tobacco Inspection Act, did not emphasize the need for "uniform" or "official" marketing standards. It authorized the adoption of marketing agreements and orders only when the Secretary of Agriculture found that economic conditions in a particular area warranted them, and even then they were to be temporary in nature. The Act further required that such orders were to be "limited in their application to the smallest regional production areas" found practicable and were to be drawn in "different terms" to give "due recognition to the differences in production and marketing" between areas. This language indicated that Congress contemplated that "there might be widespread regional variations in the standards governing production and processing,"[105] and from this inference it could be deduced that

> if the Congress of 1935 really intended that distribution would be comprehensively governed by grower-adopted quality and maturity standards, and all state regulation of the same subject would be ousted, it does not seem likely that the statute would have invited local variations at the production end while saying absolutely nothing about the effect of those production controls upon distribution for consumption.[106]

Second, the legislative history of the Triple A militated against displacement of state regulation. The House and Senate committee reports cautioned that the bill contained nothing "to permit or require the Federal Government to invade the field of the States" or "to force

States to cooperate" in any marketing agreements which might be set up under it; this implied that Congress apparently intended "to do no more than to invite farmers and growers to get together, under the auspices of the Department of Agriculture, to work out local harvesting, packing and processing programs and thereby relieve temporarily depressed marketing conditions."[107] But there was an absence of any congressional design "to deprive the States of their traditional power" to supervise "the ultimate distribution and sale of produce" to consumers.

A third factor obviously contributed to Brennan's willingness to sustain the California law. The Florida avocado maturity standards were not drafted by "impartial experts in Washington or even in Florida" but by "the South Florida Avocado Administrative Committee, which consists entirely of representatives of the growers and handlers concerned."[108] Since the Secretary of Agriculture invariably adopted the Committee's standards, it appeared that the whole marketing program was designed primarily to secure "orderly competition among the South Florida growers." In summary, the most plausible conclusion to be drawn from the federal legislative scheme was that it did not supersede state power to act in the same area.

Brennan gave short shrift to the challenge under the equal-protection clause; he merely held that the California maturity standard was not "arbitrary or devoid of rational relationship to a legitimate regulatory interest" and that it did not result in "irrational discrimination as between persons or groups of persons."[109] But the Commerce-Clause issue was more difficult; and since the record was not clear as to whether the appellant's evidence of a burden on commerce had been admitted officially by the lower court, he remanded the case for a new trial on that one question.

Justice Byron R. White registered a strong dissent.[110] He asserted bluntly that "the Agricultural Adjustment Act and regulations promulgated thereunder leave no room for this inconsistent and conflicting state legislation."[111] It was necessary, therefore, only to reach the supremacy-clause issue; and he stated the minority position clearly and forcefully:

> The central and unavoidable fact is that six out of every 100 Florida avocados certified as mature by federal standards are turned away from the California markets as being immature, and are excluded from that State by the application of a maturity test different from the federal measure. Congress empowered the Secretary to provide for the orderly marketing of avocados and to

specify the quality and maturity of avocados to be transported in interstate commerce to any and all markets. Although the Secretary determined that these Florida avocados were mature by federal standards and fit for sale in interstate markets, the State of California determined that they were unfit for sale by applying a test of the type which the Secretary had determined to be unsatisfactory. We think the state law has erected a substantial barrier to the accomplishment of congressional objectives.[112]

White proceeded to substantiate his arguments. He focused primarily upon the federal regulatory scheme. It was "comprehensive and pervasive"; the Secretary had prescribed "in minute detail the standards for the size, appearance, shape, and maturity of avocados."[113] No gap existed which would "warrant state action to prevent the evils of a no-man's land," and any supplementary state regulation could only compromise to some degree "the congressional policy expressed in the Act"—a policy "to establish and maintain such minimum standards of quality and maturity and such grading and inspection requirements for agricultural commodities . . . as will effectuate . . . orderly marketing."[114]

White pressed the point that this purpose demanded uniform standards of quality, and he attacked directly and cogently Brennan's reasoning that if Congress intended to displace all state regulation, "it does not seem likely that the [federal] statute would have invited local variations at the production end while saying absolutely nothing about the effect . . . upon distribution." Countered White:

It may not obstruct or burden commerce to admit avocados into commerce on diverse bases in different parts of the country; any individual grower in that situation would face but one standard. But it does burden commerce and frustrate the congressional purpose when each grower faces different standards in different markets. To slip from permissible nonuniformity at one end of the stream of commerce to permissible nonuniformity at the other end thus is to read the statute too casually and gloss over the congressional purpose, which expressly was to facilitate marketing in and transportation to "any and all markets in the current of interstate commerce."[115]

Furthermore, there was nothing in the AAA or its legislative history which showed "any congressional intention to accommodate or permit state controls inconsistent with federal law or marketing orders issued thereunder."[116] True, the Secretary was authorized to seek the cooperation of state officials in setting up marketing programs, but he was not directed "to defer to any State." In the present instance the state requirement was irreconcilable with the federal order, which was designed specifically to solve the problem "of moving mature avocados into interstate commerce"; and White concluded:

> We have, then, a case where the federal regulatory scheme is comprehensive, pervasive, and without a hiatus which the state regulations could fill. Both the subject matter and the statute call for uniformity. The conflict is substantial—at least six out of every 100 federally certified avocados are barred for failure to pass the California test—and it is located in a central portion of the federal scheme. The effect of the conflict is to disrupt and burden the flow of commerce and the sale of Florida avocados in distant markets, contrary to the congressional policy underlying the Act. The State may have a legitimate economic interest in the subject matter, but it is adequately served by the federal regulations. . . . In such circumstances, the state law should give way; it "becomes inoperative and the federal legislation exclusive in its application."[117]

The case of *Florida Lime & Avocado Growers v. Paul* was wrongly decided. In an ingenious fashion California seized upon the difference in ancestry of California and Florida avocados, which showed up in the oil content of the mature fruit, to erect a partial barrier to Florida competition. Its motive was clearly the protection of the economic interests of its own producers—a selfish, parochial aim which was in direct conflict with a federal marketing order, and yet the Court upheld this misuse of state power. Brennan chose to focus on the at-best ambiguous language of the AAA and to ignore the purpose behind it—the authorization to the Secretary of Agriculture to encourage and facilitate the orderly distribution of agricultural products throughout the United States via federal marekting orders; and he went on to argue that because Congress had made provision for nonuniformity of quality standards at the production end, it could not have intended to displace nonuniform state regulations at the consumption end.

With brilliant logic White exposed the fallacy of this reasoning. To provide for a variety of standards nation-wide at the production end would not obstruct commerce because any individual producer would still have only one standard to meet, but to sanction different standards at the consumption end would force a producer to meet more than one standard and hence would burden commerce; the character of agricultural commodities is just not that amenable to alteration. Such a result, of course, ran in direct opposition to the congressional policy embodied in the AAA, that is, federal help and support for American agriculture.

White also pointed out correctly that the present situation was not analogous to *Parker v. Brown.*[118] In that case no federal marketing order had been promulgated with which the California prorate raisin program could conflict; here the state regulatory scheme barred Florida avocados which had been "certified as mature by federal standards," and there was "unmistakable" conflict between federal and state law. Thus *Florida Lime & Avocado Growers v. Paul* may be seen as even more respectful of state power than *Parker v. Brown* or, to put it another way, more disrespectful of the paramount interest of the nation in freedom of commerce for its essential foodstuffs.

One point remains to be made. Although Brennan and White both addressed themselves primarily to the pre-emption issue under the supremacy clause and focused their opinions on "the intent of Congress" in the Agricultural Adjustment Act of 1935, it is obvious that they were using traditional balancing tests to reach their conclusions. Brennan found that the maturity of avocados was not a subject which demanded "exclusive federal regulation"; White contended that the Secretary's avocado marketing order was "comprehensive, pervasive, and without a hiatus which the state regulations could fill." Brennan referred more than once to California's right to protect is consumers from deception,[119] and he emphasized the fact that in actual practice it was the South Florida Avocado Administrative Committee which drafted the quality and maturity standards for Florida avocados; White quite candidly revealed his basic reason for opposing the state regulation in this statement: "The effect of the conflict is to disrupt and burden the flow of commerce and the sale of Florida avocados in distant markets." Thus one of the leading pre-emption cases of the 1960's, which was remanded for retrial on the Commerce-Clause issue, was debated and decided on what are patently *Cooley* balancing-of-interests grounds or conventional Commerce-Clause considerations.

Advertising Controls

A month later the Court decided the case of *Head v. New Mexico Board of Examiners in Optometry* (1963).[120] A New Mexico statute prohibited the advertising of eye-glasses—lenses, frames, or mountings—on the basis of price or price discounts. A newspaper (owned by Agnes K. Head) and a radio station (Permian Basin Radio Corp.), both located in

Hobbs, New Mexico (which is in the southeastern part of the state and close to the Texas border), accepted advertising from a Texas optometrist which contained price quotations on eye-glasses and spectacles. The state Optometry Board filed a complaint against the two companies; they defended their action on the ground that the state law imposed an unconstitutional burden on interstate commerce. Permian Basin also argued that the regulation of radio advertising had been pre-empted by the Federal Communications Act of 1934.

Justice Stewart spoke for seven justices in an opinion which summarily rejected both claims and upheld the state regulation.[121] He relied primarily upon his opinion in *Huron Portland Cement Co. v. Detroit* (1960) to settle the Commerce-Clause issue. The principle followed there was this:

> In determining whether the state has imposed an undue burden on interstate commerce, it must be borne in mind that the Constitution when "conferring upon Congress the regulation of commerce, . . . never intended to cut the States off from legislating on all subjects relating to the health, life, and safety of their citizens, though the legislation might indirectly affect the commerce of the country. Legislation, in a great variety of ways, may affect commerce and persons engaged in it without constituting a regulation of it, within the meaning of the Constitution."[122]

The present statute, like the smoke-abatement ordinance, was designed as a public-health measure; its purpose was to protect New Mexico's citizens against "the evils of price-advertising methods tending to satisfy the needs of their pocketbooks rather than the remedial requirements of their eyes."[123] Thus it came within "the most traditional concept" of the state's police power. Since it applied to "any person," it did not discriminate against interstate commerce; and since it impinged upon no area of commerce "which by its nature requires uniformity of regulation," it did not impose "a constitutionally prohibited burden" upon that commerce.

The pre-emption argument was equally easy to answer. Here Stewart relied upon *California v. Zook* (1949) and *Florida Lime & Avocado Growers v. Paul* (1963) to reiterate that the Court was required to judge each pre-emption case on its own merits and that the challenged state law was to be upheld unless there was found "such actual conflict between the two schemes of regulation that both cannot stand in the same area, [or] evidence of a congressional design to preempt the field."[124] He admitted that under the Federal Communications

Act,[125] the Federal Communications Commission, in passing upon the fitness of an applicant for the grant or renewal of a broadcasting license, could consider "a wide variety of factors," one of which was the content of the advertising to be offered. But this grant of federal authority "to promulgate general regulations concerning the subject of advertising" was not in itself sufficient to displace state regulation:

> Assuming this to be a correct statement of the Commission's authority, we are nevertheless not persuaded that the federal legislation in this field has excluded the application of a state law of the kind here involved. The nature of the regulatory power given to the federal agency convinces us that Congress could not have intended its grant of authority to supplant all the detailed state regulation of professional advertising practices, particularly when the grant of power to the Commission was accompanied by no substantive standard other than the "public interest, convenience, and necessity." . . . In the absence of positive evidence of legislative intent to the contrary, we cannot believe Congress has ousted the States from an area of such fundamentally local concern.[126]

Finally, Stewart could find no conflict between the New Mexico act and the federal regulatory scheme, and he was satisfied that the former would not "frustrate any part of the purpose of the federal legislation."[127] Operation of the state statute thus had not been superseded. Clearly, however, the rationale behind the decision was, in this instance, the overriding interest of New Mexico in protecting the health and physical well-being of its citizens.

Pre-Emption Or Balancing?

This concludes a survey of the most important Commerce-Clause cases of the past 30 years in which there has been a clash between federal and state legislation. On the basis of the foregoing discussion, several conclusions may now be drawn. First, it seems unnecessary to belabor further the main argument made at the beginning of the chapter that the Supreme Court, in its role of umpire of the federal system, has continued to apply Chief Justice Stone's basic balancing doctrine to decide claims of federal supersession. This does not mean that the Court is engaged in some sort of constitutional chicanery which it masks with an invocation of the pre-emption doctrine; rather, it reflects the fact that there is an element in these cases which is missing from the usual state case—the presence of a specific congressional act. In order to deal with this added factor—which, of course, it must—the Court structures its opinions in terms of pre-emption criteria and then attempts to determine whether these have been met, based upon an examination of the language and/or legislative background of the federal statute. But because Congress almost never makes its intent to pre-empt or not to pre-empt explicit, the Court is forced, in effect, to use its own wisdom as to congressional purpose; and, as was argued in the last chapter, the balancing test is the one most likely to give a workable and generally satisfactory solution to the power disputes which are endemic to a federal system. In this context, it seems fair to say that the Court is merely performing its assigned constitutional duty in this area and performing it quite responsibly.

Second, the only firm generalization which can be made about the trend of decision in these ten cases is that no really dominant pattern emerges. In general, the Court has become more lenient toward state power in the 1960's than in the 1940's, but the actual score in the cases covered is six to four in favor of federal preemption of the field. It may be argued, however, that decisions such as *Huron Portland Cement Co. v. Detroit* (1960) and *Florida Lime & Avocado Growers v. Paul* (1963) go a long way toward expanding the scope of state power over interstate commerce beyond any limits previously set by the Court. What all of the cases do demonstrate, of course, is the wide range of choice open to the Court in its role as final arbiter of national and state power, a role which it shows no inclination to relinquish and which, in fact, it should not abdicate.

A corollary to the proposition that these holdings point to no one trend of constitutional interpretation is the fact that there is no particular pattern as to the way in which the individual justices vote; most of them show a varied record. In this regard, it is interesting to note that Justice Black is much more likely to deny state power in the presence of a federal act than he is in its absence; he voted six out of ten times for exclusive congressional occupation of the field. Thus in this area Black again tends to see more eye-to-eye with his old compatriot, Justice Douglas.[128] But Douglas is by far the most consistent supporter of national power on the Court; he voted nine out of ten times for federal control at the expense of state regulation. At the opposite end of the spectrum, the second Justice John Marshall Harlan cast six out of six votes to uphold exercises of state power; and, oddly enough, Justices Brennan and Stewart, who are often on opposite sides of civil-liberties and rights-of-the-accused cases, were in perfect agreement with each other and took a generally pro-state attitude. By and large, however, most of the justices display a mixed position, sometimes voting for federal pre-emption of a field and at other times for concurrent state control. The Constitution is still what five justices say that it is.

Finally, the fact must be faced that the analysis above takes issue with the majority opinions in four cases: *Cloverleaf Butter Co. v. Patterson* (1942), *Huron Portland Cement Co. v. Detroit* (1960), *Campbell v. Hussey* (1961), and *Florida Lime & Avocado Growers v. Paul* (1963). The specific reasons for this opposing view have been spelled out previously and need not be repeated now. But it does seem necessary to aver that the defense of this dissent from part of the Court's work rests upon a fundamental constitutional position, the rationale of which is that the decisions in these cases cannot be supported by an appeal to a properly applied balancing-of-interests test. The basic argument of the last chapter was that Chief Justice Stone's balancing doctrine represented both sound constitutional law (in terms of *Gibbons v. Ogden* and *Cooley v. The Board of Wardens*) and a highly pragmatic approach to the solution of problems inherent in a federal system. But a careful study and consideration of all the relevant "facts and circumstances" were an essential part of the doctrine and necessary to its legitimate application in particular situations, and it is precisely this element which is lacking in these four cases. A second reading of the criticisms which accompany the holdings will demonstrate the validity of this contention.

If it be objected that it is somewhat disingenuous to use Stone's doctrine of the 1940's to criticize the three decisions of the 1960's[129] and thus put words in the Chief Justice's mouth which he never spoke, the blunt answer is this: (1) The brief and almost cursory majority opinion in *Campbell v. Hussey* contains none of the searching analysis and painstaking attention to detail which were the hallmarks of the Stone approach; and (2) neither *Huron Portland Cement Co. v. Detroit* nor *Florida Lime & Avocado Growers v. Paul* can be supported under the principles so clearly enunciated in *Southern Pacific Co. v. Arizona;*[130] nor, as Justice White showed, can *Florida Lime & Avocado Growers* be sustained under *Parker v. Brown.* In sum, adherence to both the letter and the spirit of Stone's maxims would require contrary decisions in the four cases. And if it be further objected that Stone does not have the last word with respect to Commerce-Clause adjudication, the short rejoinder is that no better formulation than the balancing-of-interests doctrine has yet been devised to adjust harmoniously the often conflicting needs of the nation and the states.

Notes

1. See an anonymous article, "Pre-emption as a Preferential Ground: A New Canon of Construction," *Selected Essays on Constitutional Law: 1938-1962,* compiled and edited by a committee of the Association of American Law Schools (St. Paul, Minn.: West Publishing Co., 1963), 310-23. Pre-emption is basically a Commerce-Clause doctrine, although its best-known uses were in *Hines v. Davidowitz,* 312 U.S. 52 (1941), an alien registration case, and *Pennsylvania v. Nelson,* 350 U.S. 497 (1956), a sedition case.

2. 373 U.S. 132.

3. Ibid., 143.

4. For substantiation of this point, see the article, "Pre-emption as a Preferential Ground," *Selected Essays on Constitutional Law: 1938-1962,* 310-17.

5. 331 U.S. 218.

6. Ibid., 230. Notice how closely these tests parallel those used by Chief Justice Earl Warren in *Pennsylvania v. Nelson* (1956); Warren, of course, relied heavily upon the Douglas formulations in *Rice.*

7. 315 U.S. 148.

8. For his complete opinion, see ibid., 150-69. He was joined by Justices Roberts, Black, Douglas, and Jackson.

9. Ibid., 156.

10. *U.S. Statutes at Large,* XXIV, 209; XXXII, 193; XXXVII, 273. These sections and amendments taken together were termed the Renovated Butter Act.

11. 315 U.S. 148, 167-68.

12. Ibid., 169.

13. For his complete opinion, see ibid., 170-77. He was joined by Justices Frankfurter, Murphy, and Byrnes. Justice Frankfurter added a short dissent of his own; see ibid., 177-79.

14. Ibid., 173.

15. Ibid., 174.

16. Ibid., 175.

17. Ibid., 176.

18. Ibid., 176-77.

19. Ibid., 179.

20. 331 U.S. 218.

21. Ibid., 229.

22. For his complete opinion, see ibid., 220-38. He was joined by Chief Justice Vinson and Justices Black, Reed, Murphy, Jackson, and Burton.

23. A total of nine subjects covered by both the state and federal acts was before the Commission; see ibid., 224-29. Three other matters covered by the state law but omitted from the federal statute were complained of; these the Court declined to rule on until such time as alleged conflicts with federal regulations might occur; see ibid., 236-37. In a companion case, *Rice v. Board of Trade of Chicago*, 331 U.S. 247 (1947), a unanimous Court per Justice Douglas also refused to decide as premature the Board's claim that the Commodity Exchange Act superseded any state regulations of federally designated "contract markets."

24. Ibid., 230. In *Munn v. Illinois*, 94 U.S. 113 (1877), one of the *Granger Cases*, Chief Justice Waite upheld an Illinois law which fixed the rates that warehouse owners might charge for grain storage and which provided other regulations for the business of warehousing.

25. *U.S. Statutes at Large*, XXXIX, 486.

26. *U.S. Statutes at Large*, XLVI, 1463.

27. 331 U.S. 218, 234. The citations on the congressional reports are as follows: *Senate Report No. 1775, 71st Congress, 3rd Session; House Report No. 2314, 70th Congress, 2nd Session.*

28. Ibid., 236.

29. For his complete opinion, see ibid., 238-47.

30. Ibid., 238.

31. Ibid.. 241.

32. Ibid., 246-47.

33. 336 U.S. 725.

34. For his complete opinion, see ibid., 726-38. He was joined by Chief Justice Vinson and Justices Black, Reed, and Rutledge.

35. Ibid., 728.

36. Ibid., 728. The main thrust of Murphy's later argument points to the use of the balancing test under the guise of a pre-emption issue. This will be commented upon more fully later.

37. Ibid., 728.

38. Ibid., 729.

39. Ibid., 729. The respondent's contention was based upon a statement by Justice Holmes in *Charleston & Western Carolina Railway Company v. Varnville Furniture Company,* 237 U.S. 597, 604 (1915): "When Congress has taken the particular subject-matter in hand, coincidence is as ineffective as opposition, and a state law is not to be declared a help because it attempts to go farther than Congress has seen fit to go."

40. Ibid., 729.

41. Ibid., 730-31, for the two quotations.

42. Ibid., 734-35.

43. Ibid., 735.

44. Ibid., 736.

45. Ibid., 737-38.

46. For his complete opinion, see ibid., 741-92. He was joined by Justices Douglas and Jackson. Justice Frankfurter agreed with Burton in a separate dissent; see ibid., 738-41.

47. Ibid., 742.

48. Ibid., 749.

49. Ibid., 754-55.

50. Ibid., 756.

51. Ibid., 747-48.

52. Ibid., 776.

53. Ibid., 737.

54. See *Fry Roofing Co. v. Wood,* 344 U.S. 157 (1952) and *Bibb v. Navaho Freight Lines,* 359 U.S. 520 (1959), both of which were discussed in Chapter 7.

55. 348 U.S. 61.

56. For his complete opinion, see ibid., 62-65. Justice Jackson, who had died just two months before, would surely have concurred in the decision.

57. Ibid., 63-64.

58. Ibid., 64.

59. 357 U.S. 77.

60. Ibid., 85. For his complete opinion, see ibid., 78-89. Justice Harlan, joined by Justices Frankfurter and Burton, dissented on the ground that the suit was premature because the local authorities had been given no opportunity to apply the ordinance; see ibid., 89-92.

61. *U.S. Statutes at Large,* XXIV, 379.

62. 357 U.S. 77, 87.

63. 386 U.S. 351.

64. Ibid., 358-59. For Black's complete opinion, see ibid., 352-60. The decision was 8-1; only Justice Harlan dissented. Notice that in 1967 appropriate reference could still be made to "burdens on interstate commerce" to strike down local laws.

65. 362 U.S. 440.

66. For his complete opinion, see ibid., 440-48. He was joined by Chief Justice Warren and Justices Black, Clark, Harlan, Brennan, and Whittaker.

67. Ibid., 443.

68. Ibid., 445.

69. Ibid., 446.

70. Ibid., 447. Notice the mechanistic character of Stewart's reasoning and the return to the old "direct-indirect" formula. He attempted merely to classify the local law as a police regulation and thus to escape the task of looking at its real consequences. (See Note 122.)

71. For his complete opinion, see ibid., 449-55.

72. Ibid., 449.

73. Ibid., 453.

74. Ibid., 453.

75. Ibid., 454-55.

76. Jon D. Hartman, "Constitutional Law—Federal Steam Vessel Inspection Statute No Bar to Local Smoke Control Law," *University of Illinois Law Forum* (1960), 450, 451.

77. Ibid., 452.

78. An anonymous review, "The Supreme Court: 1959 Term," *Harvard Law Review*, LXXIV (November, 1960), 81, 134-35.

79. Bernard Schwartz, "The Supreme Court—October 1959 Term," *Michigan Law Review*, LIX (January, 1961), 403, 420.

80. *Gibbons v. Ogden*, 9 Wheaton 1 (1824). It seems entirely reasonable to suppose that Marshall would never have permitted one municipality to outlaw marine equipment which had been specifically approved for use on the navigable waters of the United States by an official agency of the "general government." It is beside the point that his interpretation of the Federal Coasting Act of 1793 may have been none too sound; if he had not wished to avoid arousing the slave-holding interests, he could easily and legitimately have used the Commerce Clause per se to crush the New York steamboat monopoly. (See Chapter 1.)

81. 368 U.S. 297.

82. For his complete opinion, see ibid., 298-302. With him were Chief Justice Warren and Justices Clark, Brennan, and Stewart. The decision was 6-3; Justice Whittaker concurred in the result.

83. Ibid., 298. Here he cited *Mulford v. Smith*, 307 U.S. 38. (See Chapter 3 for details of the case.)

84. *U.S. Statutes at Large*, XLIX, 731.

85. 368 U.S. 297, 299.

86. Ibid., 300-01.

87. Ibid., 300, footnote 3.

88. Ibid., 302. Here he relied, *inter alia*, upon *Rice v. Santa Fe Elevator Corp.*, 331 U.S. 218 (1947).

89. For his complete dissenting opinion, see ibid., 302-17. He was joined by Justices Frankfurter and Harlan.

90. Ibid., 304-05. For this reason, Black thought that the District Court's "solicitude" for South Carolina growers had been "entirely misplaced." Ibid., 305, footnote 10.

91. Ibid., 306-07.

92. Ibid., 309.

93. Ibid., 310.

94. Ibid., 311-12.

95. Ibid., 313.

96. Thomas W. Christopher, "A Contentious Pre-emption: *Campbell v. Hussey*," *Journal of Public Law*, XI (1962), 341-51.

97. Ibid., 351. In Christopher's view, to find pre-emption here is to disregard *California v. Zook*, 336 U.S. 725, and *Huron Portland Cement Co. v. Detroit*, 362 U.S. 440. In *California v. Zook* and *Campbell v. Hussey* there is both "coincidence and supplementation, with stiffer state penalties, and both concern matters with which states historically have dealt." Ibid., 347. In *Huron* and *Campbell* neither federal act contained "categorical or even strong pre-emption language," and both cases involved "matters of local concern." To Christopher, "there appears to be more justification for applying the pre-emption doctrine in *Huron* than in *Campbell* due to the possibility of conflicting local rules [in *Huron*]." Ibid., 348.

98. Ibid., 351.

99. 373 U.S. 132.

100. For his complete opinion, see ibid., 133-59. With him were Justices Harlan, Stewart, and Goldberg.

101. Ibid., 142. For precedent he cited *Huron Portland Cement Co. v. Detroit,* 362 U.S. 440 (1960).

102. Ibid., 144. Here he relied upon *Plumley v. Massachusetts,* 155 U.S. 461 (1894).

103. Ibid., 145.

104. *U.S. Statutes at Large,* XLIX, 750. The marketing provisions in question were initially enacted on August 24, 1935, as amendments to the first AAA of 1933. They were later reenacted in virtually the same form as the Agricultural Marketing Agreement Act of 1937. (*U.S. Statutes at Large,* L, 246.) The second Agricultural Adjustment Act was passed in 1938.

105. 373 U.S. 132, 149.

106. Ibid., 149.

107. Ibid., 150. It is perhaps worth mentioning with respect to AAA language that Congress in 1935 had to be wary of a Court which, less than three months before, had handed down *Schechter Poultry Corp. v. United States,* 295 U.S. 495 (May 27, 1935), and which, of course, had not yet decided *NLRB v. Jones & Laughlin Steel Corp.,* 301 U.S. 1 (1937), or *Mulford v. Smith,* 307 U.S. 38 (1939).

108. Ibid., 150-51.

109. Ibid., 152. The eight percent oil-content requirement applied, of course, to all avocados marketed in California, regardless of where grown.

110. For his complete opinion, see ibid., 159-78. He was joined by Justices Black, Douglas, and Clark.

111. Ibid., 160.

112. Ibid., 166.

113. Ibid., 167.

114. Ibid., 170.

115. Ibid., 171.

116. Ibid., 172.

117. Ibid., 176-77.

118. Ibid., 168.

119. Ibid., 144, 145, 146, 150.

120. 374 U.S. 424.

121. For his complete opinion, see ibid., 425-32. The decision was unanimous (9-0). Chief Justice Warren and Justices Black, Clark, Harlan, White, and Goldberg joined Stewart; Justice Douglas concurred in the result, and Justice Brennan wrote a concurring opinion which treated the pre-emption issue in more detail.

122. Ibid., 428. Quoted from *Huron Portland Cement Co. v. Detroit,* 362 U.S. 440, 443-44. Part in quotation marks from *Sherlock v. Alling,* 93 U.S. 99, 103 (1876). Notice again Stewart's effort simply to classify the state law as an exercise of the state's police power (and not as a regulation of interstate commerce per se) in order to sustain it. In view of the fact that the Court has long taken the position that the states possess at least a partially concurrent power over commerce (*Cooley*), this return to the mechanistic classification of powers which predominated in the Marshall era seems odd and inexplicable. The present author surmises that it reflects a desire on the part of the Court to be unduly lenient toward the states.

123. Ibid., 426. Quoted from the Supreme Court of New Mexico in the decision below, 70 N.M. 90, 94.

124. Ibid., 430. Quoted from *Florida Lime & Avocado Growers v. Paul,* 373 U.S. 132, 141. (The bracket is Stewart's.)

125. *U.S. Statutes at Large,* XLVIII, 1064.

126. 374 U.S. 424, 431-32.

127. Ibid., 432. Justice Brennan made this point the crux of his concurring opinion, ibid., 433-48 at 444-46. But he was more cautious than the majority and warned: "Our holding today intimates no view of the constitutionality of several other superficially similar forms of state regulation of broadcasting." Ibid., 447.

128. A major exception to this is their clash in *Campbell v. Hussey,* 368 U.S. 297 (1961). They also differed in *California v. Zook,* 336 U.S. 725 (1949) and *Huron Portland Cement Co. v. Detroit,* 362 U.S. 440 (1960).

129. There can be no argument about Stone's disapproval of *Cloverleaf Butter Co. v. Patterson,* 315 U.S. 148 (1942), because he wrote the major dissenting opinion in that case; see ibid., 170-77.

130. 325 U.S. 761 (1945) at 767, 769, 770, 780, 781-82. See also Bernard Schwartz' analysis above, quoted from an article cited in footnote 79; and see footnote 70 for still another criticism of the way in which the Court decided the *Huron* case.

9 State Taxation and Congressional Intervention

The final area of state power to be considered is taxation of interstate commerce. Because so much of American business is organized on an essentially nation-wide basis and because the general public now makes such large service demands upon government at all levels, the states have been forced to seek new sources of revenue and thus inevitably have imposed various kinds of taxes and charges upon the conduct of interstate business. But always the question recurs as to whether these levies run afoul of the negative implications of the Commerce Clause. The result is that this field of constitutional law is both immense and diverse—so much so in fact that it would be impossible to treat it at all adequately within the intended length of the present study. Besides the lack of space, however, there is a more legitimate reason for confining the coverage here to a somewhat superficial review of the leading cases of the past 33 years. This field of taxation is a highly technical one; to understand accurately the precise effects of various state exactions on interstate commerce requires a knowledge of economic theory which, quite frankly, goes beyond the professional competence of the present author. And yet this kind of empirical economic appraisal is necessary to any very meaningful criticism of the Supreme Court's decisions in terms of what constitutes a proper balance between state and national interests. Accordingly, the thrust of the analysis will be toward identifying only the broad trend of Court decision. What will also emerge from the survey is again the great discretion which the Court can exercise in its role as final arbiter between national and state power.

Exclusionary Taxes

As good a place to begin as any is with the rather well-known case of *Henneford v. Silas Mason Co.* (1937).[1] In 1935 Washington levied a two-percent tax on retail sales within the state; concurrently, it laid a two-percent tax on "the privilege of using within this state any article of tangible personal property." To relieve retail buyers of a double burden, several exemptions were made to the use tax; two of these were: (1) the tax was not to be collected unless the property was bought at retail, and (2) it did not apply to articles which had "already been subjected to a tax equal to or in excess of" two percent. The Silas Mason Company, a contractor engaged in the construction of the Grand Coulee Dam, brought over $900,000 of machinery and supplies, which had been purchased at retail in other states, into Washington; but it refused to pay the use tax on the grounds that it was "upon the operations of interstate commerce" and that it "discriminated" against such commerce.

Justice Benjamin N. Cardozo wrote the majority opinion which upheld the state-taxing scheme.[2] He admitted that the practical effects of the use tax were (1) to help Washington retail dealers compete with sellers elsewhere who were exempt from "a sales tax or any corresponding burden," and thus (2) to prevent "a drain upon the revenues of the state."[3] The question was whether these consequences necessitated a holding that the tax was repugnant to the Commerce Clause, and he found that they did not.

Cardozo answered the contention that the exaction was on the "operations" of commerce by asserting that the tax was "upon the privilege of use after commerce is at an end." He continued:

> Things acquired or transported in interstate commerce may be subjected to a property tax, non-discriminatory in its operation, when they have become part of the common mass of property within the state of destination. . . . For like reasons they may be subjected, when once they are at rest, to a non-discriminatory tax upon use or enjoyment.[4]

The machinery and materials had seen "continuous use in Washington long after the time when delivery was over," and they came within these rules.

Cardozo had equally little trouble in refuting the claim that the tax discriminated against interstate business transactions. He reasoned that

Equality is the theme that runs through all the sections of the statute. There shall be a tax upon the use, but subject to an offset if another use or sales tax has been paid for the same thing. This is true where the offsetting tax became payable to Washington by reason of purchase or use within the state. It is true in exactly the same measure where the offsetting tax has been paid to another state by reason of use or purchase there.

. . . When the account is made up, the stranger from afar is subject to no greater burdens as a consequence of ownership than the dweller within the gates. The one pays upon one activity or incident, and the other upon another, but the sum is the same when the reckoning is closed.[5]

The tax was not a "protective tariff" imposed on the act of interstate importation; the motives of the state legislature were none of the Court's business; and "a tax upon use, or, what is equivalent for present purposes, a tax upon property after importation is over, is not a clog upon the process of importation at all, any more than a tax upon the income or profits of a business."[6] The levy was a valid exercise of Washington's taxing power.[7]

Two years later the Court did find evidence of a "protective tariff." *Hale v. Bimco Trading, Inc.* (1939)[8] involved the validity of a Florida statute which authorized the State Road Department to fix standards for all cement sold or used in the state and which imposed an inspection fee of 15 cents per hundredweight on cement brought in "from any foreign country." Justice Felix Frankfurter, in his maiden Court opinion, struck down the state act.[9] The quality standards and inspection requirement applied only to foreign cement, which accounted for approximately 30 percent of all the cement sold and used in Florida; uncontested evidence showed that the inspection fee was "sixty times the actual cost of inspection." Frankfurter's conclusion was hardly surprising; he rejected the state's police-power subterfuge:

So far as public safety demands certain standards in the quality of cement, such safety is dependent on assurance of that quality by appropriate inspection no less of the 70% domestic cement than of the 30% obtained from abroad. That no Florida cement needs any inspection while all foreign cement requires inspection at a cost of fifteen cents per hundredweight is too violent an assumption to justify the discrimination here disclosed. The other justification—the competitive effect of foreign cement in the Florida market—is rather a candid admission that the very purpose of the statute is to keep out foreign goods.

321

. . . Such assumption of national powers by a state has, ever since March 12, 1827 (*Brown v. Maryland*, 12 Wheat. 419), been found to be in collision with the Constitution. . . . [I]t would not be easy to imagine a statute more clearly designed than the present to circumvent what the Commerce Clause forbids.[10]

Florida could not effect an "embargo" on foreign cement.

A different kind of exclusionary levy was invalidated in *Best & Company, Inc. v. Maxwell* (1940).[11] North Carolina laid an annual privilege tax of $250 on every person or corporation, not a regular retail merchant in the state, who displayed samples of goods in any hotel room or house rented or occupied temporarily for the purpose of securing retail orders. Justice Stanley F. Reed spoke for a unanimous Court (9-0) in striking down the state tax.[12] He was succinct in his condemnation of the measure:

> The Commerce Clause forbids discrimination, whether forthright or ingenious. . . . Nonresidents wishing to display their wares must either establish themselves as regular North Carolina retail merchants at prohibitive expense, or else pay this $250 tax that bears no relation to actual or probable sales but must be paid in advance no matter how small the sales turn out to be. Interstate commerce can hardly survive in so hostile an atmosphere.[13]

The effect of the tax would necessarily be "to discourage and hinder the appearance of interstate commerce in the North Carolina retail market," and the state could not thus fetter that "freedom of commerce" which allowed merchants "a regional or national market for their goods." Such discrimination was constitutionally prohibited.

Property, Sales, and Use Taxes

The mid 1940's brought a series of cases before the Court, and the results for state power were mixed. The most notable victory for the states came in *Northwest Airlines, Inc. v. Minnesota* (1944).[14] Northwest, a Minnesota corporation with St. Paul as its home base, operated a fleet of airplanes in interstate commerce. None of its planes were continuously outside of the state during the year, and Minnesota sought to impose a personal-property tax on the entire fleet. By a narrow, five-to-four margin, the state's claim was upheld.

Justice Frankfurter wrote the "opinion and conclusion" of the Court in which only Justices Douglas and Murphy joined unreservedly.[15] He based the decision entirely upon the special relationship which obtained between the company and the state:

322

No other State can claim to tax as the State of the legal domicile as well as the home State of the fleet, as a business fact. No other State is the State which gave Northwest the power to be as well as the power to function as Northwest functions in Minnesota; no other State could impose a tax that derives from the significant legal relation of creator and creature and the practical consequences of that relation in this case. On the basis of rights which Minnesota alone originated and Minnesota continues to safeguard, she alone can tax the personalty which is permanently attributable to Minnesota and to no other State.[16]

The present situation was precisely analogous to that in *New York Central & Hudson River Railroad Co. v. Miller* (1906);[17] there Justice Holmes had held that New York could tax all of the railroad's rolling stock because none of the cars were "continuously without the State during the whole tax year" and thus had not acquired a "tax situs" elsewhere. On an identical basis, that of the domiciliary rights of the state, the Minnesota tax had to be sustained.

On the same day the Court decided the case of *McLeod v. J.E. Dilworth Co.* (1944).[18] Dilworth, a Tennessee manufacturing corporation which was not qualified to do business in Arkansas and which had no sales office or other place of business in that state, made sales of machinery and mill supplies for delivery there. Orders for the goods, which were solicited by traveling salesmen who were domiciled in Tennessee, had to be confirmed at Dilworth's Memphis headquarters where title passed to the purchaser. Arkansas sought to impose its gross-receipts tax on the sales made to its residents. By a vote of five to four, the Court invalidated collection of the state exaction.

Justice Frankfurter wrote the majority opinion.[19] He held that the tax was a "retail sales tax" which the state had "no power to exact." The present situation was different from the one in *McGoldrick v. Berwind-White Coal Mining Co.* (1940), and that case was not controlling. Berwind-White maintained a sales office in New York City, took orders there, and made actual delivery there; this activity constituted a local sale which might be taxed. Here Dilworth maintained its offices in Tennessee, the sales were made in Tennessee, and delivery was consummated "either in Tennessee or in interstate commerce." Under these circumstances, it was clear that the transfer of ownership occurred in Tennessee, and Arkansas could not be allowed "to project its powers beyond its boundaries and to tax an interstate transaction"; to do so would sanction "an assumption of power by a State which the Commerce Clause was meant to end. The very purpose of the Commerce Clause was to create an area of free trade among the several States,"[20] and the tax was in conflict with that purpose.

At the same time, a very similar use tax was sustained in *General Trading Co. v. State Tax Commission* (1944).[21] General Trading, a Minnesota corporation which had not qualified to do business in Iowa and which maintained no sales office or other place of business there, made sales of merchandise which were sent to purchasers in Iowa. Orders were secured by salesmen headquartered in Minnesota and were taken subject to acceptance in Minnesota. Iowa attempted to collect a two-percent use tax from General Trading on the property shipped by it to purchasers in Iowa. By a vote of seven to two the Court upheld the tax.

Justice Frankfurter again spoke for the majority.[22] He relied almost wholly on past precedents, including *Henneford v. Silas Mason Co.* (1937), to vindicate the state:

> The tax is what it professes to be—a non-discriminatory excise laid on all personal property consumed in Iowa. . . . The exaction is made against the ultimate consumer—the Iowa resident who is paying taxes to sustain his own state government. To make the distributor the tax collector for the State is a familiar and sanctioned device.[23]

Iowa could collect her use tax from an out-of-state seller.

Transition Year, 1946

In 1946 the Court decided two cases of some importance. One was *Nippert v. City of Richmond.*[24] At stake was the validity of a municipal ordinance of Richmond, Virginia, which imposed an annual license tax of "$50.00 and one-half of one percentum of the gross earnings, receipts, fees or commissions for the preceding license year in excess of $1,000.00" upon persons or firms "engaged in business as solicitors." For five days in January, 1944, Dorothy Nippert solicited orders in Richmond for the American Garment Company of Washington, D.C. She was arrested for failing to procure a license, fined, and ordered to comply with the ordinance. She appealed on the ground that the statute violated the Commerce Clause.

Justice Wiley B. Rutledge wrote the five-to-three opinion which invalidated the license tax.[25] He relied primarily upon the rationale of *Robbins v. Shelby Country Taxing District* (1887) and distinguished as inapposite the *Berwind-White* case. The sales in *Berwind-White* were regular and continuous, and the New York two-percent sales tax was "directly proportioned to the volume of business transacted." Here all of the evidence pointed to the conclusion that the solicitation was at best casual and spasmodic. Furthermore, the tax bore "no relation to the volume of business done or of returns from it";[26] legally, not a single sale could be made without the intial payment of a "fixed substantial sum" which would be increased in any subsequent year.

The Richmond tax imposed "substantial excluding and discriminatory effects" in other ways. The small operator or even the larger operator with a highly specialized product (and therefore a limited market) would both "find the tax not only burdensome but prohibitive, with the result that the commerce is stopped before it is begun";[27] the fact that it was a municipal tax merely added to its potential of exclusion because a similar flat exaction could be levied by every city in Virginia, and "the cumulative burden will be felt more strongly by the out-of-state itinerant than by the one who confines his movement within the State or the salesman who operates within a single community or only a few."[28] The inevitable result could only be "the stoppage of a large amount of commerce."

This was the real vice in the appellee's position; it did not take into account the "practical consequences" of the measure; the tax inherently was

> highly variable in its incidence and effects with reference to the manner in which one organizes his business and especially in respect to its location and spread in relation to state lines. It was exactly these variations, when they bear with undue burden upon commerce that crosses state lines, which the Commerce Clause was intended to prevent.[29]

Richmond could not discriminate against drummers in interstae commerce "in favor of local competing business."

The other leading case of 1946 was *Freeman v. Hewit*,[30] which involved the constitutionality of the Indiana Gross Income Tax Act of 1933 as applied to receipts from the sale of intangible securities on the New York Stock Exchange. The securities, part of the estate of a deceased Indiana resident, were delivered to an Indiana broker who arranged for their sale through his New York correspondent and who then remitted the proceeds (less expense and commissions) to the seller-trustee. Indiana sought to impose its one-percent gross income tax on the transaction; the trustee of the estate paid the levy under protest and brought suit for recovery.

In a six-to-three decision the Court found for the trustee. Justice Frankfurter spoke for five justices in holding that the tax constituted a direct burden upon interstate commerce.[31] He began with a restatement of a fundamental and familiar canon:

> In two recent cases we applied the principle that the Commerce Clause was not merely an authorization to Congress to enact laws for the protection and encouragement of commerce among the States, but by its own force created an area of trade free from interference by the States. In short, the Commerce Clause even without implementing legislation by Congress is a limitation upon the power of the States. *Southern Pacific Co. v. Arizona,* 325 U.S. 761; *Morgan v. Virginia,* 328 U.S. 373.[32]

Frankfurter recognized that the power to tax was "a dominant power over commerce"; thus, historically, state attempts to impose "a direct tax on commerce" had been "more carefully scrutinized and more consistently resisted than police power regulations of aspects of such commerce."[33] He likened the present situation to the one in *J.D. Adams Manufacturing Co. v. Storen* (1938), but he did not rest his reasoning on that case;[34] instead, he simply struck down the Indiana tax on the ground that it resulted in an "interference by a State with the freedom of interstate commerce."[35] Trade was "a sensitive plant," a gross-receipts tax was "a direct imposition" on the free flow of goods, and a state could not subject the former to the latter without violating the "immunities implicit in the Commerce Clause." The Indiana exaction as applied was unconstitutional.[36]

The Court Abdicates and Congress Acts

The 1950's saw the Court develop a generally more lenient attitude toward state taxation of interstate commerce. A good example is *City of Chicago v. Willett Company* (1953).[37] A Chicago ordinance levied an annual license tax on all trucks operated for hire within the city; the tax was graduated according to capacity in tons, and the penalty for failure to pay it was a fine. Willett, an Illinois corporation, owned a fleet of trucks which it used to transport goods within Chicago and between Chicago and other points in Illinois, Indiana, and Wisconsin; it refused to pay the license tax on the ground that it could not separate its intrastate business (upon which the tax fell) from its interstate business which was beyond Chicago's reach under the Commerce Clause. By a vote of eight to one the Court sustained the tax.

Justice Frankfurter delivered the majority opinion.[38] He relied heavily upon *New York Central & Hudson River Railroad Co. v. Miller* (1906) and his own *Northwest Airlines, Inc. v. Minnesota* (1944) to uphold the city ordinance:

> The central and decisive fact in this case is that respondent's business has, as much as any transportation business can have, a home. That home is Chicago. To the extent that respondent's business is not confined within the City's limits, it revolves around the City. . . . It receives . . . the City's protection, and it benefits from the City's public services. In the circumstances, a tax of reasonable proportions such as the one in question, not shown in fact to be a burden on interstate commerce, is not inconsistent with the Commerce Clause.[39]

All of the Willett Company's trucks could be taxed.

On February 24, 1959, the Court handed down an important decision. *Northwestern States Portland Cement Co. v. Minnesota*[40] held that net income from the exclusively interstate operations of an out-of-state corporation might be taxed by a state provided the exaction was nondiscriminatory and was properly apportioned to local activities. Northwestern, an Iowa manufacturer of cement with its one plant at Mason City, sold about 48 percent of its product to independent dealers in Minnesota. It maintained a three-room sales office in Minneapolis which was occupied by two salesmen and a secretary; two other salesmen used the office as a clearing house. These four salesmen solicited orders from eligible dealers and contacted potential end-users to secure orders for the dealers; all orders were transmitted to Mason City for acceptance, filling, and delivery. Minnesota imposed an annual tax upon the net income of Northwestern, apportioned to the amount of business done in the state and computed at the same rate as for residents. Northwestern resisted payment with the argument that the tax violated both the Commerce Clause and the due-process clause of the Fourteenth Amendment.

Justice Tom C. Clark spoke for five of the six-man majority.[41] He rested his approval of the Minnesota income tax primarily on past precedents. The first important one was *United States Glue Co. v. Town of Oak Creek*, 247 U.S. 321 (1918), in which "the Court distinguished between an invalid direct levy which placed a burden on interstate commerce and a charge by way of net income derived from profits from interstate commerce."[42] The second was *Norfolk & Western Railway Co. v. North Carolina*, 297 U.S. 682 (1936), in which

"North Carolina was permitted to tax a Virginia corporation on net income apportioned to North Carolina on the basis of mileage within the State."[43] Clark read this to mean that "the entire net income of a corporation, generated by interstate as well as intrastate activities, may be fairly apportioned among the States for tax purposes by formulas utilizing in-state aspects of interstate affairs."[44]

The clincher was *West Publishing Co. v. McColgan*, 328 U.S. 823 (1946), a unanimous *per curiam* decision in which the Court sustained a California tax "on the apportioned net income of West Publishing Company, whose business was exclusively interstate."[45] There the California Supreme Court had found: "It is settled by decisions of the United States Supreme Court that a tax on net income from interstate commerce, as distinguished from a tax on the privilege of engaging in interstate commerce, does not conflict with the Commerce Clause."[46] Clark was succinct: "We believe that the rationale of these cases, involving income levies by States, controls the issues here."[47] The state income tax was not a regulation of commerce "in any sense of that term" and did not discriminate against or burden unduly the operations of Northwestern. As to the possibility of multiple taxation, the short answer was that no such showing had been made. In sum, the tax did not offend the prohibitions of the Commerce Clause.[48]

Justice Charles E. Whittaker wrote a long and well-documented dissent to show that no past precedents directly supported Clark's conclusion and that the Court was breaking new ground in its present decision, ground which was forbidden by the Commerce Clause.[49] Justice Frankfurter agreed with Whittaker and indicated his major concern in opposing "this new step":

> My objection is the policy that underlies the Commerce Clause, namely, whatever disadvantages may accrue to the separate States from making of the United States a free-trade territory are far outweighed by the advantages not only to the United States as a Nation, but to the component States.[50]

The Court's ruling would actively burden commerce for two reasons. First, since the states would undoubtedly act now to tax proportionately income from exclusively interstate commerce, thousands of small or moderate-size corporations soon would be buried under the bookkeeping and accounting systems which would be necessary "to meet the divers and variegated tax laws" of the states; the cost of these systems well might "exceed the burden of the taxes themselves." Second, the extensive litigation which would develop as a result of challenges to apportionment formulas would create legal expenses which would cast a further burden on businesses conducted across state lines.

Frankfurter was not "unmindful of the extent to which federal taxes absorb the taxable resources of the Nation, while at the same time the fiscal demands of the States are on the increase."[51] But he thought that the allocation of tax revenues could not be made "wisely and smoothly through the adjudicatory process," and he issued an appeal for legislative action:

> The problem calls for solution by devising a congressional policy. Congress alone can provide for a full and thorough canvassing of the multitudinous and intricate factors which compose the problem of the taxing freedom of the States and the needed limits on such state taxing power. Congressional committees can make studies and give the claims of the individual States adequate hearing before the ultimate legislative formulation of policy is made by the representatives of all the States.[52]

In less than seven months Congress responded to this suggestion and to the concomitant cries of anguish from the business community. On September 14, 1959, it demonstrated its displeasure with the Court's extraordinary new leniency toward state power by passing the Interstate Commerce Tax Act.[53] This statute contained two main provisions. First, it prohibited any state from imposing a net income tax on income derived from interstate commerce by any out-of-state person (or corporation) if the only business activity in the taxing state was "the solicitation of orders by such person, or his representative, in such State for sales of tangible personal property, which orders are sent outside the State for approval or rejection, and, if approved, are filled by shipment or delivery from a point outside the State." A more direct slap at the decision in the *Northwestern States Portland Cement Co.* case could hardly be imagined. Second, the Act called for the House Committee on the Judiciary and the Senate Committee on Finance to

> make full and complete studies of all matters pertaining to the taxation by the States of income derived within the States from the conduct of business activities which are exclusively in furtherance of interstate commerce or which are a part of interstate commerce, for the purpose of recommending to the Congress proposed legislation providing uniform standards to be observed by the States in imposing income taxes on income so derived.

329

The committees were directed to make their reports and recommendations on or before July 1, 1962. Congress had at last decided to take the matter in hand!

Further Leniency, 1960–1964

In spite of these congressional warning signals, the Court continued to sustain various exercises of the states' taxing powers. In the early part of 1960 it decided *Scripto, Inc. v. Carson.*[54] At issue was the validity of a Florida statute which imposed a three-percent use tax on sales of tangible personal property and made the dealer liable if he failed to collect it. Scripto, a Georgia corporation, sold mechanical writing instruments adapted to advertising purposes through ten wholesalers or jobbers who were residents of Florida and who solicited orders on a commission basis. It maintained no sales office, warehouse, or other place of business in Florida and had no regular in-state employee or agent. Orders were sent directly to the Atlanta office for acceptance, and all sales were consummated there. Florida attempted to collect the use tax, but Scripto objected on the grounds that the state levy as applied placed an unconstitutional burden on interstate commerce and violated the due-process clause of the Fourteenth Amendment. By a vote of eight to one, the Court upheld Florida's right to compel Scripto to act as its tax collector.

Justice Clark wrote the majority opinion.[55] He noted that the tax was "a nondiscriminatory exaction levied for the use and enjoyment of property which has been purchased by Florida residents and which has actually entered into and become a part of the mass of property in that State";[56] its burden fell on the ultimate purchaser in Florida and not upon the out-of-state seller unless, as here, "he fails or refuses to collect it from the Florida customer." The test of whether the state could collect from Scripto was the nature and extent of the corporation's activities in Florida, that is, there had to be "some definite link, some minimum connection, between a state and the person, property or transaction it seeks to tax."[57] In the present case the ten wholesalers or "salesmen," who were "conducting continuous local solicitation in Florida and forwarding the resulting orders from that State to Atlanta,"[58] provided a sufficient "nexus" for the support of the tax. The only incidence of the sales that was "nonlocal" was the acceptance of the orders, and it was obvious that Scripto's substantial Florida volume was due to the effectiveness of the local function of solicitation. Under these circumstances, the decision in *General Trading Co. v. State Tax Commission* (1944) was controlling, and the tax was valid.

330

The *Scripto* ruling merely added fuel to the conflagration of business protest which *Northwestern States Portland Cement Co. v. Minnesota* had created originally, and in 1961 Congress expanded the scope of its authorized 1959 study of state taxation to include sales and use taxes and "all matters pertaining to the taxation of interstate commerce by the states."[59] But before this comprehensive project was completed, the Court handed down another important decision in *General Motors Corporation v. Washington* (1964).[60] The state imposed a tax for the privilege of engaging in in-state business activities; it was levied at the rate of one-fourth of one percent of the gross receipts of the business. Washington sought to tax the entire gross wholesale sales made by General Motors in the state. General Motors, a Delaware corporation, protested payment on the grounds that the tax (1) was on the privilege of engaging in interstate commerce and thus was discriminatory, (2) was unapportioned and thus resulted in the imposition of a multiple-tax burden in violation of the Commerce Clause, and (3) was a deprivation of property without due process of law as guaranteed by the Fourteenth Amendment.

In a close, five-to-four ruling the Court sustained the Washington gross-receipts tax. Justice Clark, the undisputed champion of the states in these cases, filed the majority opinion.[61] He admitted that a local tax measured by gross receipts from interstate commerce presented the danger of a cumulative burden on that commerce which might destroy it and that the Court had held that such commerce could not be subjected to "multiple taxation." But he found that a "careful analysis" of past precedents revealed the principle that

> the validity of the tax rests upon whether the State is exacting a constitutionally fair demand for that aspect of interstate commerce to which it bears a special relation. For our purposes the decisive issue turns on the operating incidence of the tax. In other words, the question is whether the State has exerted its power in proper proportion to appellant's activities within the State and to appellant's consequent enjoyment of the opportunities and protections which the State has afforded.[62]

General Motors had entered Washington voluntarily and engaged in business activities therein; it had the burden of showing that its operations were "interstate in nature" and therefore exempt from the state exaction.

Clark then turned to the facts to demonstrate General Motors' inability to establish its exemption. Four company divisions maintained sales and service organizations in the state. Pontiac and Oldsmobile both had zone offices in Portland, Oregon, headed by a zone manager; district managers, who lived in Washington and used their homes as offices, called upon Washington dealers to help them work out sales estimates and take purchase orders. In-state service representatives also called on the dealers to assist them with the personnel and inventory problems of their service departments. Chevrolet conducted an identical operation, except that it maintained a branch office at Seattle to facilitate service on the dealers' orders. General Motors Parts operated two warehouses—one at Portland and one at Seattle—from which it sold and shipped parts and accessories to the dealers; it willingly paid the tax on sales from the Seattle location, but it opposed payment on sales from the Portland installation. In addition to the zone managers at Portland, other company personnel from out of state who carried on in-state activities included business management managers, parts and service managers, and used car managers—all for the purpose of helping and strengthening the local dealer network.

In view of all these facts, Clark concluded that the tax was not upon the mere "privilege" of doing interstate business, and he stated tersely his reason for upholding it:

> Thus, in the bundle of corporate activity, which is the test here, we see General Motors' activity so enmeshed in local connections that . . . we cannot say that the Supreme Court of Washington erred in holding that these local incidents were sufficient to form the basis for the levy of a tax that would not run contrary to the Constitution.[63]

In fact, the tax was "so closely related to the local activities of the corporation" that it made no difference in its constitutionality that it was unapportioned. Clark admitted that General Motors' claim of multiple-taxation presented a "difficult question," but he dismissed it with the assertion that the company had not demonstrated "what definite burden, in a constitutional sense," other state taxes placed "on the identical interstate shipments by which Washington measures its tax."[64] Thus the question was one which the Court need not answer, and the tax could stand.

Justice Arthur J. Goldberg dissented vigorously.[65] He characterized the decision as an important departure "from a fundamental purpose of the Commerce Clause" and from the established principle that state taxes on interstate sales had to be "fairly apportioned"; and he thought that it would be difficult "to conceive of a state gross receipts tax on interstate commerce which could not be sustained under the rationale adopted today."[66] That rationale was that the validity of a state tax rested upon "whether the State is exacting a constitutionally fair demand for that aspect of interstate commerce to which it bears a special relation."[67] But such a formulation was patently unworkable in practice because it afforded no answer to the question, "What is 'fair?'"[68]

Goldberg pressed the point about "fairness" and criticized the Court for side-stepping the multiple-taxation issue:

> These problems are engendered by the rule applied here and cannot be evaded. For if it is "fair" to subject the interstate sales to the Washington wholesale sales tax . . . then it would seem equally "fair" for Oregon . . . to tax the same gross sales receipts. Moreover, it would seem "fairer" for California, Michigan or Missouri—States in which automobiles are manufactured, assembled or delivered—to impose a tax measured by . . . the same gross sales receipts.[69]

He went on to show that Washington's taxing scheme, which consisted of a manufacturers' tax and a wholesalers' tax (with exemption from one if a local manufacturer-wholesaler), placed a double burden on an out-of-state manufacturer who operated in a state which had the same tax provisions as Washington; the "foreign" firm would pay a local manufacturing tax and a wholesale tax to Washington. Thus interstate commerce would be discriminated against, and the efficient allocation of resources in the national economy would be affected adversely.

To the plea that the tax was nondiscriminatory since it fell on all wholesale sales (intrastate and interstate) made to Washington purchasers, Goldberg responded bluntly:

> The Commerce Clause, however, was designed, as Mr. Justice Jackson said in *H.P. Hood & Sons, Inc. v. DuMond* . . . to create a "federal free trade unit"—a common national market among the States; and the Constitution thereby precludes a State from defending a tax on interstate sales on the ground that the State taxes intrastate sales generally. Nondiscrimination alone is no basis for burdening the flow of interstate commerce. The Commerce Clause "does not merely forbid a State to single out interstate commerce for hostile action. A State is also precluded from taking any action which may fairly be deemed to have the effect of impeding the free flow of trade between States. It is immaterial that local commerce is subjected to a similar encumbrance."[70]

In his view the only gross receipts upon which the state could collect the unapportioned tax were the sales of General Motors Parts from its Seattle warehouse;[71] all of General Motors' other in-state sales should be exempt from the Washington tax if "the common national market created by the Commerce Clause" were not to be undermined. But Goldberg's admonition went unheeded.

Congressional Response

Meanwhile, the House Judiciary Committee, with the approval of the Senate Finance Committee, carried out the mandate which had been given in 1959 and 1960. It formed a Special Subcommittee on State Taxation of Interstate Commerce, chaired by Representative Edwin E. Willis (D.–La.), which conducted a four-and-one-half-year study on the subject, aided by a ten-member advisory group of distinguished experts which was headed by Ernest J. Brown, Professor of Law at Harvard University. The results of the study were published in four volumes.[72] Briefly, the subcommittee found that the existing system of state taxation of interstate commerce worked badly for both business and the states because it contained the following defects: (1) widespread noncompliance, (2) overtaxation and undertaxation as a result of the inconsistencies in state rules and noncompliance, (3) the existence of discriminatory state provisions which were advantageous to local companies relative to out-of-state competitors, and (4) an attitude of widespread resistance to taxpayer responsibility, especially on the part of small and moderate-size companies.[73] Legislative recommendations to reform the system and to protect the "American common market" were then spelled out.[74]

The first move for legislative action came on October 22, 1965, when Representative Willis introduced a bill (H.R. 11798) which embodied the special subcommittee's major proposals. After holding extensive hearings on this bill from January 26 to April 6, 1966, the subcommittee formulated a more limited program which Willis introduced as H.R. 16491 on July 25, 1966. The House Judiciary Committee approved H.R. 16491 without amendment on September 7, 1966, but the House did not have time to consider it before the 89th Congress adjourned. The legislation was reintroduced in the 90th Congress as H.R. 2158, was amended further, and then was passed by the House on May 22, 1968; but the Senate took no action on it, and it died with the 90th Congress. Undoubtedly, however, a similar measure is likely to be introduced again in Congress. H.R. 2158 in its final form contained the following major provisions:

1. The states and their political subdivisions were denied power (a) to impose a net income tax or capital stock tax on a corporation other than an excluded corporation (one which has an average annual income in excess of $1,000,000) unless the corporation has a business location in the state during the taxable year, which location is defined as owning or leasing real property within the state, or having one or more employees located in the state, or regularly maintaining a stock of tangible personal property in the state for sale in the ordinary course of business; (b) to require a person to collect a sales or use tax with respect to a sale of tangible personal property unless the person has a business location in the state or regularly makes household deliveries in the state; or (c) to impose a gross receipts tax with respect to a sale of tangible personal property unless the seller has a business location in the state. (Nothing in the above was to be considered as repealing the 1959 law with respect to any person or as changing state power with respect to an excluded corporation.)

2. With respect to the net income tax (or capital stock tax), a corporation other than an excluded corporation is given the option of using an apportionment formula based upon the two factors of property and payroll (but excluding sales volume), and the states may not impose a tax in excess of the amount determined by this calculation.

3. With respect to sales and use taxes, an interstate sale must have its destination in a state in order for that state to impose a sales tax or require a seller to collect a sales or use tax with respect to the sale. A use tax may not be imposed on a person without a business location in the state, and the amount of any such tax shall be reduced by the amount of any sales or use tax previously paid to another state.

Thus the House of Representatives indicated that the Supreme Court had gone somewhat too far in sanctioning state taxation of interstate commerce; at least one body of the elected representatives of all the people were determined to prevent any further "Balkanization" of the most productive and most prosperous commercial entity in the history of the world—the American national economy.

While H.R. 2158 wended its way through the House legislative mill, the Court began to have some second thoughts about its recent virtual abdication as the guardian of interstate commerce. In the spring of 1967 it decided *National Bellas Hess, Inc. v. Department of Revenue.*[75] The case involved an attempt by Illinois to require National Bellas Hess, a mail-order firm incorporated in Delaware and headquartered in

Missouri, to collect a use tax on sales of goods made to Illinois consumers. National maintained no office or other place of business, had no agents or solicitors, owned no property, had no telephone listing, and did no advertising by the usual media in the state; its only contact with Illinois residents was via the United States mail or common carrier since twice a year it mailed catalogues to active or recent customers throughout the nation and supplemented these with occasional "flyers." Orders were, of course, sent in by mail, accepted at North Kansas City (Mo.), and then delivered by mail or common carrier. National contended that there was no taxable "nexus" between it and Illinois and that the use-tax liability created "an unconstitutional burden upon interstate commerce." By a vote of six to three the Court agreed.

Justice Stewart wrote the majority opinion.[76] He admitted that the Court had "upheld the power of a State to impose liability upon an out-of-state seller to collect a local use tax in a variety of circumstances"[77] and that *Scripto, Inc. v. Carson* (1960) represented "the furthest constitutional reach to date of a State's power to deputize an out-of-state retailer as its collection agent for a use tax."[78] But the *Scripto* case was not controlling because in that case the seller had ten wholesalers, jobbers, or "salesmen" who carried on "continuous local solicitation"; here, any such connection was missing, and the Court would not obliterate the valid distinction which previous cases had drawn "between mail order sellers with retail outlets, solicitors, or property within a State, and those who do no more than communicate with customers in the State by mail or common carrier as part of a general interstate business."[79]

Finally, Stewart summed up his condemnation of the state-use tax as applied and indicated his awareness of the current political support for the free flow of interstate trade:

> [I]t is difficult to conceive of commercial transactions more exclusively interstate in character than the mail order transactions here involved. And if the power of Illinois to impose use tax burdens upon National were upheld, the resulting impediments upon the free conduct of its interstate business would be neither imaginary nor remote. For if Illinois can impose such burdens, so can every other State, and so, indeed, can every municipality, every school district, and every other political subdivision throughout the Nation with power to impose sales and use taxes. The many variations in rates of tax, in allowable exemptions, and in administrative and record-keeping requirements could entangle

National's interstate business in a virtual welter of complicated obligations to local jurisdictions with no legitimate claim to impose "a fair share of the cost of the local government."

The very purpose of the Commerce Clause was to ensure a national economy free from such unjustifiable local entanglements. Under the Constitution, this is a domain where Congress alone has the power of regulation and control.[80]

Thus in this case the Court, fortified by a partial expression of congressional "intent," once again assumed its historic and necessary role as constitutional protector of the national interest in the free and unburdened flow of commerce "among the several States."

The foregoing discussion may now be summarized very briefly. Over the past third of a century the Supreme Court has been faced with the perennial problem of judging state taxation of interstate commerce. On the whole the Court has shown great sympathy for the revenue needs of the states and, particularly in the last two decades, has rather consistently sustained state taxes on out-of-state corporations if there appeared to be any reasonable "nexus" between the companies' in-state activities and the incidence of the tax. In fact, the Court has gone so far in this direction that Congress has become concerned enough about preserving the "American common market" to conduct a study of the whole complex matter; and while few corrective measures have been taken to date, the national legislature may yet act to protect and to ensure the continued vitality, efficiency, and prosperity of the commercial enterprise of the United States.

Notes

1. 300 U.S. 577.

2. For his complete opinion, see ibid., 578-88. The decision was 7-2; Justices McReynolds and Butler dissented without opinion.

3. Ibid., 581.

4. Ibid., 582. In support of the first statement he cited *Woodruff v. Parham,* 8 Wallace 123 (1869).

5. Ibid., 583-84.

6. Ibid., 586.

7. Cardozo added the cautionary remark that nothing in his opinion was meant to imply that "allowance of a credit for other taxes paid to

Washington made it mandatory that there should be a like allowance for taxes paid to other states." Ibid., 587. A state, "for many purposes," was "a self-contained unit."

8. 306 U.S. 375.

9. For his complete opinion, see ibid., 376-81. The decision was unanimous, 8-0; Justice Brandeis had retired just two weeks before and had not yet been replaced.

10. Ibid., 380-81.

11. 311 U.S. 454.

12. For his complete opinion, see ibid., 454-57.

13. Ibid., 455-56.

14. 322 U.S. 292.

15. For his complete opinion, see ibid., 292-301. Justice Black concurred in the result, but he was careful not to foreclose the right of other states to tax "transactions and properties in interstate commerce"; see ibid., 301-02. Justice Jackson also concurred in the result, but he was equally careful to assert that Minnesota's right to tax the whole fleet was "exclusive of any similar right elsewhere"; ibid., 302-08. Chief Justice Stone, joined by Justices Roberts, Reed, and Rutledge, dissented vigorously on the ground that the Court's decision exposed Northwest to "the risk of a multiple burden to which local commerce is not exposed"; see ibid., 308-26. (The risk was real since six other states had already subjected the carrier's interstate planes to personal-property taxes; Stone again had the soundest argument.)

16. Ibid., 294-95.

17. 202 U.S. 584.

18. 322 U.S. 327.

19. For his complete opinion, see ibid., 327-32. He was joined by Chief Justice Stone and Justices Roberts, Reed, and Jackson. Justice Douglas, joined by Justices Black and Murphy, dissented on the ground that *McGoldrick v. Berwind-White Coal Mining Co.,* 309 U.S. 33, was not being followed; see ibid., 332-35. Justice Rutledge dissented on the ground that he could see no difference between the Arkansas sales tax and the Iowa use tax which the Court sustained in *General Trading Co. v. State Tax Commission,* 322 U.S. 335, decided the same day; see 322 U.S. 349-62.

20. Ibid., 330.

21. 322 U.S. 335.

22. For his complete opinion, see ibid., 336-39. With him were Chief Justice Stone and Justices Black, Reed, Douglas, and Murphy. Justice Rutledge concurred in a separate opinion; see 322 U.S. 349-62. Justice Jackson, joined by Justice Roberts, dissented on the ground that Iowa had no constitutional power to make "a tax collector of one whom it has no power to tax . . . as the price of the privilege of doing interstate commerce"; see ibid., 339-40.

23. Ibid., 338.

24. 327 U.S. 416.

25. For his complete opinion, see ibid., 417-35. He was joined by Chief Justice Stone (just two months before his death) and Justices Reed, Frankfurter, and Burton. Justice Jackson was in Germany and took no part. Justice Black dissented without opinion. Justice Douglas, joined by Justice Murphy, dissented on the ground that the Court had inadequate evidence of an unconstitutional burden on interstate commerce; see ibid., 435-37.

26. Ibid., 427.

27. Ibid., 429.

28. Ibid., 430.

29. Ibid., 432.

30. 329 U.S. 249.

31. For his complete opinion, see ibid., 250-59. He was joined by Chief Justice Vinson and Justices Reed, Jackson, and Burton. Justice Rutledge wrote a long concurring opinion in which he assaulted the "direct-burden" rationale, but he agreed with the result as necessary to prevent the possibility of a "cumulative and therefore discriminatory tax burden" on interstate commerce; see ibid., 259-83. Justice Black dissented without opinion. Justice Douglas, joined by Justice Murphy, dissented on the ground that the Court had confused "a gross receipts tax on the Indiana broker with a gross receipts tax on his Indiana customer"; the former would be unconstitutional (*Gwin, White & Prince, Inc. v. Henneford*, 305 U.S. 434), but the latter would not (*Western Live Stock v. Bureau of Revenue*, 303 U.S. 250). See ibid., 283-86.

32. Ibid., 252.

33. Ibid., 253.

34. Ibid., 255. This was where Frankfurter and Rutledge parted company; Rutledge would have based the decision squarely on the *Adams* case; see Note 31.

35. Ibid., 257.

36. As a final point, Frankfurter saw no difference between the interstate sale of an intangible and a tangible; see ibid., 258-59.

37. 344 U.S. 574.

38. For his complete opinion, see ibid., 574-80. He spoke for five justices besides himself: Black, Jackson, Burton, Clark, and Minton. Justice Reed, joined by Chief Justice Vinson, concurred on the ground that the tax was a valid charge for the use of Chicago's streets; see ibid., 580-82. Justice Douglas dissented on the ground that because Willett's interstate business increased the amount of the tax by increasing the number of trucks operated, the flat fee per truck was "an unconstitutional burden on interstate commerce"; see ibid., 582.

39. Ibid., 580.

40. 358 U.S. 450. Consolidated with this case was *Williams v. Stockham Valves & Fittings, Inc.*, a Georgia case with similar facts.

41. For his complete opinion, see ibid., 452-65. With him were Chief Justice Warren and Justices Black, Douglas, and Brennan. Justice Harlan wrote his own concurring opinion; see ibid., 465-70. Justice Whittaker, joined by Justices Frankfurter and Stewart, dissented on the ground that the Commerce Clause "precludes the States from laying taxes directly on, and thereby regulating, 'exclusively interstate commerce' "; see ibid., 477-97. Justice Frankfurter dissented separately in an opinion which will be discussed later; see ibid., 470-77.

42. Ibid., 459. (In the *Glue Co.* case, Justice Mahlon Pitney upheld an apportioned and nondiscriminatory Wisconsin tax on a *Wisconsin* corporation as applied to net profits derived from out-of-state sales; the net income tax could not be considered "so direct a burden upon plaintiff's interstate business as to amount to an unconstitutional interference with or regulation of commerce among the states.")

43. Ibid., 460. (This is a fair statement; but as Justice Whittaker noted in his dissent, Norfolk & Western carried on "substantial local activities" within North Carolina. Ibid., 493.)

44. Ibid., 460.

45. Ibid., 460. Justice Harlan placed heavy reliance on the *West* precedent in his concurrence. Ibid., 467-68.

46. Ibid., 461.

47. Ibid., 461.

48. Ibid., 462-64. Clark disposed of the due-process objection in short order; he held merely that Northwestern had engaged in such "substantial income-producing activity" within Minnesota that "nexus" had been formed between the activity and the tax sufficient "to satisfy due process requirements." Ibid., 464-65.

49. For his complete opinion, see ibid., 477-97. The state tax was a direct, substantial regulation of interstate commerce, and the Commerce Clause put such "substantial regulation" exclusively in the hands of Congress. Ibid., 496-97. One who agrees that the decision embraced "novel doctrine" is Bernard Schwartz. Although he approves of the result, he criticizes the reasoning behind it: "In its *Northwestern States Cement* opinion, the Court animadverted on the 'need for clearing up the tangled underbrush of past cases' in this field, asserting that 'the decisions have been "not always clear . . . consistent or reconcilable." ' Unfortunately, the decisions discussed on commerce and state power appear only to compound the confusion. . . . The desire to appear consistent with precedent . . . hardly justifies the twisting of clear prior decisions to make them appear to mean something other than what they have always meant to the profession." Bernard Schwartz, "The Supreme Court—October 1958 Term," *Michigan Law Review,* LVIII (December, 1959), 165, 187. (See particularly 179-187.)

50. Ibid., 473.

51. Ibid., 475.

52. Ibid., 476-77.

53. *U.S. Statutes at Large,* LXXIII, 555.

54. 362 U.S. 207.

55. For his complete opinion, see ibid., 207-13. He was joined by Chief Justice Warren and Justices Black, Douglas, Harlan, Brennan, and Stewart. Justice Frankfurter concurred in the result on the basis of *General Trading Co. v. State Tax Commission,* 322 U.S. 335. Justice Whittaker dissented on the basis of *McLeod v. J.E. Dilworth Co.* 322 U.S. 327, and in reiteration of his views in *Northwestern States Portland Cement Co. v. Minnesota,* 358 U.S. 450.

56. Ibid., 211.

57. Ibid., 210-11. The words are those of Justice Jackson in *Miller Brothers Co. v. Maryland,* 347 U.S. 340, 344-45 (1954), wherein the Court invalidated a Maryland use tax as applied to a Delaware merchandising corporation which had its store in Delaware and sold to residents of Maryland who came to the store. Some of the goods purchased were delivered in Maryland by the seller's trucks, but Jackson held that this was insufficient to give Maryland jurisdiction or power to tax the Delaware vendor; thus the tax violated the due-process clause of the Fourteenth Amendment.

58. Ibid., 211.

59. *U.S. Statutes at Large,* LXXV, 41.

60. 377 U.S. 436.

61. For his complete opinion, see ibid., 437-49. He spoke for Chief Justice Warren and Justices Black, Douglas, and Harlan. Justice Brennan dissented on the ground that the tax was not "fairly apportioned to the commerce carried on within the taxing state" and hence did not meet "the standards required by the Commerce Clause"; see ibid., 449-51. Justice Goldberg, joined by Justices Stewart and White, dissented in an opinion which will be reviewed later; see ibid., 451-62.

62. Ibid., 440-41.

63. Ibid., 447-48.

64. Ibid., 449.

65. For his complete opinion, see ibid., 451-62.

66. Ibid., 456.

67. Ibid., 457. Goldberg was quoting Clark.

68. Ibid., 457. Goldberg's criticism of Clark's fairness formula is not unlike Justice James Iredell's criticism of Justice Samuel Chase's natural-justice test; neither is regulated by any "fixed standard," and "the ablest and purest men" might reach different results in applying them. The Chase-Iredell clash occurred in *Calder v. Bull,* 3 Dallas 386 (1798).

69. Ibid., 458.

70. Ibid., 461. The part in quotation marks is from Justice Frank-

furter's majority opinion in *Freeman v. Hewit,* 329 U.S. 249, 252 (1946).

71. Goldberg reached this conclusion based on his reading of *Norton Co. v. Department of Revenue,* 340 U.S. 534 (1951). In that case, Norton Co., a Massachusetts corporation, maintained a branch office and warehouse in Chicago, Illinois, through which it sold abrasive machines and supplies. The office also took orders which were sent to Norton's headquarters at Worcester, where they were filled and shipped directly to the customer. The Court, per Justice Jackson, sustained an Illinois occupation tax, measured by gross receipts from retail sales of tangible personal property, upon all of Norton's sales except the orders which were shipped directly from Worcester to the purchaser; these were immune, and Goldberg reasoned that GM sales made through the Portland, Oregon, zone offices were immune from the Washington tax, too.

72. "State Taxation of Interstate Commerce," *House Report No. 1480,* Vols. 1 & 2, 88th Congress, 2d Session (1964); *House Report No. 565,* Vol. 3, and *House Report No. 952,* Vol. 4, 89th Congress, 1st Session (1965).

73. *House Report No. 952,* 89th Congress, 1st Session (1965), 1127-28.

74. Ibid., 1129-96.

75. 386 U.S. 753.

76. For his complete opinion, see ibid., 753-60. He was joined by Chief Justice Warren and Justices Clark, Harlan, Brennan, and White. Justice Abe Fortas, supported by Justices Black and Douglas, dissented primarily on the ground that the case was controlled by *Scripto, Inc. v. Carson,* 362 U.S. 207 (1960); see ibid., 760-66.

77. Ibid., 757. He cited, *inter alia,* the decision in *General Trading Co. v. State Tax Commission,* 322 U.S. 335 (1944).

78. Ibid., 757.

79. Ibid., 758.

80. Ibid., 759-60.

10   Conclusion

Every serious student of American constitutional law knows that Supreme Court justices are not noted for their brevity of expression; and by this time the patient reader knows that the present author is no better in this respect than those of whom he writes. Nevertheless, the major findings of this study of the Supreme Court and the Commerce Clause from 1937 through the spring of 1970 need to be brought together and summarized briefly. Since, in each of the areas covered, the individual cases of importance have been reported and analyzed in detail, it seems necessary now only to reiterate the broad generalizations which those cases substantiate. There are five of these.

Federal Power

First, there is the fact of plenary national power over every aspect of interstate commerce. Congress, under the authority of the Commerce Clause, is able to reach into every nook and cranny of the highly interdependent American economic system. It has unquestioned control over any business activity which in any way "affects" commerce, regardless of how "local" that activity may be, how remote or "indirect" its effect may be, and how small or insignificant the contribution of a single instance may be if it is representative of "many others similarly situated." Nor is Congress limited to the regulation of subjects which are wholly economic in nature; by virtue of its commerce power it can strike at the primarily moral evils of gambling (*Champion v. Ames*), prostitution (*Hoke v. United States*), and racial

345

discrimination in public accommodations (*Heart of Atlanta Motel v. United States* and *Katzenbach v. McClung*), the only constitutional requirement being the showing of a connection between the prohibited activity and that commerce or intercourse which "concerns more states than one." Thus, 146 years after *Gibbons v. Ogden,* it is settled constitutional principle that the federal commerce power is the power "to prescribe the rule by which commerce is to be governed," that it is "complete in itself, may be exercised to its utmost extent, and acknowledges no limitations, other than are prescribed in the constitution," and that it is "vested in congress as absolutely as it would be in a single government, having in its constitution the same restrictions on the exercise of the power as are found in the constitution of the United States." Chief Justice John Marshall's powerful initial constructions of the Commerce Clause are now the undisputed law of the land.

Second, and in amplification of the first proposition, it may be asserted that the only constitutional provisions which the Supreme Court would allow to restrict this specifically delegated power are those which grant with equal specificity certain individual rights and liberties; in other words, only the guarantees of the Bill of Rights (Amendments One through Nine) and the prohibitions of Article I, section 9, against bills of attainder (*United States v. Brown*) and *ex post facto* laws could limit in any way congressional use of the Commerce Clause to effect national economic policy. But at least since *United States v. Darby* in 1941, the Tenth Amendment—that last refuge of the antifederalists and the states' righters—has ceased to be a barrier to the full exercise of an enumerated power. In that case Harlan Fiske Stone characterized the Tenth Amendment as a "truism," which merely declared that "all is retained which has not been surrendered," and in doing so reaffirmed the validity of Marshall's premise in *McCulloch v. Maryland* (1819) that "the government of the Union, though limited in its powers, is supreme within its sphere of action." Old constitutional heresies die hard, however, as a case decided in the spring of 1968 illustrates. *Maryland v. Wirtz*[1] concerned the validity of certain amendments to the federal Fair Labor Standards Act of 1938.[2] In 1961 Congress changed the basis of coverage from each employee "engaged in commerce or in the production of goods for commerce" to all employees of any "enterprise" engaged in commerce or production for commerce, provided that the enterprise also fell within certain listed categories. Then in 1966 Congress added to the list of categories any enterprise engaged in the operation of a hospital, a school for handicapped or gifted children, an

346

elementary or secondary school, or an institution of higher education, "regardless of whether or not such hospital, institution, or school is public or private or operated for profit or not for profit." At the same time, Congress removed its exemption of the states and their political subdivisions as "employers" within the meaning of the earlier statute.[3]

Maryland, joined by 27 other states and one school district, brought action against the Secretary of Labor to enjoin the enforcement of these amendments as they applied to hospitals and schools operated by the states of their subdivisions. Four arguments were advanced in support of this position: (1) The expansion of coverage through the "enterprise concept" exceeded the power of Congress under the Commerce Clause; (2) the coverage of state-operated schools and hospitals was beyond the reach of the federal commerce power; (3) if the remedial provisions of the law were employed against the states, such action would be repugnant to the Eleventh Amendment; and (4) hospitals and schools, "as enterprises," lacked the statutorily required relationship to interstate commerce. By a vote of six to two the Court rejected the first two contentions and declined to decide the last two.

Justice John Marshall Harlan wrote the majority opinion.[4] He looked first to the 1961 amendment, the effect of which was "to extend protection to the fellow employees of any employee who would have been protected by the original Act," and found that there were two independent bases which supported the constitutionality of this "enterprise concept" of coverage. First, the reasoning in *United States v. Darby* (1941) really settled the matter. There the Court had held that Congress was empowered to "regulate intrastate activities where they have a substantial effect on interstate commerce" and that substandard wages and excessive hours, when imposed on production employees, did indeed exert a "substantial effect" on commerce by way of altering the relative competitive position of companies engaged therein. In short, there was a "rational basis" for the congressional finding of substantial effect in the 1938 Act, and the same was true of the 1961 amendment:

> The logical inference does not stop with production employees. When a company does an interstate business, its competition with companies elsewhere is affected by all its significant labor costs, not merely by the wages and hours of those employees who have physical contact with the goods in question. Consequently, it is not surprising that this Court has already explicitly recognized

347

that Congress' original choice to extend the Act only to certain employees of interstate enterprises was not constitutionally compelled; rather, Congress decided, at that time, "not to enter areas which it might have occupied [under the commerce power]."[5]

A second line of analysis was also relevant. In the original Act, Congress had found that substandard labor conditions tended to lead to labor disputes and strikes which, in turn, affected the flow of goods in interstate commerce; therefore it had chosen to promote labor peace by regulating wages and hours—two matters which often occasioned labor strife. Although the Court had not noticed this second objective in *Darby,* it had held in other cases that the protection of commerce from disruptions due to labor strife afforded a "rational basis" for federal regulation of labor conditions in industry; the prime example was, of course, *National Labor Relations Board v. Jones & Laughlin Steel Corp.* (1937). And, obviously, "substandard labor conditions among any group of employees, whether or not they are personally engaged in commerce or production, may lead to strife disrupting an entire enterprise."[6] Thus the extension of the Fair Labor Standards Act to all employees of a covered "enterprise" was clearly sustainable under two powerful lines of precedent.

Harlan then turned his attention to the more crucial issue: Could Congress extend coverage to the employees of state-operated hospitals and schools? He noted first that the statute specifically excluded executive, administrative, or professional employees (including teachers), and he assumed that "medical personnel" likewise were excluded "under the general language." Thus there was no question of a congressional attempt to tell the states "how to perform medical and educational functions"; Congress had "interfered with" these activities "only to the extent of providing that when a State employs people in performing such functions it is subject to the same restrictions as a wide range of other employers whose activities affect commerce, including privately operated schools and hospitals."[7]

Second, he looked to the facts. It was clear that "labor conditions in schools and hospitals can affect commerce." State and local governments were spending on an annual basis $38,300,000,000 for educational instruction and $3,900,000,000 for hospital operations; furthermore, these institutions were large users of goods imported from other states. Maryland, for example, which spent $8,000,000 for school equipment and supplies in 1965, made 87 percent of these purchases out of state; and of the $576,000 spent by the University of Maryland Hospital and seven other hospitals for drugs, X-ray supplies, and equipment, over 55 percent of these goods moved in interstate commerce. Harlan drew the only possible conclusion:

> Strikes and work stoppages involving employees of schools and hospitals, events which unfortunately are not infrequent, obviously interrupt and burden this flow of goods across state lines. It is therefore clear that a "rational basis" exists for congressional action prescribing minimum labor standards for schools and hospitals, as for other importing enterprises.[8]

With this last proposition firmly established he took up Maryland's specific contention that even the federal commerce power had to yield "to state sovereignty in the performance of governmental functions." But this argument was simply "not tenable" for two reasons. First, there was "no general 'doctrine implied in the Federal Constitution that the two governments, national and state, are each to exercise its powers so as not to interfere with the free and full exercise of the powers of the other.' "[9] Harlan could not have been more unequivocal in his interpretation of this principle: "[I] t is clear that the Federal Government, when acting within a delegated power, may override countervailing state interests whether these be described as 'governmental' or 'proprietary' in character."[10]

Second, while the commerce power was not unlimited in its reach, it was still true that

> valid general regulations of commerce do not cease to be regulations of commerce because a State is involved. If a State is engaging in economic activities that are validly regulated by the Federal Government when engaged in by private persons, the State too may be forced to conform its activities to federal regulation.[11]

For support of this holding, he quoted at length from *United States v. California*, 297 U.S. 175 (1936), in which it was decided that a state-operated railroad was subject to the federal Safety Appliance Act. There, speaking for a unanimous Court, Justice Stone had reasoned:

> [W] e think it unimportant to say whether the state conducts its railroad in its "sovereign" or in its "private" capacity. That in operating its railroad it is acting within a power reserved to the states cannot be doubted. The only question we need consider is whether the exercise of that power, in whatever capacity, must be

in subordination to the power to regulate interstate commerce, which has been granted specifically to the national government. The sovereign power of the states is necessarily diminished to the extent of the grants of power to the federal government in the Constitution.[12]

This principle controlled the present case, and Harlan drove home the point of national supremacy in blunt language:

This Court has examined and will continue to examine federal statutes to determine whether there is a rational basis for regarding them as regulations of commerce among the States. But it will not carve up the commerce power to protect enterprises indistinguishable in their effect on commerce from private businesses, simply because those enterprises happen to be run by the States for the benefit of their citizens.[13]

Finally, Harlan brushed aside two further objections to the federal law as inappropriate for decision. He dismissed the contention based on the Eleventh Amendment by referring to the "separability" provision in the statute and relying on the time-honored practice of the Court not "to strike down otherwise valid portions of the Act simply because other portions might not be constitutional as applied to hypothetical future cases."[14] To the claim that "hospitals and schools are the ultimate consumers of the out-of-state products they buy, and hence none of their employees handles 'goods' in the statutory sense," he replied that such institutions put their imported commodities "to a wide variety of uses, presumably ranging from physical incorporation of building materials into hospital and school structures, to over-the-counter sales for cash to patients, visitors, students, and teachers,"[15] and that whether their employees handled "goods in commerce" might be considered as the occasion required. What was beyond dispute was that Congress had power, under the Commerce Clause, to bring a selected class of state employees under the protection of the Fair Labor Standards Act.

Justice William O. Douglas, usually an advocate of extensive federal power (see Chapter 8), dissented, joined by Justice Potter Stewart.[16] The basis for his disagreement was an appeal to the force of the Tenth Amendment:

The Court's opinion skillfully brings employees of state-owned enterprises within the reach of the Commerce Clause; and as an exercise in semantics it is unexceptionable if congressional federalism is the standard. But what is done here is nonetheless such a serious invasion of state sovereignty protected by the Tenth Amendment that it is in my view not consistent with our constitutional federalism.[17]

He emphasized the impact which the federal law would have on the fiscal policy of the states; the latter would be forced alternatively to raise taxes or to reduce the extent and calibre of their present health and educational services or to refrain from entering any new fields of governmental activity. Such federal interference with the sovereign functions of state governments, however, was not a proper object of the Commerce Clause, and Douglas conjured up his own modern-day parade of imaginable horribles:

If constitutional principles of federalism raise no limits to the commerce power where regulation of state activities are concerned, could Congress compel the States to build super-highways criss-crossing their territory in order to accommodate interstate vehicles, to provide inns and eating places for interstate travelers, to quadruple their police forces in order to prevent commerce-crippling riots, etc.? Could the Congress virtually draw up each State's budget to avoid "disruptive effect[s] . . . on commercial intercourse."? . . . If all this can be done, then the National Government could devour the essentials of state sovereignty, though that sovereignty is attested by the Tenth Amendment.[18]

But Douglas was pleading a long-lost cause.

But if *Maryland v. Wirtz* illustrates the fact that the Tenth Amendment has not been consigned entirely to the limbo of constitutional argument, the important conclusion to be drawn from the case is the way in which the Supreme Court now interprets the force and scope of the national power over commerce, that is, a power which (1) allows Congress to regulate any activity which impinges upon the nation's commerce, and (2) is subject to no limitations which the states might try to impose. Harlan's well-reasoned opinion is merely the latest proof that the Court has rejected irretrievably the doctrine of dual federalism and has accepted fully the original understanding of the Constitution that "the Federal Government, when acting within a delegated power, may override countervailing state interests"; or, as Edward S. Corwin put it so cogently in 1936:

A logical interpretation of the relevant provisions of the Constitution clearly and unavoidably forbids the idea that the reserved powers of the States comprise an independent limitation upon the delegated powers of the National Government. By the terms of the Tenth Amendment if a power is delegated to the United States by the Constitution, it is not reserved to the States; and by the supremacy clause, an act of Congress passed by virtue of a delegated power or powers of the United States is supreme over all conflicting State laws and constitutional provisions without exception.[19]

This is precisely the principle of construction which *Maryland v. Wirtz* reaffirmed in 1968.

State Power

The third conclusion concerns the present status of state power over interstate commerce and is that the states now exercise greater control over that commerce than at any time since *Gibbons v. Ogden* in 1824. As the Supreme Court has unfettered and expanded the federal commerce power since 1937, it has concurrently become increasingly lenient toward exercises of state power (both of regulation and taxation), until today in the latter area Congress has deemed it necessary at least to think in terms of enacting specific measures to protect interstate trade from undue state burdens and encroachments. On the other hand, the Court has not abandoned entirely the logically implied principles of *Cooley v. The Board of Wardens* (1852) that the Commerce Clause, of its own force, operates "to curtail state power in some measure" and "thus affords some protection from state legislation inimical to the national commerce";[20] therefore the Court continues to play its historic role as umpire of the federal system and in so doing continues to judge the validity of specific state regulations of commerce. Furthermore, whether such regulations are imposed in the absence of federal legislation or are alleged to conflict with existing congressional "occupation of the field," the Court subjects them to the *Cooley* balancing-of-interests test (as refined by Stone) in order to determine their constitutional validity or infirmity.

A very recent confirmation of this last proposition is found in the case of *Pike v. Bruce Church, Inc.,*[21] decided March 2, 1970. At issue was the application of the Arizona Fruit and Vegetable Standardization Act of 1929 to a company engaged in growing produce in Arizona and California and in shipping the harvested products in interstate commerce. The state statute provided that all cantaloupes grown in Arizona could not leave the state unless "packed in regular compact arrangement in closed standard containers." Bruce Church, Inc. had been transporting its high-quality, Arizona-grown cantaloupes in bulk to its centralized packing facilities in California, where they were sorted, packed, and shipped in containers identical to those required by Arizona. Then in 1968 Arizona ordered the company to pack its melons within the state. Since this would have entailed the expenditure of about $200,000 to build an in-state packing shed, the company contested the order on the ground that it imposed an unconstitutional burden on interstate commerce.

Justice Potter Stewart delivered the unanimous opinion which annulled the state action.[22] He first asserted the Court's "general rule" for determining the validity of state laws affecting commerce:

> Where the statute regulates even-handedly to effectuate a legitimate local public interest, and its effects on interstate commerce are only incidental, it will be upheld unless the burden imposed on such commerce is clearly excessive in relation to the putative local benefits. . . . If a legitimate local purpose is found, then the question becomes one of degree. And the extent of the burden that will be tolerated will of course depend on the nature of the local interest involved, and on whether it could be promoted as well with a lesser impact on interstate activities.[23]

Stewart then turned to a consideration of the purpose of the Arizona act. It had been passed to ensure that fruits and vegetables shipped from the state would meet "certain standards of wholesomeness and quality"; the anticipated result was the protection of "the reputation of growers within the State." This was certainly a legitimate local interest; but he reasoned that the action of the state here was "not for the purpose of keeping the reputation of its growers unsullied, but to enhance their reputation through the reflected goodwill of the company's superior produce."[24] Such a state interest was too "tenuous" and too "minimal" in Stewart's view to "constitutionally justify the requirement that the company build and operate an unneeded $200,000 packing plant in the State." The state order imposed a prohibited straitjacket on the firm "with respect to the allocation of its interstate resources" and thus placed "an unlawful burden upon interstate commerce" which could not stand.[25]

Only two brief comments on *Pike v. Bruce Church, Inc.* seem necessary. The first is that the case demonstrates the continued willingness of the Supreme Court to protect the freedom of interstate commerce from excessive interference or interdiction by the several states. The second is that the decision was obviously reached through the use of a balancing-of-interests process. Although Stewart went out of his way to denigrate "a balancing approach" and to insist that the Court has more frequently spoken "in terms of 'direct' and 'indirect' effects and burdens,"[26] it is apparent that in the final analysis he weighed the "tenuous" and "minimal" interest of Arizona in enhancing the reputation of its growers against the $200,000 cost to an interstate producer and found the former wanting. Furthermore, the Justice himself, in framing the Court's "general rule" on state power, recognized that in particular cases "the question becomes one of degree." But what does this entail if not judgments of comparative value? Whether Stewart wishes to admit it or not, the balancing-of-interests doctrine is an enduring and quite legitimate principle of constitutional law.

Final Thoughts

Fourth, this survey of the Supreme Court and the Commerce Clause would be incomplete without some small notice of those justices who have contributed the most to Commerce-Clause adjudication and interpretation. Without going into any detail, it may be argued that three justices stand head and shoulders above their fellows in terms of their influence upon this facet of American constitutional law. First and foremost, of course, is "the great Chief Justice," John Marshall; if he had never written an opinion other than *Gibbons v. Ogden,* he would still deserve that appellation and the gratitude of every American who rejoices in the fact that the United States is one nation. All of the important cases herein reviewed bear the imprimatur of his seminal exposition of Article I, section 8, clause 3 of the federal Constitution. The second giant is Chief Justice Harlan Fiske Stone, who killed dual federalism in *United States v. Darby* and returned federal power to Marshallian principles, and who lifted the judicial review of state power to the rational plane of the balancing-of-interests doctrine. For fidelity to the judicial function, for sensitivity to the needs of both the nation and the states, and for that objectivity which judges are supposed to possess, Stone is unsurpassed. The third figure is the first Justice John Marshall Harlan. While he perhaps does not quite have the claim to fame of Marshall or Stone, it was he who stood fast against the flood-tides of laissez-faire and dual federalism at a time when those philosophies were at the peak of their power and popularity. Harlan

354

alone dissented in *United States v. E.C. Knight Co.* (1895); he wrote the powerful majority opinion in *Champion v. Ames* (1903) which opened the way for the federal government to develop a much-needed national police power based on the Commerce Clause; and he imparted new vitality to the Sherman Antitrust Act in *Northern Securities Co. v. United States* (1904).[27] Truly, Harlan is one of the Court's great Commerce-Clause interpreters, and one who kept the faith.

Finally, a fifth conclusion seems in order; this is that the record of the Supreme Court in its interpretation and construction of the Commerce Clause is singularly clean and proper. While this study has been (hopefully) an exercise in scholarly research, logical reasoning, and objective analysis and criticism, it cannot have escaped the perceptive reader's notice that the author possesses a very deep-seated attachment to, and an appreciation of, the Court as one of the great institutions in the American system of government, perhaps the institution which more than any other has been responsible for giving practical meaning to the basic principles upon which the United States was founded—that all men are created equal, that the individual citizen is endowed with certain inalienable rights and liberties which the state cannot legitimately abridge, and that governmental power may properly be used in a constructive fashion to promote the general welfare, provide for the common defense, and insure domestic tranquility in society and the economy. It is, of course, in fulfillment of the last objective that the Court has construed the Commerce Clause to be both a vast reservoir of positive national power and a limitation upon devisive and parochial state power. In general, and over the long stretch of American history, the record shows that the Supreme Court has been remarkably consistent in interpreting the Commerce Clause to further the best interests of all the people of the United States; few have been the times when it has "tortured" that clause, and always this has been done only over the sharp protest of one or more of its own members. In short, the Court deserves high praise and strong public support for a job well done in an exceedingly difficult field.

With this clear declaration now made, one final admonition is in order: The Court should be careful in its exposition of state power under the Commerce Clause not to jeopardize the continued vitality of the American national economy which rests upon a free nation-wide market place for goods and services. The fact which emerges most forcefully from a study of the record is the persistent, ingenious, and always selfish attempts by the several states to cut up, restrict, and generally impair the normal operations of interstate commerce in favor of some purely local economic gain. The examples are legion: New York seeks both to keep its milk from going to Massachusetts and to exclude milk from Vermont; Florida seeks to exclude milk from Alabama and cement from foreign countries; Illinois seeks to force upon truckers the adoption of a mudguard of dubious value which is different from that required by any other state and to interfere with the orderly transfer of rail passengers between terminals in Chicago; and California seeks to insulate its avocado industry from Florida competition. The list of these self-seeking measures is endless, and the Court must be on its guard to protect the freedom of national commerce from state-imposed frustration and debilitation. Many of the recent great advances in constitutional law, which have put teeth into the guarantees of the Bill of Rights and the Fourteenth Amendment, have come at the expense of state power. It would be tragic if, as a sop to the states, the Court were to fail to apply fully the Commerce Clause's inherent limitations upon state action.

History shows, in marked contrast to the hopes expressed by Jefferson and Madison in the Kentucky and Virginia Resolutions of 1798, that it is the states which have been the great offenders against the American constitutional system, and this is as true with respect to commerce as it is with respect to civil rights and the liberties and immunities guaranteed by the first nine amendments.[28] The states simply have no claims—constitutional or moral—to any special consideration or any undue leniency from the Supreme Court in its role as ultimate guardian of the Constitution. It seems entirely appropriate, therefore, to close with two quotations which the justices should never forget when reviewing exercises of state power under the Commerce Clause. The first is from John Marshall's opinion in *Gibbons v. Ogden;* after having refuted all of the arguments of Oakley and Emmet in favor of the New York laws which created the steamboat monopoly, Marshall issued this warning:

> Powerful and ingenious minds, taking, as postulates, that the powers expressly granted to the government of the Union are to be contracted, by construction, into the narrowest possible compass, and that the original powers of the States are retained, if any possible construction will retain them, may, by a course of well digested, but refined and metaphysical reasoning, founded on these premises, explain away the constitution of our country, and leave it a magnificent structure indeed, to look at, but totally unfit for use.[29]

The second statement is from a speech made by Harlan Fiske Stone to the American Bar Association in 1928:

> Great as is the practical wisdom exhibited in all the provisions of the Constitution, and important as were the character and influence of those who secured its adoption, it will, I believe, be the judgment of history that the Commerce Clause and a wise interpretation of it, perhaps more than any other contributing element, have united to bind the several states into a nation.[30]

May that nation long endure; and may the Supreme Court continue, actively and responsibly, to make of the Commerce Clause a powerful instrument for the preservation of national unity and purpose.

Notes

1. 392 U.S. 183.

2. *U.S. Statutes at Large,* LII, 1060.

3. *U.S. Statutes at Large,* LXXX, 831.

4. For his complete opinion, see 392 U.S. 183, 185-201. With him were Chief Justice Warren and Justices Black, Brennan, White, and Fortas. Justice Thurgood Marshall took no part. Justice Douglas, joined by Justice Stewart, dissented in an opinion which will be examined later.

5. Ibid., 190-91. The part in quotation marks is from *Kirschbaum v. Walling,* 316 U.S. 517 at 522, and the brackets are Harlan's.

6. Ibid., 192.

7. Ibid., 194.

8. Ibid., 195.

9. Ibid., 195. The inside quotation is from *Case v. Bowles,* 327 U.S. 92, 101 (1946).

10. Ibid., 195. Here Harlan relied on *Sanitary District of Chicago v. United States,* 266 U.S. 405 (1925), in which Justice Holmes had held for a unanimous Court that the Sanitary District's "alledged need for more water than federal law allowed was 'irrelevant' because federal power over commerce is 'superior to that of the States to provide for the welfare or necessities of their inhabitants.' " The whole quotation is Harlan's; see ibid., 196. The inside quotation is Holmes'; see 266 U.S.

405 at 426. Harlan could also have relied upon *New York v. United States,* 326 U.S. 572 (1946), which upheld a federal tax levied upon mineral water bottled and sold by a state-owned corporation, the Saratoga Springs Authority.

11. Ibid., 196-97.

12. Ibid., 197-98.

13. Ibid., 198-99.

14. Ibid., 200.

15. Ibid., 201.

16. For his complete opinion, see ibid., 201-05.

17. Ibid., 201. Douglas bolstered his argument by harking back to his dissenting opinion in *New York v. United States,* 326 U.S. 572 (1946), in which he had asserted: "The Constitution is a compact between sovereigns. . . . If the power of the federal government to tax the States is conceded, the reserved power of the States guaranteed by the Tenth Amendment does not give them the independence which they have always been assumed to have. . . . They must pay the federal government for the privilege of exercising the powers of sovereignty guaranteed them by the Constitution." See 326 U.S. 572 at 595. Douglas' view, of course, would negate the clear teaching of *Darby* that the Tenth Amendment cannot cut down the exercise of a delegated power.

18. Ibid., 204-05.

19. Edward S. Corwin, *The Commerce Power Versus States Rights* (Gloucester, Mass.: Peter Smith, 1962), 255-56.

20. These reformulations of the *Cooley* rule were made by Stone in *South Carolina Highway Dept. v. Barnwell Bros.,* 303 U.S. 177 at 184 and *Southern Pacific Co. v. Arizona,* 325 U.S. 761 at 769.

21. 90 S.Ct. 844.

22. For his complete opinion, see ibid., 845-49.

23. Ibid., 847.

24. Ibid., 848.

25. In reaching his conclusions Stewart relied heavily upon *Toomer v. Witsell,* 334 U.S. 385 (1948), in which the Court invalidated a South

Carolina statute which required owners of shrimp boats licensed by the state to fish in its three-mile maritime belt to unload and pack their catches in South Carolina before transporting them to other states.

26. 90 S.Ct. 844, 847. It is interesting to note Stewart's somewhat mechanistic approach to problems of state power under the Commerce Clause. See his majority opinions in *Huron Portland Cement Company v. Detroit,* 362 U.S. 440 (1960), and *Head v. New Mexico Board of Examiners in Optometry,* 374 U.S. 424 (1963), both in Chapter 8, for other examples of this kind of thinking. For some reason Stewart is unwilling to accept overtly the discretion which the *Cooley* rule puts upon the Court to judge exercises of the partially concurrent power of the states over interstate commerce.

27. In view of these accomplishments, and because of his dissent in *Lochner v. New York,* 198 U.S. 45 (1905), the present author is inclined to overlook Harlan's opinion in *Adair v. United States,* 208 U.S. 161 (1908), which held that a congressional statute prohibiting "yellow dog" contracts by interstate carriers (section 10 of the Erdman Act of 1898) exceeded the federal commerce power and violated the "freedom of contract" guaranteed by the Fifth Amendment. If a study of constitutional law teaches anything, it is that Supreme Court justices are men and not angels. And see Harlan's protest against the judicially fabricated "rule of reason" in *United States v. American Tobacco Company,* 221 U.S. 106 (1911).

28. This indictment of the states is readily documented by reference to leading cases of the last few years in which the Court has been forced to deal with the following state practices: segregated schools (*Brown v. Board of Education,* 347 U.S. 483); establishment of religion (*School District of Abington Township v. Schempp,* 374 U.S. 203); denial of the freedom of association (*NAACP v. Alabama,* 357 U.S. 449); refusal to provide counsel for an indigent in a criminal trial (*Gideon v. Wainwright,* 372 U.S. 335); denial of the guarantee against self-incrimination (*Malloy v. Hogan,* 378 U.S. 1); malapportionment of electoral districts for state legislators (*Baker v. Carr,* 369 U.S. 186) and for federal representatives (*Wesberry v. Sanders,* 376 U.S. 1); denial of the right to vote because of race (*South Carolina v. Katzenbach,* 383 U.S. 301); and, again, the list of constitutional perversions is almost endless.

29. 9 Wheaton 1, 222.

30. Harlan F. Stone, "Fifty Years' Work of the United States Supreme Court," *American Bar Association Report,* LIII (1928), 259, 264.

Table of Cases

United States Supreme Court Cases

Adair v. United States, 208 U.S. 161 (1908).

J.D. Adams Manufacturing Co. v. Storen, 304 U.S. 307 (1938).

Alstate Construction Co. v. Durkin, 345 U.S. 13 (1953).

Amalgamated Meat Cutters & Butcher Workmen, Local No. 427, AFL v. Fairlawn Meats, Inc., 353 U.S. 20 (1957).

American Communications Ass'n., CIO v. Douds, 339 U.S. 382 (1950).

American Medical Association v. United States, 317 U.S. 519 (1943).

Arsenal Building Corporation v. Walling, 316 U.S. 517 (1942).

Associated Press v. National Labor Relations Board, 301 U.S. 103 (1937).

Bailey v. Drexel Furniture Company, 259 U.S. 20 (1922).

Baker v. Carr, 369 U.S. 186 (1962).

Baldwin v. G.A.F. Seelig, Inc., 294 U.S. 511 (1935).

Bank of Augusta v. Earle, 13 Peters 519 (1839).

Bell v. Maryland, 378 U.S. 226 (1964).

Best & Company, Inc. v. Maxwell, 311 U.S. 454 (1940).

Bibb v. Navajo Freight Lines, Inc., 359 U.S. 520 (1959).

Board of Trade of Chicago v. Olsen, 262 U.S. 1 (1923).

Bob-Lo Excursion Co. v. Michigan, 333 U.S. 28 (1948).

Borden Company v. Borella, 325 U.S. 679 (1945).

Bowman v. Chicago & Northwestern Railway Company, 125 U.S. 465 (1888).

Boynton v. Commonwealth of Virginia, 364 U.S. 454 (1960).

Brooks v. United States, 267 U.S. 432 (1925).

Brown v. Board of Education of Topeka, 347 U.S. 483 (1954).

Brown v. Board of Education of Topeka, 349 U.S. 294 (1955).

Brown v. Houston, 114 U.S. 622 (1885).

Brown v. Maryland, 12 Wheaton 419 (1827).

Buck v. Kuykendall, 267 U.S. 307 (1925).

Calder v. Bull, 3 Dallas 386 (1798).

California v. Zook, 336 U.S. 725 (1949).

Campbell v. Hussey, 368 U.S. 297 (1961).

Carter v. Carter Coal Co., 298 U.S. 238 (1936).

Castle v. Hayes Freight Lines, Inc., 348 U.S. 61 (1954).

Champion v. Ames, 188 U.S. 321 (1903).

Charleston & Western Carolina Railway Co. v. Varnville Furniture Company, 237 U.S. 597 (1915).

Cheney Brothers Co. v. Massachusetts, 246 U.S. 147 (1918).

City of Chicago v. Atchison, Topeka & Santa Fe Railway Co., 357 U.S. 77 (1958).

City of Chicago v. Willett Company, 344 U.S. 574 (1953).

Civil Rights Cases, 109 U.S. 3 (1883).

Clark Distilling Company v. Western Maryland Railway Company, 242 U.S. 311 (1917).

Cloverleaf Butter Co. v. Patterson, 315 U.S. 148 (1942).

Cohens v. Virginia, 6 Wheaton 264 (1821).

Colgate v. Harvey, 296 U.S. 404 (1935).

Colorado Anti-Discrimination Commission v. Continental Air Lines, Inc., 372 U.S. 714 (1963).

Consolidated Edison Co. v. National Labor Relations Board, 305 U.S. 197 (1938).

Cooley v. The Board of Wardens of the Port of Philadelphia, 12 Howard 299 (1852).

Dean Milk Co. v. City of Madison, 340 U.S. 349 (1951).

DiSanto v. Pennsylvania, 273 U.S. 34 (1927).

Duckworth v. Arkansas, 314 U.S. 390 (1941).

Edwards v. California, 314 U.S. 160 (1941).

Ex Parte Siebold, 100 U.S. 371 (1880).

Farmers Reservoir & Irrigation Co. v. McComb, 337 U.S. 755 (1949).

Florida Lime & Avocado Growers, Inc. v. Paul, 373 U.S. 132 (1963).

Freeman v. Hewit, 329 U.S. 249 (1946).

Lloyd A. Fry Roofing Co. v. Wood, 344 U.S. 157 (1952).

Gayle V. Browder, 352 U.S. 903 (1956).

General Motors Corporation v. Washington, 377 U.S. 436 (1964).

General Trading Co. v. State Tax Commission, 322 U.S. 335 (1944).

Gibbons v. Ogden, 9 Wheaton 1 (1824).

Gideon v. Wainwright, 372 U.S. 335 (1963).

Gordon v. United States, 117 U.S. 697 (1864).

Greer v. Connecticut, 161 U.S. 519 (1896).

Gwin, White & Prince, Inc. v. Henneford, 305 U.S. 434 (1939).

Hale v. Bimco Trading, Inc., 306 U.S. 375 (1939).

Hall v. DeCuir, 95 U.S. 485 (1878).

Hammer v. Dagenhart, 247 U.S. 251 (1918).

Head v. New Mexico Board of Examiners in Optometry, 374 U.S. 424 (1963).

Heart of Atlanta Motel v. United States, 379 U.S. 241 (1964).

Henderson v. Mayor of New York, 92 U.S. 259 (1876).

Henderson v. United States, 339 U.S. 816 (1950).

Henneford v. Silas Mason Co., 300 U.S. 577 (1937).

Hines v. Davidowitz, 312 U.S. 52 (1941).

Hipolite Egg Co. v. United States, 220 U.S. 45 (1911).

Hoke v. United States, 227 U.S. 308 (1913).

Holmes v. City of Atlanta, 350 U.S. 879 (1955).

H.P. Hood & Sons v. DuMond, 336 U.S. 525 (1949).

Hooper v. California, 155 U.S. 648 (1895).

Hotel Employees Union, Local No. 255 v. Sax Enterprises, Inc., 358 U.S. 270 (1959).

Howell Chevrolet Co. v. National Labor Relations Board, 346 U.S. 482 (1953).

Huron Portland Cement Company v. City of Detroit, 362 U.S. 440 (1960).

Hygrade Provision Co. v. Sherman, 266 U.S. 497 (1925).

Idaho Sheet Metal Works, Inc. v. Wirtz, 383 U.S. 190 (1966).

Industrial Ass'n. of San Francisco v. United States, 268 U.S. 64 (1925).

In re Rahrer, 140 U.S. 545 (1891).

International Brotherhood of Electrical Workers, Local 501, AFL v. National Labor Relations Board, 341 U.S. 694 (1951).

Johnson v. Virginia, 373 U.S. 61 (1963).

Jones v. Alfred H. Mayer Co., 392 U.S. 409 (1968).

Katzenbach v. McClung, 379 U.S. 294 (1964).

Kentucky Whip & Collar Co. v. Illinois Central Railroad Co., 299 U.S. 334 (1937).

A.B. Kirschbaum Co. v. Walling, 316 U.S. 517 (1942).

Leisy v. Hardin, 135 U.S. 100 (1890).

License Cases, 5 Howard 504 (1847).

Eli Lilly & Co. v. Sav-On-Drugs, Inc., 366 U.S. 276 (1961).

Local 74, United Brotherhood of Carpenters & Joiners of America, AFL v. National Labor Relations Board, 341 U.S. 707 (1951).

Lochner v. New York, 198 U.S. 45 (1905).

Lombard v. Louisiana, 373 U.S. 267 (1963).

Loving v. Commonwealth of Virginia, 388 U.S. 1 (1967).

Mabee v. White Plains Publishing Co., 327 U.S. 178 (1946).

Malloy v. Hogan, 378 U.S. 1 (1964).

Mandeville Island Farms, Inc. v. American Crystal Sugar Co., 334 U.S. 219 (1948).

Martino v. Michigan Window Cleaning Co., 327 U.S. 173 (1946).

Maryland v. Wirtz, 392 U.S. 183 (1968).

Mayor of Baltimore City v. Dawson, 350 U.S. 877 (1955).

Mayor of the City of New York v. Miln, 11 Peters 102 (1837).

McCulloch v. Maryland, 4 Wheaton 316 (1819).

McDermott v. Wisconsin, 228 U.S. 115 (1913).

McGoldrick v. Berwind-White Coal Mining Co., 309 U.S. 33 (1940).

McLeod v. J.E. Dilworth Co., 322 U.S. 327 (1944).

McLeod v. Threlkeld, 319 U.S. 491 (1943).

Miller Brothers Co. v. Maryland, 347 U.S. 340 (1954).

Minnesota v. Barber, 136 U.S. 313 (1890).

Minnesota Rate Cases, 230 U.S. 352 (1913).

Missouri v. Holland, 252 U.S. 416 (1920).

Mitchell v. Lublin, McGaughy & Associates, 358 U.S. 207 (1959).

Mitchell v. United States, 313 U.S. 80 (1941).

Mitchell v. C.W. Vollmer & Co., Inc., 349 U.S. 427 (1955).

Mitchell v. H.B. Zachry Company, 362 U.S. 310 (1960).

Morgan v. Virginia, 328 U.S. 373 (1946).

Mugler v. Kansas, 123 U.S. 623 (1887).

Mulford v. Smith, 307 U.S. 38 (1939).

Munn v. Illinois, 94 U.S. 113 (1877).

National Association for the Advancement of Colored People v. Alabama, 357 U.S. 449 (1958).

National Bellas Hess, Inc. v. Department of Revenue, 386 U.S. 753 (1967).

National Labor Relations Board v. Denver Building & Construction Trades Council, 341 U.S. 675 (1951).

National Labor Relations Board v. Fainblatt, 306 U.S. 601 (1939).

National Labor Relations Board v. Friedman-Harry Marks Clothing Co., 301 U.S. 58 (1937).

National Labor Relations Board v. Fruehauf Trailer Co., 301 U.S. 49 (1937).

National Labor Relations Board v. Jones & Laughlin Steel Corporation, 301 U.S. 1 (1937).

National Labor Relations Board v. Reliance Fuel Oil Corporation, 371 U.S. 224 (1963).

Nebbia v. New York, 291 U.S. 502 (1934).

New York v. United States, 326 U.S. 572 (1946).

New York Central & Hudson River Railroad Co. v. Miller, 202 U.S. 584 (1906).

New York Life Insurance Company v. Deer Lodge County, 231 U.S. 495 (1913).

Nippert v. City of Richmond, 327 U.S. 416 (1946).

Norfolk & Western Railway Co. v. North Carolina, 297 U.S. 682 (1936).

Northern Securities Company v. United States, 193 U.S. 197 (1904).

Northwest Airlines, Inc. v. Minnesota, 322 U.S. 292 (1944).

Northwestern States Portland Cement Co. v. Minnesota, 358 U.S. 450 (1959).

Norton Co. v. Department of Revenue, 340 U.S. 534 (1951).

Oliver Iron Mining Co. v. Lord, 262 U.S. 172 (1923).

Opp Cotton Mills, Inc. v. Administrator, 312 U.S. 126 (1941).

Overstreet v. North Shore Corporation, 318 U.S. 125 (1943).

Panama Refining Co. v. Ryan, 293 U.S. 388 (1935).

Parker v. Brown, 317 U.S. 341 (1943).

Passenger Cases, 7 Howard 283 (1849).

Paul v. Virginia, 8 Wallace 168 (1869).

Pennsylvania v. Nelson, 350 U.S. 497 (1956).

Pennsylvania v. Wheeling & Belmont Bridge Co., 18 Howard 421 (1856).

Pensacola Telegraph Co. v. Western Union Telegraph Co., 96 U.S. 1 (1877).

Pike v. Bruce Church, Inc., 90 S.Ct. 844 (1970).

Plumley v. Massachusetts, 155 U.S. 461 (1894).

Polar Ice Cream & Creamery Co. v. Andrews, 375 U.S. 361 (1964).

Polish National Alliance of the United States of North America v. National Labor Relations Board, 322 U.S. 643 (1944).

Prudential Insurance Co. v. Benjamin, 328 U.S. 408 (1946).

Railroad Transfer Service, Inc. v. City of Chicago, 386 U.S. 351 (1967).

Raymond v. Chicago, Milwaukee, & St. Paul Railway Company, 243 U.S. 43 (1917).

Reading Railroad Company v. Pennsylvania, 15 Wallace 232 (1873).

Rhodes v. Iowa, 170 U.S. 412 (1898).

Rice v. Board of Trade of Chicago, 331 U.S. 247 (1947).

Rice v. Santa Fe Elevator Corp., 331 U.S. 218 (1947).

Robbins v. Shelby County Taxing District, 120 U.S. 489 (1887).

Robertson v. California, 328 U.S. 440 (1946).

Roland Electrical Co. v. Walling, 326 U.S. 657 (1946).

Sanitary District of Chicago v. United States, 266 U.S. 405 (1925).

Santa Cruz Fruit Packing Co. v. National Labor Relations Board, 303 U.S. 453 (1938).

A.L.A. Schechter Poultry Corporation v. United States, 295 U.S. 495 (1935).

Schiro v. Bynum, 375 U.S. 395 (1964).

School District of Abington Township v. Schempp, 374 U.S. 203 (1963).

D.A. Schulte, Inc. v. Gangi, 328 U.S. 108 (1946).

Scripto, Inc. v. Carson, 362 U.S. 207 (1960).

Seaboard Air Line Railway v. Blackwell, 244 U.S. 310 (1917).

Sherlock v. Alling, 93 U.S. 99 (1876).

Shreveport Case, 234 U.S. 342 (1914).

South Carolina v. Katzenbach, 383 U.S. 301 (1965).

South Carolina State Highway Department v. Barnwell Brothers, Inc., 303 U.S. 177 (1938).

Southern Pacific Co. v. Arizona ex rel. Sullivan, 325 U.S. 761 (1945).

Stafford v. Wallace, 258 U.S. 495 (1922).

State Athletic Commission v. Dorsey, 359 U.S. 533 (1959).

Steward Machine Company v. Davis, 301 U.S. 548 (1937).

Swift & Company v. United States, 196 U.S. 375 (1905).

10 East 40th Street Building, Inc. v. Callus, 325 U.S. 578 (1945).

Texas & New Orleans Railroad Co. v. Brotherhood of Railway and Steamship Clerks, 281 U.S. 548 (1930).

Thames & Mersey Marine Insurance Company v. United States, 237 U.S. 19 (1915).

Thomas v. Hempt Brothers, 345 U.S. 19 (1953).

Toomer v. Witsell, 334 U.S. 385 (1948).

Turner v. City of Memphis, 369 U.S. 350 (1962).

Union Brokerage Co. v. Jensen, 322 U.S. 202 (1944).

United Mine Workers of America v. Coronado Coal Co., 259 U.S. 344 (1922).

United States v. American Tobacco Company, 221 U.S. 106 (1911).

United States v. Brown, 381 U.S. 437 (1965).

United States v. Butler, 297 U.S. 1 (1936).

United States v. California, 297 U.S. 175 (1936).

United States v. Carolene Products Co., 304 U.S. 144 (1938).

United States v. Darby, 312 U.S. 100 (1941).

United States v. Five Gambling Devices, 346 U.S. 441 (1953).

United States v. E.C. Knight Co., 156 U.S. 1 (1895).

United States v. South-Eastern Underwriters Association, 322 U.S. 533 (1944).

United States v. Sullivan, 332 U.S. 689 (1948).

United States v. Women's Sportswear Manufacturers Association, 336 U.S. 460 (1949).

United States v. Wrightwood Dairy Co., 315 U.S. 110 (1942).

United States Glue Co. v. Town of Oak Creek, 247 U.S. 321 (1918).

United Steelworkers of America v. National Labor Relations Board, 339 U.S. 382 (1950).

Walling v. Jacksonville Paper Co., 317 U.S. 564 (1943).

Warren-Bradshaw Drilling Co. v. Hall, 317 U.S. 88 (1942).

Washington, Virginia & Maryland Coach Co. v. National Labor Relations Board, 301 U.S. 142 (1937).

Welton v. Missouri, 91 U.S. 275 (1876).

Wesberry v. Sanders, 376 U.S. 1 (1964).

West v. Kansas Natural Gas Company, 221 U.S. 229 (1911).

West Coast Hotel Co. v. Parrish, 300 U.S. 379 (1937).

West Publishing Co. v. McColgan, 328 U.S. 823 (1946).

Western Live Stock v. Bureau of Revenue, 303 U.S. 250 (1938).

Wickard v. Filburn, 317 U.S. 111 (1942).

Williams v. Stockham Valves & Fittings, Inc., 358 U.S. 450 (1959).

Willson v. The Black-Bird Creek Marsh Company, 2 Peters 245 (1829).

Wirtz v. Steepleton General Tire Company, 383 U.S. 190 (1966).

Woodruff v. Parham, 8 Wallace 123 (1869).

Lower Federal Court Cases

The Brig Wilson v. United States, 30 *Federal Cases* 239 (1820).

Elkison v. Deliesseline, 8 *Federal Cases* 493 (1823).

Williams v. Howard Johnson's Restaurant, 268 F. 2d 845, C.A.4 (1959).

State Cases

Gibbons v. Ogden, 17 Johnson 488 (New York, 1820).

Livingston and Fulton v. Van Ingen, 9 Johnson 507 (New York, 1812).

North River Steamboat Company v. John R. Livingston, 3 Cowen 711 (New York, 1825).

Ogden v. Gibbons, 4 Johnson Ch. 150 (New York, 1819).

Bibliography

Books

Anderson, William A. *The Nation and the States: Rivals or Partners?* Minneapolis, Minn.: The University of Minnesota Press, 1955.

Baker, Leonard. *Back to Back: The Duel between FDR and the Supreme Court.* New York: The Macmillan Company, 1967.

Baxter, Maurice G. *Daniel Webster & the Supreme Court.* Amherst, Mass.: The University of Massachusetts Press, 1966.

Beveridge, Albert J. *The Life of John Marshall.* 4 vols. Boston: Houghton Mifflin Company, 1929.

Black, Charles L., Jr. *Perspectives in Constitutional Law.* Englewood Cliffs, N.J.: Prentice-Hall, Inc., 1963.

Congressional Quarterly, Inc. *Revolution in Civil Rights.* 3rd ed. Washington, D.C.: Congressional Quarterly Inc., 1967.

Cooke, Jacob E. (ed.). *The Federalist.* Cleveland: The World Publishing Company, 1961.

Corwin, Edward S. *The Commerce Power Versus States Rights.* Gloucester, Mass.: Peter Smith, 1962.

Crosskey, William W. *Politics and the Constitution in the History of the United States.* 2 vols. Chicago: The University of Chicago Press, 1953.

Dangerfield, George. *Chancellor Robert R. Livingston of New York 1746-1813.* New York: Harcourt, Brace and Co., 1960.

Elliot, Jonathan (ed.). *The Debates in the Several State Conventions on the Adoption of the Federal Constitution.* 5 vols. Philadelphia: J.B. Lippincott & Co., 1861 (2nd ed.).

Farrand, Max (ed.). *The Records of the Federal Convention of 1787.* 4 vols. New Haven, Conn.: Yale University Press, 1911.

Frank, John P. *Mr. Justice Black: The Man and His Opinions.* New York: Alfred A. Knopf, Inc., 1948.

Frankfurter, Felix. *The Commerce Clause under Marshall, Taney and Waite.* Chapel Hill, N.C.: The University of North Carolina Press, 1937.

Goldwin, Robert A. (ed.). *A Nation of States: Essays on the American Federal System.* Chicago: Rand McNally & Company, 1963.

Hendel, Samuel. *Charles Evans Hughes and the Supreme Court.* New York: King's Crown Press, Columbia University, 1951.

Jackson, Robert H. *The Struggle for Judicial Supremacy.* New York: Vintage Books, 1941.

————. *The Supreme Court in the American System of Government.* New York: Harper & Row, Publishers, Inc., 1963.

Kelly, Alfred H. and Harbison, Winfred A. *The American Constitution: Its Origins and Development.* 3rd ed. New York: W.W. Norton & Company, Inc., 1963.

Kilpatrick, James J. *The Sovereign States: Notes of a Citizen of Virginia.* Chicago: Henry Regnery Company, 1957.

Konefsky, Samuel J. *Chief Justice Stone and the Supreme Court.* New York: The Macmillan Company, 1945.

Leuchtenburg, William E. *Franklin D. Roosevelt and the New Deal: 1932-1940.* New York: Harper & Row, Publishers, Inc., 1963.

Mason, Alpheus Thomas. *Harlan Fiske Stone: Pillar of the Law.* New York: The Viking Press, 1956.

————. *The Supreme Court: Palladium of Freedom.* Ann Arbor, Mich.: The University of Michigan Press, 1962.

————. *William Howard Taft: Chief Justice.* New York: Simon and Schuster, Inc., 1964.

Mason, Alpheus Thomas and Beaney, William M. (eds.). *American Constitutional Law: Introductory Essays and Selected Cases.* 4th ed. Englewood Cliffs, N.J.: Prentice-Hall, Inc., 1968.

Mendelson, Wallace. *Justices Black and Frankfurter: Conflict in the Court.* Chicago: The University of Chicago Press, 1961.

————(ed). *The Supreme Court: Law and Discretion.* Indianapolis, Ind.: The Bobbs-Merrill Company, Inc., 1967.

Morgan, Donald G. *Justice William Johnson: The First Dissenter.* Columbia, S.C.: University of South Carolina Press, 1954.

Powell, Thomas Reed. *Vagaries and Varieties in Constitutional Interpretation.* New York: Columbia University Press, 1956.

Pusey, Merlo J. *Charles Evans Hughes.* 2 vols. New York: The Macmillan Company, 1951.

Ribble, Frederick D.G. *State and National Power over Commerce.* New York: Columbia University Press, 1937.

Schlesinger, Arthur M., Jr. *The Age of Roosevelt: The Crisis of the Old Order, 1919-1933.* Boston: Houghton Mifflin Company, 1957.

————. *The Age of Roosevelt: The Politics of Upheaval.* Boston: Houghton Mifflin Company, 1960.

Schwartz, Bernard. *The Supreme Court: Constitutional Revolution in Retrospect.* New York: The Ronald Press Company, 1957.

Smith, Alexander. *The Commerce Power in Canada and the United States.* Toronto: Butterworths, 1963.

Story, Joseph. *Commentaries on the Constitution of the United States.* 4th ed. with notes and additions by Thomas M. Cooley. 2 vols. Boston: Little, Brown and Company, 1873.

Swisher, Carl Brent. *American Constitutional Development.* 2nd ed. Cambridge, Mass.: Houghton Mifflin Company, 1954.

Williams, Charlotte. *Hugo L. Black: A Study in the Judicial Process.* Baltimore: The Johns Hopkins Press, 1950.

Articles

Abel, Albert S. "The Commerce Clause in the Constitutional Convention and in Contemporary Comment," *Minnesota Law Review,* XXV (March, 1941), 432-94.

Anonymous. "Pre-emption as a Preferential Ground: A New Canon of Construction," *Selected Essays on Constitutional Law: 1938-1962,* compiled and edited by a committee of the Association of American Law Schools (St. Paul, Minn.: West Publishing Co., 1963), 310-23.

_____. "The Supreme Court: 1959 Term," *Harvard Law Review,* LXXIV (November, 1960), 81.

Barrett, Edward L., Jr. "State Taxation of Interstate Commerce— 'Direct Burdens,' 'Multiple Burdens' or What Have You?" *Selected Essays on Constitutional Law: 1938-1962,* compiled and edited by a committee of the Association of American Law Schools (St. Paul, Minn.: West Publishing Co., 1963), 324-55.

Christopher, Thomas W. "A Contentious Pre-emption: *Campbell v. Hussey," Journal of Public Law,* XI (1962), 341-51.

Corwin, Edward S. "The Passing of Dual Federalism," *Essays in Constitutional Law,* Robert G. McCloskey (ed.). New York: Vintage Books, 1957, 185-210.

_____. "The Power of Congress to Prohibit Commerce," *Selected Essays on Constitutional Law,* compiled and edited by a committee of the Association of American Law Schools (4 vols., Chicago: The Foundation Press, Inc., 1938), III, 103-29.

Cushman, Robert E. "The National Police Power under the Commerce Clause of the Constitution," *Selected Essays on Constitutional Law,* compiled and edited by a committee of the Association of American Law Schools (4 vols., Chicago: The Foundation Press, Inc., 1938), III, 36-90.

Dangerfield, George. "The Steamboat Case," *Quarrels That Have Shaped the Constitution,* John A. Garraty (ed.). New York: Harper & Row, Publishers, Inc., 1964, 49-61.

Dowling, Noel T. "Interstate Commerce and State Power—Revised Version," *Selected Essays on Constitutional Law: 1938-1962,* compiled and edited by a committee of the Association of American Law Schools (St. Paul, Minn.: West Publishing Co., 1963), 280-97.

Frank, John P. "The New Court and the New Deal," *Hugo Black and the Supreme Court: A Symposium,* Stephen Parks Strickland (ed.). Indianapolis, Ind.: The Bobbs-Merrill Company, Inc., 1967, 39-74.

Freidel, Frank. "The Sick Chicken Case," *Quarrels That Have Shaped the Constitution,* John A. Garraty (ed.). New York: Harper & Row, Publishers, Inc., 1964, 191-209.

Hartman, Jon D. "Constitutional Law—Federal Steam Vessel Inspection Statute No Bar to Local Smoke Control Law," *University of Illinois Law Forum* (1960), 450.

Haskins, George L. "John Marshall and the Commerce Clause of the Constitution," *University of Pennsylvania Law Review,* CIV (October, 1955), 23-37.

Kendall, David W. "Mr. Gibbons and Colonel Ogden," *Michigan State Bar Journal,* XXVI (February, 1947), 22-25.

Leuchtenburg, William E. "The Origins of Franklin D. Roosevelt's 'Court-Packing' Plan," *The Supreme Court Review: 1966,* Philip B. Kurland (ed.). Chicago: The University of Chicago Press, 1966, 347-400.

Mann, W. Howard. "The Marshall Court: Nationalization of Private Rights and Personal Liberty from the Authority of the Commerce Clause," *Indiana Law Journal,* XXXVIII (Winter, 1963), 117-238.

Mendelson, Wallace. "New Light on *Fletcher v. Peck* and *Gibbons v. Ogden,*" *Yale Law Journal,* LVIII (1948-1949), 567-73.

Powell, Thomas Reed. "Our High Court Analyses," *The New York Times Magazine,* June 18, 1944.

_____. "The Child Labor Law, The Tenth Amendment, and the Commerce Clause," *Selected Essays on Constitutional Law,* compiled and edited by a committee of the Association of American Law Schools (4 vols., Chicago: The Foundation Press, Inc., 1938), III, 314-36.

_____. "The Still Small Voice of the Commerce Clause," *Selected Essays on Constitutional Law,* compiled and edited by a committee of the Association of American Law Schools (4 vols., Chicago: The Foundation Press, Inc., 1938), III, 931-32.

_____. "The Validity of State Regulation under the Webb-Kenyon Law," *Selected Essays on Constitutional Law,* compiled and edited by a committee of the Association of American Law Schools (4 vols., Chicago: The Foundation Press, Inc., 1938), III, 880-901.

Ribble, F.D.G. "The 'Current of Commerce': A Note on the Commerce Clause and the National Industrial Recovery Act," *Selected Essays on Constitutional Law,* compiled and edited by a committee of the Association of American Law Schools (4 vols., Chicago: The Foundation Press, Inc., 1938), III, 184-97.

Roper, Joseph A. "The Constitution: Discovered or Discarded," *Notre Dame Lawyer,* XVI (January, 1941), 97-124.

Schwartz, Bernard. "The Supreme Court—October 1958 Term," *Michigan Law Review,* LVIII (December, 1959), 165-208.

_____. "The Supreme Court—October 1959 Term," *Michigan Law Review* LIX (January, 1961), 403-30.

Sholley, John B. "The Negative Implications of the Commerce Clause," *Selected Essays on Constituitonal Law,* compiled and edited by a committee of the Association of American Law Schools (4 vols., Chicago: The Foundation Press, Inc., 1938), III, 933-73.

Stern, Robert L. "That Commerce Which Concerns More States Than One," *Harvard Law Review,* XLVII (1933-1934), 1335-66.

_____. "The Commerce Clause and the National Economy, 1933-1946," *Selected Essays on Constitutional Law: 1938-1962,* compiled and edited by a committee of the Association of American Law Schools (St. Paul, Minn.: West Publishing Co., 1963), 218-79.

_____. "The Problems of Yesteryear—Commerce and Due Process," *Essays in Constitutional Law,* Robert G. McCloskey (ed.). New York: Vintage Books, 1957, 150-80.

————. "The Scope of the Phrase Interstate Commerce," *Selected Essays on Constitutional Law: 1938-1962,* compiled and edited by a committee of the American Law Schools (St. Paul, Minn.: West Publishing Co., 1963), 298-309.

Stone, Harlan F. "Fifty Years' Work of the United States Supreme Court," *American Bar Association Report,* LIII (Aug-Sept., 1928), 259.

Government Documents

Congressional Record: Proceedings and Debates of Congress. various volumes. Washington, D.C.: U.S. Government Printing Office.

Hearings Before Committees of the United States Senate and House of Representatives. various. Washington, D.C.: U.S. Government Printing Office.

Records and Briefs of Cases Decided by the Supreme Court of the United States. various volumes. Washington, D.C.: U.S. Government Printing Office.

Reports of the United States Senate and House of Representatives. various. Washington, D.C.: U.S. Government Printing Office.

Small, Norman J. (ed.). *The Constitution of the United States of America: Analysis and Interpretation.* Washington, D.C.: U.S. Government Printing Office, 1964.